WINNING WOMEN'S HEARTS AND MINDS

Selling Cold War Culture in the US and the USSR

Winning Women's Hearts and Minds

Selling Cold War Culture in the US and the USSR

DIANA CUCUZ

UNIVERSITY OF TORONTO PRESS
Toronto Buffalo London

© University of Toronto Press 2023
Toronto Buffalo London
utorontopress.com

ISBN 978-1-4875-0377-2 (cloth)   ISBN 978-1-4875-1873-8 (EPUB)
                                      ISBN 978-1-4875-1872-1 (PDF)

Library and Archives Canada Cataloguing in Publication

Title: Winning women's hearts and minds : selling Cold War culture in the US
   and the USSR / Diana Cucuz.
Names: Cucuz, Diana, author.
Description: Includes bibliographical references and index.
Identifiers: Canadiana (print) 20230210586 | Canadiana (ebook) 2023021087X |
   ISBN 9781487503772 (cloth) | ISBN 9781487518738 (EPUB) |
   ISBN 9781487518721 (PDF)
Subjects: LCSH: Ladies' home journal. | LCSH: Amerika (Washington, D.C.) |
   LCSH: United States Information Agency. | LCSH: Cultural diplomacy –
   United States – History – 20th century. | LCSH: Propaganda, American –
   Soviet Union – History – 20th century. | LCSH: Women consumers –
   United States – History – 20th century. | LCSH: Consumption (Economics) –
   United States – History – 20th century. | LCSH: Women's periodicals,
   American – History – 20th century. | LCSH: Popular literature – United
   States – History and criticism. | LCSH: Women – Soviet Union – Social
   conditions.
Classification: LCC E183.8.S65 C83 2023 | DDC 327.73047–dc23

We wish to acknowledge the land on which the University of Toronto Press operates. This land is the traditional territory of the Wendat, the Anishnaabeg, the Haudenosaunee, the Métis, and the Mississaugas of the Credit First Nation.

University of Toronto Press acknowledges the financial support of the Government of Canada, the Canada Council for the Arts, and the Ontario Arts Council, an agency of the Government of Ontario, for its publishing activities.

  Canada Council   Conseil des Arts
                      for the Arts   du Canada

Funded by the   Financé par le
  Government   gouvernement
   of Canada   du Canada

*In memory of my mother –
who consistently and unwaveringly encouraged me to pursue my passions and my dreams.
Volim Te.*

Contents

List of Figures and Tables ix

Acknowledgments xiii

Introduction: Why Women, Cold War Cultural Diplomacy, and *Amerika*? 3

Part One: Shaping Women, Gender, and the Communist Threat through the *Ladies' Home Journal*

1 The "Modern Woman": The "Special Privileges" of American Womanhood in the *Ladies' Home Journal* 25
2 The "Babushka": The "Special Hardships" of Russian Womanhood in the *Ladies' Home Journal* 52

Part Two: Selling Women, Gender, and Consumer Culture through *Amerika*

3 Selling the American Way Abroad: The Beginnings of Cold War Cultural Diplomacy in the Soviet Union 99
4 Modelling the American Dream: Fashion and Femininity in *Amerika* 119
5 Living the American Dream: The Happy Homemaker in *Amerika* 146
6 *Amerika, USSR,* and a Woman's Proper Place in the 1960s 180

Conclusion: Assessing *Amerika*'s Effectiveness: Soviet Promises for the Future and Its Failures 212

Notes 229
Bibliography 287
Index 303

Figures and Tables

Figures

2.1 February 1948 *Ladies' Home Journal* cover with a typical Russian farmwoman 61
2.2 Russian women reaping the harvest on their collective farms 63
2.3 Russian women building a school overlooking the Volga River 64
2.4 Peasant girls dancing together after a long workday near Kiev, Ukraine 65
2.5 Girls sunning themselves on the Dnieper River, Kiev, Ukraine 66
2.6 A village store, with "bare" shelves, on a collective farm 66
2.7 GUM, Russia's largest department store, on a crowded day in Moscow 67
2.8 Stalingrad housewife hanging her laundry in the sun 68
2.9 "Sun Fashions Here to Stay" 69
2.10 Living room decorated with bright, stylish, and affordable items 70
2.11 A healthy and colourful homemade feast, even during winter months 71
2.12 "How America Lives" depicts the Dickson family of Rochester, New York 72
2.13 Mrs. Dickson's makeover is a "Welcome Change" 74
2.14 The "typical housewives" of Vyborg, just north of St. Petersburg 83
2.15 Elderly woman resting with her groceries and cow on Gorki Street, Moscow 88
3.1 1951 *Cleveland Plain Dealer* cartoon 105

x Figures and Tables

3.2   August 1946 *Amerika* cover, featuring a woman at a newsstand 107
4.1   First issue of reissued *Amerika*, October 1956 126
4.2   December 1958 *Amerika* cover, featuring opera singer Marion Anderson 133
4.3   "Practical Fashions" 137
4.4   College students wearing the latest in affordable evening fashions 139
4.5   Bryn Mawr students studying in their dorm rooms 141
4.6   Maternity clothes showing Russian readers that pregnancy can be fashionable 144
5.1   Debutantes and their parents enter the President's Hotel in Washington D.C. 148
5.2   A church wedding ceremony in Lumberton, New Jersey 150
5.3   Milk carton beach house in Fire Island, New York 154
5.4   Housewife and mother Peg Scoville engaging in her daily activities 157
5.5   Housewife and mother Peg Scoville hugging her young son 158
5.6   Layout of an ideal modern kitchen 159
5.7   Modern kitchen filled with bright colours and electrical appliances 160
5.8   A self-service supermarket, with an abundance of food items in one location 165
5.9   The 2,500-space parking lot of the Seven Corners Shopping Centre in Arlington County, Virginia 174
5.10 The main floor of an American department store 175
5.11 Woman shopping with her children in fabric department 176
6.1   The miniskirt as the latest trend in young women's fashion 184
6.2   March 1962 *USSR* cover, depicting the working women of the Soviet Union 190
6.3   Russian women waiting to receive free facial treatments at the Helena Rubenstein exhibit at the American National Exhibition in Moscow 194
6.4   March 1971 *Amerika* cover, including a special report on the "ideas, look, and role of American women" 196
7.1   October 1994 *Amerika* cover, the magazine's final issue 224

Tables

2.1   Workers (and mothers), Soviet women today, population by socio-occupational groups, 1959 57

4.1 Analysis of articles in *Amerika* about or designed to appeal to women, October 1956–December 1960 135
6.1 Time budgets, non-working time, men and women, 1959 211

Acknowledgments

This book represents a long journey, one filled with many people without whom it may not have been completed, and to whom I am eternally grateful. Molly Ladd-Taylor provided detailed comments, insights, and expertise that ultimately proved useful. Her generous advice, infinite kindness, and vast knowledge of American history helped guide me over the years. I am forever indebted to my editors. First, Richard Ratzlaff, whose enthusiasm for this project even before I had convocated, led me to the University of Toronto Press. This made all the difference to me as a first-time author. Second, Stephen Shapiro, who took over this project shortly thereafter and has been a consistent source of advice and unending support throughout its various stages, through my many modifications, and even as I inundated him with both big picture and mundane questions. His prompt responses and patience in seeing this come to fruition are appreciated. I cannot fully express my gratitude to him. Three anonymous reviewers at UTP generously took time out of their schedules to provide thorough and useful recommendations. Their critical eyes served to better my argument and my final output. The contributions of Anne Laughlin, my copy-editor, who shared her own experiences of growing up in postwar America, and Barbara Porter, my managing editor, were extremely valued through these final stages. In particular, the latter patiently, and thankfully, caught items that I did not. Jennifer Harris went through the much appreciated, but quite daunting, task of creating an index for this book, one which I could not imagine undertaking myself.

I owe a great deal to the hard work of the archivists at the archives and libraries I visited throughout the years; in particular I thank David Pfeiffer at the National Archives at College Park, Maryland; Randy Sowell at the Harry S. Truman Library in Independence, Missouri; Chelsea Millner at the Dwight D. Eisenhower Library in

Independence, Kansas; and the staff at the Toronto Reference, York University, and University of Toronto Libraries. Their enthusiasm for the areas in which they work, coupled with their ability to quickly and easily find the records that this Canadian historian researching the United States needed, made my work not only easier but also much more enjoyable. The conferences I attended provided invigorating forums in which to showcase my work, particularly the Popular Culture Association/American Cultural Association conferences, where I not only received feedback but made good friends in the process. Throughout the duration of my writing, I have been employed as an instructor and in other capacities at Toronto Metropolitan University and the University of Toronto. My colleagues there have been a source of wisdom and encouragement. Seeing their own meaningful work has inspired and motivated me in many ways. I would like to thank Dima Sochnyev for his assistance in translating *Amerika*'s articles from Russian into English. I would also like to thank those colleagues and friends who kindly read various versions of this manuscript and provided useful commentary and suggestions for improvement.

"Life happened" throughout the duration of this project. I could not have survived, at least enjoyably, years of graduate school, teaching, my "side hustle," this passion project, and life's ups and downs without the constant support of my family, lifelong friends, and even strangers, whose acts of kindness have made all the difference. They have been my saving graces. Some may not have always understood my career choices, but the small and large ways in which they showed their support, whether it was through telephone conversations, gatherings, dinners, and in general allowing me to feel like a human being again, has meant the world. I have a wonderful group of cousins; no matter where we are in life, we manage to get together as if no time has passed. I could not have asked for a better experience than being able to grow with them. My dear circle of friends is so special to me. Throughout the years, we have experienced both joy and tears together, and always much laughter in between. Their generosity was an enjoyable source of distraction from the stresses that come with both teaching and manuscript writing. There were two individuals that were most central in my life as I focused on this project, the first, during its inception, research, and writing stages, and the second, as it neared its critical end. You both know who you are, and I would like to thank each of you for your various methods and degrees of support. For the latter, I can unequivocally state that your support, in the most spectacular, but also in the most everyday, mundane ways, did not go unnoticed. Your endless words of encouragement further motivated me to push my own boundaries, in this project and in others. I cannot wait to see what the future holds for us.

For as long as I can remember, my older sisters have been my rocks, through good times and not-so-good times. Their support never wavered throughout this process. My sister Donna and brother-in-law Paul's house has been a second home to me. I am grateful for the encouraging words they gave me throughout these years, as well as the pride they showed in discussing my work. Throughout the duration of graduate school and this project, I have watched my nephews, Petar and Aleks, grow up. I may have frequently been distracted by my work, but they provided another set of distractions. Their sense of humour, silly nature, and playfulness made memories that I will cherish forever. My sister Tina has been an endless source of support. Among other things, she has been an attentive listener, excellent chef, thoughtful personal shopper, patient research assistant, and, mainly, a good friend. Words cannot express the immense gratitude I have for all of the sacrifices she has made, not just towards helping me achieve my goals, but also towards helping our family throughout the years. Donna and Tina, I am not sure what twist of fate allowed me to have sisters like you, but I count myself among the lucky ones.

Finally, this manuscript is inspired by two people whose life journeys converged and led to my own: my parents, Mladjen and Milka Cucuz. For as long as I can remember, my father told me stories of communist Yugoslavia during times of war and its aftermath. Whether or not he realizes it, his stories instilled in me a genuine love of history and politics. On many occasions, when I may have been deterred, my mother's words always encouraged me. Like my father, she told me stories; hers were stories of "ordinary" life, and she told them with intense nostalgia for her birthplace, a small village in northwestern Bosnia. My love of history and curiosity for life under communism were inspired by my father's epic stories, but also by those ordinary stories that my mother told, that in all actuality, were not so ordinary. Combined, they created a desire in this girl from East Hamilton to better understand her parents' experiences growing up, the broader political environment in which they lived, and how the two intersected. Their support for my pursuit of my dreams was unwavering and it pushed me throughout all of the ups and downs in life, especially after my mother passed away in the midst of my doctoral work. Mainly, this story is for you, Mama. Wherever you are, I hope that you are able to read this and understand just how much you inspired me and how much your own story inspired this one. In many ways, completing this manuscript represents the beginning of a new chapter in my life. I hope it is one that you can be proud of.

WINNING WOMEN'S HEARTS AND MINDS

Introduction

Why Women, Cold War Cultural Diplomacy, and *Amerika*?

With this issue, we present a new monthly magazine designed to mirror for Soviet readers the multitudinous aspects of American life. It is and will be a magazine about the people of the United States – how they live, work, and play. It will try to capture their moods and aspirations, their concerns and their lighter moments of relaxation … We shall attempt to portray what Americans are thinking and doing, what they are reading and saying. This and succeeding issues will contain some articles reprinted from magazines of national circulation which already have been read and enjoyed by millions of Americans. Art and science, industry and labour, culture and technology, work and leisure – all will be presented in this magazine, along with a host of other topics. But whatever the subject, the story we will be telling is the story of American people. In brief, we shall try to give you a revealing picture of the United States today -- a picture that is constantly changing and, we believe, always interesting.[1]

This description, appearing in the first issue of *Amerika*, told readers the style, structure, content, and goals of this new monthly magazine, one which would be distributed in the Soviet Union throughout the remainder of the Cold War.[2] During the early Cold War, the US government had limited access to the Russian people.[3] This changed in 1956, when it was given the first sustained opportunity in four years to reach them on a regular basis through *Amerika*, a glossy Russian-language magazine published in the United States and distributed in the Soviet Union.[4] It contained stories and pictures of American life and culture. Reappearing on Soviet newsstands in October 1956 after a four-year hiatus, *Amerika*'s re-emergence was the climax of a US Cold War overseas information program that began in 1953 and promoted ideas concerning women, traditional gender roles, and consumption, with the intention of selling the "American way of life" abroad. Just as this era became known as the "golden age of capitalism," historians have referred to it as the "golden age of diplomacy."[5] This is the first sustained analysis of how the idealized images of American women and consumer culture that dominated the postwar mass media were distributed not just at home but also abroad in the Soviet Union, through *Amerika,* for the purposes of gradually destabilizing the communist regime. While *Amerika* was not explicitly geared towards women in the same way postwar American women's magazines were, it contained a considerable amount of material about and for them. *Amerika* serves as a microcosm of the significance of women, gender, and consumption to international politics during the Cold War. Under the administration of President Dwight D. Eisenhower, the US government drew on conservative postwar gender norms in its overseas information program; through *Amerika* it deployed images of supposedly happy and fulfilled American women as feminine housewives and mothers living under a US capitalistic consumer culture. The US government believed these images would appeal to the magazine's female readers, encourage a desire for consumer goods and, by proxy, promote conservative gender roles, and ultimately undermine a Soviet regime that was known for promoting gender equality in place of the "special privileges" that women were purported to have in the United States. In other words, it hoped to win the hearts and minds of Russian women.

Much has been written about the rise of US consumerism and attempts to spread it abroad. In 1951, David Riesman wrote "The Nylon War," a satirical story of a US campaign called "Operation Abundance" that bombarded Russians with consumer goods in order to incite dissatisfaction and sway them towards the American way of life. Among those goods that Riesman highlighted were ones targeting women. They consisted of labour-saving household items, including vacuum cleaners, toasters, stoves, and refrigerators, and personal items, including soap, tampons, hair products, clothing, and, naturally, nylons.[6] Emily S. Rosenberg argues that since the beginning of the twentieth century the US government and private businesses have worked together to spread US consumer culture and the ideology of "liberal developmentalism." Rosenberg explains that liberal developmentalism includes support for private enterprise, free trade, and investment, the flow of information and culture, economic and cultural exchanges, and the belief that other nations should replicate the American experience.[7] Images of technology, consumerism, and affluence, it was thought, would further the country's appeal and lead to its association with progress and modernity. These efforts intensified in the postwar period, when government and business adopted a strategy to create a mass consumer society at home, as well as export one abroad, in order to reconstruct the nation's economy and usher in an era of prosperity.[8] Walter Hixson's path-breaking study on US Cold War propaganda and cultural initiatives shows that consumer culture, through its ability to expand US influence, heighten the discontent of citizens, and gradually destabilize communist nations, was one of the country's "greatest foreign policy assets."[9]

During the postwar period, the US government adopted a program of "cultural infiltration" in response to the Soviet government's initiation of an "anti-American" campaign, thus limiting its ability to maintain a presence in the Soviet Union and its satellite states.[10] After his 1953 inauguration, Eisenhower began to prioritize this approach. He was aware of the power of public opinion and had a strong desire to develop contact with the Russian people. The opportunity to achieve this objective increased two months after his inauguration: long-time Soviet leader Josef Stalin died in March and shortly thereafter Nikita Khrushchev rose to power. Khrushchev's 1956 "Secret Session" speech denouncing Stalin and his cult of personality before the Twentieth Congress of the Communist Party (CP) of the Soviet Union led to a new era in its diplomatic relations. Khrushchev's move away from Stalinist polices included "peaceful coexistence" and increased contact with the West. This policy change, which aligned with Eisenhower's goal of increased contact, stemmed from the changing approaches to international relations. Until the beginning of the Cold War, the US government, like most other peacetime governments, practised traditional diplomacy. Traditional diplomacy can be defined as the process of forging relationships with other nations, often relying on the interaction of high-ranking officials, in order to reach a formal agreement based on a particular foreign policy decision.[11] After World War II, new transportation and communications technologies altered the nature of international relations, allowing governments and people to interact more frequently and exchange knowledge. Eisenhower recognized that, in light of the ideological battle of the Cold War, public opinion was important and could stimulate policy formulation.[12]

Eisenhower's creation of the United States Information Agency (USIA) in 1953 reflected this new strategy.[13] In order to win congressional support for the USIA and its initiatives, the administration emphasized the distinction between its own information program and that of the Soviet Union, which it called "propagandistic" and associated with lies and deception.[14] Eisenhower went to great lengths to separate America's information program from the Soviet Union's activities, stating that the new agency would concentrate on objective, factual news and commentaries.[15] Other officials reiterated these claims, indicating that the USIA neither practised psychological warfare nor utilized propaganda techniques, but did admit it was attempting to win people over to its side. The USIA's first director, Theodore Streibert, stated that the agency's purpose was to show foreigners that US policies and objectives aligned with its own aspirations for freedom, progress, and peace, as well as to counter falsities directed by the "Soviet propaganda machine."[16] The USIA's Soviet information program was characterized by two central tenets. First, it sought to reach Russian citizens in order to convey broad information and ideas about American democratic values. At the time, this included conservative ideas surrounding gender roles and the family. Second, it sought to expose these citizens, particularly women, to the American "way of life" and consumer culture so they could develop a favourable view of the United States.

Under Eisenhower, the USIA used three channels to appeal to the Russian people. The first was radio programming, through the Voice of America (VOA). The VOA was established in 1942 and began broadcasting to Russians in 1947. However, its ability to reach them was precarious, as it was frequently jammed by the Soviet government beginning in 1949.[17] In 1953, as Eisenhower was looking to consolidate his international information activities, the VOA was transferred from the State Department to the newly created USIA.[18] The second channel used to appeal to the Russian people was print material, particularly *Amerika*. *Amerika* was first published by the State Department from 1945 until 1952, when it was discontinued owing to difficulties with the Soviet government over censorship and circulation. In 1955, a reciprocal agreement was reached that allowed for the exchange of magazines in each country. Beginning in 1956, *USSR* was distributed in the United States, and *Amerika* was reissued and redistributed in the Soviet Union, this time under the control of the USIA. *Amerika* was a glossy magazine filled with stories and pictures on American life and culture. Officials believed it was less offensive than the types of anti-American propaganda the Soviet government used and could foster a more appealing image of the United States.[19] *Amerika* provided the USIA with the ability to carefully hone the messages it used to appeal to Russian women and, in contrast to the VOA, it was able to use the power of the visual image in order to do so. The third channel used to appeal to the Russian people was the foreign exhibition, beginning with the American National Exhibition, which took place in Moscow during the summer of 1959. This six-week-long exhibition, a consumer spectacle attended by 2.7 million visitors, became the site of the famous "kitchen debate" between US vice president Richard Nixon and Khrushchev.[20]

A variety of terms can be used to describe these activities behind the Iron Curtain. "Propaganda," "psychological operations," and "warfare" or "political warfare" are and have been used interchangeably. Part of this terminological ambiguity stems from the hesitancy of the American public and officials to accept their nation's involvement in such activities. Propaganda can refer to any "technique or action that attempts to influence the emotions, attitudes or behaviour of a group, in order to benefit the sponsor."[21] It is typically concerned with the persuasion of public opinion and mass attitudes – either to change or reinforce existing attitudes and opinions. It can include a variety of tactics such as speeches, publications, radio, film, television, and exchanges.[22] Historically, Americans have viewed propaganda in a positive light, but after its extensive use during World War I, particularly by their German opponents, it began to take on negative connotations. According to Hans Tuch, a US embassy official in the Soviet Union under Eisenhower, the term was considered unsuitable as a description for the US government's activities, which were supposedly more legitimate than those of the Soviet Union.[23] Since the beginning of the Cold War, countless terms have been adopted to describe what is otherwise known as propaganda. The terms "psychological operations," and later "psychological warfare" or "political warfare," were all widely used under the Truman administration.[24] These terms can be defined as propaganda supplemented with other covert measures of a political, economic, or military nature.[25] They can include trade and economic aid, diplomacy, or the threat of force.[26] However, Truman-era officials most frequently used the term psychological warfare when appealing to Congress, which often denied funding for activities labelled as propaganda but was more open to the term "warfare."[27] Under both the Truman and Eisenhower administrations, officials privately used all of these terms interchangeably. When designating titles for agencies and addressing the public, they most often referred to propaganda as "information" activities, denoting their supposed objective and educational purposes in contrast to Soviet activities, which were considered manipulative. Another term that has been used to describe USIA activities is "public diplomacy." In 1965 Edmund Gullion, an American diplomat turned dean of the Fletcher School of Law and Diplomacy at Tufts University, used the term to describe the process of international information and cultural relations.[28] Tuch defines public diplomacy as a government's process of communicating directly with foreign publics in order to bring about an understanding of a nation's ideas and ideals, its institutions and culture, as well as its national goals and policies.[29] Public diplomacy involves top-down interaction, where governments interact and communicate knowledge to ordinary individuals, who can then communicate that knowledge to the wider public.[30] Cultural diplomacy is just one type of public diplomacy, along with political and ideological diplomacy.[31] A significant portion of the USIA's activities included interaction and communication with foreign publics. For the sake of consistency, this study refers to the USIA's long-term activities, particularly its publications, as cultural diplomacy.[32] However, when discussing specific US officials, and the ways in which they understood and approached the US information program, it retains the original language used.

This study builds on two bodies of scholarship. The first is the flourishing field of Cold War studies, including research that shows the importance of propaganda and cultural diplomacy. The second is literature on white, middle-class heterosexual women and, more broadly, on gender and its integral relationship to consumption during the Cold War. In recent years, historians have produced excellent studies on the history of cultural diplomacy, as well as on the broader objectives and tactics of US policymakers targeting citizens behind the Iron Curtain. Michael L. Krenn argues that cultural diplomacy has a long history in the United States, beginning with the country's "unofficial" attempts at cultural diplomacy, which coincided with the creation of the republic and were accelerated during World War I. However, it is generally argued that America's "official" policy of cultural diplomacy, that is, acts carried out by official government agencies to promote American culture abroad, began during World War II.[33] Eisenhower, a firsthand witness to the success of information programs in influencing foreign publics, and largely free from the domestic constraints of his predecessor Harry Truman, was keen on adopting and expanding on these tactics during peacetime.[34] Kenneth A. Osgood suggests that Eisenhower aggressively integrated propaganda into all foreign policy initiatives, and even used it at home to enlist Americans in international campaigns aimed at winning the hearts and minds of people behind the Iron Curtain.[35] Scott Lucas discusses the Cold War as an ideological battle where the US government created a "state-private network," composed of public agencies and private groups and individuals; this network established a total war effort that included propaganda activities in order to free people from communism.[36] Both studies demonstrate that by the mid-1950s, Eisenhower's administration adopted a gradual approach, with cultural diplomacy at its centre, towards destabilizing the Soviet Union. In one of the few works that connects women to this narrative, Helen Laville argues that white women's voluntary organizations worked in conjunction with the US government in spreading its anti-communist messages, and the American way of life, abroad.[37] Studies on Soviet cultural diplomacy are rare but worth noting, as they provide the unique perspective of the "other." Historians have touched on the desire of Soviet officials in the post-Stalinist era to reorient its foreign policy and increase communications and cooperation with the United States. While the United States hoped to use this easing of tensions to promote its consumer culture, the Soviet Union hoped both to better understand the "enemy" after a period of isolation from the West and to sell the socialist experiment. Historians tend to agree that this strategy may have proved detrimental to the Soviet government. For instance, Soviet cultural achievements were of little appeal to the American public while US consumer goods were coveted by its Soviet counterpart.[38] As a result, by 1960, the Soviet government was more vulnerable to ideological attack and more open to Western influence.[39]

Rich and varied histories analyse US government efforts to export American culture as part of a broader Cold War foreign policy. Historians of cultural diplomacy emphasize how specific programs were critical in the battle for cultural supremacy.[40] These programs served multiple purposes. First, they provided a means for American artists and athletes to travel abroad and promote a deeper understanding of US culture. Second, they combatted Soviet allegations that the United States lacked a refined culture. Third, by including successful African Americans such as Louis Armstrong and Dizzy Gillespie, they promoted an image of progress during a time when Soviets heavily critiqued racial inequality in the United States. Both Penny Von Eschen and Mary Dudziak extrapolate on this last point. Von Eschen shows that African American musicians toured the world as "jazz ambassadors," but also as civil rights advocates, by making impromptu public appearances, interacting with ordinary citizens, and commenting on domestic politics.[41] Dudziak paints racism as a national security issue, showing that the US government sought to mitigate Soviet criticisms of Americans race relations and, as a result, hastened the passage of civil rights legislation.[42] These studies reinforce the point that individuals largely ignored in the study of international relations were often key actors on the world stage, particularly in spreading American culture. USIA officials already knew that cultural activities could be effective when they began transmitting images of American women and consumer culture within the Soviet Union.

Among other, lesser-studied actors in relation to the Cold War are women. American women became closely associated with the newly emerging mass consumerism that enveloped postwar America. Literature on gender and consumerism shows how conservative gender norms and visions of the suburban family and domesticity were deployed at home and abroad. Several studies highlight the ways in which

American women were used and made themselves useful in combatting communism during an era known for its emphasis on conservative gender roles. In *Homeward Bound*, Elaine Tyler May discusses how the anxieties of a nation amid a hostile international setting characterized by atomic weaponry and a communist threat led to the veneration of a tranquil domestic setting. Women were called on to re-enter the private sphere, create comfortable home lives for their families, and raise children to become good citizens. However, in a unique twist reflective of the Cold War, women were also given the task of protecting their communities from the so-called dangers of communism, typically by becoming involved in organizations dedicated to promoting traditional American values.[43] These prescribed roles for women in the home and community served dual purposes. First, they justified the postwar removal of women from the workforce in order to make way for returning veterans.[44] Second, they were used in images of supposedly happy and fulfilled women to promote capitalism and consumption both at home and abroad.[45] Laura Belmonte focuses more extensively on the overseas information program by showing the myriad ways in which the Truman and Eisenhower administrations attempted to "sell the American way" by using images of women, gender, and the family to export capitalism around the world.[46] These studies firmly plant women into a discourse that typically describes Cold War institutions as masculinized settings dominated by groups of elite men.[47] They complicate the traditional narrative, as this study does, to show women's utility to Cold War decision makers, both as symbols and actors in their own right. Women were part of a larger political and cultural process in which the US government defined their roles in traditional terms, tied them heavily to America's newly emerging mass consumption society, and presented them abroad in order to appeal to Russian women.

This study is unique because of its gendered analysis of the overseas information program and of *Amerika*, a magazine which relied heavily on conservative gender norms and images of women to convey positive messages about the American way of life and its consumer culture in order to win Russian women's hearts and minds. American women became important symbols in the ideological battle of the Cold War as their so-called happier and more prosperous lifestyles were used to show the merits of capitalism. These monolithic images, reflected in the fictional characters of the postwar period such as June Cleaver, Harriet Nelson, and Donna Stone were presented in the US media and in many cases so effective that they have endured in our memories of the Cold War, in spite of the fact that women are not a monolithic group and have always had multiple and diverse experiences.[48]

Historically, images of women have frequently been used to sell a particular way of life, as well as the status other women could attain if they adopted that way of life. Since the late nineteenth century, democracy and capitalism have traditionally been associated with consumption, and consumption, in turn, allowed for the "pursuit of happiness," particularly in a rapidly industrializing society that relied on strict regimentation. Mass production and consumption allowed Americans, amid the monotony of their lives, the possibility of shaping their individual identities apart from the masses.[49] Rosenberg argues that there has been "a strong tradition in Western culture in which representations of women's roles served as emblematic markers for the degree of 'civilization' reached by society as a whole."[50] Indeed, as the United States modernized, so too did its women. Advertising was key to pushing these changes forward. Prior to World War I, advertisers relied on the printed word to convey messages, but by the 1920s approaches in advertising changed tremendously. Advertisers abandoned lengthy textual descriptions and turned to creating attractive images, particularly ones that could appeal to women. Fashions and cosmetics were the first products to be impacted by this advertising makeover.[51] Through advertising, capitalists built a culture that combined the new realities of civil society, particularly the newly emerging methods of mass production, with traditional gender roles. For the white, middle-class, heterosexual women who had been separated from the marketplace with the rise of industrialization and traditional gender roles these messages were particularly important. Advertisements offered them the possibility of achieving standards valued in Western society – and ideals of beauty, grace, and romance – through the use of modern products. Consumption, in effect, promised unhappy women, or women that perceived themselves as being unhappy once they viewed these products, a solution to their supposed problems.[52] These modern advertisements spoke to the "primal urges and sensations repressed in the everyday confines of civilization." They appealed to a woman's emotions and desires, and promised instant gratification.[53] By the start of the Cold War, the USIA hoped the same could be done for Russian women, who were typically depicted as engaged in the drudge work that was involved in rebuilding what many Americans believed to be a backwards nation. The research and knowledge accrued by the "ad men" behind these campaigns became integral to the design and promotion of the nation's overseas information program, which concentrated on expanding America's markets and exporting its consumer culture.[54] They concluded with zeal that the "art of persuasion is to give him what he wants so truthfully and skillfully as to influence his thinking in the process." The USIA, influenced by and sometimes enlisting these ad men, turned its attention to those who possessed a tremendous amount of purchasing power: women.[55]

This is precisely why it is important to understand the extent to which the USIA deployed images of women and consumption in its overseas activities, and to appreciate what these images entailed. The *Ladies' Home Journal*, from which the USIA drew much of its inspiration, is a particularly useful magazine from which to analyse the postwar gender norms and representations of women. It was pivotal in shaping and reflecting twentieth-century womanhood and consumption. Created in 1883 as a monthly magazine for predominately white, native-born, middle-class, heterosexual women, by 1903, it was the first to reach one million subscribers.[56] As the most popular women's magazine during the early Cold War period, with a monthly circulation of five million, its messages were especially important because of its ability to reach and influence vast numbers of women.[57] The *Journal* conveyed an American way of life and culture that tended to reflect and promote the privileged lives of its readers. In other words, it rarely deviated from the status quo. According to it, femininity, fulfilment, and happiness were derived from the material prosperity that was made available through a modern capitalist society.

Integral to the *Ladies' Home Journal* objectives of showcasing the supposedly happy lives of American women during the Cold War was the frequent depiction of the "other," in this case Russian women, in order to emphasize the benefits of capitalism over communism. Despite these frequent depictions of Russian women, there was a blatant absence of the racialized "other" in postwar women's magazines, namely African American women, but also those that further contributed to the country's diverse racial and ethnic makeup, including Hispanic, Asian American, and Indigenous women. Where images of unhappy Russian women were used to show the benefits of American capitalism, images of unhappy African American women who may reflect poorly on the nation were noticeably missing from both the overseas information program as well as postwar women's magazines.[58] According to images in the *Journal*, the Soviet system provided its women little of what its American equivalent did. In other words, the "special privileges" of American women were juxtaposed with the "special hardships" of Russian women. It portrayed the latter as the overworked, unfeminine, and unhappy victims of a communist state that provided them with few consumer goods. This depiction of the Russian woman as one who wanted to remain in the home, take care of her husband and children, and shop freely, but could not due to a repressive regime, was ubiquitous in the US media. Robert L. Griswold calls attention to the images of Russian women that became embedded in the American psyche during this time, arguing that a stereotypical image of the Russian woman as being "graceless, shapeless, and sexless" emerged.[59] For American women who read the *Journal*, this portrayal of Russian women provided a microcosm into the larger Soviet regime and its lack of modernity. Stories articulated the inadequacies of a so-called backward Soviet system that deprived its women not just of modern homes in the suburbs and consumer goods such as electrical appliances to fill them, but also basic necessities such as proper food and clothing.[60] Even Soviet leaders occasionally criticized their nation's low standard of living, at times going so far as to praise the US government for ensuring a higher standard of living for its own citizens.[61] To be sure, there were stories in the US media, particularly in the immediate aftermath of World War II, which gave more positive accounts. These stories tended to highlight the strength and resilience of hardworking Russian women, but they rarely depicted them as being grateful for a communist regime that allowed them to obtain affordable housing, universal healthcare, and a free education. Instead they showed women as being hopeful for a brighter future, liberated from communism.[62] These accounts showed Americans the human impact of a supposedly corrupt Soviet regime, during a time when they had little knowledge of the country. American women could deplore the Soviet government for seemingly forcing its women to engage in hard and menial labour (as if American women had never engaged in such labour), but simultaneously feel sympathy for the overburdened women. In particular, stories and images of Russian women were used to show American women that, although their Russian counterparts resided in a distant land, they had much in common with them on the basis of their gender, in particular their roles as wives, mothers, and keepers of the home. The goal was to persuade American women to adhere to a prescribed way of thinking that was in line with the ethos of the Cold War.

Ladies' Home Journal articles on Russian women served a dual purpose. Not only were they intended to "educate" readers on the supposed realities of life behind the Iron Curtain, in the process making them feel "lucky" to be American, but they were also closely intertwined with the Cold War, particularly the US foreign policy doctrine of "containment," a term first coined by State Department official George F. Kennan. In "The Sources of Soviet Conduct," his influential article that appeared in the July 1947 issue of *Foreign Affairs* under the pseudonym "X," Kennan described the Kremlin's "neurotic view of world affairs" as being shaped by a sense of insecurity. He argued that the US should avoid both outright war or appeasement with the Soviet Union, but instead adopt a "long-term, patient, but firm and vigilant containment of Russian expansive tendencies."[63] Containment can also describe the extent to which numerous venues in American life contributed to a culture that sought to curb communism *at home*.[64] May coined the term "domestic containment" to describe a strategy in which Cold War ideology and the postwar emphasis on domesticity reinforced each other. The political consensus that supported Cold War policies abroad fuelled conformity to the postwar home and family.[65] Just as the postwar home became a "sphere of influence" to contain communism, so too did the surrounding community, as white, middle-class women were called on to extend their roles beyond the home and engage in civic activities in order to combat communism. Domestic containment blurred the lines between the public and the private and became a way for women to demonstrate their loyalty and patriotism to their country.[66] As Laura McEnaney writes, civilian defence or "preparedness" in case of a nuclear attack became highly privatized, and domesticated, and therefore, feminized in the postwar era. Seemingly eager to contribute, and readily available at all hours of the day, just as they were during World War II, the government called on female volunteers to protect what were considered their "interests," namely the home, the family, and the community from the enemy.[67] According to May, this strong adherence to the family was meant to strengthen patriotism and morals and instil in individuals a love for community, God, and country.[68] To go against this norm, "to look different; to act different; to think different," signified subversion or godlessness.[69]

Stories and images that attempted to sell the idea of domestic containment were pervasive in postwar magazines such as the *Ladies' Home Journal*. In spite of the popular perception brought forward by Betty Friedan in her seminal 1963 work, *The Feminine Mystique*, that postwar women's magazines conveyed monolithic messages about women and gender, they contained multiple and at times contradictory messages.[70] Women's magazines expanded the traditional definition of "domestic" and linked the home and family to wider national security concerns.[71] Joanne Meyerowitz argues that postwar women's magazines used anti-communist sentiment to advocate for women's political participation, and to promote a positive image of politically active women who showed allegiance to their nation.[72] Others have reinforced the idea that beyond their covers, postwar women's magazines espoused a subversive form of feminism during an era widely known for its conservative values. Women did, indeed, weigh other options for their lives beyond those of housewife and mother.[73] Nevertheless, postwar magazines such as the *Ladies' Home Journal* predominantly reflected the gender norms of the time and attempted to sell them to American women. Images that highlighted women's political participation were secondary to ones that related to homemaking. Further, they reflected a white, middle-class ideal that altogether neglected the vast and varied experiences of working-class women and women of colour, those who were often unable to remain in the home.

When the USIA was established, it utilized these limited images of women. Information experts also attempted to gauge what resonated most with foreign audiences. For example, where possible, they conducted research prior to, during, and after exhibitions, and carefully tailored their strategies and tactics to appeal to different countries and people.[74] For example, USIA officials drew on surveys conducted with female visitors who attended earlier exhibitions they held in Poland and Yugoslavia. USIA officials already assumed that all women wanted to consume, and survey responses confirmed this notion, as female visitors had generally positive responses to the consumer goods available at American trade fairs and exhibitions.[75] Officials took these survey responses as further affirmation that consumption was central to every woman's life, even one who lived under a communist regime.[76] Based on these images, the USIA assumed they knew of the desires of all Russian women who, according to it, would surely want to improve their lives so that they mirrored the so-called happy ones of American women. As Belmonte confirms, USIA officials firmly believed that images of the supposedly happy housewife, mother, and consumer would be nothing but attractive to Russian women.[77]

With the approval of postwar media, and seemingly of communist women, these limited images were consistently portrayed to Russian women in *Amerika* throughout the decade. They were idealized versions of white, middle-class, heterosexual American women seen in their roles as happily feminine housewives, mothers, and consumers. The magazine's importance cannot be underestimated because, for years, it was the sole and most consistent method by which the USIA could advertise widely to Russian women the benefits of conservative US gender norms and consumer culture. *Amerika* thus became a symbol of what Lizabeth Cohen calls the American "consumer's republic." According to Cohen, the consumer's republic, characterized by a mass consumption-oriented society, deemed that the good purchaser who was devoted to "more, newer and better" was in fact, the good citizen.[78] This idea of the "purchaser as citizen," a predominately white, middle-class female figure, emerged in the postwar period. She desired products for herself and her family, but while consuming she served the national interest. When women could afford to do so, they were assumed to embrace this role with zeal, not only because it was in their nature to consume, but because it also reflected their devotion to their country and its capitalist values.[79] Female consumers exerted a tremendous amount of influence, counting both the home and the marketplace as their spheres of influence. Through *Amerika*, ideas about the female purchaser as citizen came into full view. *Amerika* was filled with articles and images of women that showcased their ability and desire to consume, including content on homes, kitchen appliances, food, clothing, and hair and beauty items. It contained images of the feminine housewife, mother, and consumer living in a capitalist culture of abundance. This study will analyse how *Amerika* was used to advertise to Russian women the same conservative gender norms and consumer culture that were used to appeal to American women at home.

In spite of clear evidence that gender, consumerism, and international politics and diplomacy were highly interconnected during the Cold War, neither these interconnections nor *Amerika* have been studied in depth.[80] However, historians have argued that bridging the gap between these seemingly disconnected subject areas can enrich our understanding of each. For example, a 1990 issue of the *Journal of American History*, entitled "A Round Table: Explaining the History of American Foreign Relations," included essays aimed at non-specialists in the field of diplomatic history who had recently embraced alternative approaches to the study of foreign relations, including those that explored culture and gender.[81] Without using the terms "culture" or "gender," Melvyn P. Leffler broadly noted that "national security policy encompasses the decisions and actions deemed imperative to protect domestic core values from external threats."[82] One cannot define America's postwar domestic core values without reference to a consumer culture that reflected and perpetuated traditional gender roles. These are among the values that the USIA conveyed abroad through its information program. More specifically, in a 1994 issue of *Diplomatic History* entitled "Culture, Gender, and Foreign Policy: A Symposium," both Rosenberg and May argued that the study of international politics and relations is deepened through cultural and gender analyses, and that these discourses often reinforce and gain power from their interrelationships. Gender and sexuality are deeply imbedded in the ideological construction of foreign policy and add new insights to historical analyses.[83] Through the study of overseas information activities such as *Amerika* we can see that the USIA's attempts to spread American consumer culture, with its central focus on women, both reflected and shaped an era during which women were thrust into the centre as the political and ideological symbols of their nation.

Attempts to spread American consumer culture abroad were highly effective. In postwar Europe, the US government promoted an American-style consumer culture which gradually pushed out Old World influences and expanded its own.[84] Europeans came to associate the United States with "wealth, a comfortable standard of living for the masses, freedom, modernity, consumption, and a peaceful life," all of which they desired for themselves.[85] However, Western Europeans did have agency over this process. Richard Pells argues they took aspects of American consumer culture and modified them to suit their own tastes and traditions, allowing them to maintain a level of cultural distinctiveness.[86] In other words, an early version of what sociologist Roland Robertson has referred to as "glocalization," the adaptation of the global into local contexts.[87] However, consumer culture in the Soviet Union has remained understudied until recently. Exciting new scholarship discusses both the evolving status of Russian women and the extent of their appropriation of US culture. The Soviet government depicted its women and their lives in an optimistic manner, just as the US government did with its own women. Lynne Attwood argues that after the Bolshevik Revolution a "rational" approach towards women's status called for gender equality and their full involvement in the public sphere. However, a "romantic" approach that called for women's continued commitment to their husbands, children, and the home lingered in the background.[88] By the Stalinist era, the Soviet Union attempted to combine its theoretical and social needs and promoted an "awkward" combination of both approaches, one which dictated that women should work like men yet still fulfil their motherly and wifely duties.[89] As Natasha Kolchevska has noted, the exemplary woman in postwar Soviet society became the "good worker," the "good citizen," and the "whole woman." In addition to her devotion to the state, she was heterosexual, maternal, loving, attentive to her home, family, and friends, susceptible to romance, and reasonably concerned about her looks. In other words, these women were "Angels in the Home and at Work."[90] Attwood argues that Russian women's magazines actively promoted this "New Woman." In a nation where the government controlled all aspects of mass communication, she calls magazines the "principal vehicles for the dissemination of 'official' images of Russian women to the female population, aimed at helping construct appropriate female identity."[91] By the Khrushchev era, official Soviet discourse called for women's active engagement in both the economy and the domestic sphere. The Soviet government heralded the equality of its women, yet simultaneously venerated them as mothers and managers of the home.[92] The Soviet government released an abundance of literature promoting these messages. Women were encouraged to fulfil their household duties by filling their homes with modern products that reflected a simpler and easier life, but without the "bourgeois" excess seen in the United States.[93] However, in spite of Khrushchev-era efforts to ease the burdens of housework and childcare, women were far from equal. They spent more time than men on housework and, as a result, had less time to improve their educations and skills and to participate in extracurricular activities.[94] Their lives were actually quite similar to those of American housewives, but in many cases, without the abundance and affordability of consumer goods. They were, in effect, expected to do it all.[95]

Naturally Russian women, like American women, had some semblance of agency over their lives. By the late 1950s/early 1960s, Russian women began to appropriate select aspects of US consumer culture when they could and ignored others, including fashion. Larisa Zakharova writes that Khrushchev-era reforms attempted to satisfy women's demands for more fashionable clothing options, but fashion was problematic for a rigidly structured Soviet economy; economists carefully planned clothing needs, as well as how long each item would last, leaving little room for the fickle world of fashion.[96] This lack of flexibility meant that formal Soviet fashion proved difficult to achieve. However, Soviet designers and female consumers increasingly defied these norms and took inspiration from Western magazines, fashion shows, and contact with foreigners.[97] Djurdja Bartlett writes that "everyday fashions" acted as an important intermediary between official Soviet fashions and Western ones. A state-sanctioned market, intended to satisfy the socialist middle classes in exchange for political support, provided options such as home dressmaking, tailors, and a black market to produce these items.[98] Similarly, in spite of Soviet attempts to portray an image of a refined culture, Russians also began to embrace Western-style films, music, and television shows. Kristin Roth-Ey writes that officials feared "Americanization," but found it difficult to control the impulses of Russian teenagers who appropriated US culture. Gradually, aspects of Soviet culture became Americanized.[99] These studies, which suggest that American cultural diplomacy was in some ways effective, and that Russians were willing to embrace new cultures once exposed to them, are useful to understanding the ways in which the USIA attempted to use cultural diplomacy to reach ordinary Russian women and promote the American way of life. The USIA's representations of women relegated them to a lifetime of marriage, motherhood, and homemaking, but at the same time, they were depicted as having well-rounded lives because consumer goods provided the much-needed convenience that allowed them to pursue other activities such as volunteer work. These representations showed women who were healthy, happy, and prosperous. They were also white, middle-class, and heterosexual. This singular image of the "free" American woman was juxtaposed with an image of an "oppressed" Russian woman, who had educational and employment opportunities, but little else in a communist state that deprived her of her basic necessities as a female.

Chapters 1 and 2 of this study discuss the ways in which postwar media shaped, reflected, and popularized notions and images of women, gender roles, and domesticity amid an early Cold War setting. While we tend to perceive the media as painting monolithic images of women, there are cases when the opposite was true. Women's magazines, particularly the *Ladies' Home Journal*, were integral in depicting varied, and contradictory, images of women. Chapter 1 focuses on America's "happy housewife heroine" and the "special privileges" the American government supposedly bestowed upon her, but also highlights the women who volunteered, were active in civic affairs, and on occasion even worked. The latter image, often absent from popular memory, was tied to a political setting in which the Cold War and anti-communist sentiment held sway.

Chapter 2 expands on the media's utilization of this postwar gender ideology to highlight the "other." In the context of the Cold War and struggle against communism, this was a far less appealing image of the Russian "babushka." She was most frequently seen as the supposedly overworked, haggard, and unhappy victim of a communist regime that provided her with few consumer goods. Her "special hardships" provided a convenient juxtaposition to the privileges of the American woman. She was a figure whom American women could view in the pages of postwar magazines, and could at times relate to, but more often pity because of her oppression. Brought together, these images signify the importance and utilization of women for explicitly Cold War–related purposes.

Chapter 3 provides an account of the Truman administration's difficulties in establishing a program of cultural diplomacy targeting the Soviet Union, particularly during a time when the concept was in its infancy, funding was difficult to obtain, and the Stalinist government obstructed foreign access to its people. As a result, the Truman administration had only two methods, both of which were limited, to reach the Russian people: VOA radio programming, which was occasionally jammed by the Soviet government, and *Amerika*, which faced continuous problems with Soviet censor approval and suspicious circulation practices before it was discontinued in 1952.[100] This chapter further focuses on the ways the Eisenhower administration overcame those difficulties to create an integrated, multifaceted, and well-funded information program. It discusses how America became heavily associated with a consumption-oriented lifestyle, and how consumption, in turn, was connected to women through their roles as housewives and mothers. The mass media reflected this "gendering of American consumer culture." When determining the direction of its information program, the USIA adopted these positive images of American women and presented them to Russian women as fact. Appealing to Russian women allowed the USIA to demonstrate that a capitalist, consumer-oriented lifestyle would indeed provide them with a better, and happier, way of life. Further, these images emphasize the point that the media and government were more heavily interrelated than ever before.

Chapters 4 and 5 demonstrate how these images and foreign policy came together through *Amerika* in its first years under Eisenhower. Remarkably little has been written on *Amerika*, but much can, and *should*, be said about it. Running from 1945 to 1952 and again from 1956 to 1994, it was one of the most long-lasting and far-reaching instruments of official US government cultural dissemination in the Soviet Union in terms of the sheer number of people that it reached across the country on a regular basis. These chapters focus on the period from 1956 to 1960. During this time, *Amerika* took on special significance, as it was the only means the USIA had to reach Russian women en masse. During this four-year period the magazine featured frequent and lengthy articles on women as feminine housewives, mothers, and consumers, as well as countless images of them in these roles. While chapter 4 focuses on fashion and femininity, chapter 5 focuses on the home and homemaking. These chapters demonstrate that women, gender, and consumption were intertwined and played an important role in Cold War cultural diplomacy.

As the 1960s witnessed the election of two Democratic administrations, and the beginning of an increasingly tumultuous domestic political and social landscape, the nature of *Amerika*'s content began to change. Chapter 6 outlines these changes, and how they reflected the ambiguity surrounding American women's roles throughout the decade. This chapter culminates in the magazine's March 1971 issue, which contained a lengthy "special report" on women and reflected the recent emergence of the second wave feminist movement. This issue provided a notable divergence from the articles that appeared in the magazine under Eisenhower's administration. A focus almost solely on traditional gender roles and consumption gave way to a more complex understanding of the diverse nature of American women's lives, as they were shown in different ages and life stages, and embracing new roles and experiences. As the government became increasingly aware of the extent of women's discontent and responded to it (in part because feminists *forced* them to respond to it), so too did *Amerika*. In other words, by 1971, the time was right for this special report. Chapter 6 juxtaposes this issue with *USSR*'s own special issue on women, which appeared almost one decade prior, in March 1962.

This study concludes by reflecting on the impact that *Amerika*, and more broadly conservative gender roles and a consumer-oriented way of life, had on the Russian people and their government. It discusses accounts by both the US media and government officials that lauded the popularity of the magazine. Indeed, *Amerika*'s influence appears to be reflected in the fact that, by the end of the 1950s, the Russian people began to demand an increase in living standards and in the availability of consumer goods. Fortunately for the Russian people, Khrushchev's ascendency signalled a new period in Soviet leadership, one which reflected a genuine desire on his part to meet these demands. Khrushchev pledged to implement key consumer reforms for his citizens and, importantly, began the construction of *Khrushchevki*. While these mass-produced single-family apartments would have never met US standards, they signalled the first attempt on the part of the Soviet government to move away from the crowded communal apartments that characterized urban life. Finally, this study examines the extent to which the USIA's cultural activities, as well as the lure of an "American way of life," could be considered responsible for the increased demands made by the Russian people, and the changes Khrushchev instituted. During the 1960s, American-style consumer reforms did not reach the level that the US *or* Soviet government desired, but *Amerika* was an important first step in heightening Russian women's desire for a higher standard of living and access to mass-produced consumer goods. Once these windows to the West were opened even slightly, there was little chance of reverting to the past. These were desires that would continue to surface throughout the remainder of the Cold War, up to the collapse of the Soviet Union on 25 December 1991. As Riesman noted in his fictional tale "The Nylon War," if the Russian people were allowed to sample the riches of America, they would "not long tolerate masters who gave them tanks and spies instead of vacuum cleaners and beauty parlors."[101]

PART ONE

Shaping Women, Gender, and the Communist Threat through the *Ladies' Home Journal*

Chapter One

The "Modern Woman": The "Special Privileges" of American Womanhood in the *Ladies' Home Journal*

> For fifteen years and longer, there has been an attempt in America to get women back into the home by glorifying feminine fulfillment – women's fulfillment as a wife and mother – as the sole aim and justification of woman's existence. The glorification of the housewife bears an uneasy, hypocritical relationship to the actual facts of woman's life today, and is responsible for the otherwise inexplicable distress of modern American women. While millions of words have been written and are being written to help women adjust to this image of feminine fulfillment, I question the image itself – the new "feminine mystique."[1]

The Winter 1963 issue of the *Ladies' Home Journal* was billed as a special issue on men. It included articles such as "10 Ways to Keep a Husband – Young," "What Men Have Done for Love," "Why Husbands Run Away," and "Masculinity, What Is It? What Makes a Man Masculine?"[2] However, not all of them focused specifically on men. They included regular columns such as "Journal about Home," "Family Money Management," and "Dr. Spock Talks with Mothers."[3] Given the subject matter of this special issue, it was ironic that it contained one of the most iconic pieces published in the magazine's history: a controversial two-pager called "Have Housewives Traded Brains for Brooms?" Excerpted from Betty Friedan's newly released and future bestseller *The Feminine Mystique*, it shed light on the "new femininity" characterized by shopping, chauffeuring, dishwashers, dryers, electric mixers, gardening, waxing, polishing, and all of the small chores that had turned housework effectively into a career for women.[4] The *Journal* happily welcomed comments from readers, and they wrote in en masse, the majority with criticism for a writer who decried the importance of the home and family in a woman's life and questioned the happiness of the housewife and mother.[5]

Friedan's iconic description of the "happy housewife heroine" was one that not only permeated postwar discourse, but also became etched in popular memory as a symbol of a supposedly simpler time. This "average" woman was white, native-born, heterosexual, middle class, married, with children, and without a job or a career.[6] She utilized modern household technology and convenience foods, and preferred consuming to producing. She created a loving and stable family life that provided the safety net needed in a world threatened by Soviet expansionism and communism. She was distinctly feminine, both in her appearance and in her demeanour. Overall, she was satisfied with her life.[7] In essence, that life symbolized a dream, one that could only be found in America.[8] The "special privileges" that allowed women the ability to pursue and enjoy traditional gender roles, without the interference of paid employment, were ones that were supposedly bestowed upon American women by a benevolent government that placed them on a pedestal.[9] Purveyors of American culture created a discourse that perpetuated and glorified this domestic "ideal," and placed women at its forefront.[10] Among the purveyors of this discourse were the mass circulation monthly magazines geared towards women, particularly the *Ladies' Home Journal*. By the postwar era, and up to the birth of second wave feminism, this discourse had come to define American womanhood, and it was idealized in the pages of these magazines in such a way that made it seem not just accessible, but also desirable, for all women. As a result, these magazines became targets of criticism from journalists such as Friedan, who condemned them for their abandonment of the independent, career-driven heroines of the Great Depression and World War II.

However, in spite of the popular perception brought forward by Friedan that postwar women's magazines conveyed monolithic messages about women and gender, these magazines contained multiple and often contradictory messages, reflective of the Cold War setting.[11] Women's magazines expanded the traditional definition of "domestic," often linking the home and family to the national discourse through major concerns of the postwar period, including health and healthcare, a crisis in education, and the ability to maintain a culture of mass consumption.[12] Further, they used anti-communist sentiment to advocate for women's political participation and to promote a positive image of politically active women who showed allegiance not just to their homes and families but also to their nation.[13] Indeed, in the early postwar period, women's magazines had a dual purpose. The first was to reflect the conservative gender norms of the time in an attempt to sell them to American women. However, they also went beyond the complacent "happy housewife heroine" that Friedan described. Their second purpose was to highlight and encourage women's political participation. While these purposes appeared at odds with each other, they were connected through a Cold War setting in which domestic events further contributed to a virulent anti-communist campaign. They included the 21 January 1950 conviction of Alger Hiss, a career government official who was accused of spying for the Soviet Union, and the 9 February 1950 address by Senator Joseph McCarthy (R-WI) to the Women's Republican Club of Wheeling, West Virginia, in which he declared that he possessed a list of the names of 57 communists in the State Department.[14] These events were followed by the 29 March 1951 convictions, and subsequent executions, of Julian and Ethel Rosenberg, private citizens accused of committing espionage for the Soviet Union. By the early 1950s, a domestic Red Scare enveloped the nation. Unlike the Red Scare of 1917–1920, its successor profoundly altered the mood of the nation, negatively impacting scores of individuals, including elected government officials, career civil servants, members of the armed forces, academics, and Hollywood actors. A deviation from the "norm," frequently perceived as an unwavering devotion to "American" values, became associated with un-Americanness, and therefore communism.[15] For women, this "norm" was predicated on a life of white, middle-class, heterosexual domesticity, epitomized in the pages of postwar women's magazines, much as it had been in other decades, but now with the backdrop of the Cold War. Women were shown that only through domestic containment could they keep the enemy at bay.

During the postwar era, a variety of media, including print, film, radio, and, of course, the newly emerging and wildly popular medium of television, shaped and reflected gender norms and representations. However, mass circulation monthly women's magazines were extremely effective for their ability to reach and influence countless numbers of women, particularly those who could not yet afford a television set. These magazines included *Better Homes and Gardens, Cosmopolitan, Good Housekeeping, Mademoiselle, McCall's, Redbook, Vogue*, and *Women's Day*, but the magazine that deserved special attention was the *Ladies' Home Journal*.[16] By the early Cold War, the *Journal* was the nation's most popular women's magazine, with a monthly circulation of five million, and was, arguably, its most influential.[17] This position was one it retained until 1960, when it was overtaken by its long-time rival, *McCall's*, after it began to adopt a more modern approach to print culture such as the inclusion of colour pages.[18] The *Ladies' Home Journal* regularly contained articles that not only reflected the gender norms and representations of the era but, through the size of its readership, also shaped them.

As a result, it was an ideal outlet from which to highlight the wider politics of the era. As John G. Morris, the *Journal's* picture editor noted, while *Life* magazine, the most popular magazine of the postwar period, claimed to be "America's most powerful editorial force," the *Journal's* influence was more pervasive. *Life* lectured American readers, but the *Journal* addressed them, calling itself "the magazine women believe in."[19] In 1935, the Curtis Publishing Company, whose publications included the popular *Saturday Evening Post,* approached married writers Bruce and Beatrice Gould to co-edit the magazine, then mockingly referred to as the "Old Ladies' Journal."[20] The September 1935 issue began an editorship that lasted for the next twenty-seven years.[21] The *Ladies' Home Journal* of the early Cold War period reflected the gender norms that its readers supposedly followed. White, middle-class, heterosexual women were generally depicted as happily embracing their roles as feminine housewives and mothers, and deeply satisfied with their ability to consume. However, in spite of this emphasis on traditional gender roles, the Goulds took a decidedly modern approach to the magazine's direction and structure when they took over its editorship. Its leanings, while not necessarily feminist, were certainly pro-feminine, and were reflected in the motto it adopted in the 1940s, "never underestimate the power of a woman." The Goulds employed female staff members and writers and encouraged women's political participation.[22] They encouraged women to extend their roles beyond the home and into the local community for the explicit purposes of combatting the spread of communism. Their interest in politics was evident in the number of articles and images devoted to it and the Cold War in general. Throughout the early postwar period, the structure of the *Journal* remained consistent. It had sections devoted to either excerpted or condensed novels, "Fiction," "Special Features," "General Features," "Fashions and Beauty," "Food and Homemaking," and "Poetry." It also contained sections on any combination of areas including gardening, interior design, and architecture. While most of the *Journal's* content clearly focused on the traditional woman, both its "Special Features" and "General Features" sections frequently delved into diverse topics, which included politics.

In the postwar period, the *Ladies' Home Journal* defined the term "femininity" for its readers. Perhaps nobody was a better expert on the topic than Louise Paine Benjamin, the *Journal's* beauty editor and author of *Why Men Like Us: Your Passport to Charm* (1937). In January 1947, she articulated to female readers what it meant to be feminine.[23]

> Femininity, in spite of the title of this article, does not begin at home, but in back of that, in the *mind*. It is an attitude. It is a feeling about one's

relationship to people – including men. As nearly as I can discover, it is a feeling about living and, in particular, a feeling about one's relationship to people – including men. As nearly as I can discover, it is true and delicious womanliness which causes its possessor to feel she is lucky to be a woman and, therefore, a potential sweetheart, wife and mother.[24]

Benjamin noted that femininity was a young girl's belief that she should "take pride and satisfaction in her sex. Her whole happiness will be largely determined by this ability, and willingness, to respect herself as a woman." Benjamin provided readers with advice on how to be a "lovely girl." This included developing proper etiquette and dress, treating older people respectfully, giving the illusion of being pursued even when already "caught," never ignoring your partner, having a pleasant voice, learning at least one "socially useful sport" to help you fit into a crowd, regularly attending church, and volunteering.[25] While Benjamin's thoughts on femininity were her own, they were also shared by the *Journal*'s editors. In October 1952, reader Nancy B. Levesque wrote to the magazine asking the editors a simple but perplexing question: How do you define femininity? The Goulds responded with a simple answer, "if you've got a man interested in you, you're feminine – enough."[26] These sentiments were reflected more broadly in the *Ladies' Home Journal*. Throughout the early postwar period, the magazine deployed images of supposedly happy and fulfilled American women as either training to be, or current, feminine housewives and mothers. Femininity, marriage, motherhood, and domesticity were shown as central elements of women's lives, all with the backdrop of consumption set against them. Because femininity was important to the *Journal*, it was assumed to be important to its readers, and a trait that should be reflected throughout all aspects of their lives. In June 1952, the magazine provided readers with "The 'How to Get Married' Chart." It noted that 93.5 per cent of all women would eventually marry and gave tips on how to avoid falling in that dreaded 6.5 per cent. It included suggestions on US states where men were most likely to marry, the clubs a woman should join, places she could meet a husband, sports she should participate in, education she should receive, and jobs she should acquire. While other *Ladies' Home Journal* articles regularly celebrated a woman's passivity, this article unusually suggested that she should be *aggressive* in her desire to get married, as this was the way to get a man to the altar. The article also gave recommendations on her appearance, suggesting that men preferred women that were shorter than them, between 100 and 140 pounds, and brunette. By odds of three to one, they preferred women in "extreme feminine dress." While the average male was lured by rich colours, such as red and royal blue, executives were lured by "dainty" colours such as peach and pink. All disliked shorts and sportswear.[27] Benjamin's earlier article also confirmed the importance of proper dress. One of her nuggets of wisdom for being a "lovely girl" was to always "dress up for a fight." She was not referring to a physical alteration, but rather noted that if a woman always looked her best, she would have more confidence in herself and be ready for any opportunity.[28] The *Journal* had a clear opinion on what it meant to be feminine and it conveyed this information to its loyal readers.

According to the *Ladies' Home Journal*, the desire to project femininity was closely related to the ideal goals of every normal, well-adjusted woman: to attract, obtain, and retain male companionship. This would lead to the achievement of her life's objectives, to become a wife and mother. In order to do so, her outward appearance, including beauty and dress, were of utmost importance. This renewed emphasis on a woman's clothing signalled a deviation from previous years, when wartime restrictions were in place, and fabric was in short supply. When magazines such as the *Journal* encouraged women to purchase new clothes, or even to make them, in order to appear feminine, it was signalling that the days of Depression era and wartime thrift were behind them. Columns such as "Little Gem of a Wardrobe" instructed women to sew their own clothing, appear fashionable, and accessorize. First appearing in February 1947, the same month and year that Christian Dior debuted his revolutionary "New Look" on the Parisian runway, it immediately articulated its rationale.[29] It indicated that many women loved the idea of having high-quality, but simple clothing that was versatile and timeless. They could accessorize outfits with items such as jewellery, flowers, apron overskirts, scarves, or belts. They preferred this approach to dressing rather than "one-season, hit-or-miss clothes." The article suggested that a good way for a woman to get exactly what she wanted in style, colour, and fabric was to make these "costumes" herself. That month's "Little Gem of a Wardrobe" provided accompanying sketches and patterns of three items, a black dress, a dark or neutral suit, and a coat that could go over both.[30] Subsequent columns followed the same approach, providing women with "Hollywood Patterns," all of which were supposedly simple to make, but appeared both luxurious and alluring on their statuesque models. "Little Gem of a Wardrobe" attempted to instil in *Ladies' Home Journal* readers a seemingly frugal approach to fashion, one that encouraged women to sew their own clothing and favour timeless fashions. At the same time, it encouraged them to appear feminine and fashionable through good designs, high-quality fabrics, and trendy accessories.

Interestingly, even the *Journal*'s non-fashion related articles took this same approach. This included one of its longest running monthly columns, "How America Lives." "How America Lives" began in February 1940 as a way to introduce readers to diverse families living across the country. While highlighting a particular family, a connecting article frequently made over the woman at the centre of the article, typically a housewife, and often did so on a budget. February 1948's "Welcome Change" made over thirty-three-year-old Mary Dickson. Dickson was a busy but happy housewife in Rochester, New York, whose frugal habits allowed her family to save money while living on just $71 a week. Her small budget left her little for a proper wardrobe. With the help of the *Journal*'s beauty editor, Mary transitioned from her "severe" look, a bulky suit with a high collar, thick stockings, practical shoes, an unfashionable hat, and "unbecoming" hair and makeup, to her "new look." This new look not only referenced Mary's makeover but also the Dior-inspired fashion and beauty trends of the postwar period. Dior's designs deviated from the unshapely, utilitarian styles of the previous decades that women like Mary wore, and now included a distinctly nineteenth-century look with rounded shoulders, a fuller and longer skirt, and a cinched waist intended to accentuate an hourglass figure, that is, a small waist and large bust and hips. Accessories, as described in "Little Gem of a Wardrobe," were central to this new look.[31] In other words, with Dior's "New Look," women would once again appear feminine, and thus ready to embrace their roles as housewives and mothers. Mary's own new look was similar. It consisted of a slender dress, sheer stockings, modern pumps, a new haircut and permanent, and more glamorous makeup. In addition, the article noted that, although she weighed only 133 pounds, she was given an "illusion of superslimness" with a high-waisted, elasticized girdle. The article concluded by telling the *Ladies' Home Journal* reader that there could be a "whole new world of beauty" for her too. With honest self-analysis, followed by the organization of her appearance, she could enhance her most attractive features. This "new look" would be a welcome change not just for her but also the people around her.[32] Similarly a March 1952 article made over Arvella Weir, a twenty-one-year-old housewife from Seattle. The mother of three-year-old triplets, Weir naturally saw to it that money went to her children first, and then to her clothing. In "Pretty Mother's Wardrobe ... $99.00," *Journal* editors helped her choose an economical and versatile wardrobe. This included a cotton dress for the park, a formal one for parties, a suit to go into town, a raincoat for year-round weather, and pedal pushers and t-shirts for regular days. Her new wardrobe reflected her feminine side yet provided her with the practical items she needed as a mother of three.[33] April 1952's "Stay in Style Wardrobe" made over Duda Kutvirt, a Czech housewife from Rochester, New York. Kutvirt described herself as a "bargain hunter" who spent practically nothing on clothes. Mrs. Kutvirt favoured quality and good designs, and the editors helped her put together a wardrobe that cost only $111.56. Unlike Dickson, however, Mrs. Kutvirt did not need a drastic makeover. She appeared to have already taken a cue from "Little Gem of a Wardrobe." Six images of Mrs. Kutvirt showed her as a slim, attractive woman with modern hair and makeup. Her wardrobe, however, was updated with spring suits, silk dresses, and printed cotton skirts. She accessorized with hats, scarves, veils, belts, and even her husband's tie. Kutvirt must have been quite popular with *Ladies' Home Journal* editors as she appeared in another article that month called "Are You an Up-to-Date Beauty?"[34] The article encouraged women to exercise in preparation for the summer, modernize their hair, and maintain a daily beauty regimen. It also included an image of Kutvirt accompanied by a complimentary caption that referred to her as slim and appealing.[35]

October 1952's issue made over thirty-eight-year-old Eugenia Simons, a Los Angeles housewife whose marriage struggles, a rarity for the magazine, were highlighted in "How America Lives."[36] The *Journal*'s beauty editor chose to replace Simons' "severe" dress with a more feminine look. The article showed images of Eugenia before, dressed in a sharply tailored suit and wearing an unattractive hat, and after, in a flowing dress and soft curls, both of which highlighted her femininity and brought out her softer side. Aptly titled "The Soft Touch," the article encouraged her to wear softer colours and lines, and to add one pretty touch a day, such as a hankie poking out of a blouse pocket or a ribbon in her hair. It also told her to invest in colourful flats and crisp aprons or housedresses, which would make her look and feel fresher while doing housework. Keeping in mind the context of that month's "How America Lives," the article intertwined fashion, beauty, and marriage by also giving Eugenia marriage advice. This advice included slowing down from her daily tasks, actively listening to her children and husband, avoiding arguments when possible, and encouraging family fun. The article optimistically concluded that the "approachable woman" was one whom children, family, and friends turned to for help and fun.[37] At the same time that the *Journal* discussed budgets, however, it also emphasized fashion trends, some of which were likely unobtainable for the ordinary reader. Articles instructed women how to dress for each season, as well as events such as holiday parties, beach days, and vacations. At times, they focused on essentials in a woman's wardrobe, including suits, black dresses, and sweaters, and other times they showcased luxury items, such as furs. They highlighted couture fashions, particularly from Paris, and they also revealed "new fashion" trends, including maternity wear.[38] Fashion articles in the *Ladies' Home Journal*, with their emphasis on budgets, were seemingly made for every woman, yet at the same time also emphasized items that were likely inaccessible to the ordinary reader. All of them, however, highlighted the necessity for a woman to showcase her feminine side for the purposes of appearing attractive in the presence of men.

As seemingly natural stages in every woman's life, weddings and marriages were frequently written about in the *Ladies' Home Journal*. This focus on the domestic "ideal" reflected postwar reality. The 1950 US census, for example, indicated that 65.7 per cent of American women over the age of fourteen were, in fact, married.[39] Articles such as May 1954's "The Big Wedding" told the story of Mary Jo Alhoff and Don Schmidt, both twenty-three years old and from St. Louis, Missouri, as they prepared for their wedding day. Mary Jo and Don had met at a high school dance while students, and had courted for seven years, two of which were spent apart while Don served in the army. They were religious and attended mass every morning, were university-educated, and had well-paying jobs, she as a laboratory technician and he as a supervisor in a printing department. They had gotten engaged three years prior and had saved for their wedding, even managing to make a down payment on a home and accumulating enough savings for furniture and a car. In essence, Mary Jo and Don appeared to be the perfect young American couple. "The Big Wedding" was an appropriate title for this article, as this was an elaborate affair given the time period. It included a one-hundred-and-fifty-person engagement party, four bridal showers, a "spinster party," a rehearsal for an eighteen-person wedding party, a fifty-six-person breakfast on the morning of the wedding, and a six-hundred-person afternoon reception. Mary Jo's wedding and subsequent marriage were long-thought-out events in her life, just as they would seemingly be for every *Ladies' Home Journal* reader. Knowing that Don was "the one" from the moment she met him, Mary Joe had planned for both early on, choosing her china pattern on her eighteenth birthday and preparing her bridal trousseau two years in advance of the wedding. In the end, Mary Jo and Don's wedding went off smoothly, and, following the reception, they immediately left for their week-long honeymoon in Florida. The *Journal*'s article did not just convey the details of their extravagant wedding, it also made clear Don's views on marriage. While Mary Jo had a good job and made the same amount of money as her husband, he did not want a "career girl" for a wife. During their first year of marriage, he intended to use his salary for living expenses, and hers for major purchases and to accumulate further savings. According to Don, if Mary Jo failed to quit her job after one year, he planned to "become so uncooperative about the house that his wife will be too tired to keep up both a job and a home."[40] In spite of Mary Jo's professional accomplishments, it appeared that within time she would eventually follow the gender norms reflected in the *Ladies' Home Journal*.

Those gender norms were firmly cemented in the happy marriage of Pat and Eddie Gorrie, the subjects of September 1955's "The Best Things in Life Are Free." The article focused on their life in Ridley Park, Pennsylvania, where they lived in a small house and managed to get by on Eddie's commensurately small salary. They had one daughter, and Pat was pregnant with their second child. The article described twenty-five-year-old Pat as a young, healthy, energetic homemaker with a spotless house. When Pat looked back on her life, she did so fondly, but admitted that the days before she met Eddie were unstable. Born in Philadelphia, she moved from one "career" to another, as secretary, government girl, and page girl, and did small jobs such as writing and working in radio and television. Pat eventually landed her dream job in New York City as a secretary to a press agent, and shared a Greenwich Village apartment with an aspiring actress. She took public transportation to her office located on Fifth Avenue. Pat appeared to live the life of a modern career women, until she became homesick and returned to Philadelphia six months later, where she accepted a job as a government stenographer. No doubt following the advice of magazines such as the *Ladies' Home Journal*, Pat began to suspect that she "didn't really want a career."[41] Her wishes came true one night, in January 1952, when she met her future husband, Eddie, at an ice-skating rink. They were married just six weeks later. Upon returning from their honeymoon, Pat quit her job to devote her "enthusiasm to learning how to be a homemaker." She wanted an old-fashioned family, with routine and normalcy. She intended to be there for her children, establish family traditions, and ensure that her daughter was taught homemaking, a skill Pat never learned from her own mother, who worked and never cooked for the family.[42] After she was married, Pat taught herself these skills, learning how to cook and sew. Her housecleaning revolved around Eddie's shiftwork. She cleaned while he was at work, so they could spend time together as a family while he was home. Her tasks included cleaning the bathroom every day and ironing everything, even sheets and towels.[43] Her lists, placed strategically throughout the kitchen, helped her to be "consistent" in her housework.[44] In essence,

Pat had transformed from a career girl into the perfect housewife. Pat's happiness was evident when she admitted that everything she had ever wanted had come true. While she was young she had a career, but she now had a wonderful husband, a beautiful daughter, and her own home. According to her, her favourite career out of all of her pursuits was motherhood.[45] When asked if her marriage had any problems, she proclaimed that, aside from being slightly pinched financially, there were none. She felt that luxuries were not important; she found ways to keep herself entertained, including visiting with family, attending church, gathering with her neighbourhood wives' club, participating in outdoor sports, and seeing free concerts in nearby Philadelphia. She proclaimed that she did not know how anyone could "complain about being a housewife – marriage is the best job there is."[46] Pat's life, while satisfying for her, was likely unrealistic for *Ladies' Home Journal* readers. It sold a version of domesticity that made the life of a non-wage-earning housewife and mother seem attainable for all. Further, Pat's comments reflected the notion that happiness for women lay solely in marriage, motherhood, and the home.

Proficiency in homemaking and motherhood was a consistent theme throughout the *Ladies' Home Journal* and was evident in its attempts to show women how to properly keep house and be good mothers. In the context of the early Cold War, these roles were of the utmost importance. As housewives and mothers, free from the supposed burdens of a career, their focus could turn to bearing children and raising them to become patriotic citizens, thus ensuring the continuation of American civilization. In an age of domestic containment, "good housekeeping" was used as a line of defence against communist attack. As McEnaney writes, for women, good housekeeping included knowledge of the basic rules of modern warfare, training family members in disaster preparedness, containing their panic and fear, and preparing the home for attack and recovery by gathering food and essential supplies and by keeping it clean.[47] In a 1955 speech, Katherine Howard, Deputy Administrator of the Federal Civil Defense Administration, indicated that good housekeeping was "one of the best protections against fire in an atomic blast."[48] The *Journal* ran countless articles on American women's efforts to keep house. Ordinary housewives like Pat, even without training from their mothers and while having to pinch pennies, turned houses into homes, made their tasks seem nearly effortless, and were happy in the process. In the few instances when the *Journal* ran articles showing the struggles of ordinary women in this role, they were often turned into life lessons for readers, so they too could become good housewives and mothers.

Articles such as August 1954's "The Scrambled Housewife" deviated from the gleeful images of women such as Pat. It focused on Dorothy Canner, a housewife and mother of four living in a new home in the quintessential postwar suburb, Levittown, New York. Dorothy was more established than Pat, but much less adept in her role. She admitted that her husband had a reasonable income, but she spent money on unnecessary items and they never had savings. She called herself disorganized, admitted she frequently woke up tired and cranky, and often got mad and yelled at her husband and her children.[49] Interestingly, the *Journal* attributed the latter trait to her Italian temperament, as if to suggest that American women could have neither impatience nor anger. Dorothy also noted the inordinate number of chores her husband did, including putting the children to bed, getting up to check on them at night, shopping for their clothes, doing weekend laundry, occasionally cooking, and washing the dishes.[50] Dorothy's case seemed like an unusual one for the typically sunny pages of the *Ladies' Home Journal*, but it had a purpose. The *Journal* portrayed Dorothy as a frivolous and frazzled wife and mother, incessantly spending on credit and exasperated with her disobedient children. She proclaimed that she hated to cook, blamed her dislike of the kitchen on the chaos that her children caused in it, and ordered groceries over the phone without knowing the cost for delivery.[51] When asked if debts were the chief obstacle in her marriage, she proclaimed that *she* was "the chief obstacle. I have no organization."[52] When Bill, Dorothy's husband, was asked the same question, he kindly proclaimed that they had no *real* ones, although he admitted they needed a budget. Turning to the help of a psychiatrist and the *Journal*'s homemaking editor, Dorothy and Bill developed a budget to trim their expenses as well as a plan to discipline their children. By the end of the article, six weeks after their initial interview, Dorothy happily declared that things were "100 per cent better." She felt more energetic and no longer "flew off the handle." The kids even did small jobs around the house, which provided them with a sense of belonging.[53] A related article showed how the Canners developed a new budget by determining Bill's average monthly salary as an insurance salesman, adding up their fixed expenses and allotting money for variable expenses. Importantly, Dorothy changed her methods as a homemaker. For the first time, she planned her menus ahead of time, created grocery lists, and shopped carefully, cutting costs whenever she could. She streamlined her tasks, setting the breakfast table the night before, and getting up half an hour before the family so she was able to serve them breakfast on time. Preparing full meals had an impact both on the family's expenses and nutrition. Bill no longer had to purchase snacks while at work to maintain his energy, and her children ate more regularly and healthily. As a result, they became sick less, thus reducing the expensive medical bills that were a source of concern. Ultimately, the overall well-being of the Canner family appeared to rest in Dorothy's hands. Once she learned to embrace her "natural role" and be a proper homemaker, their family life improved tremendously.[54] Dorothy was so successful in her tasks that she penned an accompanying article, "Interesting and Inexpensive," which showcased her newly acquired talent: cooking. Dorothy's expertise was reflected in diverse recipes such as barbequed lamb shanks with chive rice, vegetable chow mein, spaghetti with clam sauce, fried chicken, and Belgian meatballs. Her meals, of course, would be incomplete without the classic American convenience foods of the era, including a cottage-cheese mould made with gelatin, a cake made from a packaged mix, and grilled hot dogs, which allowed Bill to occasionally take over the cooking, but only in a traditionally masculine manner, through the barbeque.[55] In the first pages of these articles on the Canner family, Dorothy seemed like a frivolous and frazzled housewife, unable to maintain a budget or properly care for her children. By their end, she had turned into an expert housewife and mother, happy in her role, and proud of her newfound skills. The *Ladies' Home Journal* had successfully demonstrated how *any* woman could transform herself into the ideal housewife. The suggestion was implicit: a failure to improve one's homemaking skills could lead to serious problems that included not just an unhappy marriage but also maladjusted children. The prospect of being a "bad mother" was met with dire warnings for *Ladies' Home Journal* readers. It could result in childhood problems that continued into adulthood, including hypersensitivity, illness, obesity, alcoholism, criminality, or homosexuality. All of these ailments threatened postwar gender roles, particularly American masculinity, as well as the traditional marriage. This mentality was adopted and propagated at an early stage of the Cold War, when a November 1945 article asked the "serious" question "Are American Moms a Menace?" and warned that an "overbearing mother" was a "threat to our national existence." They could, in essence, drastically alter the entire national culture and its outlook.[56] Throughout the next decade, similar articles appeared in the magazine.[57]

Under the Goulds' editorship a host of long-running columns emphasized gender norms. They included "Diary of Domesticity," by Gladys Taylor; "Ask Any Woman," by Marcelene Cox; and "There's a Man in the House," by Harlan Miller.[58] Two of its most enduring columns focused solely on the institution of marriage. The first, "Making Marriage Work," by Clifford R. Adams, a psychologist at Pennsylvania State

College, ran from October 1947 to October 1961. Its first column, rather surprisingly, warned young women to "Be Cautious about Marrying." Adams warned women that if they sought independence, were in poor health, had unhappy parents, were set in their ways, or did not want children, a career was the wiser choice. However, if they were stable, had a happy childhood, were interested in community activities and enjoyed keeping a house, marriage was the ideal choice.[59] The implications of his words were clear, unless something was wrong with a woman or her surroundings, marriage was the norm and could provide her with happiness and fulfilment. Otherwise, she should "relegate" herself to a career. Next month's column was more forthright, asking women the question "Are You Failing as a Wife?" It recognized the tremendous amount of work that went into being a good wife and mother, and told the reader that in these roles her most important jobs were that of housekeeper, business manager, caretaker, nurse-governess, companion, psychologist, and, finally, lover. She would provide good meals and keep the house orderly and clean, create a budget, ensure household supplies were always on hand, maintain her family's household equipment and paperwork, care for her children when healthy and ill, take an interest in her husband's activities, praise him frequently, and always "respond to his mood." In other words, the postwar woman was required to act as a superwoman. Adams indicated that if she was deficient in any two of these jobs, her marriage was lacking.[60] Subsequent columns followed the same formula, asking women those important questions that could define the nature of their relationship, including "Are You a Good Housekeeper?" "Is Your Husband Bored?" "Is Your Husband Happy?" and "Am I a Responsible Wife?"[61] Each of these columns included a series of questions called "Ask Yourself?" that allowed a woman to reflect on her marriage and seek ways to improve it, mainly by improving herself. January 1955's column was entitled "Are You a Creative Wife?" Using the word creative in its title was indeed a creative way to avoid using stereotypical words such as nosy, jealous, and needy. Adams discussed the need for a wife to respect her husband's privacy, to avoid looking through his personal belongings, prying into his job or business, supervising his personal behaviour, and monopolizing his time. The article warned that denying her husband his privacy would show she had little trust in him, and that as a result, she could soon have real reason not to trust him. Adams' solutions to these problems depended on the "understanding and imagination of a thoughtful, creative wife." In an "Ask Yourself" portion of the column, he asked the reader if, in the past month, she had bought a gift for her husband, served him a new dish, made herself appear more attractive, shared new stories with him, and complimented him. Adams' questions also involved outside activities for both partners. Had they eaten out together at least once in the past month, had friends in for the evening, gone to shows together, and visited acquaintances?[62] None of these questions involved asking a woman to develop her own hobbies and interests independently of her husband. December 1948's "Changes a Husband Would Make" appeared to *finally* address the "problems of husbands," but such was not the case. Instead, changes referred to those a husband would elicit in his wife, rather than in himself. Several hundred husbands, categorized as "happy" and "unhappy," were surveyed and asked the question "What changes would you make in your wife, if you could?" The top answer for unhappy husbands was increased sexual desire. In this case, Adams noted that if a wife was less responsive than her husband wished, she could consider herself partly responsible if he turned to another woman. The changes that closely followed sexual desire included uneven temperament, a tendency to scold, an absence of affection, a lack of thrift, and a carelessness of dress. Again, Adams told wives that the answer to potential problems in their marriages lay with them and asked them questions related to their own improvement.[63] March 1949's column, "What's Wrong with Husbands?," acted as a response to December's column, asking women to list their husband's faults. The top responses consisted of "does not talk things over freely," "is impatient," "criticizes me," "does not show his affection," and "is always wrapped up in his business." Instead of focusing on how their husbands could improve, Adams asked women to find the root cause of their husband's issues, perhaps stemming from his childhood. If they could not do this, they could rather simplistically "let him know how much it hurts; he will probably try to do better."[64]

The *Ladies' Home Journal*'s emphasis on marriage was reflected in its most enduring and popular column, "Can This Marriage Be Saved?" The long-running column first appeared in January 1953 as an eight-part series and was different in format than the *Journal*'s other columns. Each column discussed the marital issues of an ordinary couple, and, rather than strictly provide advice as Adams did, gave the perspectives of both the husband and wife. The column was accompanied by the input of a counsellor, who provided guidance, as well as a concluding – often happy – update on their marriage.[65] All cases were seen at the American Institute of Family Relations (AIFR) in Los Angeles, a non-profit organization opened by Dr. Paul Popenoe in 1930. Known as the "world's largest and best-known marriage-counselling center," the institute reflected Popenoe's own views on marriage. Popenoe, referred to as the "father of marriage counselling," believed that the majority of divorces were unnecessary and undesirable. According to the *Journal*, his institute gave immediate, practical help to unhappy couples, and educated the general public on family living.[66] At the same time he believed in the sanctity of marriage, he was known for his work in eugenics and as an advocate for compulsory sterilization. However, as Molly Ladd-Taylor has pointed out, while eugenics is often associated with race and class, gender and the family were paramount to Popenoe's understanding of it. Born in 1888, Popenoe, who was interested in the connections between eugenics and marriage counselling as early as the 1910s, wrote, "I began to realize that if we were going to promote a sound population, we would not only have to get the right kind of people married, but we would have to keep them married."[67] As eugenics became closely associated with Nazi Germany and Adolf Hitler's horrific attempts to create a superior Aryan race at the expense of those he believed to be "inferior," the US government began to distance itself from its own controversial history of forced sterilizations. Popenoe began to focus on a eugenics strategy that was more compatible with postwar American political and cultural ideals, namely one that emphasized the heterosexual marriage and family.[68] The connections between Popenoe's beliefs regarding eugenics and "Can This Marriage Be Saved?" are clear. Marital advice, properly articulated by counsellors in the *Ladies' Home Journal*, could influence the millions of white, middle-class, heterosexual women who read the magazine, thus ensuring that marriages were "saved," children were conceived and raised according to "proper" values, the nation's population increased, and American civilization flourished.[69]

In the first column, the AIFR boasted of thirty counsellors who had seen 20,000 people and succeeded in saving 80 per cent of their marriages. One of these couples was Diana and Guy; married for six years, they had rushed into marriage after only six weeks of dating. Diana wanted a home of her own, children, a husband who helped with housework, and romantic attention. Guy was resentful of Diana's complaints about their rented apartment and childless marriage, her poor housekeeping skills, her newfound interest in art, and her job, which allowed her to socialize with other men. Their revelations, as well as their counsellor, caused each to see the error of their ways, stop criticizing, and start understanding each other. Guy became a more romantic lover, took an interest in Diana's art, and assisted in the housekeeping, particularly cooking. Diana began dressing more attractively for her husband and learned to keep house, and both had a common newfound interest in gardening. They compromised in purchasing a small house with a large garden; she quit her job and, at the time of printing, was expecting their *second* child. In other words, Diana and Guy now had the perfect marriage, a growing family, and were, as the column put it, "supremely happy."[70] Subsequent columns focused on marital issues related to frivolous, selfish, and career-minded wives; jealous, cheating, drunk, and even abusive husbands; sexless marriages; interfering in-laws; and homosexuality.[71] Regardless of the issue, the featured couple, but specifically the wife, consistently recognized and overcame their differences and stayed together for the sake of their marriage and, when they had them, children. Readers wrote in expressing their satisfaction with the column and the insight it brought. In March 1954, one woman wrote that she had enjoyed every single column, as she herself had benefited from the AIFR. While her husband had refused to see the counsellor after their initial appointments, she continued to do so, developing a deeper insight into herself and her relationships, thus enabling her to have a comfortable and happy home life, and become an active member of her community. The woman's name was withheld, but she claimed that she was happier than she had ever been, had a good marriage, a kind and considerate husband, and normal, happy children.[72] In January 1955, Mrs. D.L. Hubert wrote that while she was happily married, the column helped her "see lots of ways I can make even our marriage a lot happier."[73] The implication in these letters, as in the column, was that the responsibility for preserving the marriage and family largely belonged to women, not their husbands. This mentality was reflected in Popenoe's own works, including *Modern Marriage: A Handbook for Men* (1925) and *Marriage: Before and After* (1943), the latter of which included chapters such as "Eight Cures for Manhaters," "The Frigid Wives of Reno," and "Smart Wives Don't Nag."[74] The work of the AIFR, rooted in Popenoe's teachings, proved to be popular, as did the column, which ran for an astounding fifty-two years.

Tied closely to *Ladies' Home Journal* notions of femininity, marriage, motherhood, and homemaking was the postwar emphasis on consumption, particularly as it related to capitalism and democracy. No *Ladies' Home Journal* columnist advocated for this "American way of life" more than renowned American journalist and radio broadcaster Dorothy Thompson, whose column, which began in 1937, lasted until her death in 1961. The Goulds allowed her to write on any topic she chose, and while her column included "fluffy" topics such as shopping, sewing, and gardening, it often focused on civic and political issues, intertwining them with women's everyday lives.[75] June 1954's "Commercialism Takes – and Wears – a New Look" took this approach, connecting free-market capitalism with the emergence of a distinctly female space: the shopping centre. Thompson began her article with a critique of capitalism, by indicating that commercialism had been blamed for many faults in American life, including the exploitation of cheap labour, the pursuit of the superficial, and the defacing of beautiful landscapes with billboards. She tied her article into the Cold War context by arguing that socialists had declared private enterprise, characterized by cutthroat competition, incompatible with cooperative planning. She went on to defend and praise capitalism, in particular trade and the mercantilism. She argued that trade was "internationally minded and democratic, cutting across national and class divisions" and that merchants were adept at ascertaining the needs and desires of the public, and quick to adapt to fulfil them.[76] One of the recent ways they had done this was through the development of the shopping centre. Thompson outlined her visit to the recently opened Northland Center, a 1.3-million-square-foot space that served the 400,000 people who lived in the Detroit suburbs.[77] Combatting socialist critiques, Thompson called it a beautiful, yet practical, model of enlightened planning and social cooperation between merchants, architects, sculptors, artists, and citizens that could not have happened without private enterprise. For the women of the community, Northland appeared to be a shopper's paradise. They could leave their vehicles in the seventy acres of surrounding parking lots and walk to the pedestrian- and baby carriage–friendly area, which contained ten connected courts, terraces, malls, and lanes. All had central areas with gardens, fountains, sculptures, benches, and background music. Covered colonnades protected shoppers against rain and snow, and all stores were uniformly heated or cooled, depending on the season. In keeping with her sentiment that trade cut across national and class divisions, Thompson noted that shops existed for every pocketbook. She observed that tawdry signs indicating competitive prices were not plastered in windows, but rather competition was confined to quality, display, and price. The spirit was "cooperative as well as competitive" and each store seemed "to want all to succeed." She noted that Northland also served the needs of the broader community. It had two auditoriums for concerts, clubrooms with a kitchen that could be used by civic groups, five restaurants, a dry cleaner, bank, post office, hair salon, and grocery store, and a physician and nurses on hand in case of a medical emergency. Overall, Thompson described the centre's atmosphere as fun and leisurely, reporting that in the six-hour tour she took with Victor Gruen, its chief designer, she had not felt the slightest bit of fatigue. In her mind, projects such as Northland refuted the notion that civic planning could only be accomplished with government involvement. In fact, she doubted that any such project could *ever* be built by a government with the support of taxpayer money. Rather, she argued that in the United States, there was room for different models of planning; the only question was who would do it most beautifully, practically, and economically.

While many *Ladies' Home Journal* articles promoted a discourse of domesticity centred on women, others reflected the circumstances of the Cold War, encouraging women to take active roles in combatting the Soviet threat. Every person in the postwar home could do their part, and women were called upon to be good housewives, mothers, *and* citizens in the public sphere, thus ensuring their efforts in containing, domestically, the communist threat.[78] A large majority of the articles on the Cold War and communism came from Thompson herself. In August 1950, she wrote "A Primer on the 'Cold War,'" which defined the term "Cold War" for *Ladies' Home Journal* readers. She defined it as a condition in which "opponents are struggling with each other by every means except an armed clash, each meanwhile arming with ever more powerful weapons in anticipation of an attack from the other, and in the hope of deterring through fear, such an attack."[79] The article made clear the ideological position of the *Journal*, and its readers. It argued that the Cold War was justifiable because communists, by nature of their political principles, would not feel secure as long as any world power remained capitalist. Americans, therefore, were unwillingly forced into a Cold War by a Soviet Union which felt compelled to engage in a struggle with the non-communist world.[80] The threat of Soviet expansionism became a common theme in the *Ladies' Home Journal*. April 1948's "The Economical Man Is the Patriot" argued that communism had become an "instrument of the perennial Russian world conquest dream. It is compatible with Russian nationalism and no other."[81] Communism, according to the article, depended on the breakdown of the established order, an order that threatened sacred US institutions such as "churches, moralities, traditions, education, industrial leaders, non-communist labor leaders, and the popular bodies of the state."[82] February 1952's "To Protect Civil Liberties" stated that communism worked to break down faith and tradition. Communists "decry Christianity as a myth, history as a lie, national heroes as scoundrels and patriots as bigots. The criminal is a victim, parental influence is despotism, classical education is reactionism and order is tyranny."[83]

These beliefs dominated the magazine's content well into the 1950s, in spite of the death of Soviet leader Josef Stalin and a thaw in relations between the two countries. May 1958's "What Price Liberty?" compared the West to Rome, likening modern Western civilization to the Roman Empire immediately before its fall. It condemned the US government and its people for their poor response to this challenge.

While US citizens extolled the "virtues of liberty, the superiority of the American and Western standard of living, pointed out the vices and failures of the Communist regimes, and kept this country ... in a formidable military posture," they had not clearly analysed the challenge.[84] It was safe to assume, according to the article, that Soviet leaders would not launch a nuclear war, but it was not safe to assume that they had abandoned their intention of becoming the world's most powerful nation.[85] The article argued that the Soviet Union had many advantages. It was able to appeal to Asian and African nations that were resentful of years of Western colonial rule. The solution, therefore, was for the West to further expand its influence into these areas. Rather dramatically, the article argued that "it would be history's most ironic jest if the Communists proved themselves abler capitalists and traders than capitalist lands."[86] According to the article, there was no reason for this to happen except for "public and congressional apathy, indolence and indecision ... The issue must be settled in the present Congress, on a bipartisan basis. Otherwise we may lose the world of freedom ... in this generation."[87] The *Journal* presented a grave picture of the international world, emphasizing the threat of communism to sacred US institutions and to the established world order.

Foreign policy was connected to the home front; the successful defeat of communism, according to *Ladies' Home Journal* rhetoric, depended not necessarily on Russians themselves, but on the American people to do their part.[88] In a regular column entitled "If You Ask Me," readers wrote in to ask former First Lady Eleanor Roosevelt for advice on matters of a personal, professional, and often political nature. In one response to a question regarding the necessity of FBI loyalty tests, Roosevelt responded that she hoped the FBI "would not do more than it is now doing about communism in this country," and in fact, she would prefer to see it do less, and Americans themselves do more.[89] American women were encouraged to identify threats to the established order and do their part in containing communism by taking an active role in civic life. Politicians often appealed to readers' patriotism and devotion to country. In 1951's "How to Get Better Men Elected," Senator William J. Fulbright (D-AR) urged female readers to do their part in containing the communist forces that threatened Cold War America.

> Confronted as we are by a relentless attack upon our institutions by the communists, the all important thing is that we preserve the morale, the spirit and the hopefulness of the democratic tradition. Only time will tell us whether or not it is a fortunate coincidence that the most critical period in our history arrives just as the census reveals that women now outnumber

the men in our nation ... The women now have the opportunity and the power to bring our democratic system through its greatest test.[90]

Fulbright argued that women had an instinctive concern for the preservation of the race, and thereby faced a responsibility they could not escape.[91] This call to action in the *Ladies' Home Journal* may seem unusual during a period long remembered for its zealous commitment to the family, the home, and domesticity, but it became the norm for the magazine. Similarly, February 1952's "No Place for a Woman?" encouraged women to exercise their right to vote because failure to do so was "un-American." Not exercising one's right to vote was a refusal to "fight for and protect the American way of life, the American home and the American family."[92] The article explained that the rise of Adolf Hitler, Benito Mussolini, and Stalin was due to the apathy of the countries' citizens. The author urged the reader to consider the effects of voter indifference in other countries. "It has produced evil dictators' intent upon enslaving the world and destroying the United States."[93] September 1952's "The Eyes of the World Are upon Us" encouraged *Ladies' Home Journal* readers to vote in the next election by pointing out that the number of people who had voted at the national level had been on a steady decline since 1880, culminating in a new low of 42 per cent in 1950.[94] Yet, the article argued, we "are the country which is 'selling' democracy to the world. We are ... trying to persuade Asia, the Middle East, Africa, the South America dictatorships that the right of the people to rule their own destinies is the most precious political heritage men can have."[95] The article went on to salute eight women who were persuaded to take political action owing to their belief that their most valuable contribution to their country, aside from rearing their families, was active political participation. The *Journal* incorporated women's public participation as "part of a positive image of the modern American woman in the postwar world."[96] Articles such as "14 Points for Beginners in Politics" instructed women to register and vote, research candidates, attend meetings, join organizations and parties, and volunteer for political tasks. With this easy-to-follow advice, women could keep both their homes and countries safe from communism.[97]

Election years were particularly important in the *Ladies' Home Journal*, and 1952, which saw Eisenhower pitted against Democrat Adlai Stevenson, was no exception. With the Cold War firmly entrenched, the need to enlist women in the battle against communism took on a more urgent tone. January 1952's "It's Time Women Took Direct Action" told women that the country was entering an election year facing a crisis. "Shocked by revelations of corruption and moral callousness in public life, challenged by communism to prove that free government can work," the article asked "what can American women do about it?"[98] Articles assured women, and perhaps their husbands, that political involvement could be considered an extension of family life. March 1952's "You Can Ask Questions" told women that a home could not be divorced from its community. Political leaders made decisions that affected the lives of women and their families on a daily basis. Thus, women should ask questions of their local candidates in order to make informed decisions on Election Day. It encouraged women to use their leisure time towards the "common good," because as good citizens, democracy was not just something you discuss, it was "something you do."[99] April 1950's "What's the US to You?" promoted the goals of national organizations such as the non-profit League of Women Voters and urged women to become members of the party of their choice. They could start at the bottom by addressing envelopes, ringing door bells, making telephone calls, or babysitting for other mothers who were involved. It warned women that a delay in involvement "could mean trouble for your community or your nation." [100] Women were told to make politics their business. "Voting, holding office, and raising your voice for new and better laws are just as important to your home and your family as the evening meal or spring house cleaning."[101] Again, major political figures immersed themselves in these calls to action. In May 1952's "Join a Party ... Either Party ... But Join," Senator William Benton (D-CT) pointed out that American women were in a unique position of power as they had two million more votes than men. He called on women who were "willing to work" to join any party, and to persevere if faced with intimidation from others. He encouraged them to join a party committee, to know what they want and go after it, and to be persistent and good natured, no matter how menial the task at hand. Benton especially urged women with young children to get involved in local politics, as family problems were also broader community problems, and vice versa.[102]

By associating women's activism with domesticity, the *Journal* attempted to debunk the myth that the world of politics was strictly for men. Women could get involved by extending their domestic talents to the political realm. For example, women could advocate for traditionally "female" issues such as improved healthcare and education, municipal reform, neighbourhood beautification, and improved infrastructure. Men, in turn, could support their wives' endeavours because such advocacy on the part of women would simply be an extension of their traditional, more feminine roles. August 1952's "Women's Place in Politics" stated that the average man, while recognizing the right of women to vote, believed that politics, unlike housekeeping, was not the place for women. "So many women seem to agree," the article stated, but "nothing could be farther from the truth. The fact is that many public problems are quite similar to housekeeping problems and the housekeeper's viewpoint is essential to their solution."[103] While not depreciating the possibilities open to women in state and national politics, the article argued that local government was a natural expression of female interest and power, and it placed tremendous pressure on them to get involved. It grimly warned that democracy is engaged in a "struggle for survival … If we fail to govern our home localities well, popular government will collapse all along the line. If we succeed at home, we shall similarly succeed at Washington."[104]

It was not enough to simply tell women to get involved; the *Journal* also showed them how. In October 1951, its editors began a monthly column called "Political Pilgrim's Progress." Its first column argued that the greatest danger posed to democratic society was America's "do-nothing" citizens, those who had become apathetic and lazy. In order to encourage political involvement, the column showcased "average" women who integrated democracy into their lives by becoming active community members.[105] Throughout the postwar period, the *Journal* frequently invoked examples of these types of women. For example, January 1952's "It's Time Women Took Direct Action" depicted two politically active women, Mrs. Dorothy McCullough Lee, the first female mayor of Portland, Oregon, and Mrs. N., the state chairman of a women's organization that had created better schools, parks, sewage plants, and assembly halls.[106] In November 1954, the *Ladies' Home Journal* devoted an article to Estes Kefauver's senatorial campaign in Tennessee. The lengthy piece focused on Edna Jamison, a woman who worked tirelessly as a manager. Jamison was chosen primarily for her volunteer activities in her hometown of Jackson, Tennessee, which included her prominent role in her church, in education reform, and in establishing the town's first League of Women Voters chapter. Rather humbly, she declared that her main motivation, aside from having a son in the armed services, was, like that of mothers everywhere, her deep concern for the frightening state of the world. She believed it was more important than ever to send Washington the best the country had to offer.[107] February 1952's "Women Like You and Me in Politics" told the stories of thirteen "normal" women in public office, all chosen because of their appeal to the average *Ladies' Home Journal* reader.[108] Dorothy Davis, for example, was elected mayor of the small town of Washington, Virginia. With the help of her all-female council, she was able to use her domestic skills to institute the most efficient system of "town housekeeping" that Washington had ever seen, and with its first-ever surplus of $300.[109] The remainder of the article highlighted twelve other "average" (but in reality rather remarkable) women, who, according to the article, easily and effectively ascended to political office. February 1953's "They Say It with Action" stated that more than 2,000 women serve in city, state, and federal government positions. It offered an intimate look at nine of them in order to spur more women to action. The nine included Los Angeles city councillor Rosalind Weiner. At twenty-four years old, she was the youngest woman ever elected to council. She was recently married and successfully combined marriage and a career. Another was Katherine Elkus White, the mayor, or "city mother" as she called herself, of Red Bank, New Jersey. She was the married mother of two who prided herself on her ability to bake a "mean cake."[110] Finally, there was Mrs. John B. Sullivan. As Missouri's first congresswoman, she ran in 1952 after her late husband's sudden death and won. When voters complained that a woman's place was in the kitchen, she agreed, but explained that certain circumstances sometimes forced a woman to earn a living. She was also, of course, a great cook.[111] "Political Pilgrim's Progress" had a considerable impact on *Journal* readers. The September 1952 issue featured eight women, each citing the column for somehow instigating their civic participation, whether it encompassed writing letters, canvassing, creating women's organizations, or even running for Congress.[112]

Even the *Journal*'s long-running "How America Lives" turned political at times.[113] From its inception in February 1940, in the midst of a war raging in Europe, it ominously claimed that the United States was perhaps "the last stronghold of democracy in the world." Readers needed to know now, more than ever, what exactly was the American way of life. This way of life was represented through the families the *Journal* depicted each month through this column, the families that it claimed lived in the "greatest experiment in self-government the world ever saw." These families, according to the *Journal*, were incredibly diverse. They lived in all parts of the country, both rural and urban, and represented a range of income levels.[114] Of course, they did have one thing in common: all were American patriots. The column concluded that the families they would get to know through the column were "as real, warm and American as pumpkin pie right out of the oven. They are yourselves. And you are democracy."[115] November 1952's column, "We're Polls Apart ... in Politics Only," discussed the Upshaw family of Dallas, Texas.[116] Catherine, a housewife and mother, supported Eisenhower, while her husband, Banks, a textbook publisher, supported Stevenson. Their four children were split down the middle. The

Upshaws inherited their interest in politics from their parents. Banks, a lifelong Democrat and conservative, was the chairman of Precinct 20 in Dallas County, the largest in Texas. He supported the decentralization of power in Washington, states' rights, low tariffs, and an interest in the "common man without being so darned socialistic about it." He was worried the government had taken over everything and was "trying to give people their security on a silver platter."[117] Catherine, on the other hand, had been a state treasurer for the League of Women Voters for fifteen years before she left to work in Eisenhower's local campaign headquarters. While she agreed with her husband on most issues, her reason for "liking Ike" was based on his international stance. According to her, "he knows the foreign situation and can do the most about solving it."[118] She firmly agreed with the new internationalist sentiment of the postwar Republican Party. That sentiment appeared to be echoed by others within her community, as the article indicated that Ike's popularity had grown among the "urban and well-to-do" in Texas. Nevertheless, their neighbours still found their "rivalry" confusing, even though the Upshaws insisted it was natural for them. They had political differences and felt that marriage was more stimulating, even fun, if you did not always agree.[119] In spite of these differences, and in addition to her political advocacy, Catherine still maintained a proper home for her husband and children, albeit with the help of her husband's reasonable salary and their long-time maid. The article described forty-nine-year-old Catherine as eager and full of pep as a schoolgirl, even with her four children and household duties. In addition to campaigning, she did editorial work for the League, attended meetings of the Association of University Women, served as a treasurer for the First Unitarian Church, and was a bookkeeper for Banks Upshaw & Co., her husband's company. When asked "Isn't all this enough without campaigning for General Ike too?" Catherine replied that she did not think so. "One thing I can't give up is my job as a citizen. I think I do a little better as a mother and housewife because I'm interested in things outside my home. Besides, I have to admit I enjoy it."[120] The *Journal* walked a fine line in letting its readers know that women *could* be politically active while simultaneously fulfilling their traditional roles as housewives and mothers. Catherine's unique case proved just how successful women could be both inside and outside the home. After all, in a Cold War context, and during election years in particular, nothing was more important than women fulfilling their duties as active citizens by campaigning for their candidate of choice and casting their ballots.

These discourses complicated the role of Cold War–era women and encouraged them to expand their horizons beyond the complacent "happy housewife heroine" that Friedan described. *Ladies' Home Journal* articles, as well as letters to the editors, indicate that "average" American women *did* listen to these calls to action and *were* politically active during the Cold War in many ways, small and large. Readers believed that these acts contained communism and protected American democracy. Journalists like Friedan, therefore, were not wrong in their belief in the existence of a discourse of domesticity that permeated postwar women's magazines, but that interpretation can be expanded to include the multiple, often contradictory, discourses that also existed. In fact, it was this unique approach, these mixed messages, that acted as a double-edged sword for the *Journal*. By the time Friedan's article was published in 1963, well after the height of a domestically driven postwar ideology, the *Journal* saw a gradual drop in circulation (although it remained influential, second in circulation only to *McCall's*), a decline in advertising revenue, financial problems on the part of its publisher, and editorial changes.[121] As a Madison Avenue executive put it, the magazine "tended to attract older readers rather than the young married couples that advertisers wanted to reach."[122] As Jean E. Hunter has noted, during the decade, of all the women's magazines, the *Journal* was the one that "most frequently and favorably discussed the changes in American society which had given rise to the new feminism." It was the magazine most consistently concerned about women as individuals, rather than as housewives and mothers.[123] An analysis of domestic containment in the *Ladies' Home Journal* shows that politics can be greatly enriched through analyses of culture and vice versa. In intertwining the seemingly separate realms of culture and politics, our understanding of the place of women in a given society can be deepened. During the Cold War, the *Journal* promoted a discourse of domesticity that at times relegated women to the home, but it also promoted a discourse that put them implicitly, and at times explicitly, on the front lines in upholding white, middle-class American values, and thus containing domestic communism and the Soviet threat. It has been well documented that throughout American history, in spite of popular perceptions, "private" women have been active in the public sphere in various guises, particularly during times of upheaval.[124] The situation in the Cold War was no different. Stories and images that attempted to sell this idea of domestic containment were pervasive in postwar magazines such as the *Ladies' Home Journal*. These stories and images were the same ones that were consistently portrayed to Russian women in *Amerika*. *Amerika* presented only idealized versions of white American women happily seen in their roles as feminine housewives and mothers, just as postwar magazines for American women did. Women were, on occasion, depicted as working in full-time professions, but these jobs were secondary to their other roles. Just as magazines such as the *Journal* highlighted to American women the benefits of a democratic, capitalist society, particularly in regard to consumerism, *Amerika* sought to convey the same images to Russian women, albeit in more subtle ways. During the early Cold War period, magazines in both countries, particularly the *Ladies' Home Journal* and *Amerika*, had striking similarities. Both were used to advertise gender norms and consumer culture to women at home and abroad.

Chapter Two

The "Babushka": The "Special Hardships" of Russian Womanhood in the *Ladies' Home Journal*

The USIA's ideas about how best to appeal to Russian women were shaped to a remarkable extent by the idealized images of white, middle-class housewives and mothers that postwar women's magazines presented. There was a deep connection between the USIA's information program and these magazines, as the latter were surprisingly political. Just as it did during World War II, in the postwar era the US government forged partnerships with media outlets so they could report on and sell American values, namely democracy, consumerism, and capitalism. These partnerships also involved telling the story of its political enemies.[1] As a result, a common journalistic approach during the Cold War was to contrast the so-called freedoms and liberties of the United States with the tyranny and oppression of the Soviet Union.[2] Postwar women's magazines such as the *Ladies' Home Journal* frequently highlighted the differences between the two countries, as well as the possible ramifications of communism on any given society. They attempted to show the inadequacies of a Soviet system that deprived its women not just of freedom and liberty but also of the supposed "special privileges" that American women had, namely the ability to pursue traditional gender roles: to appear feminine, enter into a heterosexual marriage, stay home and care for their families in single-family suburban homes, and fulfil their roles as consumers without the necessity of taking on full-time employment. According to these accounts, the American capitalist system was superior because it created a privately run, competitive marketplace in which women could afford to stay home, and actually wanted to do so, in part because of the abundant affordable goods and services available to them. Mass consumption set them apart from Russians, impacting all facets of their lives, and supposedly making them happier as a result.

The *Ladies' Home Journal* used depictions of "the other," in this case Russian women, to draw a contrast between American and Soviet life and culture.[3] Common themes consisted of the non-traditional gender roles, low living standards, and lack of consumer goods in the Soviet Union. These aspects of Soviet life deeply and disproportionally affected women, who were most responsible for caring for the home and family and making purchases for the household. Historians have corroborated these claims, writing that under the postwar Stalinist regime, both rural and urban Russians experienced shortages, and despite rationing could not obtain adequate access to housing, food, or clothing, as supplies were limited.[4] Living standards did improve under Khrushchev, but women's magazines continued to paint a negative portrait of Soviet life throughout the 1950s, arguing that it had taken a tremendous toll on the nation's women, who were not able to express their femininity and were unhappy as a result. While American women enjoyed "special privileges," Russian women endured "special hardships" bestowed upon them by their government – an inadequate and oppressive one.[5] In pursuing this discourse, these magazines intended to "educate" American readers on the supposed realities of life behind the Iron Curtain, ones which inevitably benefited the United States in its propaganda war with the Soviet Union. This discourse could, in turn, further evoke anti-communist sentiments in their readers. It could make them feel "lucky" to be American, while simultaneously allowing them to develop a better understanding of "the other," and to sympathize with the plight of Russian women. As a result of these accounts, stereotypical images of Russian women as being "graceless, shapeless, and sexless" became embedded in the American psyche.[6] These articles rarely acknowledged that the destruction of World War II was still being felt in the Soviet Union, and blamed the Soviet regime for the adversity Russian women experienced. In 1953, when the USIA began developing its overseas information program, these images guided its attempts to appeal to women. Thus, representations of women are important for understanding the USIA's cultural program. The agency believed that the supposed wants, needs, and desires of Russian women were akin to those the postwar American media imagined for their own women, and as a result, invoked images of an America that supposedly provided a better way of life for its women. These were the same values the USIA began to espouse in *Amerika* when it was reissued in 1956, although in a way that was less overt than in US magazines.

Media representations of the Soviet Union were tied to the tumultuous nature of the US-Soviet relationship, and as a result, fluctuated throughout the twentieth century. During World War II, when the two nations worked as allies in defeating the Axis powers, postwar women's magazines produced articles that were sympathetic and even complimentary both to the Soviet regime and its people. February 1943's "Our Allies, The Russians," by Ella Winter, was one such example.[7] Winter began by introducing *Ladies' Home Journal* readers to Stalin, but instead of the critical approach the magazine would take during the Cold War, she simply referred to him as "probably the most photographed man in history," yet noted that his personal life was a well-kept secret. She never elaborated on the secrecy that permeates dictatorial regimes or used the words communist or socialist to describe the nation's political system. Winter focused on the lives of the Russian people, including the professional and personal lives of its women. Rather progressively and without judgement, she noted that all women were mobilized for the war, and that they worked in all fields, in the professions, in industry, and on the farms. She noted that married women kept their maiden names, divorce was easier to obtain than in the United States, and nurseries cared for young children. Other topics she discussed included the country's limited food supplies, anti-religious government propaganda, a lack of private enterprise and commercialism, restrictions on land ownership, universal healthcare and education, and low unemployment. Winter's article was remarkable in that she pointed out diverse elements of Soviet life, yet refrained from criticizing the government. For example, food shortages were simply referred to as "tragic," freedom of religious worship had "returned," radio free of commercials was a "paradise" for those who did not like them, state-owned land meant that Russians never lost value on their property, Soviet medical care was "the best," and low unemployment would likely remain for decades. Finally, Winter deemed pay inequity and the concept of savings meaningless as most services were free and consumer goods were minimal. In the years after this article was published, when the Cold War was at its peak, *Ladies' Home Journal* writers heavily critiqued these aspects of Soviet life, particularly those that impacted women, such as their mass mobilization in the work force and their inability to purchase consumer goods. However, in the context of World War II, and in the interests of the US-Soviet alliance, the article either remained neutral or applauded characteristics of Soviet society.[8]

In the postwar era, as the Cold War materialized and the nature of the US-Soviet relationship altered, the media's approach followed suit. It initially took on a sympathetic tone towards the Soviet Union, but as the US-Soviet relationship unravelled, its stance became increasingly critical. In these initial years, Americans expressed an immense curiosity about the Soviet Union, especially its women. This resulted in a plethora of news stories and articles, some based on concrete observations and others on speculation. In November 1946, Joseph

Phillips, a foreign affairs columnist for *Newsweek*, argued that in order to fully understand the Russian people, attention needed to be paid to the "character and habits of Russian women," who experienced a "special hardship" under communism.[9] This wording is noteworthy, given the US government's and media's lauding of the "special privileges" American women enjoyed. Similarly, in February 1947, LaFell Dickinson, the president of the General Federation of Women's Clubs, wrote in *Redbook* that it was impossible "to understand any country without understanding something of its women." Americans got their first glimpse of the postwar hardships that Soviets experienced in June 1947, when *The March of Time*, a newsreel company owned by Time, Inc., released *The Russians Nobody Knows*, an eighteen-minute-and-twenty-four-second newsreel that played in movie theatres nationwide.[10] The footage, filmed by Peter Hopkinson, the British cameraman for the United Nations Relief and Rehabilitation Administration (UNRRA), an international relief agency that provided food, clothing, and medical supplies to the victims of German-occupied Europe, was intended to document UNRRA work in Minsk, Kiev, and Odessa during that past winter.[11] Hopkinson recalled in his 1969 memoir, *Split Focus*, that at the time there was increasing suspicion between the two countries, but he hoped his footage would "contribute towards a better understanding" between them. His images captured a brief moment in time that he believed would simultaneously evoke sympathy in Americans for the plight of the Russian people and "bring home to the Russians the good will that the United States" had shown to them through UNRRA, thereby easing the emerging tensions in US-Soviet relations.[12]

The Russians Nobody Knows vividly demonstrated the level of sheer destruction in Minsk brought on by the war, when Nazis had invaded homes, broken down doors, smashed windows, and drove people onto the streets, often killing them.[13] Filmed just one year after the war, the film showed a harsh winter, with images of women labouring on farms and praying in churches, a government-run grocery store, and a clothing cartel and boot factory where UNRRA supplied materials. Although *The March of Time* heralded the footage as the "first uncensored film the Russians had ever permitted anyone to make in their country," in his memoir, Hopkinson wrote of Soviet efforts to control his filming. For example, he noted that they refused to allow him to film German prisoners of war laying bricks – there were still more than one million living in the Soviet Union. They did not want him to film the decrepit exterior of a boot factory. Finally, when he was taken to a government-run grocery store he was given a bottle of champagne and told to film it, because it would show the "high standard of living" enjoyed in the Soviet Union.[14] Hopkinson's most poignant footage showed the 30,000 orphans of Minsk who lived in a government-run orphanage that depended on UNRRA for their food and clothing. However, he did acknowledge that these orphans appeared "healthy and happy."[15] *The Russians Nobody Knows* showed a hardworking people who had suffered tremendously. Hopkinson himself noted that the majority of the Soviet people he encountered "recoiled with horror" at the thought of another war.[16]

The Russians Nobody Knows conveyed the immeasurable suffering the war brought to the Soviet people; during the Nazi invasion almost every family lost at least one member, more than 70,000 towns and villages were burned and looted, 32,000 industrial enterprises were left in ruins, and 65,000 miles in railroad tracks were destroyed. Life was difficult as homes were overcrowded, products were in short supply, clothes and shoes were worn out, and food was rationed.[17] Even years later, the devastating effects of the war were still evident. As late as the 1959 census, women outnumbered men by more than twenty million (table 2.1).[18]

The destruction of industry and infrastructure, coupled with the extent of male casualties, meant that women played a critical role in the labour force during the war and after. In the category of "employees" they exceeded men by almost 3 per cent, and in the category of "workers" they remained behind by only 6 per cent.[19] As a result of their high rates of workforce participation, when Russian women were depicted in the US media, particularly in those early years after the war, they were often shown with other women and engaged in manual labour.[20] These images were corroborated in American research. From 1950 to 1951, social scientists Alex Inkeles and Raymond Bauer, based out of the Soviet Research Center at Harvard University, conducted a study of refugees who had left the Soviet Union between 1942 and 1944 and moved to Central and Western Europe, the United States, Canada, and Australia. The Center accepted large government contracts, and both Inkeles and Bauer acted as consultants to the Eisenhower administration. The study of the Harvard Project on the Soviet Social System, *The Soviet Citizen: Daily Life in a Totalitarian Society*, was released in January 1959. Rather than focusing on the political and economic regime, it focused on the Soviet people and their daily lives within the family, at school, in work, recreation and politics, as they had experienced them while living in the Soviet Union. The study also sought to explore not only people's experiences but also their values and beliefs, their desires and frustrations.[21] Inkeles and Bauer acknowledged that

Table 2.1. Workers (and Mothers): Soviet Women Today Population by Socio-occupational Groups, 1959 Urban and Rural Population

	Both Sexes	Male	Female
Total population (workers and dependants)	208,826,650	94,050,303	114,776,347
Workers	100,763,579	48,249,150	52,514,420
Employees	41,903,081	17,398,728	24,504,353
Collective farmers	65,548,826	28,104,754	37,444,072
Individual peasants and independent craftsmen	557,998	269,918	288,080
	Percentage		
Total population (workers and dependants)	100	45	54.9
Workers	48.2	51.3	45.8
Employees	20.1	18.5	21.3
Collective farmers	31.4	29.9	32.6
Individual peasants and independent craftsmen	0.3	0.3	0.3

Source: *Itogi vsesoiuznoi perepisi naseleniia 1959 goda* (Results of the All-Union Census of 1959) (Moscow: Gosstatizdat, 1962), 90–1, table 27. Reprinted in Mark G. Field, "Workers (Mothers): Soviet Women Today," in Donald R. Brown, *The Role and Status of Women in the Soviet Union* (New York: Teachers College Press, 1968), 27.

their findings were limited as they pertained to the period before and during World War II, but they supplemented their work with a historical account of the development of Soviet policy and institutions in each of the major areas they addressed, as well as with observations and interviews they conducted during their visits to the Soviet Union in 1956 and 1957.[22] Theirs was one of the rare studies of everyday life in the Soviet Union, and as a result, it informed State Department and USIA viewpoints on life behind the Iron Curtain.

The official Soviet line was that *all* of its women worked and enjoyed working, but statistics demonstrate that just as postwar American women had a variety of different roles, so too did Soviet women.[23] Inkeles and Bauer attempted to find out if larger numbers of Soviet women actually began participating in the workforce after the Revolution. They interviewed émigrées and asked them questions about their own working lives, as well as those of their mothers. The study found that older generations of women resisted pressure to work full-time and instead stayed at home. In contrast, women born after the Revolution were more likely to participate in the labour force. In particular, white-collar workers had a broader acceptance of Soviet values, believing that they should work in order to free themselves from the "slavery" of the household.[24] They expressed their desire to have a career, freedom, and independence from the confines of the home. One woman, an economist, asserted that she pursued her career after marriage because she "did not want to be dependent upon a man" and "did not want to sit in the kitchen and take care of children."[25] Inkeles and Bauer's study revealed that, by 1949, half of all people employed in the Soviet workforce were women.[26] However, in spite of comments by Soviet women to the contrary, Inkeles and Bauer ultimately concluded that the regime acquired the increased participation of women in the workforce only out of economic necessity. White-collar women desired a career, but working-class women, who encompassed the majority of the population, worked only to supplement the family income and maintain an adequate standard of living. They simply could not afford to stay at home after they married and had children.[27] These findings are reflective of a class divide in which women of a certain status were able to obtain educations and enjoy careers that took them out of the home, while others toiled in jobs that they possibly loathed, thus ensuring that homemaking remained the more attractive option. In spite of this divide, what is clear is that Inkeles and Bauer did indeed interview women who clearly expressed their discontent with paid employment. One Soviet respondent gave a traditional viewpoint on the subject, arguing that women should be different. "A woman can't be equal because when a mother works it's bound to weaken the family."[28] Writing in the context of the conservative domestic ideology of the 1950s, they argued that these women, like American women, would have stayed home if they were able to do so. When the USIA shaped its overseas information program, these images and studies were central to their understanding of Soviet women's lives and were aligned with the dominant gender narrative of the postwar period.

Curiosity about the threat of communism created a demand for information about life in the Soviet Union. One of the first postwar magazine accounts on this topic appeared in the February 1947 issue of *Redbook*, where Dickinson wrote of her thirty-five-day visit to "war-torn areas" that included Moscow, Leningrad, and Stalingrad during the summer of 1946. Dickinson travelled as part of a seven-person delegation for the American Society for Russian Relief to "observe the distribution and use of American relief supplies." However, as the president of the General Federation of Women's Clubs, and the only female in attendance, she demonstrated an interest in the conditions of Russian women. She wrote that while there had been a number of US missions to Russia, these delegations were almost solely comprised of men and because of this little had been written on Russian women. When she visited, she made it her purpose to study Russian women and compare them to American women. Dickinson wrote of the devastation wreaked by the war, the ravaged cities, and the women who toiled to clear the debris, often without wheelbarrows or shovels. She noted their difficult working conditions and that every woman she encountered had lost at least one family member during the war. At the same time, they never complained or appeared unhappy. While she wrote admiringly of these women, applauding their exceptional parenting skills, their unrelenting belief in God, and their work in traditionally male fields, she also declared that she did not care to live in their country.[29] In an earlier account in the *New York Times*, she again praised Russian women, even admitting that they seemed happy in a country which, unlike the United States, provided them with equal rights to men, but carefully noted that "we don't want their way of life here."[30]

The most notable magazine account of postwar Soviet life emerged in 1948, from the collaboration between renowned American writer John Steinbeck and Hungarian-American war photographer Robert Capa.[31] During a time when only a small number of Americans had the firsthand knowledge of the subject, the *Ladies' Home Journal* commissioned features by a number of famous people, like Steinbeck and Capa, to cover life in the Soviet Union. *Journal* articles described the repressive conditions of the country. The two men developed a friendship during the war, and during the summer of 1947 they travelled throughout the Soviet Union for the purpose of showing Americans that "Russians are people too."[32] Their travels through rural and urban Russia, Georgia, and Ukraine resulted in 1948's *A Russian Journal*.[33] However, before its release they also published "Women and Children in the USSR," an elaborate sixteen-page account with forty-seven images, thirteen of which were in colour, that appeared in the February 1948 issue of the *Journal*.[34] The Goulds hailed the article as the first full report on day-to-day life in the Soviet Union in a US magazine, adding that it was good for *Ladies' Home Journal* readers to have a glimpse into the lives of Russian women and children, and they hoped that one day it would also be possible to show such a story about Americans to Russians.[35] The Goulds intended the article to revolve around Capa's captivating images.[36] As picture editor John Morris noted, when Steinbeck and Capa returned from the Soviet Union, he personally offered Capa $20,000 for his photographs, while the Goulds, who "handled" Steinbeck, offered him only $3,000 for his accompanying text and captions. Steinbeck was unhappy about this inequitable arrangement and that he would have to fit his text to the layout of Capa's images, but he agreed to it as a favour to his friend.[37] The cover image alone indicates the power of Capa's work (figure 2.1). The colour photograph of a solitary Russian woman – with her aging face, muscular arms, and peasant garb – working on her hands and knees on the farm – evoked the Depression-era photographs of the Farm Security Administration a decade earlier.[38] It showed American women that life in the Soviet Union was just as difficult as it had once been in the United States. Images such as these took on special significance. For Americans, travel to the Soviet Union was extremely restricted, and as a result, the few accounts and images that existed of Russian women, particularly in reputable magazines such as the *Ladies' Home Journal*, could exert tremendous influence.

The Soviet government was aware of the power of photography. When looking to travel to the Soviet Union, Steinbeck, who was well known and admired there for his writing on the effects of the Great Depression, was able to obtain a visa easily. Capa, on the other hand, found it difficult to do so, in part because Soviet authorities were suspicious of foreign photographers who might capture and share unfavourable images of Soviet life. Capa received a visa only after Steinbeck appealed for one on his behalf, informing the Soviet consulate in New York City that they worked as a team.[39] Once the two men arrived in Moscow, Capa's efforts were thwarted. He waited days for his photography permits, Soviet police frequently stopped him for questioning, and his requests to photograph factories were denied.[40] He eagerly awaited the opportunity to leave Moscow and move on to the countryside, where he would be away from the watchful eyes of the Soviet police. However, as Capa biographer Alex Kershaw writes, these efforts were thwarted on many occasions. The deputy chairman of the Ukrainian Society for Cultural Relations (UOKS) wrote in a secret report to his staff that Capa needed to be "watched to prevent him from taking pictures of what he shouldn't."[41] In Ukraine, Steinbeck and Capa's guides took them on a "vodka tour." The two men overate, drank excessively, and interacted with "pretty girls" as part of Soviet attempts to distract them from the harsh realities of Ukrainian life.[42] Soviet officials further attempted to control the outcome of Capa's work by reviewing his pictures before he flew home. The two that were removed, one of a woman lying in front of an altar in a damaged chapel crossing herself, and the other of a group of uniformed German prisoners of war walking down the streets of Moscow guarded by a soldier, showed signs of distress

The "Babushka" 61

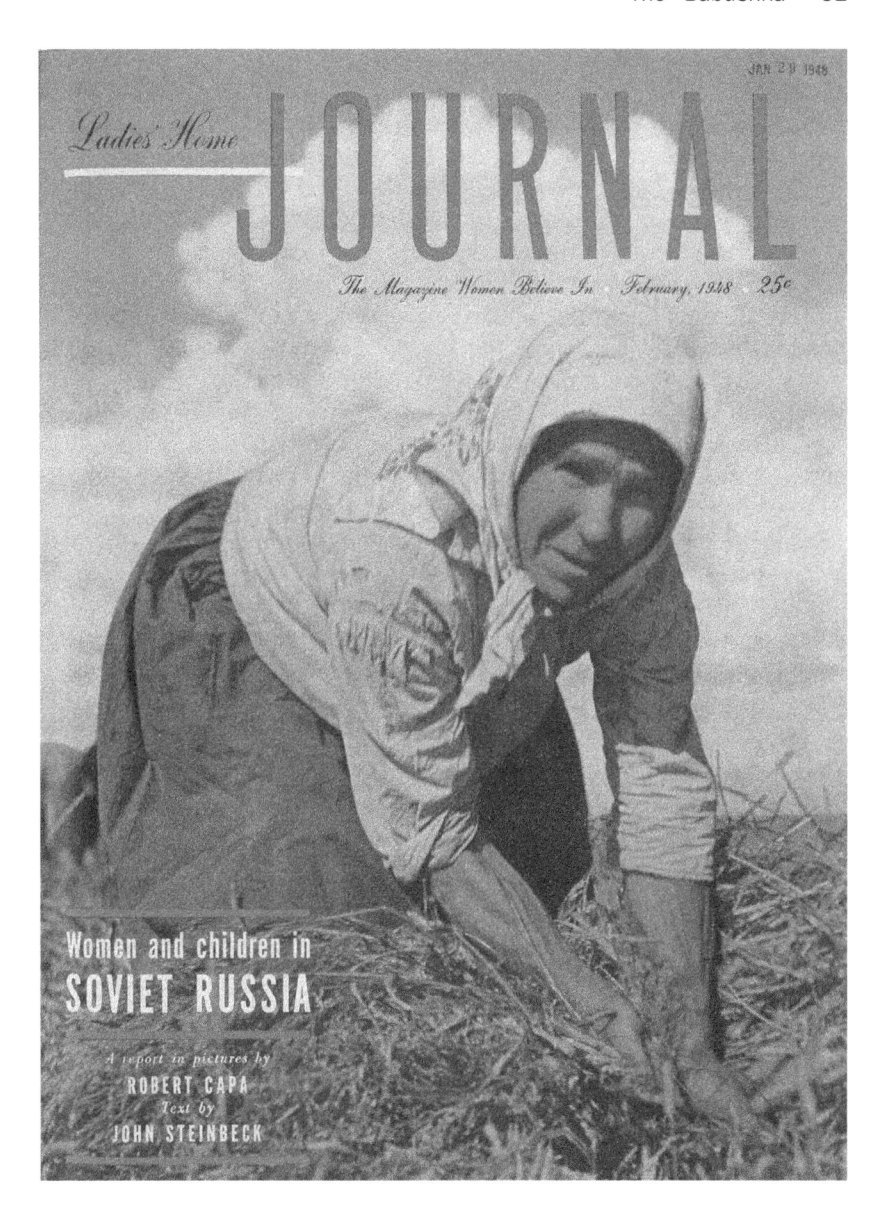

Figure 2.1. This *Ladies' Home Journal* cover put a human face to communism. It showed American women the hard work and haggard appearance of a typical Russian woman farm worker. Her appearance contrasted with the images of American women, shown as both happy and feminine, in the magazine. Robert Capa, *Ladies' Home Journal*, February 1948.

within the Soviet Union.[43] Perhaps unaware of the larger implications of these images, Capa wrote, "Nothing that mattered ... was withheld."[44] But these images were impactful. For Soviet officials, they may have proven much more detrimental to their international reputation than the image of a hardworking female farmer that graced the cover of the *Ladies' Home Journal*, but it was exactly these types of images that postwar media used to tug at the heartstrings of American women.

In "Women and Children in the USSR," Steinbeck and Capa were intensely critical of what they called a totalitarian regime. According to Steinbeck, Stalin's image was everywhere. His "portrait hangs in every room of every museum. His bust is in front of all airports, railroad stations, bus stations. His picture in needlework is undertaken by school students. Every house has at least one picture of him."[45] In spite of these criticisms, Steinbeck and Capa's forays into the countryside to observe farm life first-hand and interview ordinary Russians resulted in some of their most intriguing accounts and photographs. This aspect of their journey resulted in a sympathetic account of the life of the Russian farmer. Capa's images, according to Steinbeck, showcased the "real Soviet Union" and the human effects of communism, but more importantly, they showed that, although the war had ended three years prior, its effects were long-lasting.[46] "Women and Children in the USSR" provided powerful visual evidence of the vastly different lives that postwar Russian and American women led. In particular, Steinbeck and Capa were struck by how hard Russian women worked. In cities, women alone rebuilt the infrastructure destroyed by the war; drove trucks, buses, and streetcars; and worked in factories. On farms, they "ran the house, did the cooking, took care of the chickens, pigs, goats and cows ... They traded, and bought and sold."[47] Capa's images revealed women working in difficult, and even unusual, circumstances. Figure 2.2, for instance, depicts women doing farmwork, which American women had always done, but figure 2.3 shows barefoot women laying bricks to build a school, something which would have seemed more unusual to *Ladies' Home Journal* readers. The majority of these images contained only women and reflected, and even explicitly acknowledged, the male losses incurred during the war, as well as the fact that women needed to work in order to ensure their own survival as well as that of the nation.[48] According to Steinbeck, even young women worked long hours in the fields. They "come home, eat, rest for an hour, bathe, put on clean clothes and go to their clubs to dance violently until one o'clock in the morning. We do not know when they slept."[49] Capa's images showed these lighthearted aspects of Soviet society: young women happily dancing barefoot with each other, or

Figure 2.2. Images such as this one showed the extent to which Russian women worked in the postwar era, in many cases simply because the loss of the men in their lives forced them to do so. Original caption: Women reap the harvest on the collective farms, for many men are dead or maimed. They laugh and talk, but seldom pause in their work. Robert Capa, *Ladies' Home Journal*, February 1948.

sunning themselves on the beach, much as they would have done in the United States (figures 2.4 and 2.5). Steinbeck's accompanying text stated that they "found more gaiety and laughter" among people in Kiev than in Moscow. The irony of these images appearing in the *Ladies' Home Journal* was that America's postwar magazines rarely showed its own women participating in similar activities with each other. In an era that focused heavily on home and hearth, media depictions of homosocial relationships appear to have been erased entirely. Instead, women were shown individually, or with their husbands or children, as if to suggest that American women did not need female friendships when they had families, or even that these friendships may lead to homosexual tendencies.[50] When American women were shown participating in "leisure" activities, it was most often in the domestic sphere or in volunteer activities in connection to schools, churches, and local politics. In other words, they participated in activities that were extensions of their family lives and communities. Steinbeck's captions are indicative of this postwar mindset. The original caption to figure 2.4, for example, states, "So few men are left that peasant girls gather to dance in their club."

Figure 2.3. As part of their newfound roles in rebuilding the nation, Russian women frequently engaged in hard labour that would have been considered unacceptable for American women. Original caption: Barefoot women bricklayers build a new school overlooking the Volga. Robert Capa, *Ladies' Home Journal*, February 1948.

The implication being that *only* when men were absent, would women engage in such activities with each other. As much as Capa's images were unique to the *Ladies' Home Journal*, they were important. During a time when few images existed of the Soviet Union and its people, these emphasized the ramifications of war but also the humanity of Russian women, many of whom had lost the men in their lives yet appeared to find happiness in the simple things. These sympathetic media images

Figure 2.4. Images such as this one showed that, in spite of the heavy losses they suffered and hard work they engaged in, Russian women managed to find time for fun at the end of a long workday. Original caption: So few men are left that peasant girls gather to dance in their club when day's work is done. "And besides, the men are bashful," one told us. Robert Capa, *Ladies' Home Journal*, February 1948.

acknowledged the devastation brought on by the war and its implications for women's lives.

In spite of their different circumstances, Russian and American women were portrayed by Steinbeck and Capa as sharing two basic characteristics: the desire to shop and to be feminine. Steinbeck wrote that, like "everywhere else in the world, the women are the great shoppers."[51] They went in droves to department stores, even if items were not available. Steinbeck wrote that clothing was scarce, options were minimal, and makeup and perfume were rarely seen. Capa's images, however, depict a country that provided its people with, at the very least, basic necessities. Figure 2.6 shows a rural store with what the caption refers to as shelves that are "quite bare," but items are available, and women appear ready to make their purchases. Additionally, figure 2.7 shows a well-stocked downtown Moscow department store filled with both female and male shoppers. However, according to Steinbeck, these items were often expensive and, as a result, inaccessible to ordinary Russians. According to Steinbeck, Russian women, like American ones, had a desire to appear feminine, but did not have the same comforts, clothes, and cosmetics. However, they combed their hair, wore neat clothing, and had a "stride about them when they walked."[52] Figure 2.8 depicts what Steinbeck refers to as a Stalingrad "housewife" hanging laundry on a sunny day

66   Shaping Women, Gender, and the Communist Threat

Figure 2.5. On the beaches of Kiev, women enjoy a welcome break from work. Original caption: At Kiev in the Ukraine, we found more gaiety and laugher than in Moscow. Couples danced at a night club on the River Dnieper and sunned on the beach. Robert Capa, *Ladies' Home Journal*, February 1948.

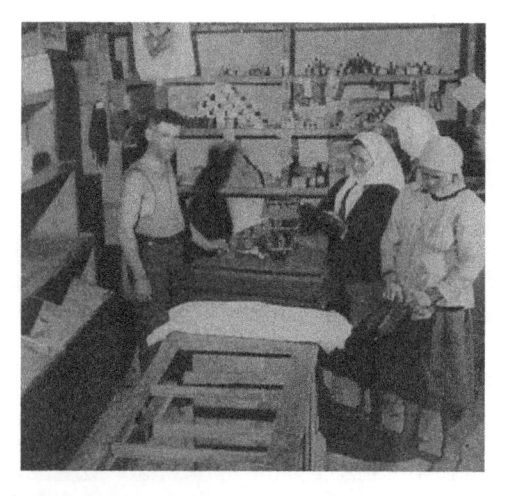

Figure 2.6. While Steinbeck's captions indicated that the shelves of this village store were "quite bare," they appeared to contain the basic necessities that Russian women needed. Original caption: In village store on collective farm, women look over new shipment of galoshes. Shelves are quite bare. Robert Capa, *Ladies' Home Journal*, February 1948.

Figure 2.7. This crowded image of GUM, Russia's largest department store, showed the Russian demand for consumer goods was just as high as it was for Americans. The caption, however, suggested that high prices made it difficult for these women to afford many items. Original caption: Commercial, state-owned food store in Moscow sells delicacies ranging from caviar to wines, but prices are very high. Robert Capa, *Ladies' Home Journal*, February 1948.

amid what he called the "cave" that had once been her home. He and Capa were amazed at how, in spite of their conditions, these women still managed to appear feminine, "neat and fresh."

For Steinbeck, another characteristic connecting Russian and American women was their curiosity about the "other." Russian women wanted to know how American women lived: the food they ate, the clothing they wore, the healthcare and school systems they had access to.[53] Steinbeck and Capa maintained that many erroneously believed that American women were "overdressed, neurotic and kept," but were pleased to hear that they milked cows, kept chickens, and washed diapers. They told readers that Russian women were surprised, "just as you may be surprised at our report of how like us" they are.[54] In spite of Steinbeck's observation that these women lived on the hope that tomorrow would be a better day, Capa's images reflected their at times daunting existence. They demonstrated the differences between Russian and American women, particularly regarding the nature of their employment, comfortable home lives, and access to consumer goods. According to them, "the women we met were poor, industrious and hospitable. They did not live so well as we do, and they work very hard."[55]

68   Shaping Women, Gender, and the Communist Threat

Figure 2.8. Capa's image of this Russian housewife hanging laundry outside, with her home in rubble, provided the starkest contrast to images of American housewives, with their comfortable suburban homes, within the *Ladies' Home Journal*. Original caption: This Stalingrad housewife, hanging out her laundry in the sun, is one of many we saw who continue to live right on in the caves they have constructed of what once were houses. We were amazed not only that they could survive such conditions, but that they also remained feminine, managing to look neat and fresh. Robert Capa, *Ladies' Home Journal*, February 1948.

Capa's portraits of Russian women were vastly different from those of the American women depicted in that same *Ladies' Home Journal* issue. Although the *Journal* occasionally showed working and politically active women, the majority of the magazine still focused on femininity, marriage, motherhood, and domesticity as central elements of women's lives. For example, the same February issue that contained Steinbeck and Capa's account also included a six-page spread on the latest in summer fashions, called "Sun Fashions Here to Stay." Highlighting the importance of clothing in appealing to *Ladies' Home Journal* readers, thirteen of its fifteen images were in colour, and all showed modern clothing on tall, slim, and attractive models (figure 2.9).[56] Another article, "What Can Young Marrieds Afford?," presented an idealized image of suburban life, showing the luxurious living room of a newly married couple (figure 2.10). It included couches, chairs, and drapes in matching fabric; a coffee table; end tables; a fireplace; and accents including lamps, flowers, and a mirror, all decorated for the supposedly "low"

Sleeveless beige crepe sheath dress by Josct Walker. Kenneth Hopkins' cartwheel hat. Headley's gold link necklace strung with pearls.

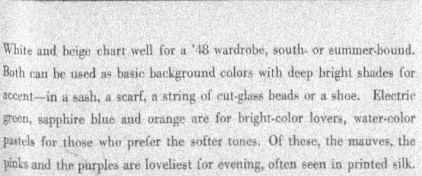

Corded cotton in banana beige by Claire McCardell. Orange and black, the accent.

White and beige chart well for a '48 wardrobe, south- or summer-bound. Both can be used as basic background colors with deep bright shades for accent—in a sash, a scarf, a string of cut-glass beads or a shoe. Electric green, sapphire blue and orange are for bright-color lovers, water-color pastels for those who prefer the softer tones. Of these, the mauves, the pinks and the purples are loveliest for evening, often seen in printed silk.

The petticoat dress for evening: pure silk pink-and-purple print over two full petticoats in organdy, by Adele Simpson.

Figure 2.9. Light, bright, and feminine ready-made summer fashions such as these, appeared, during the heart of winter, in the *Ladies' Home Journal*, providing yet another contrast to Capa's dismal black-and-white images of poorly dressed Russian women. "Sun Fashions Here to Stay." Wilhela Cushman, *Ladies' Home Journal*, February 1948.

Figure 2.10. Juxtaposed with figure 2.8, this image shows the bright, stylish, and affordable items available for American women when decorating their first homes. Original caption: All the furniture pieces in this room are basic, chosen to remain in good style, and be re-covered when the scheme is changed. The carpet is basic also, but the accessories are wedding presents or pickup pieces accumulated as one goes along. Harold Fowler, *Ladies' Home Journal*, February 1948.

cost of $945.03.[57] Yet another, "February Fare," included colourful photographs and recipes of a homemade feast that included an abundance of fresh and canned fruits and vegetables, many of which were not normally available to Russians during their harsh winters. Recipes included a curried chicken and apple soup, swiss cheese tart, baked tomatoes, a beet and onion salad, as well as an arrangement of pineapple, peaches, apricots, and cherries (figure 2.11).[58]

The closest semblance to Steinbeck and Capa's Russian women consisted of the families portrayed each month in the long-running and popular *Ladies' Home Journal* series, "How America Lives."[59] February 1948's "How America Lives" featured the story of Lewis Dickson, a war veteran and advertising copywriter, his wife Mary, and their two young daughters. Lewis himself penned the article that discussed their

Figure 2.11. An abundance of healthy and colourful food, available at any time of the year, was one of the key advantages that American women believed distinguished them from their Russian counterparts. Harold Fowler, *Ladies' Home Journal*, February 1948.

life in a four-room, pre-furnished apartment located in a temporary war housing project. Lewis wrote that some would call their simple home a "slum," but it was affordable and had a lawn and flowerbed.[60] The young couple were saving to buy a home and car so they could live the American Dream (figure 2.12). Lewis made seventy-one dollars per week and claimed their plan worked because of "careful planning, budgeting and ... cooperation between spouse and spouse."[61] Their

Figure 2.12. "How America Lives" discussed the life and spending habits of the Dickson family. While Mrs. Dickson did not engage in paid work as Russian women did, she worked hard at maintaining her home, family, and budget in the hopes of one day purchasing a home. Original caption: Lew Dickson's housing tip: "Make something else 'do' until you can get a better deal on your dreams." They rent four rooms for $36.50 in a project. Otto Hagel, *Ladies' Home Journal*, February 1948.

savings were spearheaded by Mary, a conscientious homemaker who "ruthlessly trimmed" all frills. She saved on food, made their clothing, and rarely engaged in outside entertainment. She was portrayed as a busy, but happy, housewife, whose job was to lighten the "do-without days," before they purchased their dream home, with laughter and understanding.[62] On the surface, if any *Ladies' Home Journal* article remotely resembled the lives of Russian women, it was this depiction of the Dickson family. Although the article emphasized their struggles of "doing without," it showed much faith in US capitalism to carry them through those struggles. This hopeful attitude was clearly intended to provide a juxtaposition to the dreary life of the Russian woman. Dickson, seemingly aware of the special nature of this issue that included "Women and Children in the USSR," wrote that while their food bill averaged $19.92 per week, an amount that would seem "spartan" to many Americans, it would still be "heaven on earth" to "ration-harried" Brits or Europeans who survived on "below subsistence calorie levels." The Dickson's home, with its green space, appeared palatial in comparison to the small communal apartments of Moscow, known as *kommunalki*, in which tenants, sometimes strangers to each other, shared kitchens and bathrooms. The destruction of World War II, particularly to infrastructure and housing, as well as a sudden influx of Russians to urban centres, had made living space one of the Soviet Union's most pressing domestic concerns. According to historian Donald Filzer, in 1946 Moscow's 3.8 million residents had an average living space of 4.4 square metres. By Stalin's death in 1953, its population had grown to roughly 4.8 million, yet its average living space remained almost the same.[63] In part, this was due to Stalin's postwar priorities, namely his efforts to reconstruct Moscow as a model socialist city intended to rival those of the West. This included the building of costly and elaborate neoclassical skyscrapers, which came at the expense of much-needed housing to accompany the rise in population.[64] After Khrushchev came to power, he denounced Stalin's excesses and effectively put an end to further construction projects of this nature. To address housing shortages, he introduced the building of *Khrushchevki*, low-rise standardized apartment buildings designed for single nuclear families. They included individual kitchens and bathrooms, and represented the first attempts on the part of the Soviet government to introduce privatization.[65] These construction efforts, however, were still nearly a decade away by the time Dickson's 1948 article was published. As a result, the conditions of the postwar, Stalinist-era home became notorious in the US media.

    A related article seemingly appeared to do away with Mrs. Dickson's frugal life altogether by providing her with a makeover and

74   Shaping Women, Gender, and the Communist Threat

Figure 2.13. "Welcome Change" detailed Mrs. Dickson's well-deserved makeover. Hal Reiff, *Ladies' Home Journal*, February 1948.

new wardrobe (figure 2.13). Her "new look," which the magazine called "groomed, gracious and slender," was apparently a "welcome change" not just for herself, but for others around her.[66] These *Ladies' Home Journal* images reflected postwar gender norms of women as feminine housewives, mothers, and consumers. They contrasted tremendously with the magazine's cover image of a Russian woman labouring on the field, and the images taken by Capa that appeared within its pages.

Although Steinbeck and Capa's account came early in the Cold War, during a time when the Soviet Union was still recovering from the massive losses of World War II, it provides an important glimpse into the lives of the Russian women who appeared to have worked tirelessly and endlessly for the good of their nation. Furthermore, it provides a glimpse into the ways that America's cultural leaders portrayed the repercussions of the war, as well as the human element of what they believed was a repressive regime. Indeed, when Morris reviewed Capa's images, he noted that they reflected a Soviet Union he had "never imagined," one that consisted of ordinary people rather than a communist regime and World War II battlefronts. According to Morris, these images were a "plea for peace and sanity in a world that was becoming mad with fear."[67]

Similarly, in 1954 famed reporter Harrison Salisbury wrote "Russia Re-Viewed," a fourteen-part series for the *New York Times* based on his five years as a correspondent in the country. Like Steinbeck and Capa, he touched on "the common man"; he profiled three Russians, including sixty-year-old Maria. Maria had a difficult life. Her husband was sent to Siberia during the 1937 purges, her son died in the army in 1944, and, according to Salisbury, since then she had "not really lived." She worked forty-eight hours a week in a Moscow factory as a medical worker, had her own room (her daughter had moved out because they "got on each other's nerves"), and few possessions. She never read the newspaper, as she lost interest long ago in public events, and rather sadly proclaimed that if war ever came again, she would kill herself. For Salisbury, Russia was not just a nation solely defined by its socialist ideology; rather he embraced the "real Russia," a land filled with a rich history, thriving intellectual culture, and a simplicity of life characterized by its people. For him, this "Mother Russia" was highly feminized, and victimized by the bureaucratic, authoritarian nature of the Stalinist state.[68] Salisbury's series proved to be so impactful that it earned a Pulitzer Prize for International Reporting.[69] Through their work, he, Steinbeck, and Capa wanted Americans to see the humanity of Russian women and even sympathize with them and their daily lives because they were victims not just of communism but also of war. Six months after the publication of Steinbeck and Capa's article, the August 1948 edition of the *Ladies' Home Journal* included a letter by a German-American woman asking Eleanor Roosevelt if she believed it would be possible to reach out to and unite with Russian women to "work for peace." Having escaped from Nazi Germany, the woman noted that "it must be the mission of the women to unite against war." However, Roosevelt doubted it would be possible as communications between the two countries were difficult, information was restricted, and friendship was not encouraged.[70] In spite of Roosevelt's less-than-hopeful response, the *Journal*'s approach, demonstrated through Steinbeck and Capa's article, appeared to be effective. As they noted, "Russians are people too." They concluded, "Their hopes are not foreign to us. They want to raise fine children and to educate them. They want to live better and more comfortable lives. They work incredibly hard to that end."[71] The female readers of the *Ladies' Home Journal* appeared to recognize this. Accounts that emerged in the following years took on a similar purpose, but were less sympathetic and more overtly political, reflecting the intensification of the Cold War. They failed to acknowledge the continued devastation in the Soviet Union brought on by World War II, instead solely blaming the regime for the difficulties its women faced.

As the Cold War escalated, so too did the postwar media's emphasis on the bleak conditions that existed behind the Iron Curtain. While earlier accounts noted the impact of the war on the Russian people, later ones either downplayed or entirely ignored the possibility that it could have long-term effects, instead focusing solely on the inability of the communist regime to provide for its citizens, particularly its women. The magazine's emphasis on the Soviet Union's supposedly repressive nature stemmed in part from the Goulds. The Goulds had a particular interest in the Soviet Union, even travelling there for four weeks in 1956 on assignment for a feature entitled "We Saw How Russians Live" that appeared in the February 1957 issue. It was accompanied by "Report on Russia's Youth," written by American student Robert Griscom, based on his own 1956 visit. Both accounts detailed the rigidities of the Soviet system, but simultaneously provided a sympathetic account of the Russian people, discussing women's employment, motherhood, and the home.[72] From the outset, the Goulds confirmed that they had no desire to meet with Kremlin officials, who they believed would toe the party line; rather they wanted to know how this "iron regime" affected the lives of ordinary citizens. In a joint interview with the *Journal*'s editorial staff, they each described Russians as a "busy, determined and stolid people engaged in an enormous enterprise." However, they also led "grim" lives. Bruce Gould described the Soviet Union as a society without a middle class, where the masses were peasants and workers were incredibly poor and oppressed.[73]

Both the Goulds and Griscom emphasized the repressive nature of the Soviet regime. Beatrice Gould said her most vivid impression of the country was the discovery that the majority of Russians were cut off from outside news and information. Ignoring the anti-communist activities that her own government conducted at home, as well as the anti-communist sentiment in her own magazine, Beatrice noted that Russians received a distorted image of their government, which did not convey the truth regarding their corrupt political practices at home and abroad. According to the Goulds, Russians realized they were not getting the whole truth, but had little power to bring about change. While in Moscow the Goulds received some outside information, particularly from the partially jammed VOA, Radio Liberation, and British Broadcasting Corporation (BBC) broadcasts; outside of Moscow they were entirely blacked out. They described the inability of Russians to obtain information on US life and culture. For example, a library visit revealed that no Western newspapers or periodicals – with the exception of one old issue of *Life* magazine – were available.[74] Griscom also confirmed the difficulties Russians faced in obtaining access to foreign broadcasts and publications that depicted life and culture in the United States. Despite visiting numerous libraries, only after visiting the Institute of Foreign Languages, and after much interrogation, was he was able to view popular US periodicals such as *Colliers, Life*, and the *New York Times*.[75] According to Griscom, Russian youth knew official government news did not tell the whole story and noted that, whenever possible, they took advantage of the relaxed regulations that accompanied de-Stalinization to gain knowledge of the outside world. They recognized him as a Westerner and frequently stopped him to engage in conversation and ask questions about life in the United States. Like Steinbeck and Capa, Griscom described the similarities between Russian and American youth, but also highlighted the former's desire for consumer items such as clothing and cars, fondness of jazz music, preference to socialize with friends rather than family, and relaxed notions of morality.[76] Similarly, the Goulds maintained that Russians were intensely interested in life in the United States, at least for the sake of comparing it to life in their own country. They were asked most frequently, "Is it true that you are worse off in America than we are?" and "Is it true that you have a great deal of unemployment?"[77]

The Goulds' critique of the Soviet Union included the fact that it "forced" women to take on non-traditional roles and lead unconventional lives, ones that ran counter to America's postwar gender norms. Both Bruce and Beatrice described the working conditions of Russian women, indicating that they did the hardest work in the country. They described women taking on non-traditional positions that included building roads, loading and unloading trucks with heavy materials, and sweeping streets while their male colleagues simply looked on. They noted that some women received an education and were able to obtain professional positions, but said their heavy workload resulted in a hardship that impacted all aspects of their lives. For example, according to the Goulds, Russian women bore very little physical resemblance to American women. They wrote that a Russian woman of forty-five looked sixty and it was rare to see well-groomed hair and accessories such as ribbons, scarves, and handkerchiefs. According to Beatrice, it seemed as if these women did not want to appear too feminine, but, she and her husband, in keeping with postwar American gender norms, concluded that Russian women's unfeminine appearance was more likely because their hard work left them "little energy to charm."[78]

78   Shaping Women, Gender, and the Communist Threat

According to the *Ladies' Home Journal*, the fact that Russian women had wage-earning positions also meant that they had little time to be "good mothers" in the sense that America's pronatalist ideology dictated. Instead, they typically left their children in government-supported nurseries. The Goulds acknowledged the children were in good care; they were well fed, clothed, and provided with toys, but they spent all day there and approximately one-third slept at school because their mothers worked at night.[79] The Goulds intended to show readers that the Soviet government forced women into long shifts and heavy work that impacted all facets of their lives, including their ability to properly mother their children. Their descriptions fed into dire postwar warnings on the separation of mother and child. "Mother-bashers," as they became known in the United States, saw the sudden influx of women entering the paid workforce as a problem, arguing that their selfish desire to remove themselves from the home led to increased instances of abandonment and juvenile delinquency.[80] The assumption was that the Soviet regime, by forcing women to engage in paid labour and leave their children in the care of strangers, was causing potential damage to future generations of Russian citizens. Naturally, Russian women, if given the opportunity, would choose to stay at home and raise their children but lacked the opportunity to do so under communism. This was, of course, a rather interesting stance considering Beatrice was a writer before taking the helm of the *Journal* at the relatively young age of thirty-seven, a choice that would have undoubtedly impacted her ability to raise her only daughter. In fact, one year prior, in June 1955, the *Journal* ran "They Let Us Talk to the Russians," an interview with Gay Humphrey and Ted Curran, two of four students at the Russian Institute at Columbia University who were granted visas to travel to the country in the spring of 1955. The interview revealed that Russian women would likely have approved of Beatrice's decision to continue working after her child was born. Humphrey noted that women who worked and had families tended to look down upon those who stayed home to care for their children, commenting disapprovingly that they stayed home "all day."[81]

Another area in which the Goulds painted a stark contrast between American and Russian women was in their home lives and general living conditions. In an effort to see the homes of average Russians, the Goulds knocked on apartment doors hoping to find individuals who would let them inside. This approach proved successful in Leningrad, but unsuccessful in Moscow, where people seemed fearful of the repercussions of allowing Americans into their homes.[82] In her study on the communist conflation between the public and private spheres, Deborah

A. Field notes that while many Russians expressed pride in their peaceful co-existence with their neighbours, and the creation of a helpful community surrounding them, they lacked privacy. At times, crowded conditions facilitated surveillance and denunciations of individuals to the secret police, particularly during the Stalinist era. This behaviour continued under Khrushchev, but it was of a less sinister nature and typically revolved around issues related to sexual behaviour, family relations, and child welfare. [83] When the Goulds were able to enter urban homes, they described what to them were abysmal living conditions, with multiple families crammed into small apartments. Beatrice described one apartment that contained thirteen people. Each family had one room, and all shared a communal kitchen and toilet. There was no bathroom. The kitchen contained one gas stove, one sink, no refrigerator, and three small tables, one for each family, with shelves and cupboards above and below each table for pots, pans, and dishes.[84] Griscom described similar conditions.[85] Beatrice attempted to humanize Russian women, relating their lives to their hardworking counterparts in America. She stated that in spite of their circumstances, Russian women, "like women round the world, were trying to make the best of what they had."[86] Although they complained about their living conditions and lack of space, they tried hard to turn their apartments into homes and were proud of the few possessions they had. Overall, while being extremely critical of the Soviet government, Beatrice felt an admiration and sympathy for these friendly, dignified, and hospitable women.[87]

While the Goulds and Griscom, like Steinbeck and Capa, were more or less sympathetic, other *Ladies' Home Journal* correspondents provided more scathing descriptions of life under communism and the status of Russian women. From March to May 1952, the *Journal* published a three-part series called "Letters from Moscow," written by Lydia Kirk, the wife of Admiral Alan G. Kirk, former US Ambassador to the Soviet Union, who was stationed in Moscow from June 1949 to October 1951. Unlike other *Ladies' Home Journal* writers, Lydia Kirk was married to a man with an extensive naval and diplomatic career and as a result, she had a vested interest in politics and international affairs. During World War II, her husband's work stationed them in England, France, and Italy.[88] From 1946 to 1949, they lived in Brussels, while her husband was US Ambassador to Belgium, and following his ambassadorship in the Soviet Union, he served as director of the Psychological Strategy Board (PSB), an agency established in 1951 by Truman to provide for the "effective planning, coordination and conduct, within the framework of approved national policies, of psychological operations."[89] Kirk's letters were written to her three children in order to maintain contact with them while she and her husband were stationed in Moscow. Although the *Journal* provided only a brief sample of her "Letters from Moscow," later that year she released *Postmarked Russia*, which contained almost one hundred letters in their entirety. Knowing that first-hand accounts of life behind the Iron Curtain were rare, particularly from women, Kirk had her letters published because, according to her son, she wanted to act as an effective representative for her family and her country.[90] However, her motives were likely more politically oriented. A confirmed Democrat, Lydia was fiercely patriotic.[91] "Letters from Moscow" and *Postmarked Russia* were released in 1952, almost immediately after her return from the Soviet Union and just prior to her husband taking on his directorship of the PSB.

In March 1949, Lydia's husband accepted his new post in Moscow, a moment she greeted with a sense of shock as well as "duty and responsibility." She knew she would have to sacrifice "much that was easy and pleasant," but Moscow was a post he could not refuse.[92] In a 1952 *New York Times* interview, Kirk admitted she had a distinct opportunity to convey to Americans the "nightmare of life in Soviet Russia."[93] For example, in a letter dated 30 July 1949, just one month after arriving in Moscow, she informed her daughters that she was expecting to find Moscow a "working city, alive and growing, a vital expression of the people's recovery from a long and terrible war and of their hope and dream of a new world." Instead, she found it a "dingy muddle with nothing to offer of beauty, but the stark, terrifying mass of the Kremlin itself."[94] Kirk wrote her letters with impressive clarity and detail, but often failed to acknowledge that she lived in the Soviet Union just several years after the end of a devastating war. She appeared to believe that the country should have recovered by the time of her arrival, and blamed the wretched circumstances of Russian women's lives on a "wicked system."[95] She expressed her hope that Russians could be reached through the type of "propaganda" that gave them what they needed and wanted. For example, she described a situation at Spaso House, the US Ambassador's official residence, in which servants got hold of her Sears, Roebuck & Co. catalogue and begged her to order items for them.[96] Kirk believed Russians needed propaganda emphasizing consumer values in order to challenge the illusion that they were living in a "paradise."[97] Kirk's letters reflected the opposite, as they showed the difficulties Americans faced living in Moscow, and provided a glimpse into what, according to her, was a repressive regime for all Russians. Her letters detailed the rigidities of the Soviet system, including the difficulties US embassy employees faced in obtaining visas and the frequency with which they were sent home for no apparent reason; the Soviet stronghold on religion and culture, which was reflected in the closing of her Catholic Church, the jamming of English-language radio broadcasts, and the general inability to establish meaningful connections with Russians, many of whom feared the consequences of American friendships.[98]

Kirk painted a dismal picture of the lives of Russian women, focusing on their work and work-life balance, appearance and clothing, and consumption habits. In August 1949, she described women in Mokhovaya Square, whom she had seen repaving the street, pouring and smoothing asphalt, and operating steamroller machines. She noted that working with asphalt was a hard and dirty job, but there was no job that was too rough and hard for Russian women. They cleaned streets, lifted and laid stones and bricks, loaded and unloaded trucks, shovelled sand and gravel, and plastered and painted walls. At the same time, she found them to be submissive workers. According to her reports, these "girls" arrived in Moscow from the countryside, with little education, eager to work, and frequently ended up engaging in hard manual labour, often at the expense of their health.[99] One morning in August 1950, she described the working conditions of women laying cement outside of her window. She remarked that these women, aged twenty to twenty-five, barely spoke to each other and worked with little enjoyment. In her view, they reflected the general attitudes of Russian labourers, who were chosen from the ranks of those who did the most poorly in school. They were put into trades and had no hope for advancement, but they never complained and accepted their circumstances. She called them a "robot group condemned to forced labor."[100] This comment of course ignored the conformity rampant throughout postwar America. Throughout her time in Russia, Kirk claimed to have repeatedly witnessed women engaged in hard labour, which was a far cry from the circumstances in her own country. In the postwar period, increasing numbers of American women engaged in full-time, permanent wage work.[101] However, they were frequently relegated to pink-collar occupations, including healthcare, education, and service work, that were reflective of their supposed nurturing, moral, selfless, and docile nature.[102] In contrast, Russian women did what in the United States would have been seen as men's work. Kirk admitted that throughout her stay, she had little direct contact with Russian women, and while she said many appeared fearful to speak to Westerners, that did not stop her from commenting on their status. She noted that in terms of so-called equal rights in the Soviet Union, women seemed to get the "short end" of the stick. Indeed, scholars have noted that, professionally, Russian women were unequal. Although they did have increased opportunities in education, healthcare, and engineering, they dominated in industries where pay was lower and, overall, were paid below the national average in all fields. Men retained the most powerful positions, particularly within the Communist Party.[103] According to Kirk, these women worked immensely hard, but did not seem to enjoy the same pleasures that Russian men did. She occasionally saw young women at restaurants and engaging in cultural and leisure activities, but older women tended to stay home to care for the children. Even when Kirk attended social functions in an official capacity, she said she rarely saw the wives of Soviet officials. She noted that she never saw them in public with their families and never saw them driving, failing to acknowledge that vehicles were rare commodities in the Soviet Union, particularly in urban centres with mass transportation networks.[104] Kirk's letters described a way of life that differed from that of elite American women such as herself, who were often seen in public socializing and engaging in a variety of activities.

Appearing four years after Capa's moving images were published in the *Ladies' Home Journal*, the ones accompanying Kirk's account were intended to show the magazine's readers that the lives of Russian women had barely improved. Kirk added to her devastating depiction of Russian women by emphasizing their unfeminine appearance. She wrote that the young women laying cement in front of her window appeared to be older than their years and barely resembled the feminine-looking women in the United States.[105]

She remarked that women's dresses lacked variety in shape, fabric, and colour. They resembled "sacks," typically loose-fitting throughout the body, with high necks and long sleeves. They were made of cheap cotton or rayon in the summer and coarse wool in the winter. Dresses were rarely any colour but dark brown, plum, or blue.[106] Russian women also found themselves limited in the forms of clothing available to them. No matter how cold the weather, women always wore dresses and never slacks (figure 2.14).[107] Kirk described women's undergarments as "rudimentary" in nature.[108] The items she saw in department stores lacked variety. Others items were simply non-existent. Nylon stockings and girdles were a rarity, and Kirk claimed she had never seen nightgowns for sale. Women's panties resembled bloomers, often in bright blue or purple cotton. Matching brassieres were available but were made according to the same model, heavy and with little consideration for the individual shape and size of a woman. Breasts were shoved into "dome-like pockets and held high, almost under their chins."[109] They were stacked on store shelves like "cups in a china shop."[110] Kirk wrote that better-dressed women appeared to wear old-fashioned chemises of white cotton, edged with cheap lace. She also included prices, with

Figure 2.14. This image showed the clothing of the Soviet Union's "typical housewives." Although it was taken in Vyborg, just north of St. Petersburg, with its frigid temperatures, it is noteworthy that the woman on the left is wearing thin stockings. Original caption: These typical housewives were photographed in Viborg [sic]. Boots are felt valenkis. Blackstar, *Ladies' Home Journal*, April 1952.

bloomers at $7 and brassieres at $4.50.[111] Highlighting the importance of gender and consumerism in the Cold War, Emily S. Rosenberg has noted that among the first items the United States attempted to export into the Soviet Union women were indeed undergarments. In 1963, the US Commerce Department invited Ida Rosenthal to a trade mission in Moscow. Rather fittingly, Rosenthal was a Russian Jew from Minsk and the founder of Maidenform, a manufacturer of brassieres and girdles.

During a time when American women's roles were gradually changing, she was an example of a successful female entrepreneur.[112] Maidenform products were sold in 115 countries, and the company hoped to expand to the Soviet Union.[113] It claimed it manufactured undergarments that were intended both to accentuate women's figures and provide them with support and comfort.[114] When Rosenthal returned from her trip, she was just as critical as Kirk in her assessment of Russian undergarments, claiming that they resembled those worn in the United States forty years earlier. Bras, for example, used fabrics with no stretch and came in only four sizes, from small to "quite big." Rosenthal noted that she would like "Russian women to wear Maidenform bras. They'll look better, they'll feel better, and maybe we'll get along better."[115] Of course, Maidenform bras were never actually made available on the Soviet market, but the attempt to market them emphasized the lengths the US government went to cater to these supposedly unhappy and unfeminine women. As Kirk noted a decade earlier, it was difficult for Russian women to appear feminine given their limited, and frequently expensive, clothing options. According to her elite sensibilities, the purchase of an item as common as a coat or a pair of shoes required much consultation and was as serious as purchasing a car in the United States.[116] This was, of course, in contrast to her own fashion options. She noted that no matter how plainly she was dressed, she was stared at on the street. Showcasing her Western wardrobe appeared to be a priority for Kirk, as she lamented the delay of her clothing trunk upon her move to Moscow; this mishap forced her to wear a simple red-and-white summer print, rather than a white brocade, to the embassy's 1949 Fourth of July reception. She was also unable to wear sports clothes and bathing suits during the Russian summers because travel was heavily restricted for Western diplomats.[117]

Kirk's account reveals a class divide between Russian women. She wrote that wives of high-ranking officials could afford more fashionable clothing and expensive jewellery. Occasionally, she would go to the opera or theatre and see these women dressed fashionably, at least for the Soviet Union, wearing full-length dresses made of satin or velvet, with silver-fox furs draped over one shoulder.[118] While wedding rings were not generally worn, they would wear "dinner rings," fancy rings of oval shape often placed on the index finger.[119] A watch was a sign of social status in the Soviet Union.[120] According to Kirk, though, these privileged women were a rarity and the masses of Russian women had minimal access to the types of clothing and jewellery that existed in the United States. Again, she failed to recognize that the slow economic recovery and a lack of consumer goods were due, in part, to the massive destruction caused by war. By 1951, towards the end of her stay in Moscow, Kirk did write of improvements in the availability of consumer goods. The Soviet government was beginning to import items from the satellite states, and clothing and shoes appeared to be more affordable, warmer, and of better quality than when she first arrived in Moscow. However, she wrote that none were as stylish as anything sold in the United States.[121]

Kirk detailed another element of Soviet life of interest to American women: food. In contrast to Steinbeck's description of the hearty meals that he and Capa were served in the countryside, Kirk's account painted a portrait of a city with limited food options. She wrote that the daily meals of the Russian worker typically consisted of *kasha*, or porridge, for breakfast, eaten plain or with oil. Lunch was soup, sauerkraut, or pickled or fresh cucumbers, and bread. Dinner always included bread, made and sold in government-controlled shops, which Kirk admitted was excellent. Flour was difficult to find and expensive. There was none for sale aside from 7 November (the celebration of the October Revolution) and 1 May (May Day). According to Kirk, because flour was available only on these two national holidays, it appeared as if it were a generous gift from Stalin.[122] Kirk wrote that in many instances, embassy staff asked her for flour, which she brought in from Germany or Finland in place of holiday gifts.[123] Meat was expensive, and the most common variety was stewing beef rather than the roasts that were popular in the United States. At times, she would see women carrying this meat home, unwrapped, and in their bare hands. Vegetables, even during the summer months, mainly consisted of cabbage, carrots, parsnips, cucumbers, and onions. Dairy products were difficult to obtain. Kirk stated that she used powdered milk since fresh milk was often handled poorly in stores. She had seen that milk, brought in from farms in huge cans, was rarely refrigerated and ladled directly into any containers that customers brought with them.[124] Russian women were known to have carried their own containers and bags with them during their shopping trips because stores and markets did not provide them. Additionally, they regularly carried with them an *avoshka*, a net or mesh expandable bag "just in case" they happened to come across difficult-to-find items.

In February 1958, Nancy Jones Levine, the wife of NBC news correspondent Irving R. Levine, wrote to the magazine to briefly describe her life as a newlywed in Moscow.[125] She called her twice weekly trip to the market a "workout," accompanied by much pushing and elbowing for items. It also required her to carry bags and jars from home in which to place her purchased items. She had learned her lesson the hard way, when her first purchase, berries, were dumped directly from the scale into her hands.[126] Even dining in a restaurant, according to Kirk, was a lacklustre affair. In July 1951, she described dining atop the Moscow Hotel with five ambassadors, an evening that may have seemed remarkable to some, but not for her. Although the restaurant had a view overlooking the Kremlin, and an orchestra and dance floor, she described an overcrowded atmosphere with poorly dressed servers and patrons dining on questionable food. Their meal consisted of cold meat, raw fish, caviar, cucumbers, whole tomatoes, and toasted bread. Later this was accompanied by what she referred to as "greasy, fried shoestring potatoes" and a "chicken cutlet buried beneath a layer of hard, fried fat." Dessert was ice cream and an apricot compote. She described the dining experience as poor and lamented the amount it cost their hosts.[127] Even in restaurants items were limited. Levine wrote that during their stay at the National Hotel, they never needed to review the hotel restaurant's menu, as it was the same all year, and the majority of the items listed were not available.[128] While both Kirk and Irving described negative food and dining experiences, it should be noted that they stood in contrast to those of official delegations who were invited to the Soviet Union. For example, in December 1949, US chess champion Gisela Kahn Gresser travelled to the Soviet Union for five weeks for an international women's tournament. In October 1950's "I Went to Moscow," she wrote that while she experienced difficulties in obtaining her visa and in travelling to Moscow, she and the other delegates received five-star treatment. This included their nightly dinners which were "convivial affairs" with a large variety and abundance of food including meat and fish, as well as a concluding banquet that flowed with caviar, wine, and vodka.[129] It was clear that when Americans visited the Soviet Union on "official" business for a short period of time, the government spared no expense, but in the day-to-day life of an American living in the country, circumstances were far different.

Overall, Kirk's accounts reflected her displeasure at the lack of consumer goods available in Moscow. She noted that department stores could hardly be called that as they contained very little. In fact, they contained mainly "trash" that one would find in an American attic.[130] Years later, "They Let Us Talk to the Russians" reaffirmed that the Russian eagerness to buy consumer goods, at least in the eyes of Americans, was still not satiated by 1955. Humphrey and Curran's visit to Moscow's largest department store, GUM, showed them that there were large crowds attempting to buy items, but in certain months they were simply not available.[131] In the words of these writers, Russian women seemed to face a particularly daunting task. They were eager to attract men, but lacked the necessary consumer goods, makeup, perfume, and clothes that would enable them to do so. In contrast, the US capitalist system created a marketplace in which women could enjoy an abundance of items at affordable prices. December 1946's "America's Greatest Problem" outlined the centrality of this distinguishing characteristic to postwar America. It stated that the greatest problem facing the country was "maintaining the uninterrupted production of abundant goods of all kinds." Rather dramatically, it stated that a serious crisis in production would not only affect the happiness of Americans but also "adversely influence the whole world."[132] More than ever, during the Cold War, US capitalism became associated with consumption, and, in turn, happiness. *Ladies' Home Journal* editors intended their readers to recognize this and sympathize with the deprived women of the Soviet Union.

Even the photographs that accompanied Kirk's account reflected what appeared to be an exhausting shopping experience. Figure 2.15, for example, depicted an elderly woman, dressed in heavy and unattractive, but warm, clothing, who had completed her daily shopping, which consisted only of her single "avoshka." The ordeal appears to have worn her out so much that she has decided to rest on a bench. What makes this image even more intriguing, however, is that she is resting on a bench on one of Moscow's busiest streets while holding on to her cow, perhaps the cow she had intended to sell on that day.[133]

These images contrasted with the articles and images in the *Ladies' Home Journal* which portrayed shopping as a relaxing, even joyful, experience rather than an exhausting one. The advertisements that appeared on the same pages of Kirk's article emphasized that contrast. March 1952's advertisements, which contained Kirk's first instalment of letters, appeared strategically selected for their ability to enhance a women's femininity. Advertisements for Old Spice Toiletries, Lassie Jr. 100 per cent wool tweed coats, Corocraft jewellery, and Van Raalte stockings and slips were placed directly beside Kirk's letters. The latter consisted of two-colour advertisements that included prices, only $1.65 and $5.95 for each item, and the statement that whether you were tall, average, or petite, Van Raalte products were made for all shapes and sizes, would suit your length, and hug your waistline perfectly.[134] Just three pages earlier, Kirk had included her detailed descriptions of the "rudimentary" women's undergarments that existed in the Soviet Union, and provided a list of their expensive prices, no doubt meant to horrify the reader.[135] Directly embedded in Kirk's letters on page 198 of March 1952's *Ladies' Home Journal* was an advertisement for the Brand Names Foundation, a non-profit organization that advocated for this continued use of advertising, brand names, and brand-based media. This Cold War–era foundation was fiercely patriotic in its promotion of the centrality of choice and brand-name goods to democracy and free-market capitalism.[136] Its advertisement directly appealed to the average female reader, asking

88 Shaping Women, Gender, and the Communist Threat

Figure 2.15. This image showed *Ladies' Home Journal* readers the difficulties, as well as the exhaustion, Russian women experienced while shopping, even in the nation's capital. Original caption: Leading her cow, this Russian woman stops to rest on Gorki Street, Moscow's chief thoroughfare, after shopping. Cotton-wadded coat is usual winter wear. Blackstar, *Ladies' Home Journal*, April 1952.

"Who is the girl in the dreams of ten thousand men?" The answer: "the American consumer." For she was the target of US manufacturers when they were dreaming up new products and new improvements. The advertisement took on a patriotic tone, noting that free competition meant freedom of choice for the buyer, and a multitude of good things for her to choose from. The comparison was clear: under a Soviet regime, government dictated the manufacture, availability, and price of all products, to the detriment of women, but under a US system of government, the female consumer was boss.[137] "They Let Us Talk to the Russians" affirmed the lack of brand names in the Soviet Union. Curran noted that advertising was simple and direct, and there was only one type of each product available, if you could even afford to buy it.[138]

Kirk's dissatisfaction with the Soviet regime intensified when she experienced brief periods of escape. In July 1950, she and her husband visited West Germany. According to her, after the initial novelty of living in Moscow had worn off, and she once again had a glimpse of the outside world, it was hard to return to Moscow. "More and more we seem cut off from all contact and communications with these people. The gulf of ideas, of taste, of sympathy even, grows deeper and deeper."[139] Her final letter, dated 4 October 1951, expressed her sadness at leaving behind the friendships she and her husband had developed, but excitement at leaving the country she had lived in for two years but could never quite call home. She concluded with the statement that "Russia one never forgets." While Kirk's letters reflected some positive aspects of the Soviet system, for example, the emphasis placed on literacy, the impressive transportation system, and the official Soviet line encouraging family unity, for the most part, her letters reflected her dissatisfaction with life in Moscow. They showed the difficulties women faced under a communist regime, even those that were just living there temporarily. While Kirk's letters are important because they were among the first accounts written by an American woman on life in Cold War Moscow, they are even more important for two other reasons. First, they were written by an American woman living in the Soviet Union for a sustained period of time, and from a rare perspective as the wife of a diplomat, a role that provided her with valuable knowledge of the inner workings of the Soviet regime, particularly in its diplomatic relationships with other nations. Second, her letters were extremely thorough and detailed, particularly in relation to her dissatisfaction with what she believed to be a repressive communist regime. Despite espousing equality for women, the regime denied them the privileges associated with womanhood considered commonplace in the United States, including the ability to cultivate a feminine appearance, to marry and care for their families without the "burden" of difficult wage work, and to freely purchase consumer items.

Throughout the early Cold War, the most frequent and ardent *Ladies' Home Journal* critic of the Soviet government and its treatment towards women was Dorothy Thompson, whose monthly column addressed political issues.[140] Thompson had a long history of anti-communist writing. In 1928, a decade after the Russian Revolution, she wrote *The New Russia*, a scathing review of the communist regime and life within the Soviet Union. While she painted a picture of a quaint countryside, she described Moscow as simultaneously the "most progressive and the most pitifully backward capital in Europe."[141] According to Thompson, Moscow in the 1920s was a capital city in disarray, characterized by high poverty rates, buildings in disrepair, and massive housing shortages. In discussing living conditions, she compared the apartments where many Muscovites resided to nineteenth-century New York City tenements.[142] She argued that very few people in Moscow lived a decent existence by Western standards. Many of Thompson's critiques focused on women's status and the family. According to her, the Soviet introduction of free divorce without the consent of both parties and the transfer of childcare from the home to the daycare centre led to increased marital instability.[143] She lamented the communist regime's attempts to negate the importance of love and emotions in society and that, in a land once famous for women of wit, charm, and soul, one seldom saw a beautiful woman. The majority of women were badly groomed, had tired, flaccid skin, and were pale. While she admitted that their appearance could in part be the result of genes, as well as the "adverse material conditions of life," she ultimately believed that it was the result of living in a society where women were not encouraged to love and be loved.[144] She stated that women had essentially become "de-womanized."[145]

In earlier years, *Ladies' Home Journal* writers were not always as critical of Russia. In March 1917, as the February Revolution was unravelling, and as the United States was still allied with Russia, the magazine included "The Russian Woman That Is Coming," one of a series of articles that addressed the changes to women's status due to the war.[146] The article heralded the Russian woman's newfound independence after years of suffering and degradation, noting that she was "at last" attaining self-support and self-respect. According to the article, these changes were launched more than fifty years earlier, when noblewomen began establishing industrial schools for local "peasant women" on their estates and under their supervision. There, peasant women learned skills such as jewellery and lacemaking, embroidery, and hat and basket weaving. The article noted other progress for peasant women in recent years: rising literacy rates; the abolition of the village "vodka shop" in favour of educational and recreational centres; sewing and cooking courses; employment opportunities in nursing, administrative work, and banking; and the opening of universities and professions, particularly medicine, law, engineering, and architecture.[147] Just as the *Ladies' Home Journal* may have acknowledged the contributions of white, middle-class, progressive women in improving the status of early twentieth-century American women, it did the same for Russian women, likening their historical circumstances. The article outlined a class divide and attributed progress largely to the noble women who provided opportunities for peasant women, the middle-class women who moved to remote villages to become teachers, and the "cultured" Russian women who travelled to those areas to volunteer their services. The article failed to address the intellectual and revolutionary tide that would soon sweep the nation, and its impact on Russian women.[148] June 1918's "The After-the-War Woman" did the same, attributing the Russian woman's "new authority" to the March 1917 overthrow of the tsar, not the February Revolution, calling it the moment that "democracy was born." It outlined women's wartime contributions and noted these strong women would be the ones to help the nation recover after the "poison of Bolshevikism had run its course."[149]

While the *Ladies' Home Journal* remained relatively silent on the Russian Revolution and the nation's women during the 1920s, by the 1930s it began criticizing the new regime and its impact on them, further reflecting that either positive or negative commentary depended on the fragile state of the US-Soviet relations. Only three articles appeared in the magazine, all in the first half of the decade, but they were lengthy and foreshadowed the tone the magazine would adopt during the Cold War. October 1931's "What's What in Russia" condemned the first Five-Year Plan as being both unrealistic in its goals and inefficient in its methods, and attributed its successes to the country's embrace of American engineers, as well as its adoption of US methods of manufacturing and farming. The article made clear that the Five-Year Plan did not yet stipulate manufacturing consumer goods, but rather simply building the factories that would eventually make them, noting that it may take "six to ten" Five-Year Plans to produce consumer goods at US levels. In the meantime, even the "everyday necessaries" that were found in America's five-and-ten-cent stores were difficult to obtain, and food shortages were rampant.[150] Just one month later, "The Twilight of Russian Family Gods" was even more critical. The article began by noting that "perhaps the most beneficial product of the Russian Revolution" for the American woman was that it allowed her a "perfect laboratory demonstration of what the complete emancipation of her sex entails." It noted that, in practice, the Russian woman found that being "freed" from the drudgery of the kitchen to lead a life of equality was not as satisfactory as she thought it would be. While some women entered the professions, the majority entered the dangerous and physically exhausting trades and industries, were unable to adequately care for their children, banned from practising formal religion, and lived in communal apartments where nurseries were the norm. The article told the story of the fictional "Olga," a wife and mother whose life went on a rather dramatic downward spiral as a result of women's "emancipation." Olga and her husband "Peter" lived in one of these communal apartments. Exhausted from caring for a baby and living in a small space, the couple decided to place their baby, "Ivan," in a nursery. With her newfound free time, Olga worked full-time, attended night school, and earned a promotion. Dissatisfied that Olga was rarely at home, Peter began seeing another woman and eventually obtained a divorce, an easy task in the Soviet Union. Olga, meanwhile, came to believe that romantic love was "bourgeois" and began living her sex life as a man would, by taking on a new husband every eight months or so. When she saw her child, he no longer seemed like he was her own. The article indicated that, while there were still "ten million reactionary housewives" who refused to be "freed from their kitchens to work as hard as the men," there were more than "three million Olgas in Russia." These new Russian women were "communist-bred robots" who were eager to "preach the gospel of Revolution and the Marxian theory to the far corners of the capitalistic earth." To drive home its points, the article was accompanied by images of women operating heavy machinery in factory settings, and children in nurseries.[151] April 1934's "Russia Now Laughs" was written by renowned journalist Anne O'Hare McCormick and was more sympathetic, perhaps in part due to the US government's 1933 recognition of the Soviet Union, which she noted. However, she also confirmed the seemingly complete transformation of the new Russian woman, which was likely an unappealing image for *Ladies' Home Journal* readers. Profiling twenty-two-year-old Alla Petrova, who worked on the construction of Moscow's new subway system, McCormick wrote of her decidedly unfeminine characteristics. According to her, she lived like a soldier in a barrack, was "hard as nails and husky as a stevedore," and had "about as much feminine allure as the Rock of Gibraltar."[152] Still, McCormick remained certain that if she asked Russian women what they desired most, they would say kitchens of their own, despite their newfound freedom. To her, the happiest woman she had met in Moscow was a pretty housewife who had a rare three-room apartment for her entire family. Even while discussing Russian women's emancipation, these articles could not help but tie women to the home, family, and consumerism.

Thompson's own critical views of the Soviet Union came as a result of a larger migratory trend that took place during the interwar period. Following the Russian Revolution, progressive American women, including journalists, suffragists, social reformers, educators, and artists, flocked to the Soviet Union. While journalists such as Thompson held a decidedly negative view of the Soviet Union, others, as Julia L. Mickenberg notes, were lured by the prospect of a revolutionary socialist experiment that promised them gender equality, and new economic, political, and sexual opportunities. Even into the 1930s, when the "Soviet Experiment" turned dark with its purges and famines, and the "gap between Soviet rhetoric of women's equality and the reality of women's lives" became evident, many of these women still remained outwardly committed to the cause because it promised emancipation, even if they began to question its effectiveness privately.[153] For African American women, particularly the artists of the Harlem Renaissance, the revolution provided an enticing opportunity to experience a country where racism had been legally outlawed, and to witness first-hand the extent to which the lives of Soviet national minorities had been altered.[154]

Thompson's stature grew after the publication of her 1932 book *I Saw Hitler,* in which she interviewed future German chancellor Adolf Hitler and warned of the possible repercussions of his rise to power.[155] The book resulted in her being the first American journalist expelled from Nazi Germany. After Thompson's warnings proved correct and Hitler invaded Poland in 1939, she was named the second most influential woman in the United States, only after Eleanor Roosevelt. After World War II, Thompson came to believe that Soviets would replace Nazis as the enemies of the West. In a 1946 diary entry, she wrote, "nothing will stop the Russians except fear."[156] Thus, her *Ladies' Home Journal* columns were fiercely critical of the communist regime. March 1952's "I Write of Russian Women" contrasted the professional and personal experiences of Russian and American woman. Thompson claimed that while communism had proclaimed the emancipation of women, Russian women were expected to work from the age of eighteen to fifty-five and were the most "exploited toilers" in the country.[157] She described the working conditions of women in both the factory and the farm, all of them overworked, underpaid, and saddled with the bulk of the housework and family responsibilities. According to Thompson, their husbands were not "helping with the dishes at night. That's beneath the dignity of the Russian male … They're probably drowning the cares of the day in vodka – while mamma mends their socks."[158] Of course, Thompson and the *Ladies' Home Journal* distinguished these women from their idealized female readers, who were supposedly unburdened by heavy work, relieved by the conveniences of modern capitalism, and rewarded with loving husbands who actually helped them. Postwar women's magazines repeatedly emphasized the father figure as a willing contributor to the care of the suburban home and family, of which childrearing was central. This contrasted with media portrayals of Russian men who were unwilling to do the same, mainly owing to a fear of embarrassment or emasculation if they engaged in "women's work." This dated mentality was seen as amplifying the Russian woman's double burden, thus increasing her unhappiness. However, as Margaret Marsh has noted, the American concept of "masculine domesticity" did not actually mean that household duties were equal, it simply meant that men "increased" their childcaring responsibilities.[159] As men engaged in paid labour away from the home, masculine domesticity was often relegated to evenings and weekends, as well as more "rugged" household and familial tasks that included physical activities and the outdoors. In another column, Thompson wrote that while Europeans saw American wives as "bossy" women who dominated their husbands, American men were the "world's best husbands."[160] If true, this belief may have represented a sad acknowledgment, or even resentment, over the fact that so many of their own husbands had been killed during the war. Aside from a privileged few who were highly educated with important jobs, Thompson did not believe that "Russian women liked the regime." In contrast to the more positive descriptions of Russian women by writers such as Steinbeck that appeared in the *Ladies' Home Journal* during the late 1940s, Thompson wrote that her "woman's eye" noticed that "Russian women, as a whole, look unhappy."[161] This stance reflected a change in direction on the part of the magazine. By the early 1950s, it began taking on a more aggressive stance towards communism. It continued to depict women as hardworking, but, instead of happy and hopeful, they were now shown as unhappy living under a repressive regime.

Other columns took this narrative even further. April 1952's "How America Lives" explicitly contrasted democratic and communist institutions. "Escape to Freedom" told the dramatic journey of the Kutvirts: husband Otakar, wife Duda, and their sons, Tommy and Daniel. Native Czechs, the couple had travelled from Rochester, New York, to Czechoslovakia to visit family after the war.[162] Family illness and a communist coup in 1948 forced them to remain in the country for three years under what they called a "repressive regime." They were forced to flee by foot from the Czech mountains into West Germany, but according to them no risk "was too great to escape." [163] Their lengthy ordeal in communist Czechoslovakia taught the Kutvirts to cherish democracy. After returning to America, Otakar began teaching economics at the University of Rochester, often condemning communism in his lectures, and Duda began giving speeches on living conditions under communism, an undertaking she believed was her duty as an American. As a result of their ordeal, and their disdain for the communist system that had drastically altered their beloved homeland, the family embraced their new cultural surroundings. The American dream was well within their reach. With Otakar working multiple jobs, and Duda a "champion bargain hunter," they were able to purchase their first home for $13,000. Czech was no longer spoken in their household, Czech holidays were no longer observed, and their children would "inherit a proud heritage … They are to be middle-class Americans, and we intend them to know it."[164] The Kutvirts' story endorsed the *Ladies' Home Journal* principle that an idealized middle-class existence was attainable for anyone living in the United States, including those fleeing from communism.

These images of "graceless, shapeless, and sexless" Russian women dominated the media, as well as the pages of the *Ladies' Home Journal*, and they became embedded in the American psyche throughout the late 1940s and early 1950s. Further, they shaped popular conceptions of communism.[165] Russian women were depicted as doing it all, mainly because the repressive regime under which they lived gave them no other choice. Given a choice, however, they would certainly choose to live under a capitalist system, much like the Kutvirts did when they courageously escaped Czechoslovakia. During their 1955 visit to Russia, the Goulds described the interest of young people in learning about American life and culture. Beatrice's copies of the *Journal* were so popular that she found them difficult to hold on to. According to her, the articles that most fascinated women were pictures of homes, kitchens, and fashion.[166] The hope of US government representatives, as well as ordinary Americans, was that increased exposure to the outside world, even if only through a magazine, would lead to an increase in political, economic, social, and cultural freedom in the Soviet Union. Descriptions of Russian women in the *Journal* were important in that they showed how and to what extent communism affected the human soul, and in the pages of the magazine, they were treated seriously. However, as Jochen Hellbeck has noted in his analysis of Stalinist-era diary entries, the process whereby ordinary Russians chose to either embrace or reject socialism was frequently much more complex and characterized by internal struggles. Many early Russians were in fact interested in conforming to a socialist model that promised them much, and to the idea of belonging to a larger collective that served a greater purpose. As a result, even amid their hardships, many grappled internally with the concept of socialism in their lives, as well as their place within the socialist state. This "socialist subjectivity," as it has come to be known, complicates the narrative that Russians lived under an authoritarian regime that survived only through propaganda and terror. Rather, it shows a process of self-negotiation defined by sincerity and conviction on the part of ordinary Russians.[167] For *Ladies' Home Journal* readers, the accuracy of these representations was further reinforced by the fact that they came from the seemingly objective observations of average people who had travelled to, or even lived in, the Soviet Union, and who did not have an overt political agenda. They depicted a superior American way of life, contrasted with a Soviet one in which women were unfeminine, unfulfilled, and unhappy, all of which were evidence of the potential dangers of communism to the social order and to the privileged position of American women. These images were further reinforced by accounts such as those of the Kutvirts, Czech natives who willingly *chose* to escape their conditions. It was assumed that femininity and happiness were derived from the home, family, and material prosperity that were made available to American women because of democratic freedom and capitalism. In reading about the repressive conditions of a proud Russian people, American women could sympathize with them and recognize that by "containing" communism at home, or even doing something as small as handing over an issue of the *Journal*, they could perhaps one day alter the wretched circumstances of Russian women. *Ladies' Home Journal* articles were clearly intended to appeal to the emotions of its female readers. They capitalized on the common bonds that existed between American and Russian women in order to encourage the former to take a stand against communism. These common bonds included the ability to maintain their femininity, stay at home and raise their families without being burdened by outside work, and to experience the joys of consumer culture. Beginning in 1956, the USIA began spreading these images more rapidly through the distribution of *Amerika* magazine. The magazine became a central component of the USIA's cultural program. As part of a wider foreign policy effort to discredit the Soviet Union, it took the messages that were conveyed to American women through magazines such as the *Ladies' Home Journal* and transported them overseas in their attempts to win the "hearts and minds" of Russian women.

PART TWO

Selling Women, Gender, and Consumer Culture through *Amerika*

Chapter Three

Selling the American Way Abroad: The Beginnings of Cold War Cultural Diplomacy in the Soviet Union

> We should portray the American woman above all as a thoroughly human, hard-working, feminine person. Primary emphasis should be on the "average" American woman, particularly as wife and mother, but material on outstanding women and on the status which women have attained in America continues to have special program value.[1]

During the early Cold War period, the USIA adopted this approach in its attempts to appeal to foreign women. In 1959, the USIA formally put these ideas into writing when it developed a policy planning paper entitled "Women's Activities," a guide for portraying the American woman in its overseas information program. It stated that in almost every culture, the woman held an important position, as she represented "the family, the primary stabilizing force which holds society together." However, it recognized that many countries had "highly distorted images" of the American woman that could negatively impact foreign judgments of the broader state of the nation. The most common of these distortions were the views of her as, first, an "irresponsible glamor girl" and, second, an "unfeminine, materialistic being whose main interest in her life was her job." While the paper admitted that some American women fit these moulds, it noted that the vast majority were "characterized by devotion to family, womanliness and industriousness." To combat the negative images, the USIA's information program, through its country posts, emphasized the American woman in her most typical activities and attitudes. She was not to be portrayed as unique or perfect, but rather a person trying to solve problems. She was to be shown as compassionate and hard-working, a conserver of values, and possessing the feminine characteristics with which women throughout the world could identify and respect.[2] Her primary roles were, first and foremost, those of wife and mother.[3] In spite of this traditional orientation, the paper did support, to an extent, progressive ideas. It pointed out that the American woman had choices. Before marriage, most likely she went out to work, and, once her children were grown, she may return to work or volunteer within her community. The American woman was also free to remain single and to concentrate on a career, in which she had many options.

In essence, the paper emphasized the concept of freedom of choice in determining one's roles in life. Conveying messages about women's choices was considered especially important because, according to the USIA, Russian women lacked the ability to choose their roles in the same way that American women did. The USIA also acknowledged that around the world women's roles were changing. It indicated that in certain instances, its country posts should provide material on the status that women had attained in the United States, and offer examples of outstanding women and their significant contributions. Overall, the posts were to reflect any changes in gender roles in the countries in which USIA personnel were stationed and in the programs that catered to those women.[4] However, while the USIA acknowledged that women's lives and roles were changing, it continued to maintain that the average American woman, like her counterparts around the world, was primarily interested in the home and family, and therefore her roles as wife and mother were the ones that should be emphasized to overseas audiences. This was the approach the USIA used consistently in the Soviet Union, in spite of the fact that women's lives there had changed dramatically in terms of their active participation in the paid workforce.

During the early Cold War, the US overseas information program in the Soviet Union was shaped in large measure by the idealized images of suburban domesticity that were shown in prominent women's magazines such as the *Ladies' Home Journal*. Cold War tensions between the United States and the Soviet Union meant that the USIA had limited opportunities to convey information to Russian women. However, when it was able to do so, the USIA showed them a carefully constructed image of America as a land of democracy, freedom, capitalism, and consumption, centred on the woman. USIA officials took the idealized roles of feminine housewife, mother, and consumer and extended them to all women, regardless of their geographical location. Through their cultural activities, the USIA deployed images of hardworking and content American women that rarely, if ever, reflected the actual diversity of women's experiences in terms of their race, ethnicity, class, or sexuality. Their geographical location was occasionally touched on, but only to display wholesome suburban or rural women; the lives of their potentially non-traditional urban counterparts were rarely addressed. These monolithic images were meant to appeal to Russian women, who, for their part, were depicted by the postwar media as overworked and unhappy. Equally monolithic images of Russian women were important in shaping popular perceptions of what life behind the Iron Curtain was "really like." Although not necessarily accurate, many in the public and private sectors, as well as the general public, took these images as factual depictions of Russian women and their lives. When the USIA implemented its policies on "Women's Activities," media images of both American and Russian women shaped the form and content of its cultural program.[5]

America's overseas information program had come to full fruition by the end of the decade. However, in spite of the clear success of the nation's wartime overseas information programs, it took considerable time for a peacetime program of a similar nature to be established. The early postwar years witnessed a complex, aggressive, and costly struggle between Truman and Stalin over global supremacy, or at least supremacy over war-torn Europe. Robert Dean argues that, during this time period, a "politics of manhood" dominated international politics and shaped a strongly interventionist approach to the Cold War in which leaders did not want to show weakness in public.[6] Indeed, Truman-era officials took an aggressive approach to foreign policy decision-making and actions, devoting massive resources to national defence in an effort to combat the Soviet threat. Meanwhile, for those officials that believed in the gradual effectiveness of a propaganda or information program promoting American ideas and culture abroad, it was a struggle to amass adequate support and funding. Part of this struggle stemmed from the fact that, historically, overseas information programs had a minor role in US foreign policy.

Prior to the twentieth century, the US government had a limited global role, and there was little need to appeal to foreigners in order to win them over to American policies. This approach changed during World Wars I and II, when the necessity of swaying citizens, both domestic and foreign, towards supporting the American war effort became apparent. During these wars, Presidents Woodrow Wilson and Franklin Roosevelt created the Committee on Public Information (CPI) and the Office of War Information (OWI), respectively. Both were propaganda agencies charged with the task of directing, creating, and disseminating material intended to influence Americans at home and foreigners abroad to support the Allied war effort.[7] Women were integral to these information programs. For example, during World War II, the OWI, in coordination with private agencies, created press material, radio programs, and motion pictures to entice women to support the war effort.[8]

Much of this material vilified the enemy and encouraged American women to demonstrate their support and patriotism by working in wartime industry, volunteering, growing victory gardens, rationing food items, collecting scrap material, and purchasing war bonds. On the home front, women were integral to building and maintaining morale.[9] Artist J. Howard Miller's 1942 poster of Rosie the Riveter, wearing a red bandana, flexing her muscles, and emphatically declaring "We Can Do It!," became an icon for American women during the war and to this day remains a revered feminist symbol.[10] In spite of these programs' successes, however, peacetime information agencies were unheard of in the United States. In 1946, Truman dismantled the OWI and its activities were subsumed by the State Department, where they received little support. Senior-level State Department officials were indifferent and at times even hostile towards these additional duties.[11] Congress viewed the OWI as a relic of Roosevelt's New Deal, which they associated with large government and reckless spending. It continually cut funding for the information program, which meant that specific departments, such as State and Defense, ran their own ad hoc information programs.[12]

By 1947, as the Soviet Union further extended its influence in Eastern Europe and the threat of a Cold War loomed, the State Department, the Department of Defense, and Truman himself began to slowly recognize the importance of creating an adequately funded program to promote American ideas and culture abroad.[13] Their change in attitude stemmed from the recognition that the traditional practices of international relations were evolving. Until the beginning of the Cold War, the US government, like most governments, practised traditional diplomacy. Traditional diplomacy can be defined as the process of forging relationships with other nations, often relying on the interaction of high-ranking officials, in order to reach a formal agreement based on a particular foreign policy decision.[14] After World War II, new transportation and communications technologies altered the nature of international relations, allowing governments and people to interact more frequently and exchange knowledge. In light of the ideological battles of the Cold War, public diplomacy emerged as a method for governments to communicate directly with ordinary individuals, with the hope that public opinion could stimulate policy formation.[15] In these initial years of the Cold War, important inroads were made to expand the overseas information program. In January 1948, after significant debate over the necessity and expense of expanding the program, Congress passed the United States Information and Educational Act. Otherwise known as the Smith-Mundt Act. Named after Senator H. Alexander Smith (R-NJ) and Representative Karl E. Mundt (R-SD), respectively, it was intended to "increase mutual understanding between the people of the United States and the people of other countries."[16] The Act called for the exchange of persons, knowledge, and skills, the assignment of specialists to serve in other countries as needed, and the "dissemination abroad, of information about the United States, its people, and its policies, through press, publications, radio, motion pictures, and other information media, and through information centres and instructors abroad."[17] During its first year of operations, the program received $31.2 million in Congressional funding, double the amount spent on the foreign information program the previous year. Under Smith-Mundt, the Truman administration expanded the US press service, the VOA, and the Motion Picture Service, and created international US information centres, which held books and hosted small exhibitions.[18]

In spite of these advancements, early attempts to reach Russian audiences were frustrated by Soviet attempts to limit cultural ties between the two nations as well as the State Department's reaction to these attempts. A 1948 State Department report detailed the difficulties under Smith-Mundt in arranging exchanges with the Soviet Union and its satellite states. It attributed these difficulties to the Soviet government's fear that exchanges would expose its citizens to foreign influences and attitudes. The Soviet government prevented its own citizens from travelling abroad for a lengthy period of time and rarely permitted Americans the opportunity to enter the Soviet Union.[19] On the rare occasions that Americans were granted visas, Russians, particularly those living in large cities and in close proximity to the secret police, were hesitant to interact with them because they feared harsh repercussions if they were caught doing so.[20] As noted in chapter 2, accounts by American diplomats and journalists confirm the hesitancy, and in some cases fear, that Russians had in interacting with them. Hixson argues that efforts to limit personal interactions were part of a larger effort by the Soviet government to limit American influence. As he points out, the US government, as well as private organizations, attempted to maintain a foothold in the Soviet Union, but an "anti-Western campaign" sought to limit their presence.[21] As early as 1948, the State Department wrote that Soviet leaders were trying to block democratic nations from obtaining authentic information about conditions in the Soviet Union by imposing severe restrictions on foreign correspondents.[22] By 1950, the newly created Central Intelligence Agency (CIA) reported that since the end of World War II, the Soviet Union had been attempting to reduce Western influence among the Eastern European satellite states in order to accelerate their "Sovietization." According to the CIA, Soviet activities consisted of the expulsion of Western cultural, religious, and humanitarian agencies and the curtailment of diplomacy. By that time, political and cultural ties between the Soviet Union, Eastern European satellite states, and the West were almost completely severed.[23] The State Department, which considered cultural exchange programs with the Soviet Union and its satellite states a sign of weakness and a form of appeasement, vetoed efforts to negotiate agreements with communist regimes.[24] During the early Cold War, this hostile relationship meant that the US government had limited opportunities to reach Russian citizens, particularly its women. There were only two ways to reach Russian audiences. The first was through radio programming. However, Russians were required to register their radios and pay a subscription, and broadcasts were occasionally jammed by the Soviet government.[25] The second was through *Amerika* magazine, the Russian-language picture magazine that was published by the USIA in Washington, DC, and distributed in Russia by Soyuzpechat, the Soviet agency responsible for distributing publications in the country.[26]

The idea of *Amerika* came to fruition in 1944, when US Ambassador to the Soviet Union Averill Harriman and Soviet Foreign Minister Vyacheslav Molotov negotiated an agreement for the distribution of *Amerika*. The magazine acquired as its first editor-in-chief famed journalist Marion K. Sanders. A freelance writer and author, Sanders was hired in 1944 as a news editor with the Overseas Branch of the OWI. By the end of the war, she had risen to become the assistant chief of the Publications Bureau, which published magazines in over twenty languages. In addition to her editorial duties at *Amerika*, in 1950 she became chief of the State Department's Publication Branch, heading its New York office. The Publication Branch was responsible for issuing literature for foreign distribution, including *Amerika*.[27] *Amerika* was first published in January 1945 for ten rubles per copy, and had a circulation rate of ten thousand copies. It proved to be so popular that within one year, Ambassador Walter Bedell Smith obtained permission to increase circulation to fifty thousand copies beginning in June 1946.[28] Even if government officials had not yet recognized its value, the US media had long heralded the benefits of bombarding Russians with information on America. For example, a 1951 cartoon (figure 3.1) depicted booklets on "US Living Standards" being blasted behind the Iron Curtain, while a Russian woman instructed her husband, Ivan, to look at the "electric washing machines, sewing machines and refrigerators" within its pages.[29]

For Sanders, *Amerika* was this cartoon come to fruition. Sanders recognized that Russian readers would likely open the magazine with a "bias against it," but admittedly did not care because its appearance and content would win over readers. The magazine, according to her, was "as

Figure 3.1. Cartoons such as this one mocked a Soviet system that provided its citizens with few consumer goods, suggesting that although Russians were in awe of modern appliances, their country failed to provide them. Edward D. Kuekes, *Cleveland Plain Dealer*, 25 January 1951.

American as a Sears, Roebuck catalogue" and likely appealed to people because it matched the lure of a "mail order fairyland."[30] For example, Sanders noted that the August 1946 issue, with a front cover that showed a woman at a newsstand, and a lead story on the concept of the American free press, was likely to appeal to "feminine readers" (figure 3.2). Additionally, the cover model's outfit, including her blue purse and red shoes, may have been of "special interest" to women.[31] While *Amerika*'s first run made attempts to appeal to women, as Sanders may have insinuated, it did not do so with the same vigour as it did under Eisenhower's administration. Of the articles that were geared towards women, the majority focused on fashion. Those on marriage, the family, the home, and consumption were minimal. Those on working women, even if they focused on traditionally female occupations, were practically non-existent. Instead, *Amerika*'s first run focused on topics of wide appeal that explained America's political institutions, highlighted its economic prosperity, showcased its technology and ingenuity, and proudly displayed the wholesomeness of its people and culture. Occasionally, issues focused more heavily on specific topics, such as the free press, the judicial process, the South, modern transportation, publishing, communications, education, farming, and medicine.[32] On one rare occasion *Amerika* included a lengthy article on the African American experience, entitled "The Negro in America Life."[33] However, none of these issues were billed as "special" ones, as they were during its second run.

During this first run, journalists and US embassy officials alike boasted about the mass appeal of *Amerika*. Sanders observed that issues were widely circulated among colleagues, family, and friends, and could have been seen by as many as twenty people. This meant that if all copies sold, the readership of a single issue could have approached one million. Copies went to libraries and institutions, and others remained in homes, which allowed them to circulate even after their initial release date.[34] The ability to reach any readers was considered a feat since the process of disseminating information in the Soviet Union was lengthy and burdensome. For example, all of *Amerika*'s articles were compiled or written in New York and sent to Moscow for translation. After the magazine was translated, it was reviewed by the Soviet censor and then distributed. While an article was rarely rejected, it could take six to eight months between the time an article was written or rewritten and a finished magazine arrived in the hands of a Russian reader. As a result, content needed to be planned well in advance and much of its material needed to be "timeless."[35]

In spite of *Amerika*'s apparent popularity, problems arose as early as 1947, when sales began to fall dramatically. Suddenly, Soyuzpechat

Figure 3.2. This August 1946 cover issue of *Amerika* showed a fashionable woman examining a variety of reading materials at an American newsstand, and, in the process, demonstrating the freedom of speech that was possible in America. Cover, *Amerika*, August 1946.

officials stated that Russian readers had "lost interest" in the magazine, consistently reporting a decline in sales. The July 1947 issue sold only 19,018 copies.[36] The embassy in Moscow responded by reducing the price of *Amerika* from ten to five rubles per copy, but it never came close to being sold out, as it had been in the past.[37] The July 1948 issue fell to an all-time low, selling only 14,765 copies.[38] State Department officials blamed this decline on the Soviet government and Soyuzpechat, which they claimed delayed the magazine's distribution in an effort to restrict its sales in light of its popularity. For example, the January 1950 issue of *Amerika* arrived in Moscow for Soyuzpechat's review on 27 December, but it did not appear on Moscow's streets until 2 February. Prior issues had appeared as little as five days later.[39] State Department records reveal that there were forty newsstands in Moscow, but *Amerika* appeared at only seven of them, all located in the centre of the city, ostensibly where they could be monitored. When the magazine was displayed, US embassy officials reported it was often poorly placed, concealed beneath counters, or hidden under other publications.[40] On the last day of 1949, the Soviet International Book Agency advised the embassy that effective 1 January 1950, all unsold copies of *Amerika* would be returned to the US embassy in Moscow.[41] It returned twenty-five thousand copies, claiming it could not sell them.[42] When Ambassador Kirk brought up the issue of unsold copies to Foreign Minister Andrei Gromyko, the latter refused to take responsibility for the magazine's distribution.[43] The State Department, however, continued to ship fifty thousand copies of every issue to the Soviet Union. It, along with Sanders, made a concerted effort to remedy the problem of unsold copies, suggesting to Soyuzpechat a variety of methods to increase circulation, including wider distribution throughout the country, the distribution of courtesy issues to institutions, and the inclusion of subscription coupons in the magazine. Secretary of State Dean Acheson believed it was highly unlikely these suggestions would be implemented, but he was hopeful they would deter returns.[44] When these suggestions went ignored, the US embassy began shipping unsold copies to Germany, Austria, Hungary, Israel, Iran, and Brazil, in hope of reaching Russian-speaking groups abroad.[45]

These complications, which became known in the State Department as the "*Amerika* crisis," led to the decision to suspend its publication in July 1952. The difficulty of producing, publishing, and circulating a magazine that needed to go through so many channels, as well as the "crisis," hardly seemed worth the State Department's efforts. Further, Sanders had resigned her posts as editor-in-chief of *Amerika* and chief of the State Department's Publications Branch just one month earlier, protesting a reorganization plan which would see the abolition of its

New York office in favour of consolidation in Washington DC, a move which the State Department said would lead to greater efficiency, reduce costs, and avoid duplication of effort. Sanders made attempts to halt the move, writing to members of the United States Advisory Commission on Information, a statutory body that reported to Congress on the operations of the information program, asking for a hearing regarding the issue. According to Sanders, she received sympathetic replies, but members had questioned whether a hearing could be held in time to prevent the changes. Sanders rather correctly predicted that the move would have a "crippling effect upon the nation's written propaganda effort in a crucial moment of battle."[46] *Amerika*'s discontinuation was a pivotal moment in Truman's overseas information program, as it was one of the last avenues through which the US government could freely reach a large Russian audience. The VOA continued to operate, but the Soviet government frequently jammed its broadcasts. Journalists and diplomats visiting the Soviet Union discussed their frustration at being unable to receive non-Soviet radio broadcasts, particularly outside of major cities such as Moscow and Leningrad. As discussed in chapter 2, they commented on Russians' shocking lack of knowledge about America. *Amerika*'s discontinuation symbolized the loss of one of the last connections the State Department had with ordinary Russians in the early Cold War, undermining its ability both to counteract Soviet propaganda and to promote the American way of life.

Additionally, Truman's overseas information program was plagued by decentralized leadership and infighting. In April 1951, he created the Psychological Strategy Board (PSB), a committee that provided for the "planning, coordination and conduct, within the framework of approved national policies, of psychological operations."[47] By "psychological operations" he meant propaganda supplemented with other covert operations measures of a political, economic, or military nature.[48] The PSB consisted of the under secretary of state, the deputy secretary of the Department Defense, the director of the CIA, a representative from the Joint Chiefs of Staff as principal adviser, and a director appointed by the president. It reported to the National Security Council.[49] In spite of its ambitious mandate and high-level members, the PSB was characterized by interagency conflict and failed to unite the executive branch departments and agencies behind a single and sustainable campaign of psychological warfare.[50] The PSB was disbanded in September 1953, but its short history highlights the Truman administration's failure to launch a unified program of psychological warfare that aimed to undermine the Soviet regime, one that centred on common themes, targeted specific people, and consisted of similar objectives.

The nature of America's overseas information program changed from the moment Eisenhower took office in January 1953. Eisenhower sought to develop a more centralized, coherent, and sustainable overseas information program than the one that existed under Truman. As a five-star general who commanded the Allied forces in Europe during World War II, he understood the importance of undermining enemy morale and saw the value of cultural diplomacy as a means of directly engaging with foreign citizens abroad in order to influence their conceptions of the United States. In other words, he was aware of the power of public opinion, and wanted information activities to become a central component of America's Cold War strategy.[51] As early as his first State of the Union address on 2 February, Eisenhower affirmed these beliefs. He articulated the need to "make more effective all activities related to international information," and declared that a "unified and dynamic effort in this whole field is essential to the security of the United States and other peoples in the community of free nations."[52] The opportunity for Eisenhower to achieve his objectives increased exponentially upon the death of long-time Soviet leader Josef Stalin on 6 March. Eisenhower's determination, as well as changes in the international climate that resulted from Stalin's death, allowed his vision to slowly come to fruition. On 16 March, Stalin's successor, Georgi Malenkov, spoke before a meeting of the Supreme Soviet, the highest legislative body in the Soviet Union, and announced his government's reformist agenda. He stated that there were no problems between the East and West that could not be solved by negotiation. In the weeks following his speech, he adopted a host of measures that included increased negotiations and contact with the West in order to demonstrate Soviet goodwill.[53] Eisenhower responded to Stalin's death and Malenkov's speech that April with his "Chance for Peace" speech to the American Society of Newspaper Editors, in which he addressed America's commitment to a peaceful world. There, he stated that "every gun that is made, every warship launched, every rocket fired signifies, in the final sense, a theft from those who hunger and are not fed, those who are cold and are not clothed. This world in arms is not spending money alone" but is spending it in the "sweat of its laborers, the genius of its scientists, the hopes of its children." He went on to compare the cost of arms production to the cost of building items that were more productive for the nation and its citizens.[54]

Stalin's death, and changes in the Soviet position, were sudden, and the Eisenhower administration had done little preliminary planning for such an event, but he used the opportunity to enhance the legitimacy of an information program. Kenneth A. Osgood argues that

Eisenhower's "Chance for Peace" speech was an attempt to take the peace initiative away from the Soviet Union. The United States worried that Malenkov's anti-Stalinist approach and overtures towards peaceful negotiations would soften the image of the Soviet Union and make communism more appealing to other nations. To Eisenhower, Stalin's death meant that more than ever, an overseas information program was necessary.[55] In the first months of his administration, Eisenhower created the foundation for a viable and uniform information program. He surrounded himself with advisers that were not only knowledgeable on the topic of propaganda, but also fiercely passionate about it. His closest adviser was Charles Douglas (C.D.) Jackson, the vice-president of Time Inc., assistant to its owner and founder, Henry Robinson Luce, and the man whom Eisenhower hired in 1943 to head the wartime Psychological Warfare Division.[56] Time Inc. published the most prestigious news magazines of the postwar period, including *Time* and *Life*, established in 1923 and 1936, respectively. In addition, Luce ran the *The March of Time*, which started as a radio program in 1931 before evolving into a newsreel series in 1935. By the postwar period, Time Inc. was the largest magazine publisher in the world and its publications were well known for espousing American values. As a highly influential media executive, Jackson admitted that psychological warfare was "near and dear" to his heart.[57] In February 1953, Eisenhower named Jackson the first special assistant to the president for Cold War planning, even giving him an office in the White House.[58] This administrative move further solidified the connection between the public and private sectors, particularly the US overseas information program and media.

To advance his agenda of creating an overseas information program, Eisenhower formed two committees. On 24 January 1953, he established the President's Advisory Committee on Government Organizations, led by Nelson Rockefeller, and the President's Committee on International Information Activities, chaired by William Jackson, a former CIA deputy director. Although neither committee's reports and recommendations mentioned women, both were important in affirming the need for an overseas information program and for creating and shaping the vehicles through which women were reached. The Rockefeller Committee was tasked with making recommendations on the bureaucratic structure of the executive branch in order to consolidate White House authority over various government departments. The most important outcome of its report, released on 7 April 1953, was the recommendation that overt overseas information programs be removed from the State Department and established under a separate agency. Taking these recommendations into consideration, on 1 August 1953, Eisenhower established the USIA as a separate organization, one that reported to the White House through the National Security Council (NSC).[59] With this plan, the State Department provided foreign policy guidance, but relinquished control over all overt overseas information activities. The VOA, overseas libraries and information centres, the motion picture service, and press and publication agencies were joined under the name United States Information Service (USIS), which is how they were known abroad. These programs came under the authority of the new USIA, as it became known at home.[60] The director of the new agency, Theodore Streibert, was a Harvard business graduate and, like Jackson, a seasoned professional in the media industry. In 1933, Streibert joined the staff of radio station WOR-AM in New York City, rising to the rank of president by 1945. He was also a founder of the Mutual Broadcasting System.[61] During a time when the information program struggled to justify its existence, Streibert was prepared to handle the administrative and operational challenges that came with the creation of the new agency. [62] His appointment further solidified the creation of the postwar "state-private network." After years of infighting among separate agencies, and a lack of proper leadership and support, the overseas information program was finally given a sustainable bureaucratic foundation, and personnel and media expertise that lasted throughout the duration of the Cold War. The importance of the USIA's creation cannot be underestimated; it marked a turning point in the postwar era. Its creation contributed to a more aggressive approach to reaching the Soviet Union, and its women. This approach included the revival of *Amerika*.

Another major organizational change in Eisenhower's information program stemmed from the report of the Jackson Committee, which was tasked with evaluating the "international information policies and activities of the Executive Branch of the Government."[63] The Jackson Committee report, released on 30 June 1953, shaped the direction of the overseas information program. It reaffirmed National Security Council Paper 68 (NSC-68), written in 1950, which argued that the Kremlin wanted to establish a communist world and that doing this required the destruction of its principal enemy, the United States. It recommended the rapid building of US political, economic, and military strength in order to defend the free world and reduce Soviet power and influence.[64] However, the Jackson Committee report endorsed a multifaceted approach to combatting communism, one that reflected the 1947 suggestions of State Department official George F. Kennan to adopt a "long-term, patient, but firm and vigilant containment of Russian expansive tendencies."[65] The Truman administration largely ignored Kennan's recommendations in favour of those contained in NSC-68.[66]

The Jackson Committee Report suggested that an information program be integrated on an equivalent level with political, economic, and military initiatives and not be separate in the organization and conduct of foreign policy.[67] It noted that the Soviet Union was ahead of the United States in this regard, as it had a well-developed and coordinated propaganda campaign, one that was directed by a central government with no political opposition and had central themes that consisted of land reform, peace, anti-imperialism, and youth. Radio was the primary medium of Soviet propaganda, but publications such as the *Soviet Union*, a heavily illustrated monthly magazine, and the *New Times*, a weekly news journal, circulated widely throughout the satellite states and the Third World. The United States would have to use similar methods. The Jackson Committee Report recommended disbanding the ineffective PSB in favour of a new organization that would coordinate an overt overseas information program.[68] In September 1953, Eisenhower established the Operations Coordinating Board (OCB) as an adjunct body of the NSC.[69] The OCB was comprised of the under secretary of state as chair, the special assistant to the president as vice-chairman, the deputy secretary of the Department of Defense, the director of the Foreign Operations Administration, and the director of the CIA.[70] In 1955 the director of the USIA was made a permanent member.[71] The purpose of that move was to strengthen and bridge the gap between policy and foreign operations by providing for the "integrated implementation of national security policies."[72] Within the OCB, the agencies responsible for carrying out each policy developed a statement defining each of their responsibilities, coordinated their operational plans and organized their execution, and assessed each action so that they achieved policy objectives. The OCB then reviewed their agencies' progress, reported on it to the NSC, requested additional policy guidance if necessary, and outlined any operating problems.[73]

Eisenhower's formation of both the USIA, to consolidate overseas information activities into one agency, and the OCB, to coordinate national security policies, deviated from Truman's decentralized and often passive approach to overseas information.[74] These organizations were intended to serve several purposes. First, the information program would retain a central place in US foreign policy for the duration of its existence; second, the work of relevant departments and agencies would align, but not overlap, with national security policy; and third, the president would maintain direct contact with those involved in the information program, thus ensuring USIA and OCB support and advocacy from the White House.[75] Even the names of the USIA and OCB, and the language of their mandates, reflect the changes that accompanied Eisenhower's presidency. The Jackson Committee Report recommended abandoning the term "psychological warfare," which had been preferred under Truman, because it failed to adequately describe US efforts to build a world of peace and freedom. According to the report, the term "information program" better reflected the nation's goals and the "solidarity of freedom-loving men and women everywhere."[76]

Four principles guided the purpose, coordination, and direction of the new information program, which closely resembled a modern-day advertising campaign. First, the primary purpose of the information program would be to persuade foreign peoples around the world that their personal and national self-interests were aligned with American objectives. The United States had to find out "what other peoples want, to relate their wants" to the United States, and to explain their common goals in ways that would cause them to "join with the US."[77] Second, a continued and coordinated effort would be made to inform the world of the American position on major issues.[78] Third, officials stationed abroad would be granted discretion in adapting their information activities to local situations.[79] Finally, information needed to be dependable, convincing, and truthful, without being "excessive or blatant."[80] According to US officials, the United States had advantages over the Soviet Union, and information programs should stress these advantages to appeal to foreign audiences. These advantages consisted of the supposed commonalities that Americans shared with men and women around the world: a "belief in God, belief in individual and national freedom and the right to ownership of property, belief in a peaceful world and in the common humanity of men and nations."[81] It suggested that the benefits of the US economic system and the aspirations on the part of all people to maintain a decent standard of living, when conveyed in a modest way, were appropriate subjects of information programs.[82] The USIA, as the agency tasked with implementing the nation's information program, incorporated these recommendations into its work, but at the heart of its program was a directive given by Eisenhower himself. In carrying out its mission, he directed the USIA to delineate the "important aspects of the life and culture of the people of the United States, which facilitate understanding" of US government policies and objectives.[83]

The USIA's activities included communication and interaction with foreign publics; appealing to the hardworking women of the Soviet Union in particular was part of its mandate. The USIA's information program in the Soviet Union was characterized by two central tenets. First, it sought to reach Russians in order to convey broad information and ideas about American values, particularly in relation to democracy and capitalism. Second, it sought to expose Russians, particularly Russian women, to the American "way of life," so they would develop a favourable view of the United States. The USIA's 1959's planning paper outlined three topics that USIA material should stress to show Russian women the wholesome and fulfilling lives that American women led. The first was woman's role as "homemaker." USIA material should indicate that American women were primarily interested in creating a close-knit, loving home and family life. Access to modern conveniences and household technology did not mean that American women did not work, but rather that they were not overworked. The second was woman as "volunteer," for the roles as homemaker naturally extended into the desire to improve society and the general well-being of others. USIA material should demonstrate that women were primarily responsible for maintaining civic and non-governmental organizations, including ones related to their communities, churches, and schools. The final, and most contentious, role was woman as "wage earner." The USIA believed that this role should be approached with caution. USIA material aimed to show women in their traditional roles first, and as wage earners second, highlighting that most American women joined the labour force before marriage and after their children were grown.[84] This contradicted their reality during World War II, when they were actively encouraged to enter the labour force regardless of their age and circumstances. With some recognition of women's changing roles, and a need to appeal to the women of communist countries, the paper concluded that USIA material should demonstrate that many educational and professional opportunities existed for American women, and that the wage gap was gradually decreasing.[85] Ultimately, however, the USIA believed that Russian and American women could find the most common ground in their mutual devotion to their homes and families. While the role of women as "consumer" was not one clearly defined by the USIA, it was a by-product of her other roles, particularly that of "homemaker." In combining women's roles as "consumers" with their more wholesome domestic roles, the USIA could counter images of American women as "irresponsible glamour girls" and "unfeminine, materialistic beings," while simultaneously promoting American consumer culture, as Eisenhower had directed.[86]

In spite of the speed with which Eisenhower had established a coherent, funded, and well-led overseas information program, opportunities to develop contact with Russian women were still limited. By the middle of the decade, however, major inroads had been made. In light of Stalin's death, and developments in Soviet foreign policy, the international situation changed even further, resulting in a new era of diplomatic relations between the Soviet Union and the West. In July 1955 the "Big Four," Eisenhower, Prime Minister Anthony Eden of Britain, Premier Nikolai A. Bulganin of the Soviet Union, and Prime Minister Edgar Faure of France met in Geneva, Switzerland, to discuss world peace. The meeting was intended to discuss global security, but the most important outcome of the talks was the establishment of a framework for a cultural negotiation and a general lessening of tensions, which became known as the "Spirit of Geneva." The rise to power of Nikita Khrushchev further solidified the beginning of a new diplomatic era. That rise to power was consolidated on 14 February 1956, when the then secretary of the Communist Party gave a controversial speech before the Twentieth Congress of the Communist Party of the Soviet Union that denounced Stalin and his cult of personality. Khrushchev's move away from Stalinist policies included the establishment of measures to promote "peaceful coexistence" and increased contact with the West.

In keeping with the "Spirit of Geneva," in July 1956, the US embassy in Moscow sent a letter to the Soviet Foreign Office proposing the exchange of English- and Russian-language magazines in their respective nations.[87] The resulting agreement began a decades-long exchange of two magazines: the revitalized *Amerika* and its Soviet counterpart, *USSR* (renamed *Soviet Life* in 1964). Each side would sell fifty thousand copies, five thousand through subscriptions and the remainder at newsstands. Neither were censored. Beginning in October 1956, select newsstands throughout both countries began selling each of these magazines. USIA officials welcomed the opportunity for the US government to resurrect *Amerika* and reach Russian readers, particularly women, in a new post-Stalinist era. The new agreement between the United States and the Soviet Union, officially renewing the magazine, stipulated an equitable arrangement for both parties. However, in July 1956, Fyodor Konstantinov, head of the Soviet Union's Department of Propaganda and Agitation, made it clear that the signing of such an agreement did not mean that the Soviet government condoned *Amerika* or its content. He signed the agreement for other reasons. First, in the post-Stalinist area, the Soviet government wished to show the world that it was making a concerted effort to establish increased contact with the West. Second, it wanted to counter US propaganda by issuing a magazine that would inform Americans of the Soviet way of life.[88] Rosa Magnusdottir notes that following World War II, the Soviet Union appeared to be winning the propaganda war in Europe, but less than one decade later the United States' aggressive propaganda techniques and the lure of consumerism drove the Soviet Union on the defensive.

Further, the isolationism of the Stalin era meant that Soviet officials also found themselves with very little knowledge about the United States with which to counter its claims. After Stalin's death, the Soviets reassessed their strategy and determined that cultural diplomacy was a necessary tactic to better understand the "enemy" and even to attempt to gain American followers.[89] Consequently, while the US government initiated the move to exchange magazines, the agreement was very much a strategic signing on the part of the Soviet government. It was aware of what American cultural diplomacy would entail and made attempts to limit US influence from an early stage. Konstantinov warned that in the pages of *Amerika*, publishers would make a concerted effort to extol the economic and cultural achievements of the United States and show that Americans had a better standard of life than the Russians. The magazine would present a one-sided view and avoid the ills and contradictions of American society, including unemployment, poverty, racism, and crime. Accordingly, it was important that the magazine did not fall into the hands of "politically immature" Russians who could succumb to *Amerika*'s influence. Konstantinov advised that subscriptions should go only to "politically literate, ideologically steadfast" people. In order to achieve this, he advised that the magazine be sold only in spaces that could be controlled. Subscriptions would be filled through an employer or social or political organization.[90] The magazine would now be sold at newsstands in eighty cities, and for that reason attention was needed as to its proper placement. Main streets and theatres were ideal because they could be monitored, but public places with large concentrations of people, such as parks and transit stations, were to be avoided. Konstantinov acknowledged that the CP would need to actively refute *Amerika*'s claims through propaganda in the Soviet press. He cautioned that this work be done carefully, as any clear efforts that disrespected the agreement would result in the restriction of their own magazine in the United States.[91] The efforts of the CP to maintain control over who obtained and read *Amerika* were similar to the tactics it used during the magazine's previous run, but were much less overt. In the post-Stalinist era, circumstances were different. The Soviet desire to establish diplomatic relations with the West, as well as to distribute its own propaganda material, ensured that it took careful measures to avoid repeating its past actions which had led to the original discontinuation of *Amerika*. Further, in an effort to maintain a positive cultural relationship, the magazine was no longer subject to approval by Soviet censors before it was placed on newsstands.

For the most part, a lessening of international hostilities, and improvements in the US-Soviet relationship by 1956, ensured that both *Amerika* and *USSR* would remain in distribution for a lengthy period of time. Indeed, *Amerika* was issued throughout the remainder of the Cold War, and even beyond, as its final issue appeared in 1994.[92] The new *Amerika* was similar in structure and content to its predecessor, but in contrast to the situation in the past, proper circulation procedures and the removal of the need for approval by Soviet censors meant that *Amerika* could land in the hands of the Russian reader more quickly and efficiently. For the USIA, these organizational changes ensured a maximum number of Russian women were able to obtain and read copies of *Amerika*. *Amerika's* resurrection provided a significant turning point for the USIA in its attempts to reach Russian women and educate them about American life and culture, however selectively presented or idealized that life and culture may have been. Under Truman and in the early years of Eisenhower's administration, the US government had limited opportunities for this type of interaction, so when *Amerika* was resurrected, USIA officials had high hopes for its impact on Russian women stemming from its supposed original success. *Amerika's* importance cannot be underestimated because it was the sole vehicle by which the USIA could advertise widely and consistently to Russian women the benefits of postwar American gender norms and consumer culture. US officials believed that when a Russian woman picked up *Amerika*, she would be offered a glimpse of an alternative way of life, a hope for happiness, and a better future for herself and her family.

Chapter Four

Modelling the American Dream: Fashion and Femininity in *Amerika*

> *America Illustrated* [sic] will provide the Soviet reader with a continuing portrait of life in America. The first issue, and succeeding ones, have the goal of giving the reader the next best thing to an actual visit to the US. It will take him through our schools, to our farms and factories, theaters and art museums, into many different families – wherever he can see for himself what Americans are thinking and doing and feeling. It will not preach. It will present the facts.[1]

After a four-year hiatus, *Amerika* resurfaced on select Soviet newsstands in October 1956. During a time of decreasing tensions between the United States and the Soviet Union, it became a central component of the USIA's cultural program, as it was one of the few means that the agency could use to reach Russian women directly. The words above, articulated by USIA deputy director Abbott Washburn in July 1956, demonstrate the agency's renewed hopes for the magazine. In obtaining a copy of *Amerika*, a Russian woman could read its glowing text, view its colourful images, and, even if she was unlikely to ever visit the United States, witness the American way of life, in all of its supposed glory, from afar. The years between 1956 and 1960 were pivotal in the US overseas information program in the Soviet Union. The USIA, which had the full support of the president and Congress, was skilfully led, well-developed, and adequately funded, and clearly benefited from the initial thaw in the US-Soviet relationship. During this period, the USIA used *Amerika* to appeal to Russian women.

The idealized depictions of American women promoted in the pages of *Amerika* were the same ones that influential women's magazines shaped and propagated in the early twentieth century and later solidified in the postwar period. These depictions, described in chapter 1, defined twentieth-century American womanhood. This "average" woman, white, native-born, middle-class, heterosexual, and most often married without a job or a career, was distinctly feminine.[2] The *Ladies' Home Journal* was integral to creating this "ideal," as well as reaching the women that managed to achieve it, and the ones that desired to, a fact which did not go unnoticed by the USIA and *Amerika*'s editors. October 1960's *Ladies' Home Journal* noted its historical importance, indicating that since its inception in 1883 it had been an influential source of information in the field of "home economics." Its five million monthly readers, referred to as "housewives," turned to it in all matters relating to the home and childrearing as well as to other areas, including fashion.[3] The USIA and *Amerika*'s editors promoted the same images of American women as the *Ladies' Home Journal*. As the USIA articulated in 1959, *Amerika* showcased the American woman as being devoted to her "family, womanliness and industriousness." She was to be shown as compassionate and hard-working, a preserver of values, and possessing the feminine characteristics with which women throughout the world could identify and respect.[4] Her primary roles were those of homemaker, wife, and mother.[5] However, her secondary roles may have included work, either before marriage or once her children were grown. *Amerika* showcased American women content in their roles as housewives, mothers, and consumers, and occasionally even as workers. The USIA wanted to convey that American women had *vast choices* in their lives, but ultimately always chose femininity and family. *Amerika*'s editors, under the influence of the USIA, walked a fine line in portraying American women as feminine and at the same time downplaying their image as "irresponsible glamour girls."[6] Fashion and accessories were indeed showcased regularly in the pages of *Amerika* and were done so in much of the same way as in the *Ladies' Home Journal*. Fashions were consistently and simultaneously attractive, practical, and affordable. The pursuit of fashion appeared to be justified because it contributed to a woman's femininity, and in the process, allowed her to appear more attractive to the man in her life, or at least the future husband she was pursuing. USIA officials expected that these depictions would win the "hearts and minds" of the "graceless, shapeless, and sexless" Russian women frequently depicted in America's postwar magazines – the women that supposedly had *few choices* in their major life decisions.[7] They believed that these women yearned for a domesticated, consumer-oriented lifestyle that, according to the USIA, could only be found in democratic, capitalist countries.

When *Amerika* was resurrected in 1956, USIA officials had high hopes, based on its original success, for its impact on Russian women. An analysis of *Amerika*'s content between 1956 and 1960 reveals the goals and methods the USIA, under the Eisenhower administration, used in attempting to reach and appeal to Russian women. While mimicking the images of women seen in the *Ladies' Home Journal*, *Amerika*'s style and format emulated the most popular magazine of the postwar era: *Life*. In 1936, Henry Robinson Luce, founder of the Time Inc. mass media empire, documented his ideas for a new picture magazine where one would be able "to see life; to see the world; to eyewitness great events; to watch the faces of the poor and the gestures of the proud." That year, he purchased the rights to *Life*, a magazine founded in 1883, and turned it into the most popular picture magazine in the United States. From its first issue on 23 November, *Life* became an instant success, selling out of its 250,000 newsstand copies on the first day.[8] Each issue contained approximately 100 to 150 pages, primarily of images and advertisements, and minimal text. It consistently had one major cover story, at least one editorial, and sections on "Letters to the Editors," "The Week's Events," and "Photographic Essays," which were filled with images. The remaining sections discussed various aspects of US culture, including music, art, literature, movies, theatre, television, fashion, and sports.

By 1956, *Life* had a readership of almost 5.8 million, slightly above that of the *Ladies' Home Journal*. It both reflected and advanced American ideals and influenced the Eisenhower administration and its broader cultural activities.[9] Luce's ambitions for the magazine were best exemplified in his 1941 essay heralding the twentieth as the "Great American Century." He argued that it was America's time to spread its ideals of freedom, equality of opportunity, self-reliance, independence, and cooperation throughout the world.[10] According to *Life* writer and editor Loudon Wainwright, the magazine's success could be attributed to the fact that during a time of Cold War hostility *Life* showed its predominately white, middle-class readers images of their nation's political, economic, and cultural advancements in a way that seemed both authentic and reassuring. The magazine was a place where they could discover modern American life, be inspired by it, and feel part of it.[11] With the advent of a picture magazine, Luce wanted to "educate people to take pictures seriously." If properly mastered and appropriately viewed, they could shape and direct popular opinion, or at least the opinion Luce wanted to be popular.[12] Luce seized on the power of visual culture as an ideal means to influence "men's minds."[13] To Luce, an ardent anti-communist, that visual culture became increasingly important during the Cold War. Indeed, *Life* used the work of the twentieth century's most notable photographers, including Ansel Adams, Margaret Bourke-White, Alfred Eisenstaedt, Dorothea Lange, Edward Steichen, and Robert Capa, to showcase images of US life and culture. As Capa biographer Alex Kershaw notes, in many instances these photographs were captioned to support Luce's worldview.[14] Luce's publishing empire reflected not only US ideals, but also the close relationship between the media and Eisenhower's overseas information program. Luce was an ardent Republican and, during Eisenhower's years in office, he often used his publications to show his approval of the president's foreign policy.[15] Further, Luce's close confidantes and aides, particularly C.D. Jackson, were well known for their influence in Eisenhower's overseas information program, particularly the establishment of the USIA and the OCB.

Similar to *Life*, *Amerika* was a glossy magazine of approximately sixty pages that contained anywhere from fifteen to twenty-three articles per issue.[16] It included information on American culture, society, institutions, and ways of life, but it avoided overtly political issues and contained no editorials, for fear of aggravating the Soviet government. It only minimally covered science and industry, but did showcase consumer technology, such as automobiles and household appliances, and how it improved the lives of ordinary Americans. Unlike American magazines, *Amerika* had no advertisements, but was filled with many pictures, in black and white and in colour, that supplemented the articles. Hixson refers to *Amerika* as a form of "polite propaganda" because it did not include hard-hitting political news stories and critiques of the Soviet regime. Rather, it contained soft news stories on everyday life in the United States, the same types of articles and images seen in postwar magazines, all of which attempted to advertise the American way of life to its readers.[17] Stories written and published specifically for *Amerika* were likely to be slightly propagandistic in nature, focusing on areas such as the structure of the US government, the roles of elected officials and the press, the electoral process, labour, and management.[18] For example, March 1957's "The Role of the President," January 1958's "The Congress of the United States," and February 1958's "The Supreme Court of the United States" each explained to Russian readers the three branches of government.[19] All were written by Cornell University historian and political scientist Clinton Rossiter. The first, in particular, discussed how the functions of the presidency had grown yet still remained within the limits of the Constitution. It stated that there had been five forces that had strengthened the presidency: the rise of industrialization, the entrance of the United States onto the world stage, the series of emergencies the country had previously gone through, the turning of Congress to the president for legislative leadership, and the growth of public participation in government. This last point was notable, given the lack of political opposition, and of free and fair elections in the Soviet Union. In contrast to these more clearly propagandistic articles, those that pertained to women's issues and consumerism mainly consisted of reprints from nationally circulated magazines such as *Colliers, Glamour, Ladies' Home Journal, Look, Mademoiselle, McCall's, Pageant, Seventeen, Vogue,* and, of course, *Life. Amerika*'s editors worked on a limited budget, so their tendency to reprint articles from popular national magazines not only ensured the quality of *Amerika*'s work but also brought Russian women the same articles that millions of American women also read.[20] Occasionally, however, images were eliminated and text was condensed to account for space limitations.[21] *Amerika*'s content was carefully constructed in order to adequately adapt to the unique audience the USIA was attempting to reach.[22]

Amerika's editors strove to find content they believed would accurately reflect the United States but also appeal to Russian women. On the one hand, they wanted to present informative articles and images that would help women appreciate the free, diverse, and dynamic nature of American society. On the other hand, they knew that presenting a full and accurate picture of the country meant including its less-appealing aspects. However, Llewellyn Thompson, US ambassador to the Soviet Union between 1957 and 1962, wanted to avoid discussing problems that plagued US society, including unemployment, crime, and racial tensions. Of course, these subjects were contentious in postwar America, and officials wanted Russian readers to view an idealized version of the country. He argued that the magazine should not be published as though it were intended for an American audience, pointing out that Russian readers had never experienced a free press and had no way of evaluating self-criticism, especially in a publication put out by a foreign government.[23] According to Hans Tuch, a press and cultural attaché under Thompson, *Amerika*'s editors, not clearly identified within the magazine in its early years or in USIA records, were aware that they were publishing a magazine for readers relatively unfamiliar with the United States and sought to carefully explain the stories they presented so that they would inform, not confuse, the reader.[24] In the view of US embassy officials, *Amerika* had tremendous appeal. Through its glossy format and colourful illustrations of the country and its people, it told the idealized story of an idealized nation.[25] In an instant *Amerika* could transport Russians into a distant land filled with welcoming people and a rich consumer culture.

When determining what to include in *Amerika*, USIA officials took their inspiration from multiple sources, including letters from Russians written during *Amerika*'s first run. State Department documents indicate that readers wrote to the US embassy in Moscow requesting

124 Selling Women, Gender, and Consumer Culture

stories on the way Americans lived and worked, their homes, how they dressed, their taste in music, their hobbies, books they read, their holidays, customs, and art, as well as new technology and products.[26] USIA officials also tried to gauge reader interest in other ways, including conducting surveys in other communist nations. For example, when the State Department began issuing *Sad* (meaning "Now"), the Yugoslav equivalent to *Amerika*, in December 1951, it attempted to gauge public reaction to the magazine. The first issue, which was widely distributed to libraries, People's Committees in towns and villages, local branches of women's organizations, press and radio personnel, and visitors to US information centres, contained a questionnaire asking readers to submit their opinions of the new magazine.[27] Two thousand respondents indicated that their favourite articles were those on "science and technology," but "life in the United States" ranked a close second. In the comment section of the questionnaire, readers indicated that they wanted to see information about the lives of different types of Americans, including workers, women, Yugoslav immigrants in the United States, intellectuals, farmers, youth, and minority groups. Interest in workers overall appeared in 164 comments, but interest in women ranked a close second, at 156. The survey showed that readers were interested in articles on economics and labour, followed by politics and the military.[28]

By 1956, embassies behind the Iron Curtain began reporting that fashion and house and garden magazines were extremely popular and in great demand. The USIA had always sent mainstream newspapers and magazines, and even catalogues such as Sears, Roebuck, to these posts, but now began regularly sending issues of women's magazines such as *American Home, Better Homes and Gardens, Family Circle, Glamour, House and Gardens,* and *Vogue* to each, including Moscow.[29] *Amerika*'s editors strove to provide Russian readers with the information they wanted to know about the United States, but they took a cautionary approach. A 1960 USIA Office of Research and Analysis report entitled "What Works and Does Not Work in Communicating with the Soviet People" claimed that while the Russians resented almost any criticism of their own country by foreigners, they were eager to know about life in the United States and had a tolerance for good things said about the country. It indicated that the best way to present commentary on the United States was with a "calm, factual description" of US freedom, political participation, and high living standards. If done properly, there was little danger of displaying an air of superiority.[30] From the first issue onwards, the USIA took this approach in publishing *Amerika*. The idea was that Russian women who read *Amerika* would gain a better sense of the consumption-oriented lifestyle that permeated US culture and society. While US politics and institutions had been featured prominently in the past, *Amerika* turned its emphasis to living standards in an effort to promote the success of the postwar American economy, and to appeal to its primary consumers: women.[31]

The first issue of the new *Amerika* reflected the structure and content of subsequent issues throughout the remainder of the 1950s. This sixty-four-page issue, its cover with a lone little girl in red gazing before the Pacific Ocean, her back turned to the viewer, contained twenty articles and twelve colour images, and sold for five rubles ($1.25) (figure 4.1).[32] Its editors described *Amerika* as a

> magazine about the people of the United States – how they live, work and play. It will try to capture their moods and aspirations, their concerns and their lighter moments of relaxation … We shall attempt to portray what Americans are thinking and doing, what they are reading and saying … Art and science, industry and labor, culture and technology, work and leisure – all will be presented in this magazine along with a host of other topics. But whatever the subject, the story we will be telling is the story of American people.[33]

What was the story of the American people? According to "America Today," the 166 million people in the United States could not be neatly summarized. However, it did indicate that there was a distinct American character, way of life, and way of looking at life that had emerged over the past two and a half centuries. All were the products of "an inheritance and environment both complex and varied."[34] This initial description, a rather humble one, noted that the twentieth-century march towards technological and scientific progress had led to social changes in families and communities, and in increased freedom and responsibility.

> Today, some 65,000,000 Americans – 44,000,000 men and 21,000,000 women – are the hands and minds that run the US economy, the most abundant and stable the country has known. Their collective output in 1955 amounted to 387,000,000,000 worth of goods and services, which, in actual buying power, is nearly double the country's output fifteen years ago. A remarkably large share of this 1955 production – $116,000,000,000 worth – represents an increase in things people need and use – houses, automobiles, clothes, food, entertainment and thousands of other items.[35]

Figure 4.1. This first issue of *Amerika* paved the way for the style, structure, and content of future issues. *Amerika*, October 1956.

According to the article, Americans could purchase new products because their income was not only higher but also spread more evenly among the population than ever before. Income taxes reduced the net earnings of many in the top pay brackets, while higher wages improved the standard of living for lower-income groups. The middle class included over half the population. This was the group that *Amerika*'s editors would highlight consistently throughout the magazine's initial years, just as they did in US women's magazines. It noted postwar changes in living, writing that within the past ten years rising living standards, as well as the affordability of the automobile, had allowed ten million Americans to relocate from the cities to the suburbs with its open spaces. To satisfy the demand for houses, assembly-line methods were applied to home building. Of the 45,000,000 homes in the country at the time, one out of five were built in the last decade. The article also noted other successes in the United States, including the rise of automation, and advances in science, particularly towards combatting disease. In a rare display of humility, it noted that that there had been a lack of progress in the building of roads and schools, but attributed this deficit to an increase in automobile production as well as a large jump in the birth rate. The article noted that although Americans were known to brag about their country, they were also among its fiercest critics. It named notable authors such as Henry David Thoreau, Mark Twain, Theodore Dreiser, Sinclair Lewis, H.L. Mencken, Upton Sinclair, John Steinbeck, and others, noting that all of them, in some way, called out injustice and suffering. Implicit in all of their works, however, was an overwhelming sense of social responsibility and loyalty to the American Dream and democratic ideals. Ultimately, the article concluded by indicating that the nation and its character were in the process of development and that that development was open to change. The future promised to be as exciting as the past.

This first issue of *Amerika* set the stage for how American women would be portrayed in the magazine for the remainder of the decade. In contrast to the multiple and often contradictory messages that postwar women's magazines contained regarding women's roles, *Amerika*'s editors featured only the most idealized visions of white, middle-class American women in their magazine.[36] This first issue established four themes, intended to appeal to Russian women: 1) fashion and femininity, 2) marriage, motherhood, and family, 3) the home and homemaking, and 4) consumption.[37] USIA officials assumed that *Amerika*'s articles, accompanied by colourful images, were ones that Russian women, who were inundated with dull, state-sanctioned stories on politics, the economy, and labour, wanted to read. Articles such as "Summer Fashions" capitalized on the supposed desire of Russian women, like women everywhere, to appear beautiful and feminine. It showed what American women were wearing in the summer of 1956. Their dresses were made from durable, but comfortable, material, and were stylish, yet affordable.[38] One article, "New Member of the Family," sought to establish commonalities between Russian and American women, highlighting their roles as mothers. It discussed the ways in which a Florida couple prepared their three children for the arrival of a baby sister.[39] Although "America's 1956 Model Automobiles" may have seemingly appealed to men, it showed Russian women the benefits of US technology and how it applied to the country's culture of abundance. Although automobiles were once an expensive piece of machinery, they were now mass-produced, increasingly affordable, and depicted as an integral part of suburban family life. The article described the benefits Americans derived from their newfound mobility, the construction of an extensive highway network that allowed them to travel easily, and suburban shopping centres, where countless consumer goods could be found under one roof.[40] Of the articles that appeared in this first issue, "Ten Young Women of Distinction," was certainly the outlier. It showcased the achievements of women under the age of thirty in music, literature, science, law, theatre, film, and sport, but its most noteworthy examples comprised the profiles of three women of colour. They included Gloria Lockerman, a twelve-year-old African American girl who shocked the nation in 1955 when she appeared on *The 64,000 Question*, answered a host of difficult questions correctly, and won $16,000. African American singer Leontyne Price was highlighted for her successful career, which included touring the United States and Europe in lead roles in operas such as *Porgy and Bess* and the *Magic Flute*. Finally, the article profiled Machiko Kyo, referred to as the first "world famous" actress from Japan. It stated that she was enormously popular in the United States for her role in the critically acclaimed Japanese film *Gate of Hell*.[41] The remainder of the articles in this first issue focused on healthcare technology, agriculture, urban architecture, music, and vacations, and profiled ordinary and extraordinary Americans. All demonstrated themes that *Amerika*'s editors continuously highlighted in subsequent issues. From 1956 to 1960, they rarely strayed from this established pattern, with the exception of "Ten Young Women of Distinction," which was unique in its depiction of racial minorities. In particular, these issues showed hard-working, yet feminine, American women, alongside the families they cared for, the homes they lived in, and the consumer goods and services that capitalism provided them with.

Amerika's Soviet equivalent, *USSR,* was similar in format and basic intention. Its first issue comprised sixty-four pages filled with reports on advances in Soviet science and technology; heartwarming stories on the Russian people, their work, and their lives; and accompanying images. There were no advertisements. Both *Amerika* and *USSR* sought to advance the interests of their respective nations and their political and economic systems, and to encourage a deeper understanding of their proud people and their accomplishments – or at least the "understanding" that each nation wanted to convey to the other. *USSR* noted that both wanted to "tell their readers in word and picture about life in their respective country, thereby meeting the growing desire of the people of the two most powerful countries in the world to learn more about each other."[42] November 1960's issue contained a letter written by Khrushchev himself, addressing the American people. In it he noted, "The Soviet people sincerely want friendship between the peoples of our two countries. This can be fulfilled by getting to know each other better. The purpose of *USSR* magazine is to spread truthful information about the life of the Soviet people, thus contributing to better understanding between our two countries."[43] It appeared that the format and goals of these reciprocal magazines were indeed similar; however, their content proved to be quite different. In contrast to *Amerika*'s emphasis on the benefits of capitalism, *USSR*'s was on the benefits of communism. The Soviet Union was depicted as a land of scientific and technological progress led by a government that provided its citizens with housing, health- and childcare, educations, jobs, and high culture. In contrast to the dreary portrayals of hardworking Russians that appeared in US publications, *USSR* emphasized the humility and happiness of its people. The Soviet government could claim that it did not provide its citizens the luxuries seen in the United States because they neither needed nor wanted them. Rather, it sought to provide them with the necessities for a simple, but happy, life.

This attitude was best presented publicly in the 24 July 1959 "kitchen debate" between Nixon and Khrushchev on the opening day of the American National Exhibition in Moscow. Held in the General Electric "model kitchen" of the $14,490 one-storey, six-room ranch-style home of a "typical" American family, Khrushchev dismissed the items on display. They included an automatic lemon juicer, which he referred to as "silly," arguing that a housewife could simply "squeeze a lemon faster by hand."[44] Khrushchev's mocking message, intended to distract a Russian audience rapt by the consumer goods on display, was clear: American technological advances were not necessarily efficient, possibly made its women lazier, and, further, did not necessarily make them happier.[45] This mentality was reinforced in the pages of *USSR*. In March 1962's issue, journalist Yekaterina Sheveleva contributed an article entitled

"The Standard of Living and the Standard of Happiness." According to Sheveleva, in her conversations with foreign journalists, they claimed that Russian journalists pointedly ignored the high living standards of other countries. She acknowledged her country's shortcomings, but noted that what was more typical of her country was the happiness of its people. She wrote that refrigerators were not a "sufficient yardstick by which to measure happiness," but rather happiness derived from a "man's aspirations," and in the case of her fellow countrymen these were the sacrifices they made for the sake of "just ideals."[46] This mindset, exemplified in Sheveleva's writing, is corroborated by historian Jochen Hellbeck, who writes that after the Revolution, Russians were encouraged to achieve an "aligned life," an ideal form of being that called for individual sacrifice for the sake of the collective, and which was intended to lead to authenticity and meaning.[47] Indeed, the socialist conception of a "high standard of living" was clearly different from the Western conception. It included services traditionally promised by the socialist state, such as free education, medical and hospital care, and social insurance, all of which provided a substantial addition to the family income, thus raising its overall standard of living.[48] Sheveleva's article, and *USSR* more broadly, toed the government line: they argued, first, that each nation's conception of living standards differed, and, second, that in the context of the socialist state, living standards were largely immaterial when compared to the long-term goal of achieving socialism. Accordingly, *USSR* focused on scientific and technological advances, as well as society and culture. Articles on achievements in aviation and space were juxtaposed with the human aspects of everyday life. Russian citizens, particularly women, were shown as engaging in vast and varied work and enjoying it. Part of this was made possible by the availability of free and equal education, as well as the nurseries and kindergartens available to Russian citizens, all of which were regularly highlighted in *USSR*.

Just as *Amerika* did in its early years, *USSR* utilized its women to showcase the benefits of the nation, albeit with less regularity. For example, December 1956's "Woman's Place in Soviet Life" was a rare article that specifically addressed the place of women in the Soviet Union. It noted the equality that emerged out of the Russian Revolution, the hundreds of thousands of women who held positions in public office and in high level administration, the female factory workers who were ascending into managerial positions, as well as the scientific achievements of women. It argued that while foreigners frequently expressed their displeasure in seeing large numbers of Russian women working in physically demanding jobs, this current state of affairs was necessary given the heavy male casualties of World War II. The article pointed out the special provisions that working mothers received. They were given four months maternity leave, a rarity in the United States even today. Childcare was readily available in the form of nurseries, kindergartens, and affordable summer camps. Additionally, the article noted that "more and more of the thankless round of household chores – washing, sewing, even cooking – were being taken over" by others, giving women more time to contribute to the "economic, cultural and social progress of the country." It concluded that the "talented hands of women have added immeasurably to the nation's welfare."[49] This article presented an idealized image of the Russian woman, as did the magazine as a whole, just as *Amerika* attempted to do with its own women. It showed Russian women as more grounded and hardworking than their American counterparts. *USSR*'s editors struck a careful balance in promoting the "new woman" of the era: the "rational" worker and the "romantic" wife and mother. As Lynne Attwood points out, this was an image that the Soviet government and publishers had already honed in domestic women's magazines, just as their US counterparts had. For example, magazines such as *Soviet Woman* had existed for over a decade before *USSR* emerged. First published in November-December 1945 on a bimonthly basis, *Soviet Woman* was unique because it targeted not just Soviet women but also women of the major combatant countries of World War II. It was published in multiple languages, including English, French, German, and Russian. According to Alexis Peri, *Soviet Woman* created a feminine ideal designed to inspire both domestic and foreign audiences and advance Soviet interests. Soviet publishers were reluctant to "spotlight the rough edges of Soviet life," which might compromise efforts to promote socialism.[50] Those "rough edges" could easily extend to include the status of Russian women, particularly those that were saddled with the double burden of paid work and home and familial responsibilities, without the benefit of easy, affordable access to consumer items. In this case, the *USSR* differed markedly from *Amerika* in its portrayal of women's roles. According to the magazine, Russian women had the support of the state, engaged in fulfilling paid labour, and reaped the benefits of socialized daycare to assist them in raising their children. In contrast, *Amerika* principally depicted its women within the home. When not in the home, they were engaged in activities related to maintaining it or caring for their families. Their happiness derived from their roles as homemakers and consumers.

Amerika presented an idealized vision of the United States, and despite claiming to provide an entirely factual description of the country, it rarely acknowledged its problems. Throughout the 1950s, civil rights was undoubtedly the most contentious domestic issue in the United States, yet it was rarely addressed in the pages of *Amerika*, even though the "Negro question" was one of the Soviet Union's principal propaganda themes in attempting to expose US hypocrisy and heighten anti-American sentiment.[51] The Soviet government recognized the power of drawing attention to racial inequality in the United States to highlight the racial equality that supposedly existed in the Soviet Union. As early as 1932, Mezhrabpom film company, a Russian-German studio, began work on *Black and White*, a film billed as depicting the true struggles of African American workers in the United States, and as being "devoid of sentimentality as well as of buffoonery."[52] Twenty-two African Americans, many of them notable Harlem Renaissance figures, were lured to the Soviet Union to star in the film; they were treated like celebrities and given excellent food and accommodation, but the film was ultimately cancelled.[53] Several of the participants, including activist and professor Louise Thompson, remained in the Soviet Union for an extended period to travel, and commented on its "emancipation of women" and "elimination of national antagonisms." Writing home to her mother, she stated that those days were "the greatest of my whole life."[54] Kate A. Baldwin writes of the relationship between African American artists and the Soviet government. Many of the African American artists and literary figures were moved by the rhetoric of the Russian Revolution, the Soviet Experiment, and comparisons between historically oppressed, but newly emancipated, Russian peasants and themselves.[55]

Despite the ongoing controversy surrounding civil rights, it was not until December 1958 that *Amerika* contained a full-length article on an African American, celebrated opera singer Marian Anderson (figure 4.2). By this time, Anderson was only the third woman to individually grace the cover of *Amerika*: the other two were white, seemingly middle-class women, one dressed as a nurse and the other wearing travel clothing.[56] She was also just the fourth African American female to be profiled, after twelve-year-old Gloria Lockerman and singer Leontyne Price were included in October 1956's "Ten Young Women of Distinction," and eighteen-year-old Jean Walburg appeared in March 1957's "First Ball."[57] Anderson was a fitting choice to grace the cover of *Amerika*. She was the first African American to sing on the steps of the Lincoln Memorial, had performed at the White House and at New York's Metropolitan Opera, had toured the Soviet Union, and was a civil rights advocate.[58] Promoting artists such as Anderson was part of the USIA's larger plan to use "cultural ambassadors" to spread US music and win converts to the American way of life, as well as to assuage foreign criticism about

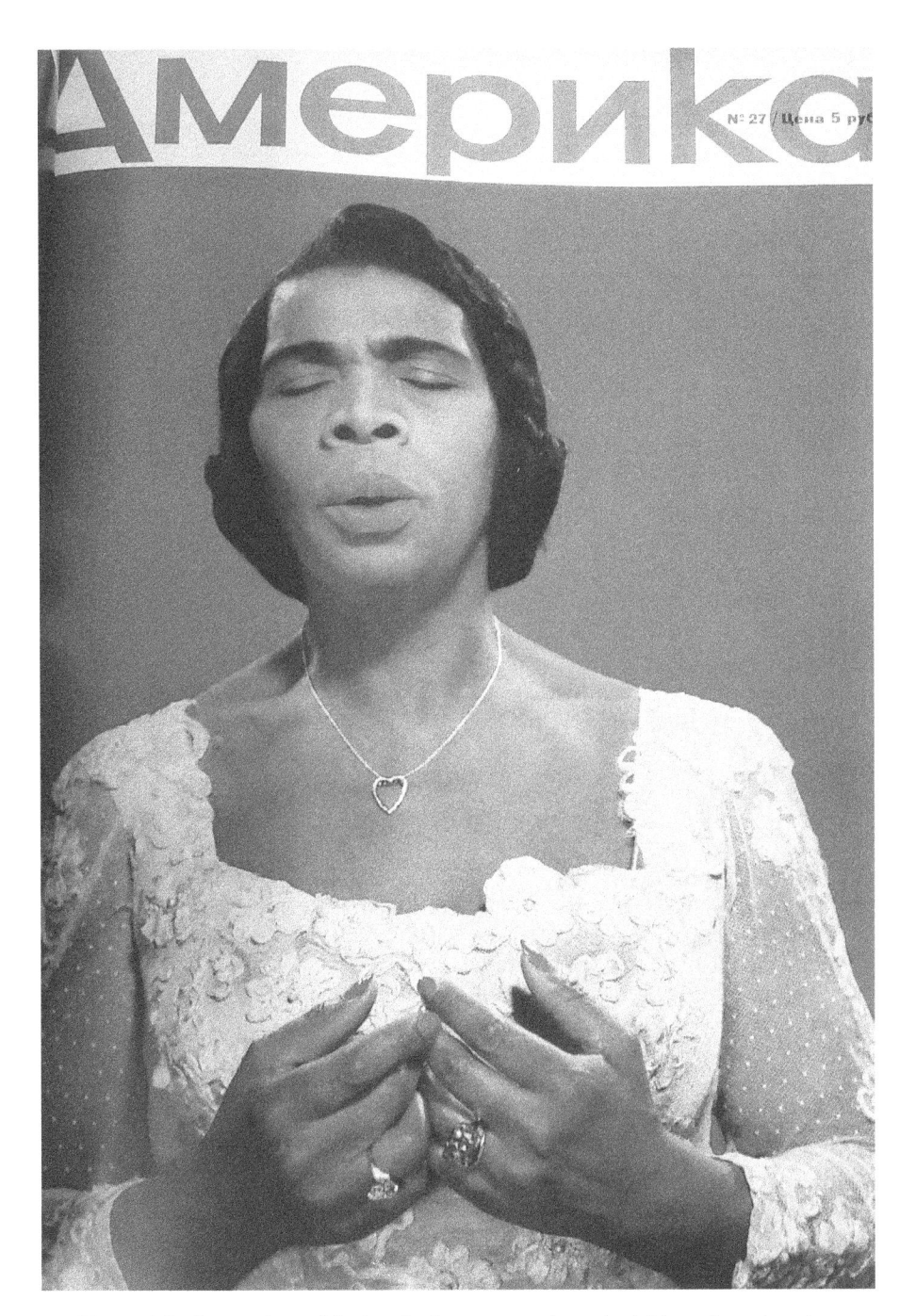

Figure 4.2. Opera singer Marian Anderson was the only African American to appear on the cover of *Amerika* during the 1950s. *Amerika*, December 1958.

the country's race relations.[59] Anderson's life, which was hardly representative of that of the average African American woman, was to serve as an example for the world to see how far American race relations had come. An excerpt from Anderson's autobiography, "My Lord, What a Morning" was included.[60] However, the lack of actual race-related content inside this issue is notable. *Amerika*'s editors wanted to highlight Anderson's professional success, particularly given that the Soviet Union heavily publicized the contradictions between US democracy and racism. However, *Amerika*'s editors missed an opportunity in this and other issues to address Soviet criticisms and discuss US race relations in a sensitive and timely manner. The February 1959 introduction of a new column called "Facts about the US" appeared promising when its first story, "The Negro Today," discussed the strides African Americans had made in education and work since 1940.[61] However, even articles that put a positive spin on the topic were a rarity, just as they were in mainstream US magazines at the time. Instead, "Facts about the US" addressed issues such as organized labour, wages and benefits, agriculture, cities, elections, and clothing.[62] Throughout the 1950s, *Amerika*'s attention to race and civil rights was minimal, although the ongoing controversy and racial violence generated significant attention and criticism domestically and internationally, particularly from the Soviet Union. Images of 1958's Little Rock Crisis, for example, generated such negative publicity around the world that Secretary of State John Foster Dulles told the *Arkansas Gazette* the publishing of such images was "not helpful to the influence of the United States abroad."[63] *Amerika* largely neglected topics that would present the country in a negative light. The unequal status of women, during a period which saw the government and media push many women out of the paid workforce, was among those neglected topics. Instead, the magazine focused on an idealized white, middle-class version of the United States, showing American women as the feminine housewives, mothers, and consumers that the editors believed would appeal to Russian women.

Amerika's editors believed that Russian women, like American women, were drawn towards glossy magazines filled with articles and colour pictures of consumer goods that could improve their lives. In the same vein as American postwar women's magazines, they used attractive clothing and accessories as a way to appeal to Russian women and their supposed feminine aspirations. The reality, however, was that while these images were visually pleasing, and the clothing stylish and tasteful, much of it was impractical for the Russian women who not only engaged in paid labour but also experienced long, harsh winters. The majority of *Amerika*'s issues from

Table 4.1. Analysis of articles in *Amerika* that were either designed to appeal to women or contained women as central figures (October 1956–December 1960).[64]

Issues	Year	Fashion and accessories	Marriage and family	Home and homemaking (including decor)	Technology and consumption	Work
1–3	1956 (Oct.–Dec.)	2	2	1	1	1
4–15	1957	11	10	3	2	3
16–27	1958	10	7	6	7	6
28–39	1959	6	5	4	8	4
40–51	1960	10	2	21	5	1
Total		39	26	35	23	15

October 1956 to December 1960 devoted at least one article to women's fashions. With respect to the four themes introduced earlier in the chapter, articles on fashion were the most frequent. Thirty-nine articles appeared on fashion, textiles, shoes, and/or accessories that were geared specifically towards adult and young women. Additionally, four included children's fashions and shoes. Reflecting the postwar emphasis on women as consumer, only three such articles appeared on men's fashions (table 4.1).

Fashion articles were similar in format to those that appeared in US women's magazines. They consisted of minimal text, a mixture of black-and-white and colour images and emphasized fashionable but supposedly practical and affordable clothing. Of all the articles in *Amerika*, ones on fashion were most likely to contain colour images. All showed tall, slender and attractive white women wearing skirts and dresses. They only occasionally wore pants or shorts.[65] In contrast to the drab, shapeless, and heavy clothing that Russian women were frequently depicted wearing in US women's magazines, *Amerika* showed its readers colourful, light, fitted, and fashionable clothing. While US women's magazines may have seemed overly critical in their depictions of Russian women, early editions of *USSR* frequently avoided the topic of fashion, or even of consumer items in general, for that matter. On the rare occasion that fashion was showcased in the magazine, it was often in its last pages. Otherwise, women were depicted in their daily tasks, working alongside men in the factory or farm and participating in cultural activities. Just as American women were shown enjoying their lives, so too were these women. *Amerika*, however, focused much more heavily on fashion and femininity. For example, November 1956's "Practical

Fashions" appeared to be anything but practical for the average Russian woman. It included four images of women wearing summer dresses, skirts, and blouses. The captions stated that the cotton garments, frequently shown in *Amerika*, were lightweight to accommodate the summer heat, practical, easy to wash, and ranged in price from only six to eighteen dollars.[66] In the description accompanying each picture, the top right (figure 4.3) was the only one that made note of its background setting, an eighteenth-century New Mexico Catholic church, perhaps alluding to what should have been an important presence in the lives of all women, but was frowned upon in the Soviet Union: religion.

Similarly, March 1957's "Fashions" contained twelve images of women in various types of clothing for spring and summer. It included eleven images and all but two outfits consisted of cotton skirts or dresses. The article stated these cotton clothes were affordable, easy to wash, and versatile, suitable for different outings such as shopping, visiting with friends, or parents' night events at school. Just as the *Ladies' Home Journal's* "Little Gem of a Wardrobe" did, the article pointed out that accessories, including hats, gloves, and jewellery, could transform a small and simple wardrobe into an extensive one. Again, the article focused on trends, noting that bright colours were fashionable for the season. However, it noted that the most fashionable trend of the season was to wear clothes that "make you happy."[67] An instruction that Russian women, who consistently experienced clothing shortages, could not easily follow. August 1957's "Fashions under Twenty Dollars" showcased eighteen images of inexpensive clothes that American women were wearing, all at affordable prices. All consisted of sleek or full skirts and dresses.[68] Like the *Ladies' Home Journal* the magazine depicted fashions for special occasions. September 1957's "Holiday Fashions" showed inexpensive holiday chic: dresses for the seaside, picnics, or "'round the world vacations."[69] Such dresses and occasions in which to wear them were luxuries that were simply out of reach for most Russian women.

There were rare attempts on the part of *Amerika*'s editors to showcase women's dress in the workplace. In spite of evidence that white, middle-class women retreated to the home during the postwar period, the US census revealed that throughout the decade women's employment levels rose. The 1950 census indicated that 33.9 per cent (18.3 million) of the nation's 54.2 million women over the age of sixteen were in the paid labour force. By 1960, that number had increased to 37.7 per cent (23.2 million) of the nation's 61.5 million women.[70] A May 1957 article was one of the few that acknowledged that a woman's wardrobe could apply not just to the home and social gatherings, but also to the workplace. "Tailored for the City" featured

Figure 4.3. These images showed Russian women what may have been considered "practical fashions" in the United States, but were likely extremely impractical for harsh Soviet winters and unpredictable springs.
Original caption: "Practical Fashions".
Upper left corner: Dress with a wide turn-down collar and a fluffy skirt. Price – around $18 (72 rubles)
Upper right corner: Satin blouse and a skirt. Price – around $13 (52 rubles) Background: church in New Mexico, built in the eighteenth century.
Bottom left corner: A very open summer dress with a low square neck. Bright colours and catchy pattern. Price – around $11 (44 rubles)
Bottom right corner: Blouse with stripes and a one-tone skirt for a contrast. Price of each item – $6 (24 rubles)
Amerika, November 1956.

fashions designed for a day in a busy urban centre. It showed five images of women dressed in tailored clothes that, according to the article, would remain fresh after a long day of shopping or working in the office. Only two images were of women in what appeared to be a city, both showing them shopping at a newspaper and flower stand. None of the images actually showed women working or in an office setting, and their captions focused on their clothing's practicality, as the items were made of washable cotton. However, the article did note the differences between urban and suburban styles of dress, indicating that city styles should be formal, and their lines attractive and practical. These fashions would allow one to board and exit trains and cars comfortably, as well as shop at crowded malls. Their fabrics did not crease, which meant they still looked fresh after a long day. The article provided tips to the Russian reader: only the most modest accessories should accompany formal dresses; in contrast, suburban- or country-style dresses could consist of bright colours and full skirts.[71] March 1958's issue included a rare article devoted solely to women's workplace attire. "Wear Them to Work" showcased six tailored outfits, consisting of jacketed suits, as well skirts and blouses, described as "neat, not gaudy." Further diminishing the role of professional women, the article stated that each of these outfits were suitable for "girls" who liked to feel dressed up, even at work.[72] Just two months later, May 1958's issue included "Office Dresses." It showcased three dresses and indicated that when buying a dress for work, women must consider elegance, style, and comfort, and fabrics that would stay fresh throughout the "eight to five" workday. All were affordably priced at $11 to $23.[73] The irony of these articles was that none actually showed women working. "Wear Them to Work" showed one woman standing in front of a filing cabinet, and another in front of a typewriter, both wearing formal gloves, an accessory certainly not practical for the workplace. The remainder of the images showed women shopping, or simply posing in front of simple backdrops. With articles like these, *Amerika* may have seemed tone deaf to the Russian woman who did not have access to such clothing, especially for work purposes, or for those who worked in settings that were not suitable for such styles of dress.

Fashion spreads also included girls, teenagers, and young adults. For example, February 1958's "College Girls Dressed Up" reflected the postwar emphasis on a new and expanding consumer market: the American teenager. The article showed the casual and affordable, yet fashionable, clothing that college girls wore throughout the day while studying in their dormitories. By night, they did their hair, and wore

Figure 4.4. These students, wearing the latest in affordable evening fashions, appeared ready either for a night out with friends or for dates with their beaus. Original caption: Trio in taffeta are Barbara Foster of Smith in blue (Anne Fogarty, $25), Carol Mahon of Manhattanville in red (Henry Rosenfeld, $18), and Helga Hoffmeister of Western College, Ohio, in plaid (Nelly de Grab, top $6, skirt $15), *Amerika*, February 1958.

colourful dresses and shoes for an evening on the town (figure 4.4).[74] The article showed seven colour images of girls who were forgoing the long evening dresses of the past and were instead choosing short evening dresses with full skirts. These dresses were deemed practical because they were easier to pack for a weekend getaway, less prone to getting dirty, and made doing new dance crazes, like the bunny hop, easier. The article stated that college girls were buying these clothes as short- rather than long-term investments because fashions changed so regularly. This was a unique revelation, given *Amerika*'s previous emphasis on practicality. However, given that every outfit cost less than $25, *Amerika*'s editors may have assumed that the affordability of the clothing, as well as the necessity of appearing fashionable, could justify minimal wear. To the predominately white, middle-class Americans who read this article, which originally appeared in *Life* magazine, these images may have represented the average college-aged girl, a status that was more attainable than ever before, but the reality was that most young women did not attend college. According to the US Census Bureau, in 1950, only 5 per cent of women had completed four or more years of college. By 1960, that number had only risen to 5.8 per cent.[75] Further, these images appeared during a time when white, middle-class American girls were widely stereotyped as attending college solely to meet a future husband and obtain a "Mrs. Degree." In contrast, the 1959 All-Union Population Census indicated that 16 per cent of all Russian women had completed college.[76] To those who had or were attending college, these images may have seemed unusual for their representations of students engaging in acts that hardly resembled the pursuit of higher learning. June 1958's "College Girls Like These Shirts," for example, showed the "favourite garment" of the University of New Mexico student, "the versatile, economic shirt," worn by women in four different images. All were accessorized with scarves, belts or jewellery.[77] March 1959's "Best Dressed College Girls" also showed colourful and clean-cut fashions that were the favourite campus wear of five college girls.[78] None of the images showed these girls in the classroom or studying, but all appeared well dressed and happy in their supposed academic environment.

"College Girls Dressed Up" went even further, showing student living conditions. Female students had turned their dormitories into well-decorated temporary homes, making them bright and colourful with affordable furniture and creative décor, including paintings, curtains, and throw pillows (figure 4.5).[79] Articles such as this one purported to show Russian women the myriad ways in which young American women could purchase items to improve both their appearances and surroundings, as well practise for their future roles as housewives. The transition of a dormitory from a dreary, communal residence to a colourful and comfortable home was, in effect, a practice run for the homes these girls would one day decorate as married women. These images contrasted with the homes in which Russian women lived. While Russian women's living spaces were also small and communal, they lacked the affordable and colourful items that American women could purchase to turn their quarters into attractive living spaces. Although the article appeared in 1958, it was reprinted from a 1953 *Life* magazine article. The editor's selection of an article published five years earlier

Figure 4.5. These Bryn Mawr students were shown studying in their well-decorated and colourful dorm room. Original caption: Bryn Mawr suite in Pembroke East has café curtains of muslin ($1.50 a yard), bedspreads, window-seat covers, and cushions of striped denim and foam-rubber floor cushions covered in solid denim (85 cents a yard). Luggage rack ($6.50) with tray serves as table. Lanterns (left) are hung on dog leashes. *Amerika*, February 1958.

reflected their interest in including, as previously noted, "timeless" articles.[80] Indeed, in spite of the five years between original publication and reprinting, the outfits in "College Girls Dressed Up" still appeared fashionable and the home décor still modern. Editors assumed that five-year-old American-produced clothing and décor would still be more fashionable than Soviet fashions, and that Russian women, with their limited access to information on the Western world, would believe that these were in fact the latest trends, in spite of the large gap between original printing and republication.

Articles such as these exemplified the vast differences between Russian and American students. For example, March 1958's "Soviet

Students Visit Washington D.C." was an account of twenty students, men and women, who went on a month-long tour of the United States as part of a cultural exchange with the Soviet Union. The article depicted their weekend in Washington, where they met the press, visited the Capitol Building, lunched with members of Congress, and spoke with labour officials on the role of unionization in a capitalist country. The article noted that some of their warmest recollections may have been their informal discussions with American students, who, much to their surprise, spoke Russian. The article took on a more serious tone than many of *Amerika*'s articles which focused solely on female students, noting that topics ranged from education to politics.[81] This decision, however, may have been due to the larger strategy of the USIA's information program. Through material such as *Amerika*, officials went out of their way to avoid criticizing the Russian people, trying to remain serious and respectful on behalf of the US government and its people. Including information on style of dress may have made Russian students appear carefree, even frivolous, particularly as they engaged in an official capacity on behalf of the Soviet government. Articles on clothing and fashion, therefore, were relegated to American students, particularly female ones. The clothing shown in the pages of *Amerika* was carefully selected not only to show Russian women styles of modern dress but also to inspire them to create their own. Larisa Zakharova confirms that, whenever possible, Russian women looked at Western magazines and studied the trends, in part, because fashion was downplayed in their own country. Russian women were encouraged by the Soviet government to value products made by socialist labour and to keep all goods until they were worn out, including clothing, making keeping up with fashion trends virtually impossible. Zakharova says that as far as economists were concerned, fashion was antithetical to socialist economics and hindered the planned production, distribution, and consumption of clothing. As a result, Soviet clothing was practical, functional, and comfortable rather than extravagant.[82] While *Amerika*'s articles claimed that clothing could be all of these things, January 1959's "Wardrobe for Mother-to-Be" was unique. It was the only article in the first years of the magazine that explicitly showed pregnant women. The majority of its articles showed either young women, mothers, or grandmothers, all of them slim by Soviet standards, and none of them ever shown to be "expecting" – an irony considering the magazine's emphasis on a domestic, pronatalist ideology. They were typically shown either without children or already with children, but never in between. Further, the article was aimed to undercut the Soviet economic system. The article contained four images of pregnant, but still surprisingly slim, women. Their clothing was conservative in comparison to the fashions typically shown in the magazine, but the article noted that slim skirts and elegant jackets were the secret behind fashionable maternity clothes, as they were both comfortable and attractive (figure 4.6).[83] However, maternity clothes, with their limited shelf life, were simply not practical for Russian women. By the middle of the 1950s, more diverse fashions began entering the Soviet landscape, but many of them were still inaccessible or expensive for ordinary Russian women.

For Russian women who were interested in fashion but unable to access the clothing seen in the pages of *Amerika*, the magazine provided alternatives. Most notably, it offered them patterns they could use to sew their own clothes.[84] December 1959's "A Smart Coat You Can Make Yourself" provided a "versatile" pattern that assisted Russian women in making a coat that, if accessorized with a belt or scarf, could act as a raincoat, a hostess robe, an evening gown, or even a beach dress.[85] Other articles encouraged teenagers and young girls to take up sewing. July 1957's "4-H Girls' Fashions" showcased forty-nine teenage girls who proudly modelled the stylish clothes they had made themselves in an annual "All-American 4H Club Rally" held in Chicago. These amateur designers were chosen from the approximately 700,000 girls who took part in the 4-H sewing program. 4-H is a national organization devoted to teaching young people from the rural US practical skills.[86] In the previous year, they had taken courses with the goal of learning how to sew, and the winners of their local fashion exhibitions were invited to the rally to show their handiwork. Each girl was judged on the attractiveness of her design, needlework, materials, accessories, and presentation, and although no winner was chosen, each received a souvenir from the event. Five images showed models in casual dresses, evening gowns, coats, and hats, all of which exhibited the hard work of these young fashion designers and seamstresses.[87] The message was implicit. If these young girls could sew their own fashionable clothing, so too could Russian women. January 1957's "Patch Fashions" even suggested that little girls could join this trend by adding bright and fun patches of materials to their skirts or by sewing clothing for their dolls.[88] While little girls were likely not reading *Amerika*, their mothers, as the main consumers of the household, were. These articles would demonstrate to Russian women and by extension, girls, that with the right pattern and material anyone could learn to sew, and that under a communist regime anyone could appear fashionable, even by Western standards. Women could see fashionable clothing within the magazine, and even if they were not readily available to them, they could attempt

Figure 4.6. These maternity fashions showed Russian women that even while expecting they could still be fashionable.
Original caption:
Top left: Semi-woollen costume, 50 dollars; blouse with a big bow, 8 dollars.
Upper right: Cotton blouse that fits any skirt, 9 dollars.
Mid right: Combination of tweed jacket and a cotton blouse, 20 dollars.
Bottom right: Combination of synthetic flannel cloth and woollen blouse, 20 dollars.
Amerika, January 1959.

to recreate these items themselves. Those who sought fashionable clothing could use a variety of strategies depending on their income. If material was available, high-income earners or elite women could have garments made to order at professional tailor shops, middle-income earners could go to semi-professional private tailors, and low-income earners could make clothing themselves.[89] Through these methods, Russian women could find ways to create distinctive and fashionable articles of clothing, even when their socialist economy failed to provide them with these items.

The pages of *Amerika* that contained the latest trends in fashion, hairstyles, and accessories proved to be important propagandistic pieces. Each issue of the magazine, which consistently contained at least one article on fashion, could be viewed by the reader and then passed from woman to woman for years. By bypassing the Soviet government, which normally produced clothing for the entire country, and by appealing directly to women, *Amerika*'s editors prevailed, and, by proxy, so too did the US government, in its Cold War battle for cultural supremacy. If women could not directly purchase fashionable clothing, they could attempt to copy the individual items they saw in the magazine, and even the full "looks" themselves. They could then take their newfound tastes and styles to the streets of Moscow, spreading them in the process. As Zakharova has noted, magazines such as *Amerika* became "timeless manuals of good taste" for consumers.[90] Russian women attempted to emulate not just the fashions but, more broadly, the ways of life they saw in *Amerika*, in the process subtly breaking down barriers between East and West. For the supposedly "graceless, shapeless, and sexless" Russian women, the articles and images in *Amerika* may have appeared as a promise, not of a future where they had to relinquish their "equal status," but one that allowed them to retain it and still appear feminine in the process.

Chapter Five

Living the American Dream: The Happy Homemaker in *Amerika*

Just as *Amerika*'s editors promoted the materialistic world of women's fashion and femininity, they also adopted an alternative approach in portraying American women. Throughout *Amerika*'s first years, they went to great lengths to convey a wholesomeness in American women that could refute the stereotypes of them as the "irresponsible glamour girls" or "unfeminine, materialistic beings" that the USIA was eager to debunk.[1] It is well known that a domestic, pronatalist ideology, with its emphasis on marriage and motherhood, shaped postwar America and consistently appeared in popular culture.[2] This ideology was well represented in the pages of *Amerika*, just as it was domestically in America's postwar women's magazines. *Amerika*'s editors regularly conveyed to readers the image of the happy homemaker, surrounded by modern household technology and convenience foods, and content in her life as wife and mother. From 1956 to 1960, twenty-six articles focused on marriage and the family, and thirty-five focused on the home and homemaking, all emphasizing the central role of the housewives and mothers who were at the heart of those families (see table 4.1). While images of the fashionable female and wholesome housewife may have seemed contradictory, they were in fact complementary in that they showed women of various ages as reaping the rewards of a distinctly American way of life. First, women were able to enjoy the benefits of *being* with their families. *Amerika* contained countless articles and images of mothers with their children, and at times, these articles even included what according to the US media were elusive figures in the Soviet family: fathers.[3] American parents were shown as present in the lives of their children, and always happy in being present. Second, women were shown as eager consumers, first solely for themselves and later in life for their themselves *and* their families. *Amerika*'s editors believed that Russian women, particularly the working housewives and mothers who were saddled with a double burden and unable to stay at home and raise their children, could read these articles, see the accompanying images, and witness the conveniences available in a capitalist country. Just as American women reading the *Ladies' Home Journal* could better understand and feel sympathy for Russian women, the USIA intended for *Amerika*'s images to evoke specific feelings in Russian women, ones which would help them both to better understand the "other," and to develop a sense of envy for a Cold War rival's way of life.

Articles on family life in *Amerika* often emphasized gendered customs and traditions, many of which were uniquely American. Introduced to girls at a young age, these rites prepared girls and women for their ultimate Cold War role: that of the happy housewife and good mother. The articles pointed out the differences between American and Russian women's lives. For example, March 1957's "First Ball" discussed the American tradition of the "debutante ball," or "coming out," of eighteen-year-old Jean Walburg of Rockville, Maryland.[4] This article was unique in that it marked the first time that an African American female and her family were chosen as the main subjects of an article.[5] Jean's mother, a high school teacher, made her daughter's debut a memorable affair by bringing together the parents of her thirteen friends to host an "affordable" ball for their children at a Washington, DC, hotel. Each girl's parents paid only forty-two dollars in expenses. This formal event was a special occasion in the life of a teenage girl, as well as her parents. Subtly emphasizing the importance of religion, even in the life of a teenage girl, and foreshadowing her wedding day, each father led his daughter separately into the hall, where a priest presented her before a waiting crowd.[6] She and her date then joined their friends at the side and waited for the ball to begin. The girls wore elaborate white dresses, the boys wore tuxedos, and together they took part in a rehearsed dance (figure 5.1).[7] While these images represented young people who were far removed from the Soviet way of life, and even from the lives of many Americans, they showed that an extravagant event was within reach of all Americans, including African Americans, in part because of the economical ways of hard-working mothers who wanted to ensure these time-honoured traditions lived on through their daughters.

According to *Amerika*, another joyous event in the life of a young woman was her wedding day. June 1958's "A Young Couple Gets Married" attempted to bridge the gap between the lives of American and Russian women by stating that everywhere in the world a young girl's wedding was a source of joy and hope for the future. Just as the *Ladies' Home Journal* did when it described newlyweds Mary Jo Alhoff and Don Schmidt, the article reveals the details involved in preparing

Figure 5.1. Images such as this showed Russian readers the time-honoured traditions Americans held dear. In this case, elaborately dressed debutantes and their parents enter the President's Hotel in Washington, DC, as guests look on. *Amerika*, March 1957.

for a typical American wedding, that of eighteen-year-old Jenny Peters and her high school sweetheart, Bud Millinghausen, in their hometown of Lumberton, New Jersey.[8] The article discussed Jenny's joyous but busy moments leading up to the big day, including writing a wedding announcement for the local newspaper, preparing her dress, collecting and opening presents, packing her honeymoon clothes, and attending the wedding rehearsal. The article culminated in the couple's church wedding, presided over by one of their college friends. At the conclusion of the ceremony, the bride, in a white gown and veil, was shown exiting the church with her groom, surrounded by family and friends (figure 5.2).

Articles such as this and "First Ball" were centred on milestones in a young woman's life; focusing heavily on customs and traditions surrounding dating and marriage, the articles emphasized affordability and accessibility. Religion played a prominent role. Russian women typically married in civil ceremonies; American women, in contrast, organized elaborate church ceremonies and receptions that took weeks and even months to prepare, but were made possible because of the couple's hard work and that of of their families and friends. Articles like this assumed that events such as weddings were milestones for the women of both countries and did not acknowledge that Russian women frequently did not have the means and access to supplies to organize, or perhaps even the interest in, such elaborate ceremonies.

In *Amerika*, marriage was a frequent topic, and couples young and old were celebrated. May 1957's "Golden Anniversary" depicted Alfonso and Rosaria La Falce, a couple who had just celebrated their fiftieth wedding anniversary by renewing their marriage vows and throwing a reception for one hundred relatives and close friends. The article not only recounted the love story that took them from Italy to the United States but also the quintessentially American rags-to-riches tale. Arriving in New York in 1903 at the age of nineteen, Alfonso obtained a job and sent for his teenage sweetheart, Rosaria. They had no money or education and were unable to speak English, but the article noted they could offer the country their "strength, hard work, frugality, faith and courage." While they were not wealthy, they lived well in a spacious nine-room home in Poughkeepsie, New York. Their family consisted of fifty-three people, and they could revel in their eleven children, their many grandchildren, and the respect and affection of their community. *Amerika* presented the La Falces as a couple who came from humble Italian beginnings but had embraced and eventually achieved the American Dream.[9] Further, their children's participation in the capitalist economy – three owned businesses – furthered that dream.

Figure 5.2. The church wedding ceremony was another time-honoured tradition shown in *Amerika*. Original caption: A moment of joy: smiling couple exit the church while guests sprinkle them with rice and confetti. *Amerika*, June 1958.

The family, particularly as it centred on children, was another popular topic in *Amerika*, just as it was in America's postwar women's magazines. October 1956's "New Member of the Family" highlighted women's roles as mothers, showcased the importance of the family, and provided Russian readers with ideas for preparing for an important event in the lives of many families: the arrival of a new sibling. It discussed the ways in which Florida couple Jim and Jessie Wilson prepared their three older children, ages four, three, and two, for the arrival of their baby sister, Jill. The children were brought to the hospital, where they were each given a doll they could watch over themselves. Reinforcing the gender roles they would be expected to embrace themselves one day, the article noted this gift would provide them with an opportunity to do what "all kids love to do: imitate their parents."[10] The idea was so successful that all of the children, even two-year-old Jay, spent hours playing with their dolls. Eleven photographs showed the Wilson children not only meeting their new sister but also playing the role of parent by dressing, feeding, and washing their dolls, just as their mother did with baby Jill. During an era which emphasized heteronormative gender roles, it may have seemed unusual for the article to contain descriptions and images of the Wilson's son caring for his own doll, but the article made clear that Jay was not as proficient in his role as his older sisters. He was shown playing with his new doll, but in a more careless, childlike manner. The article noted that his mother had to caution him against putting his finger both in his doll's and in his baby sister's eyes. Both mistakes were captured on camera.[11] Ultimately, however, the simple gift of a doll served its purpose in welcoming a new addition to the family: it allowed the Wilson children to feel included in raising their sister, and it meant that they were too occupied to be jealous of the attention she was receiving.

Even in those cases where biological children were not an option, the magazine showed that women could fulfil their maternal desires and intended roles through adoption. In postwar magazines, including *Amerika*, families came in different shapes and sizes, albeit always in two-parent, heterosexual households with children, and March 1957's "Adopting a Five-Year-Old" demonstrated this. It told the story of John and Mary Walker, a Los Angeles couple; unable to have a family of their own in the traditional way, they decided to make their familial dreams come true through adoption. The article captured the adoption process, including the Walker's decision to adopt, their three years of applications and interviewing with government and private agencies, their first meeting with five-year-old Billy, acquainting themselves with him, and, finally, taking him home from the orphanage. The article described Billy's delight with his new family and suburban surroundings, riding his tricycle in the yard, eating Mary's cooking, playing with his new toys, animatedly chatting over breakfast, visiting the toy store, sitting in a grocery cart, and being read a bedtime story. Ultimately, the article noted that the home had become "warmer for the jubilant couple." Similarly, November 1960's issue told the story of adoption through "Sister from the Far East." However, Dick and Polly Samuelson of Brockton, Massachusetts, already had four boys before welcoming Ling Kuen, a young orphan from Hong Kong, into their "happy American family." Based on the article, Ling's heritage appeared to have been abandoned as she quickly acclimated to her new surroundings. Her name was changed to Lori, and, just like Billy, she had discovered all things American: television, ice cream sodas, hot dogs, games, and what she wanted most of all, "love."[12] These articles emphasized that children not only made the family complete but they also enhanced it. And in cases with families such as the Samuelsons, who already had four children, more children brought even more happiness.[13]

Almost all of *Amerika*'s content reflected the harmonious white, heterosexual, middle-class version of postwar America that USIA officials wanted to convey abroad. Central to this vision was the single-family, detached home in the suburbs. In the postwar world, young couples joyously flocked to these suburban safe havens that contained private spaces at inexpensive prices, convenient amenities, and safety from the outside world.[14] Between 1956 and 1960, thirty-five articles appeared specifically on the home or homemaking (see table 4.1). Once again, these articles were meant to demonstrate the difference between American and Soviet styles of living. While Khrushchev had introduced the concept of *Khrushchevki*, these single-family apartment buildings took years to come to fruition, and even then, were a far cry from the seemingly luxurious postwar American suburban home. Reflecting this preoccupation with home ownership as a symbol of the American Dream, or anyone's dream for that matter, October 1958's "Housing Ideas on Display" informed the Russian reader that over one million homes had been built each year during the past decade and homeownership was at an all-time high.[15] The August 1960 issue of *Amerika* devoted ten of its twenty-one articles to the home and home construction.[16] "Housing in America," by Charles E. Silberman, an associate editor of *Fortune* magazine, stated that the number of homeowners had doubled in the last fifteen years. The housing industry had built more than twenty million new dwellings, 80 per cent of them single-family homes. Silberman noted that these trends were influenced by factors such as larger incomes, expanding suburbs, and improved building materials. The average new house had three bedrooms and one and one-half baths. One of the most popular new trends was the "family room," a room for adults to watch television and children to play. Silberman argued that the rise in housing construction had changed the US landscape, resulting in thousands of new suburbs. It also affected the way Americans lived. Furniture became simple and cleaner, men worked shorter weeks, and families had more time for recreational activities. Silberman concluded that, although the future direction of consumer choices was unclear, in a large and free economy there was room for separate markets to cater to the specific needs and desires of different people.[17]

This issue reflected the vast options that Americans had when choosing their dwellings, all of which appeared spacious compared to the small, crowded, and often communal housing that Russians, particularly those living in the city, inhabited. These conditions gradually changed as *Khrushchevki* were built, but in *Amerika* it was implied that US housing options would always be more plentiful and conditions far superior. This was made even clearer when the magazine depicted those seemingly rare postwar Americans who shunned the suburbs, or, in the case of racial and ethnic minorities, were shut out of them entirely, and chose to live in apartment buildings. "A Day in an Apartment House" deviated from the norm of the detached, single-family home and featured the first high-rise apartment facility in Arlington County, Virginia. Opened in 1955, Arlington Towers reflected the "new look of apartment living," which combined elements of both the city and the suburb.[18] "Second Homes for Family Vacations" reinforced the notion that Americans had more disposable income than ever and were using it to purchase vacation homes. It stated that two million Americans owned vacation homes and would purchase 75,000 more in the next year. The article noted that they were being built both in the country and along coastal areas only hours away from home. Because of affordable automobiles, improved highway systems, and longer vacation times, families could vacation more frequently, even on weekends. The article included colour images of vacation homes, both rustic and modern, and showed happy families enjoying them (figure 5.3).[19] One that stood out in particular, located in Fire Island, New York, was known as the "milk carton beach house" (figure 5.3). This vacation home, unique if not entirely impractical, was designed by Andrew Geller, the architect who had designed the "typical" American house that appeared at the 1959 American National Exhibition.

A home such as this may have appeared ridiculous to Russian women. However elite urban residents did have their own version

Figure 5.3. This milk carton beach house showed Soviet architects and designers the uniqueness, but also impracticality, of American vacation homes. Original caption reads: Milk carton beach house, designed by Andrew Geller for Irwin and Joyce Hunt, faces the ocean on Fire Island, NY, cost $7,000. Living area is in the centre downstairs. Master bedroom is above. Roof panels, which open up to give ocean view, can be closed in bad weather. *Amerika*, August 1960.

of the vacation home. Known as "dachas," these were weekend or summer dwellings located near the city, but far enough to provide a temporary refuge from it. They were certainly not the norm among the working classes.[20] In any event, *Amerika*'s articles portrayed owning a home, even a second home, as a fundamental aspect of American life – rather than the unattainable luxury that it was for many Americans.

While home ownership was central to the American Dream, homemakers were central to the ideal postwar home. *Amerika*, like postwar American women's magazines, devoted a significant portion of its content to the everyday life of the homemaker, often in relation to the technology that helped her care for her home. Articles on the home frequently showcased the life of the homemaker in relation to advances in technology and her purchasing power. They portrayed American women as maintaining strong values and a solid work ethic, yet able to take advantage of the modern-day conveniences and consumer goods that supposedly made their lives easier. The idea of modern household technology as a "household revolution" which freed women from drudgery was first put forth by home economist Christine Frederick in the 1920s.[21] New technology and products, however, did not always alleviate a woman's household burdens. As Ruth Schwartz Cowan and Jessamyn Neuhaus have noted, during industrialization men entered the marketplace, children attended school for longer periods, and chores went from being the responsibility of the entire family to falling primarily on women's shoulders. With the advent of new technology and products, and an increased emphasis on health and hygiene, expectations increased for cleaner homes and better-prepared and more nutritious meals.[22] The advertising industry played a major role in the association of domesticity with women, as agencies catered specifically to white, middle-class women who remained in the home, thus creating new consumer markets.[23] While the reality is that many non-white, non-middle class American women could not and did not take on these domestic roles, these images were the ones that appeared in *Amerika* to appeal to supposed Russian "housewives." The magazine walked a fine line in conveying the impression that American women worked hard but still had leisure time, thanks to modern-day conveniences. This work-life balance was something USIA officials believed Russian women lacked. In fact, many Russian women did face a double burden in their daily lives. They participated in the paid workforce on a full-time basis, but their government failed to fully socialize childcare and housework. The same was true for the many American women who also faced a double burden. However, the double burden of American women was generally unacknowledged in postwar media, and that certainly applied in the case of *Amerika*. Further, it was believed that Russian women faced added constraints brought on by inadequate housing, a scarcity of abundant and affordable resources, and the absentee husbands and fathers, who rarely contributed to household duties.[24]

Amerika depicted housewives and mothers in many geographical locations, not just the suburbs, as benefiting from advances in technology and the abundance of consumer goods. June 1957's "Farm Wife" purported to depict the lives of the five million farmwomen that lived in the US through the story of Peg Scoville, a housewife and mother of three children living on Paradise Farm, one hour north of New York City. The article discussed how new advances in technology made a difference in Peg's life, even as a rural housewife removed from urban and suburban centres. Peg's busy daily activities included childcare, cooking, cleaning, and occasionally helping her husband on the farm, but modern technology, including electricity, home appliances, telephones, television, and automobiles, lightened her work and helped her overcome the "worst enemy of a farmer's wife – loneliness."[25] The four images in figure 5.4 show that, while Peg had daily chores, she benefited from the luxuries the US economy generated, including a washing machine and dryer, a car, and an abundance of products to choose from at the supermarket. The article made it clear that, while modern technology alleviated the burdens of farm life and homemaking, Peg still worked hard, and engaged in many of the tasks her mother and grandmother did. However, modern luxuries now allowed her additional time to engage in cultural and volunteer activities, such as drawing, singing with a band, and participating in the local parent-teacher association. The article pointed out that, in spite of modern technology, Peg derived satisfaction from living off the land and creating a life centred on her home and family. At the end of the day, Peg was the centre of her family life, just as her mother and grandmother had once been. To further reinforce this notion, the final photograph provided a wholesome image of her hugging her son (figure 5.5).[26]

Just as technology was intended to improve isolated farm life, it was also intended to improve the kitchen. March 1958's "Kitchen Appliances: Today and Tomorrow" featured the vice president of General Electric, Charles K. Rieger, discussing the modern kitchen appliances that eliminated "hard and boring" work and were slowly restoring the kitchen to its traditional position as a "favoured place" in the home. He stated that modern homes typically contained one room for each individual, leaving "poor mothers" to sit in the kitchen alone. Once again, the differentiation between American and Russian life was clear. The solitary kitchen would likely have been a blessing, rather than a problem, for the urban Russian woman, who under the Stalin and Khrushchev years often shared her kitchen with others in communal accommodations. The article further noted that companies such as GE had begun modelling kitchens with the input of American women, rather than making design and functionality decisions for them. Women wanted time-saving devices, and the advent of modern appliances was once again making the kitchen, now larger, cleaner, and brighter than ever before, a desirable place for women and their families.[27] For example, a plan of GE's "Oyster Family Kitchen" (figure 5.6) laid out a dinner table, oven, housewife's nook, corner closet, refrigerator, dishwasher, and electric range in a horseshoe shape designed to maximize space, reduce clutter, and improve efficiency. It stated that it reduced the thousands of steps that housewives took in their daily tasks and made the space more

Figure 5.4. This image shows housewife and mother Peg engaging in her daily activities, including laundry, washing dishes, grocery shopping, and dropping her kids off at the bus stop. *Amerika*, June 1957.

Figure 5.5. While Peg is clearly a modern farmwife and mother, she still retains her traditional role within the home and among her family. Original caption: The appearance might change, yet the substance remains. Peg is a centre of family life, in the same way as her grandmother once was. *Amerika*, June 1957.

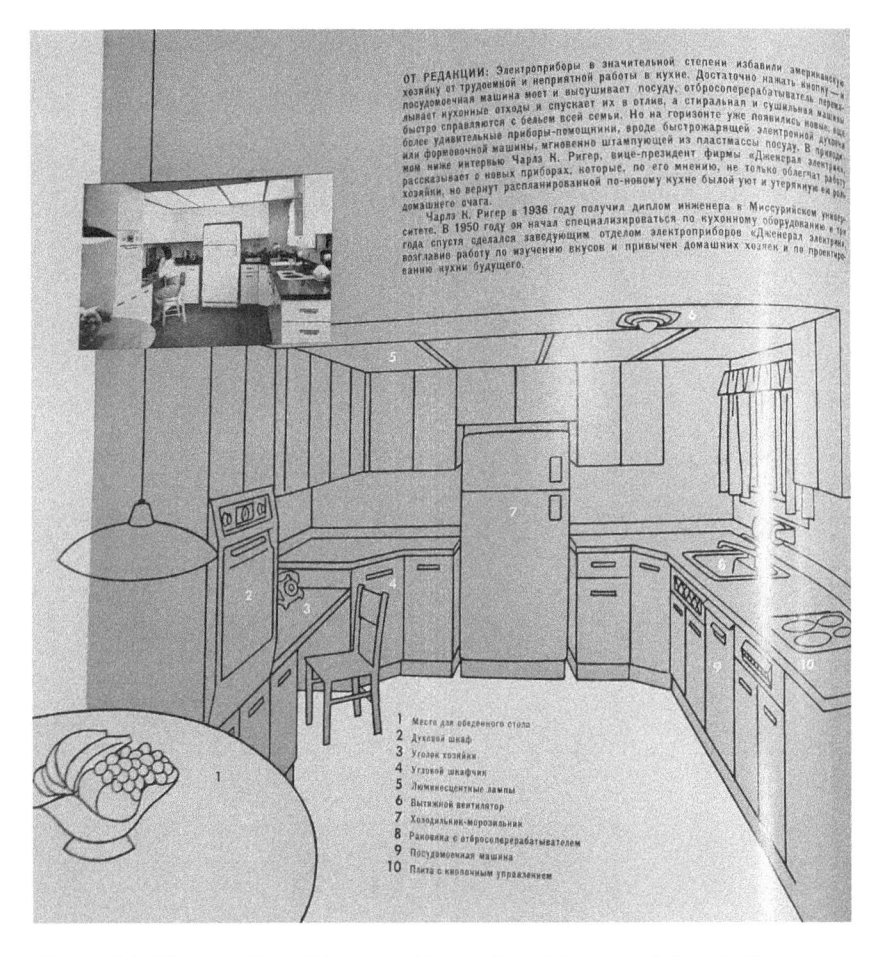

Figure 5.6. Plans such as this one, with numbered items and descriptions, clearly showed *Amerika*'s readers, and perhaps even Soviet home architects and designers, the layout of the ideal kitchen. It not only provided women with modern conveniences but also streamlined the process of meal planning and preparation. *Amerika*, March 1958.

Original caption:

1. A place for a dinner table
2. Oven
3. Housewife's nook
4. Corner closet
5. Luminescent lamps
6. Exhaust ventilation
7. Fridge
8. Garbage disposal
9. Dishwashing machine
10. Electric range

Figure 5.7. Bright colours, electrical appliances, and a well-stocked pantry helped turn a kitchen into a modern space for the housewife's daily tasks. *Amerika*, July 1960.

comfortable for them. It also included significant storage space. The embedded black-and-white image brought this plan to fruition, showing a housewife seated at her nook speaking on the telephone. While there, she could listen to the radio, read cookbooks, and make budgets and shopping lists. The article made clear that she was afforded this additional time because the kitchen was easy to keep clean. Its bright appearance also made it a place where she *wanted* to spend her time.[28]

July 1960's "Kitchen Workroom" showed Russian women a colour image of a "typical" American kitchen, highlighting the bright turquoise and white décor and the gleaming appliances that American women supposedly possessed (figure 5.7). In contrast to Rieger's argument that improvements in technology and décor had begun to re-establish the kitchen as a place for the entire family, "Kitchen Workroom" emphasized the centrality of the kitchen in the housewife's life specifically and showed her in it alone. The kitchen was a unique space for her and rarely were other individuals shown within its walls. Although the article made the kitchen sound like a desirable space for women, it also noted that new technology could mean she spent less time there and more time on things she "liked to do," a rare comment given that *Amerika*'s articles tended to emphasize the enjoyment women derived from homemaking.[29] Indeed, a focus on the kitchen was a notable addition to *Amerika*'s efforts to promote the high standard of living in America, especially for its women. The importance of the kitchen as a political tool for cultural diplomacy was demonstrated during 1959's "kitchen debate" between Nixon and Khrushchev. The debate saw Nixon laud the convenience of the GE model kitchen, arguing that Americans wanted to "make more easy the life of our housewives." Khrushchev responded by noting that such items were unnecessary in the homes of Russian women because the "capitalistic attitude" that dictated women should be homemakers rather than workers did not exist under communism, with its official policy of gender equality.[30] Their opinions clearly diverged, but the debate proved to be one of the most important cultural events of the Cold War and signified the extent to which the government connected women, consumerism, and the "American way of life."[31]

While many of the items displayed within *Amerika*'s kitchens, as well as at the American National Exhibition, may have been commonplace in the kitchens of America's white, middle-class, suburban families, they would have been considered luxury items by Russian women. As Kirk and the Goulds noted in the *Ladies' Home Journal*, even if Russian women did have the money to purchase these items, they likely would have been unavailable because Soviet government industries did not produce the same consumer goods in mass quantities as US private industries did.[32] Furthermore, the communal kitchens of cities such as Moscow made it difficult for women, even if they could obtain the latest items, to find space to store them in their shared quarters.[33] Nevertheless, in spite of the lack of attainability of the kitchens and items in these images, the USIA assumed they contained a lifestyle that would appeal to Russian women after reading *Amerika*.

Within the pages of *Amerika*, food played an important role in promoting the conveniences of American life, just as it did in the *Ladies' Home Journal*. The food industry found a new market based on the wartime development of the canning, freezing, and dehydrating of food, and this new food culture played a prominent role in the postwar United States. New "convenience foods" such as Spam, Minute Maid frozen orange juice, and Swanson TV dinners became popular and were said to "liberate women."[34] February 1958's "Revolution in the Kitchen" stated that the average American housewife spent less than half the time in her kitchen that her mother did, yet her family was getting a better-balanced diet and larger variety of food. William B. Murphy, president of the Campbell Soup Company, referred to this as a "revolution in the kitchen," made possible by the rapidly growing use of prepackaged and prepared foods. Murphy indicated that thirty years ago the average woman spent up to six hours a day making meals, but by 1958 that time was cut in half. Women were purchasing nutritious convenience foods such as cake and biscuit mixes, conserved fruits, frozen vegetables, canned soups, precut and partially cooked meats, and ready-made ice cream. Just as "Kitchen Workroom" pointed out that new technology meant women could spend less time in the kitchen, Murphy stated that young housewives did not want to be "kitchen slaves." They could cook, if necessary, but were not as concerned about their skills in the kitchen as women had once been. In contrast to typical postwar magazines, he concluded that these skills were not considered essential to being good homemakers. Instead, women were concerned about value, nutrition, and their family's health and happiness.[35] Laura Shapiro argues, however, that during the 1950s most women actually *preferred* cooking to other household tasks. They took advantage of foods that had been processed and packaged, such as sliced bread, ground beef, and bagged potatoes, but were suspicious of partially prepared foods that needed to be heated or mixed. Although convenience foods rose in popularity, women still cooked, in part because cooking was indeed faster and easier than it had ever been and convenience foods did not always meet the standard of fresh ones.[36] As Anna Zeide notes, it took over a century for the canned food industry, arguably the first convenience food, to convince Americans whose diets were limited by their geographical locations and the given season that these mass-produced metal cans with their well-preserved, but concealed, contents could be trusted.[37] While *Amerika* endorsed these convenience foods, it also celebrated America's diverse culture by including descriptions of and recipes for ethnic foods, many of which took significantly more time to prepare. May 1958's "From Pelmeni to Sukiyaki" described the "rich potpourri of America cuisine," indicating that it could please gourmets, travellers, and immigrants. It connected the history of US immigration to food and stated that since its inception, "Native Indians," British settlers, French voyageurs, Spanish, German, and Scandinavian immigrants, as well as newer waves of migrants from India and Japan, had contributed to America's diverse food culture. It listed the popularity of specific foods, including Italian pizza, French onion soup, German *sauerbraten* (marinated roast beef), Chinese rice, Pakistani curry, Hungarian goulash (beef stew), Polish *golombki* (cabbage rolls), Syrian stuffed grape leaves, Armenian shish kebab, and Mexican enchiladas. The article noted there were at least three cafes in New York where Russians could find comfort foods such as *blinchiki*, thin crepe-like pancakes, and *polmeni*, filled dumplings. The article recognized that some of these foods were authentic, while others had been Americanized, but noted that Americans were open-minded towards food. According to it, foreign foods were welcomed warmly in the United States, the "United Nations of Food."[38]

Regardless of American women's preference for convenience or fresh foods, *Amerika* demonstrated that access to plentiful, healthy, and delicious food was as much of a concern for American women as it was for Russian women as the main purchasers of household items for their families. It was fitting then, that even prior to August 1960's issue devoted extensively to housing, February 1960's issue devoted ten of its nineteen articles to food. The issue began with an image of Nixon and Khrushchev taken on 24 July 1959, the opening day of the American National Exhibition, and led with an article, "The Fair in Moscow," which noted that 2.7 million visitors had "swarmed" to see displays on facets of American life.[39] Perhaps in light of the heated "kitchen debate" between the two leaders, in this issue *Amerika*'s editors decided to focus on the production, distribution, and preparation of food. Articles such as "We Are What We Eat," "Easy Cooking in Today's Kitchen," "Food Invades the Arts," "It's Lunch Time," and "Protecting the Consumer" discussed a multitude of topics that included convenience foods, modern appliances, consumer protection, and even cookbook art, and the various ways Americans spent their lunch hours.[40] *Amerika*'s editors, assuming that women, regardless of their geographical location, enjoyed shopping, placed an importance on content that not only showcased consumer items, but also the places where American women shopped. The longest article from February 1960's issue on food was a seven-page spread channelling the postwar American obsession with the modern supermarket, which rose in popularity along with a suburban, automobile-centred culture. In 1946, there were 10,000 supermarkets in the United States, but by 1953 that number had grown to 17,000.[41] "The Supermarket in an Age of Distribution" showed a modern US supermarket that was a far cry from the cramped quarters of the mom-and-pop shops that Americans frequented before the war (figure 5.8) as well as the small, government-run food stores of the Soviet Union. This modern supermarket typically had a floor space of fifteen to twenty thousand square feet, up to one hundred staff members, and clean and brightly lit aisles with fully stocked shelves of food and other household products.

The article stated that the supermarket was a symbol of an efficient and streamlined distribution system that supplied the American people with food at the world's most affordable prices. According to the article, the supermarket was not only vital to US consumer culture, but also to housewives, due to its self-service format and convenience. In the past, housewives were forced to visit several shops before finding everything they needed, but by the 1950s they visited the supermarket once per week for one hour at a time. Contradicting Rieger's claim that housewives worked in their kitchens to methodically plan their meals, shopping lists, and budgets, the article stated that housewives did not have shopping lists, and instead engaged in impulse shopping, walking down aisles and planning their meals based on whatever caught their eye. The article noted that supermarkets had earned such fame abroad that even foreign leaders visiting the US requested to see them.[42] It cited Queen Elizabeth II and Khrushchev himself as just two examples of those who had toured supermarkets while visiting the United States.[43]

This supermarket obsession was not unique to those visiting the country, as accounts of US fairs in Italy, Poland, and Yugoslavia during the 1950s discussed the crowds that flocked to see supermarket displays.[44] At the Fifty-Seventh Zagreb International Trade Fair in Yugoslavia in September 1957, the USIA displayed "Supermarket USA," a ten-thousand-square-foot self-service "American Way" supermarket. It included over four thousand items that women could see and touch, including fresh fruits and vegetables, dairy products, frozen foods, self-service packaged meat, chicken, and fish, and convenience foods. Yugoslav president Josip Broz Tito supposedly lingered over the items with his wife, Jovanka.[45] The supermarket proved so popular that the Yugoslav firm Jugoelektro purchased the entire display after

Living the American Dream   165

Figure 5.8. Images such as this one showed Russian women the concept of the self-service supermarket, where an abundance of food items were available in one convenient location. *Amerika*, February 1960.

the fair closed, and by April 1958 had opened the country's first supermarket in Belgrade. While it was smaller than the average American supermarket, it signalled the communist country's first foray into an Americanized self-service shopping experience.[46] Jugoelektro was part of a broader attempt on the part of the Yugoslav government to provide the "good life" to its people. Indeed, Patrick Hyder Patterson notes that by the 1960s the Yugoslav people actively pursued the "Yugoslav Dream," which aimed to mirror the postwar prosperity of the American Dream.[47] It was made possible by a flexible government which permitted increased exposure to the West and its culture and allowed for foreign travel.[48] This Yugoslav "third way," as it became known, acted as an effective compromise between East and West. It not only appeased ordinary Yugoslavs, but also increased acceptance of the communist regime.[49] Of course, the USIA was aware that Western exposure could have long-lasting impacts on both governments and ordinary citizens. In 1959, the American National Exhibition in Moscow included a supermarket. Images of American supermarkets, then, were intended to entice readers, much like they did with fairgoers.[50] To *Amerika*'s editors, these articles on the home, the kitchen, and food promoted US democracy and the free market by promising Russian women a better life based on their circumstances as housewives and mothers. They not only showed spacious homes and kitchens but also modern technology and an abundance of food which, according to *Amerika*, were affordable for the "typical" American family.

There were articles in *Amerika* that deviated from the norm and depicted women as wage earners. From 1956 to 1960, *Amerika* contained twenty-five articles focusing on career women, but the overwhelming majority showed them employed in fields that were considered acceptable for women at the time, as teachers, nurses, actors, singers, musicians, dancers, designers, and writers. Occasionally articles showcased female athletes, but only through their participation in "feminine" endeavours such as ballet dancing, figure skating, and tennis.[51] The majority of the careers that were featured reinforced the notion of woman as caregiver and nurturer, or in a supporting role to the men that surrounded her. Additionally, when these career women had children, images of their families were juxtaposed with those of them as professionals, as if to suggest that the family could never be neglected, even when a woman had a career. September 1958's "New Teacher" showcased Jean Goodloe of Belmonte, California, in perhaps the most nurturing role of all, that of elementary school teacher.[52] The article showed the first day of school for the new teacher and contained eleven images of her with her thirty-six students engaged in various activities, including teaching the children, playing games with them, and supervising them on the playground before seeing them off at the end of the day. For the American woman, however, no postwar profession was more popular than that of office receptionist or secretary. March 1958's "The 2,700 Lives of an Office Building" was a lengthy piece on the customs, habits, and contacts formed by the 2,700 employees at a Madison Avenue office building. The article highlighted both men and women working predominantly in advertising, but while it showed men in varied positions, from the janitors and newsstand owners, to the salesmen and bookkeepers, to the copy chiefs, bankers, and directors, its depictions of women were stereotypical and secondary to those of the men in their offices. "Elevator girls" were discussed in the context of their free time and appearance rather than their jobs. They were shown in their clubhouse, a locker room where the article indicated they dressed, gossiped, chatted, smoked, and played cards. Unusually, it also noted that the building's managers required the women's hair to be coloured black or red, for which they were permitted free treatments. The majority of the women, however, were receptionists and secretaries, and while several images showed them engaged in work, the remainder showed them filing their nails, eating their lunches, awaiting drives to dinner and the theatre, and participating in celebrations honouring the next logical stages of their lives: marriage. In this office building, workplace bridal showers were commonplace, particularly as engagements typically foreshadowed the end of a woman's full-time employment, and the beginning of her new "career," that of housewife.[53]

With this emphasis on traditionally female employment, *Amerika*'s editors showcased women in non-traditional, professional roles on only three occasions. November 1957's "Two New Doctors in Town" depicted Will and Coll Kamprath, husband and wife physicians in the small town of Utica, Nebraska. November 1960's "Judge Ann Mikoll" featured the youngest city court judge of Buffalo, New York.[54] The lengthiest article was January 1960's "Busy Mother," which highlighted Breg Cunningham of Westport, Connecticut. Cunningham had a loving husband, six children, a comfortable home, and, in an unusual twist, her own real estate business. She had taken on a job to increase her family's income after insurance failed to cover a fire that burned down a portion of her home. The article stated that Cunningham enjoyed her job of "finding nice homes for nice people." She worked forty hours per week, received a minimum of five hundred calls per week, and had sold homes worth a total value of $400,000 in the past year. In spite of the postwar stigma attached to working mothers, the article presented her busy schedule as an asset for her children, for it taught them responsibility and the value of hard work. They helped with meals and laundry and cleaned their rooms. Her husband also helped by taking the children out for activities on weekends, when she showed homes. Overall, the article described a loving and supportive home and family life that allowed Cunningham the opportunity to combine "peeling potatoes with selling houses."[55] While these three articles were exceptional in highlighting the devotion of these women to their professions, all made sure to discuss their satisfying personal lives. All stressed the comfortable home lives and supportive husbands, as well as cooperative children, that made it possible for these extraordinary women to combine families and careers. It was only with their household "help" that they could achieve career success. In spite of the seemingly progressive nature of these articles, they were typical in that they emphasized that family always came above career. Cunningham's central role was still that of wife and mother, and her career was secondary.

The historical relationship between American women and consumption has long been studied, but the same cannot be said about Russian women, who lived under a Soviet regime, which for many years had de-emphasized and even discouraged consumerism in favour of agricultural and industrial priorities. For postwar Americans, this outlook was absurd. When Steinbeck and Capa visited the Soviet Union during the summer of 1947, they wrote that Russian women appeared to be the "great shoppers" in their country. They wanted to buy more consumer goods, including clothing, toiletries, and cosmetics, but these were too difficult to find and too expensive.[56] Their account came during the difficult immediate postwar period, and improvements were later made in the production and availability of consumer goods, but the amount of consumer goods available in the Soviet Union was never as plentiful as in the United States, nor was it ever good enough for Americans looking in. USIA officials sought to capitalize on this, and between 1956 and 1960, *Amerika* contained seven articles that focused on specific American shopping centres or department stores that offered women an abundance of goods and a variety of services (see table 4.1). While this number may seem insignificant, it is important to note that countless other articles in *Amerika* underscored the theme of consumption and highlighted consumer goods, but these seven articles are noteworthy because they discussed specific outlets as feminized spaces and as part of the built environment. Their titles were chosen to draw the female reader in and demonstrate that they were intended specifically *for her*. They presented the American shopping experience as convenient, affordable, and fun.

This approach was most evident in June 1960's "Give the Lady What She Wants," which featured the department store as a distinctly female space. Over the course of the past century, it had become associated with the growth of urban life. The department store, with its distinctive merchandising, sales, and labour practices, was one of the primary formative forces of consumption, and women were at its centre.[57] *Amerika* reflected this priority when it showed women shopping in department stores amid a sea of products and people, predominantly women. "Give the Lady What She Wants" depicted a rural woman who, for her seventieth birthday, requested that her daughters turn her "loose for a whole day" in Marshall Field's, Chicago's largest and most famous department store. Her daughter, and the author of the piece, Violet Wood, stated that for a rural Midwestern woman, a visit to Marshall Field's was a special event. When it first opened in 1852, founder Marshall Field recognized that he was living in a time when women's activities were restricted, but they were becoming increasingly recognized for their importance as consumers. As a result, he developed the slogan "Give the Lady What She Wants!" Marshall Field's Chicago flagship store contained seventy-three acres of floor space. It had two connecting air-conditioned buildings, each with ten floors, and over four hundred departments. According to Wood, Marshall Field's was not just a place to shop, it was a city within a city. It was billed as a place that offered a woman exactly what she wanted: a large selection of goods from around the world in one stop and with excellent service. In addition, it had a variety of services to ensure a comfortable shopping experience, including the first personal shopping service, package delivery service, and tearoom in a retail store, as well as seven restaurants and snack bars, a beauty salon, and fashion shows. The article reiterated the benefits of capitalism, noting that Marshall Field's was not owned by one individual, but rather by sixteen thousand shareholders who represented a cross-section of American life.[58] "Give the Lady What She Wants" presented to the Russian woman an idyllic image of the urban department store. Further, it acted as a subtle critique of the Soviet government and its strained relationship with the female consumer. In emphasizing Marshall Field's century-long recognition of the important relationship between women and consumption it was also acknowledging that over one hundred years later the Soviet government had been slow to recognize this supposed fact of life. What were, in fact, consumer luxuries were presented by *Amerika* as necessities in the everyday life of women throughout the world, and actual realities for American women. Other articles similarly highlighted the urban department store's ability to lure women. The aptly titled "Shopper's Paradise" appeared in September 1959, conveniently during the American National Exhibition, and discussed the vast selection of goods and services offered by J.L. Hudson's, a department store headquartered in downtown Detroit.[59] Built in 1881, Hudson's had been frequently expanded and by 1959 it was the tallest department store in the world. The first ten of its twenty-five floors contained accessory counters, travel items, fabrics, gifts, clothing, and shoes for the entire family, home décor, and housewares. More than 500,000 items were placed on open display so that customers could examine and pick up them on their own without the assistance of a sales clerk. The article invoked a common criticism of the Soviet shopping experience in that customers had limited access to items carefully placed behind counters, and out of their reach. It implied that Soviet shopping was akin to the outmoded, impersonal, and sometimes off-putting shopping experience that had existed in the United States the century prior. The remainder of Hudson's floors included offices and storage space. The article claimed that Hudson's retained customers through their loyalty programs. Telephone and mail orders allowed customers to have products delivered to their homes, charge accounts allowed them to pay at the end of each month, and a liberal return policy allowed them to return unused items years after purchase.[60] These articles, demonstrating how stores such as Marshall Field's and Hudson's strategically used their resources, services, and products to appeal to women, were intended to convey to Russian women that their department stores simply did not measure up.

Lengthier pieces discussed mass retailing in the United States, its history, its connections to the rise and success of capitalism, its ability to adapt to the times, and stores' dedication to their employees and the broader communities in which they were situated. These large retail stores were unique in that they established chains that expanded rapidly and were able to reach all parts of the country irrespective of geographical location, and in some cases different parts of the world. The articles in *Amerika* did not only relay success stories, but also recounted the supposedly "human" and "humane" aspects of the capitalist system. They told of the humble beginnings of American entrepreneurs who had worked hard to "make it," the extent to which they had changed the lives of Americans, and their desire to give back to their dedicated employees and communities. One example was June 1959's "Sears, Roebuck and Company," which documented the history of what it called one of the world's "great retailing giants." The company was founded in 1873, when Richard Warren Sears began to sell watches in the small town of Redwood, Minnesota; four years later he partnered with Alvah Curtis Roebuck to create Sears, Roebuck and Company. To access more consumers, they soon began distributing mail order catalogues throughout the rural United States. The article discussed how the company, close to "the heart of rural America," had been partly responsible for effecting uniformity in US living standards by bringing city refinements to the farm. Through its catalogues, farm families had access not just to the items necessary for farm life but also to items such as watches, sewing machines, furniture, dishes, baby carriages, bicycles, musical instruments, clothing, and shoes. The article noted that Sears had attracted men at first with the sale of hard goods such as tools, but soon, with the availability of attractive soft goods such as clothing, they lured in the entire family. Sears was also able to forecast trends and adapt its operations to capitalize on them. For example, during the 1920s, Sears recognized the narrowing gap between urban and rural life. With the increased affordability and accessibility of the automobile, rural farmers could travel easily, and some moved permanently to the city. As a result, Sears expanded its catalogue operation to include retail stores, and by 1959 it operated 730 of them globally. Prices were guaranteed to be "below all others" and unhappy customers were assured refunds. These principles were reflected in the Sears maxim to "treat people fairly and generously and their response will be fair and honest and generous." The success of Sears was clearly based on its capitalist formula. This included competitive prices; proper advertising; good public relations, particularly in rural communities, positive employee relations that included savings, profit sharing and pension funds, and advancement opportunities, innovations and expansion. According to the article, the "Sears formula" worked. While Sears had started by serving rural customers, it now served primarily urban ones. According to the article, Sears had not only grown with the country, it had also "changed with the country." Three of the article's six pages showcased the vast array of items available in the Sears catalogue for the ordinary American, regardless of location, to purchase. They included household items to satisfy the interests of every member of the family, including power drills, sewing machines, accordions, and bicycles. A postwar Sears catalogue would not have been complete without America's most desired technological device: the television set. The final page of the article was even more impressive, with a full-colour page of modern fashions for the entire family.[61]

September 1960's "Woolworth's House of Pennies" similarly discussed another rural retailer turned discount department store giant, one that went on to become the world's largest chain with thirty-three hundred stores. The store thrived under the ingenuity of Frank Winfield Woolworth, the son of a Utica, New York, farmer. As a young man, Woolworth recognized the reluctance of farmers to travel to the city to shop, and in 1879, he opened his first store in Lancaster,

Pennsylvania. His intention was to fill it with affordable "five and ten cent" merchandise that could be touched or examined. Woolworth's literal hands-on approach proved to be a success. According to the article, as Woolworth's stores started to carry more expensive merchandise and expanded to larger cities and around the world, business boomed. Connecting capitalist principles with democratic values, the article portrayed Woolworth's as a "community asset." Woolworth's provided local residents not just with employment opportunities but also with a tax base that supported local government and schools; it encouraged its employees to volunteer, and funds from its national budget were specifically earmarked for local civic projects.[62] In other words, these were not the corrupt bosses seen in Soviet depictions of capitalist greed, but caring, community-minded business owners. Increased profits on the part of companies were reflected in increased benefits for labour and wider communities, and the overall happiness of all. The number and variety of articles devoted both to the history of retailing and the female shopping experience demonstrate the points that Thompson regularly drove home in the *Ladies' Home Journal*. First, that successful retail in the United States was rooted in capitalist values, namely the ability to open private businesses, nurture their expansion, and watch them flourish for the benefit of all in the free-market economy; and second, that shopping was an inherently democratic experience, catering to all individuals, but women in particular, regardless of their location and socio-economic status. In the postwar marketplace, customer satisfaction was integral to the success of the retailer.[63]

Amerika featured another distinctly American method of shopping that directly coincided with the rise of the suburbs, the creation of sprawling communities of single-family homes, and the increased popularity of the automobile: the shopping mall. Cohen has discussed the shopping mall as another symbol of the American Dream. Built on the fringes of cities, it fuelled the mass consumption of the postwar era because it gave suburban women greater opportunity to purchase products, access to part-time and seasonal employment, and the ability to spend quality time with their families and socialize with others.[64] By the 1950s, a visit to the urban department store was still seen as an occasional "treat" for a woman; however, a visit to the suburban shopping mall and the department stores that anchored them became a regular occurrence for the middle-class suburban housewife who favoured convenience. Further, in keeping with the pronatalist ideology of the postwar era, the shopping mall was geared towards the entire family. Across the country, downtown department stores in major cities such as Detroit, Pittsburgh, Boston, Chicago, and New York began to shut their doors in response to middle-class Americans' mass exodus to the suburbs.[65] Articles in *Amerika* continued to highlight prominent American department stores, but emphasized that, in light of suburban growth, shopping excursions were no longer just an urban luxury.[66] These department stores were adapting to the needs of the marketplace and quickly followed Americans to the suburbs. April 1958's "City of Stores for the Suburbs" discussed the tremendous popularity of the shopping mall, which offered a vast variety of goods and services to satisfy the entire family's needs in one convenient location. It drew on the example of the Seven Corners Shopping Center in Fairfax County, Virginia, which in 1956 became the first mall to open in suburban Washington, DC. At 600,000 square feet, it had forty-seven air-conditioned stores and 2,500 parking spaces. Aerial photographs (figure 5.9) of the mall showed an expansive property filled with vehicles, undoubtedly driven by women eager to shop in the company of their children.

The reader was taken on a tour of the centre that included its largest store, Woodward and Lothrop, a department store chain based in Washington, DC, with four floors and ninety departments.[67] Additionally, the centre contained a supermarket, drug store, flower shop, beauty salon, barber shop, tailor, laundry service, and shoe and watch repair departments. For a comfortable shopping experience, the centre provided spaces to rest, a cafeteria, escalators, and air conditioning. A woman, and possibly her family, could spend virtually an entire day in the centre and never be compelled to leave. The article compared shopping at Seven Corners to the excitement of a "rural county fair or an Oriental bazaar," but with the comforts of modern technology. It indicated that families viewed a trip to the centre as a "holiday excursion" (figures 5.10 and 5.11).

Shopping malls were a new development but appeared to represent the future of shopping in the United States. While they did not exist in the Soviet Union, the USIA hoped that Russian women would admire these large shopping spaces with their abundance of goods and services conveniently located under one roof. To further their appeal, *Amerika*'s articles showed shopping malls as family-oriented spaces where women were able to bring their children. Figure 5.11, for example, contrasts with Capa's 1947 image of the Moscow department store, which showed only adults. While Americans imagined that this Moscow department store reflected the lonely Russian woman's exhausting pursuit of expensive consumer goods, the shopping malls in *Amerika* appeared as sites of relaxation,

Figure 5.9. This image of the Seven Corners Shopping Center in Arlington County, Virginia, with the majority of its 2,500 parking spots full, showed Russian readers the popularity of shopping centres. Further, it reinforced the notion that vehicles were accessible to and affordable for the masses. Original caption: Seven Corners Shopping Center, with its 2,500 parking spots, in Arlington County, Virginia. *Amerika*, April 1958.

affordability, and family. In reality, however, the sheer size and dominating presence of shopping malls on the suburban landscape may have seemed unrealistic for a Russian audience that lived either in the city or countryside – with nothing in between – and rarely owned a vehicle.

Amerika's editors certainly promoted this consumption-oriented lifestyle, but, as they did with images of women, they attempted to strike a balance, going to great lengths to assure readers that Americans still knew the value of hard work and a dollar, thus attempting to defy the stereotype that Americans were frivolous in their lifestyles and approaches to spending. February 1959's "Four Family Budgets" documented four families from across the country to see how each lived and spent their money. The Goodhues of Vermont, the Hallwells of Florida, the Hazis of Indiana, and the Smiths of Colorado were selected for their similarities, including their number of children and annual family income – seventy-five hundred dollars, an amount selected because it reflected an average family income. Each

Figure 5.10. The main floor of a department store, with its variety of consumer goods, showed Russian readers the abundance that was available in America. Original caption: Main floor of four-storey department store sells clocks, jewellery, silverware, handbags, cosmetics, leather goods. *Amerika*, April 1958.

family believed they had achieved the "good life," and throughout the article, they demonstrated the various ways in which they spent their hard-earned money.[68] Of the four families, the Hallwells and the Hazis led the most extravagant lifestyles. The former owned a sixteen-thousand-dollar home with a swimming pool, while the latter readily borrowed money for new household items. In contrast, the Goodhues and Smiths were thrifty, the former saving one thousand dollars per year and the latter saving by fixing up their house themselves, purchasing discounted appliances, and sewing their own clothing. The article depicted all four families, regardless of their spending, as epitomizing the American Dream. All had a home, at least one car, and a television. Similarly, May 1959's the "Great Shopping Game" included a personal account by a typical husband and father, Carl Rieser, on how his Connecticut family went shopping. Rieser began with the annual "pilgrimage" that millions of Americans took each year – back-to-school shopping. Rieser emphasized

Figure 5.11. Unlike *Ladies' Home Journal* images of Soviet females shopping on their own, this one showed a woman conveniently shopping with her children. The message was clear: in the US mall shopping was a family affair. Original caption: Women who make their own slipcovers or curtains head for the fabric store. Materials include chintz, damask, brocade. *Amerika*, April 1958.

his wife's central role in this process, one in which she reviewed catalogues months in advance, compared prices, and took note of new styles and colours before planning a day trip into New York City to make her purchases. Her trip was capped off with a meal and an excursion to a play, movie, or art exhibit. Mrs. Rieser's annual trip was supplemented with smaller trips throughout the year to the local shopping mall in her suburban community. Mr. Rieser explained the concept of instalment buying, the ease of exchanging items, and the shopping possibilities available for car owners. In addition to shopping, the Riesers made use of modern services that came right to their door, including egg delivery, a laundry service, and garbage collection. His account showed the myriad ways in which retailers conveniently served the American consumer.[69]

These articles highlight the extent to which *Amerika*'s editors followed USIA guidelines in their magazine's content. As the USIA articulated in 1959, its goal was to portray the American woman's "devotion to family, womanliness and industriousness."[70] *Amerika*'s articles and images of American women enthusiastically reflected this domestic ideology. American women were to be shown in their "typical activities and attitudes."[71] Seemingly happy housewives and mothers were consistently portrayed in the home, surrounded by their children, and occasionally even assisted by their "helpful" husbands. When they ventured outside of the home, they were shown engaging in tasks that could be considered an extension of home life, such as shopping for their families. Nonetheless, *Amerika* did, in fact, showcase women working, as the USIA had advised in 1959. However, they were most often seen in traditionally female occupations. Further, if "career girls" were pictured on the job, the images were frequently juxtaposed with images of their families, thus allowing the Russian reader to see that the family remained their top priority. The postwar American woman was connected to postwar notions of mass consumption, which *Amerika*'s articles discussed at length. An abundance of goods and services, as well as the brick-and-mortar stores that housed them, showed that mass production and consumption were intended to make the lives of American women more convenient and fulfilling. As fashion and accessories were intended to make women appear and feel more feminine, items such as the latest kitchen appliances, home décor, and furniture, vehicles, and suburban homes were intended to make them content in their roles as housewives and mothers. All were intended to show Russian women that, regardless of their age or status, an abundant consumer culture could alleviate their burdens and make their lives more satisfying.

In effect, whether or not Russian women knew it at the time, USIA officials and *Amerika*'s editors wanted to show them that it was possible to have *options*, and these options should include Americanized notions of what was considered acceptable for women. They wanted them to develop a deep dissatisfaction with their lives, as working women unable to care for their families on a full-time basis, and for their limited access to consumer goods and services. They wanted them to yearn for another life, one based on the US model. *Amerika* conveyed that easy access to consumer goods allowed women to become more feminine, to "catch" husbands, and to lessen their household workloads, thus providing them with more time for their families and other activities. Consumption provided the backdrop for countless articles related to women; even when these articles appeared to focus predominantly on the lives of young women, the family, and the home, elements of mass consumer society were never far behind. These articles contrasted with the limited choices that Russian women supposedly had, in terms of their ability to choose their life paths, as well as to purchase consumer goods. To an extent, the pages of *USSR* appeared to corroborate US government and media claims that Russian women's options were limited, as the magazine rarely depicted women in familial settings. Women were most often shown at work, in the company of adults, or engaged in cultural activities or sports, many of which naturally glorified the Soviet Union in its attempts to spread its own culture. When children were included, they were consistently in nurseries or kindergartens, surrounded by other children or by the women that actually cared for them, ones who were clearly not their mothers. Interestingly, however, even in nurseries, women, never men, were shown as the caregivers of small children. A rare exception was March 1962's "The Male in the Apron," which showed a dishevelled scientist caring for his baby as his wife was writing a paper on volcanoes. While presenting a seemingly progressive portrait of a man caring for his child, with the male author even stating that this was "one of the things our sex has got to get used to" when our wives are busy, he also concluded that "as one man to another, personally I'd feel happier with a woman in the house."[72] While circumstances appeared to have changed for women in the Soviet Union, in many cases they still remained the same. Of course, *USSR* always showed its women as being happy, much as *Amerika* did with its own women. In many cases, *USSR*'s images resemble those of many modern-day women, albeit in different clothing. In the context of the 1950s, these were images that were lauded by the Soviet government, even if they did not always reflect reality and were subject to disapproval by a US government that advocated a pronatalist ideology. For its part, *Amerika* promoted a postwar domestic ideology and consumer culture, both of which were closely intertwined, and appeared to impact all elements of a woman's life. By 1961, and the beginning of a new administration, it appeared that de-Stalinization, the lessening of tensions between the United States and the Soviet Union, and the USIA's overseas information program, of which *Amerika* was a central component, were beginning to have an impact. Russian women knew more about the United States than they ever had before. US officials believed that the cultural programs administered through the USIA, such as *Amerika,* had laid a strong foundation that enabled them to further infiltrate the Soviet Union. These cultural programs provided ordinary Russian women with more stories and images of the United States and its way of life and culture. Ultimately, US officials believed that, moving into the next decade, these programs would give rise to Russians' aspirations for a way of life enhanced by the types of consumer goods and conveniences available in the United States.

Chapter Six

Amerika, USSR, and a Woman's Proper Place in the 1960s

In November 1960, a young, charismatic Democratic senator named John F. Kennedy was elected president of the United States. The liberal ideals associated with his candidacy and his administration signalled the beginning of a new era, one in which women, African Americans, young people, and countless others were inspired to advocate for change and put an end to longstanding systemic discrimination and the conservative values of the previous decade. As early as January 1961, when the newly elected Kennedy graced *Amerika*'s cover, the magazine's content began to reflect this changing political climate. From that point onwards, *Amerika* was more ambiguous in its approach to women; articles devoted to women's traditional roles as housewives, mothers, and consumers were less frequent and enthusiastic than in the period from 1956 to 1960. Articles on women in general were also less frequent. Towards the end of the decade, articles of this nature dropped off almost entirely, as if the magazine's editors were unsure of how, or even if, to address the emerging women's movement. In fact, they did not do so on a large scale until March 1971, when they included a "special report" on the "ideas, look and role of American women." The magazine's approach again proved similar to that of the *Ladies' Home Journal*. In its Winter 1963 issue it had taken the progressive step of publishing an excerpt from Betty Friedan's seminal *Feminine Mystique,* and in June of 1964 devoted a special issue, edited by Friedan, to "A Daring New Concept" for American women. Friedan's "Woman: The Fourth Dimension" argued there was more to life for a woman than her roles as housewife and mother. Rather, women had broken through to another dimension, the "career."[1] However, these articles were a rarity. As Jean E. Hunter notes, because the magazine was plagued by a string of editorial changes and financial troubles at the time, its editors were open to using controversial issues and "attention grabbing gimmicks" to generate headlines and increase revenue. They did not mean that the magazine would go on to actively promote women's rights. Subsequent issues contained letters to the editor, as well as feature articles, that expressed opposition to its special issue. *Ladies' Home Journal* editors stood firmly on the fence, refusing to support either side, and in the process ignoring the burgeoning feminist movement.[2]

Throughout the 1960s, *Amerika* displayed this same ambiguity towards women, albeit in a way that took into account US foreign policy objectives and the negative ramifications of supporting the antiwar movement before a foreign audience. The magazine still contained articles on marriage, motherhood, and the family, but they were less frequent than in the past, and shorter in length. July 1961's "They Met in Moscow" told the love story of Sam Driver and Claire de Saint-Phalle, who had met at the American National Exhibition and married on their return to the United States.[3] It was not until January 1968 that another wedding was included in the magazine. "Wedding Bells of America" depicted the wedding day of Mary Wingire, *Amerika*'s picture editor. The article was only one page long, and it had a dual purpose; it gave readers a look at an American wedding as well as the people who put the magazine together.[4] Articles on the role of the housewife and mother were few and far between. March 1968's "Housewife on the Go" told the story of Mrs. Gil Truax, of Fairbault, Minnesota, who, according to the article, successfully juggled several different roles, and thrived on the demanding pace she set for herself.[5] Farm women were featured on two occasions, but, unlike June 1957's lengthy "Farm Wife," these articles did not focus on the family. July 1961's "Farm Women's Festival" showed farm women at the San Luis Obispo Fair in California, participating in lighthearted contests that included butter churning, cake baking, and even nail driving.[6] July 1962's "Women of the American Farm" portrayed diverse groups of women of various ages and geographical regions "living on the land." This article was notable because the images were taken by well-known photographer Dorothea Lange and included – a rarity for *Amerika* – an image of an African American woman. The article noted that these were not "well-advertised women of fashion" but women who exhibited a "great American style."[7]

Articles about the home also appeared less frequently throughout the decade. March 1961's "Facts about the US: The American Home" provided images and statistics on the "average" American home, depicting it as spacious, with room for a yard and garden.[8] November 1962's "Shopping for a New House" documented Ken and Carol Barnhart's "exasperating and exciting" search for a larger home for their growing family. The magazine included images of the twenty-four spacious homes they viewed in the suburb of Burbank, California, each one with at least three bedrooms, two bathrooms, a lawn, and a driveway. Most important to Carol was the kitchen ("it's where I live"); with its own eating space, it was a "delight." The article concluded by showing the happy couple standing on the front porch of their new home overlooking Burbank, declaring that it was a "luxury," and that they would never move again.[9] March 1964's issue contained a "special survey" on architecture, and included articles on the home, as it profiled a suburban San Francisco community and provided data on homeownership.[10] March 1965's "A Place of Our Own" featured the Switzer family, who, after eight years in an apartment, had moved to a home in Strathmore, New Jersey, a "pleasant" suburb with schools, churches, shopping centres, and recreation areas. Images showed the Switzers and their three children, like the Barnharts, moving into and enjoying their spacious new home, lawn, and driveway.[11] In the pages of *Amerika*, the detached, nuclear family home still presented the ideal form of living, but throughout this decade it was shown less frequently to the Russian reader.

Food production, consumption, and preparation were also less prominent in the magazine than in the previous decade. But articles focused on various conveniences that allowed women to spend less time in the kitchen. For example, October 1966's "Ready-made Pastries with Homemade Taste" featured the Sara Lee factory in Deerfield, Illinois. It stated that Sara Lee's baked goods tasted "every bit as good as mother used to make" but did not require time-consuming preparation.[12] September 1968's "There's a Factory in the Kitchen" noted that households across the country benefited from increasingly popular convenience foods because they allowed families to spend less time in the kitchen and more time on activities outside the home.[13] May 1969's "Technology Takes the Package" discussed the increasing efforts of food manufacturers to create modern packaging that was not only convenient but also appealing to the consumer. According to the article, items such as easy-open and -close containers, individual portions packages, and cook-in packages were enticing to housewives and allowed even those who only knew how to boil water to easily make a "fancy" vegetable dish.[14] January 1964's special issue on agriculture extended to food consumption, and convenience. "Grocery Chain Brings Food to Market" centred on A&P, noting that both the city dweller and suburban housewife were only minutes away from produce fresh from the farm. "Mrs. Dixon Buys Her Groceries" described Nancy Dixon's convenient once per week trip to her local Super Giant Market in Glen Burnie, Maryland, where for only thirty dollars she could shop for her entire family of five.[15] Similarly, March 1967's "What Do Americans Eat?" profiled the McIntyres, a family of six from Silver Spring, Maryland, and their trips to the supermarket, daily routines of breakfast, lunch, and dinner, and entertaining. The article still centred on Marie's role as a housewife, but also presented grocery shopping and meal preparation as a team effort, with her helpful sons carrying home groceries, and her husband barbecuing in their backyard.[16]

As in the past decade, this consumption-oriented focus extended into fashion and accessories.[17] The magazine continued to include pieces on both timeless and seasonal clothing, but by the end of the decade it began to highlight modern, and frequently controversial, fashions. May 1966's "No Blues for Jeans" showcased the casual trend that American youth had recently and eagerly embraced: blue jeans.[18] Their inclusion in the pages of *Amerika* was particularly noteworthy. While the article itself was not geared towards women in particular, historians have noted that they were the first article of Western clothing that Russian youth eagerly embraced en masse. Their enthusiastic adoption of jeans, along with rock 'n' roll, symbolized their acceptance of an exciting and abundant Western culture, one that vastly differed from their own.[19] The article noted that jeans were indeed the "Great American Leveler," as they were worn by "millionaires, movie stars and mechanics alike." Reflecting on their recent popularity, it stated that they were a favourite souvenir of foreigners after visiting America.[20] Also emerging in popularity during the decade was the risqué miniskirt. November 1966's "Short and Snappy" and August 1967's "High Style – Then and Now" showcased this latest fashion trend, one that had alarmed older generations and yet won the hearts of young women. The former referred to it as "trim as a tutu and twice as sassy" and called it the "big fashion news for today's cool young swingers."[21] Indeed, it included three young, attractive women modelling this new article of clothing and accessorizing it with coats, gloves, boots, and jewellery (figure 6.1). These images were a bold deviation from the conservative long, full skirts previously shown in the pages of *Amerika* (see figure 4.4).

Amerika's articles once again highlighted US clothing manufacturing and the extent to which it met the needs of the consumer. November 1964's "Behind the Scenes of Fashion" discussed the Butte Knitting Division of Jonathan Logan, the largest US manufacturer of women's ready-to-wear clothing. The article noted that by consolidating its supplies and operations, including fabric and tailoring, the plant could respond quickly to consumer reaction, increasing "production on winners and stopping output on duds."[22] As in the past, *Amerika* continued to showcase the convenient but complex locations where women could purchase these items. Articles on US retail giants, as well as the

В моде все возможно: это белое замшевое пальто оказалось длиннее клетчатого, желтого с красным, платья. Впрочем, и оно настолько коротко, что прохожий невольно обернется.

Этот наряд вызовет укоризненный взгляд матери, но зато доставит большое удовольствие дочке. Белые сапожки и коричневый с клетчатым воротником жакет выглядят чрезвычайно эффектно.

Figure 6.1. These images of the miniskirt, the latest trend in young women's fashion, deviated from the traditionally long, full skirts that had been depicted in *Amerika* since its inception. Irving Penn, *Amerika*, November 1966.

suburban shopping mall, showed Russian readers the abundance available to the American consumer, frequently under one roof. December 1961's "Shoppers' Mecca" took the reader behind the scenes of a modern department store, Macy's.[23] February 1969's "How the World's Number One Retailer Got to the Top" attributed Sears, Roebuck and Co's eight-billion-dollar earnings to intense brand merchandizing, an extensive catalogue, a loyalty program, and exclusive products sold under the Sears brand name.[24] December 1964's "The Magic of Store Windows" showed Russian women brightly coloured window displays that included home settings, kitchen appliances, table settings, clothing, and accessories. For *Amerika*'s editors, dazzling displays of well-arranged products were just as important as the products themselves. In that vein, May 1969's issue included articles that highlighted the importance of "packaging" in appealing to consumer needs. February 1967's "Finding Out What the Consumer Really Wants" examined the rise of market research, as companies increasingly attempted to understand the mind of the consumer. It noted that for consumers, the decision-making process was a multifaceted one that included factors such as performance, quality, price, convenience, aesthetic appeal, and, at times, emotional considerations, including self-enhancement, popularity, and social identity. The article attempted to put a positive spin on what readers may have perceived as manipulative tactics to lure in consumers, by noting that the purpose of consumer research was to "find out what the consumer really wants." According to the article, American consumers had many choices, and most successful US businesses were not built on advertising, which Americans had become "resistant to," but rather on consumer satisfaction and repurchase.[25] In that same month, "The Lure and Fascination of Seven Fabulous Stores" featured stores ranging in size and geographical location. The article noted that they were "great," not because of their prices or range of wares, but rather because they turned the "simple act of shopping into a real event." The people who ran them created an aura that made a trip to that store as "thrilling as a safari."[26] Similarly, "Tyson's Corner: Everything and Anything in One Package" centred on what it referred to as the largest single level shopping centre in the world, located in the suburb of Mclean, Virginia. The article compared the centre to a bazaar, and noted that its 125 stores under one roof, convenient services, highway access, and free parking drew in an "audience" from surrounding states. In other words, the centre was "packaged" so as to lure in the female shopper and entice her to stay for the entire day.[27]

Undoubtedly, the most notable change in *Amerika*'s approach during the decade was in relation to working women. While these articles still leaned conservative, they were more varied and frequent than other types of articles about, or geared towards, women. They were also ambiguous in their tone, on the one hand showcasing women in traditionally feminine roles and, on the other hand in male-dominated ones. Articles showcased both ordinary and extraordinary working women. Many were still relegated to occupations that were deemed acceptable for women, such as teacher, nurse, nun, flight attendant, garment worker, fitness instructor, dancer, singer, songwriter, designer, model, and actress.[28] However, women were also shown in non-traditional roles, in one instance each as a logger, a scientist, a heart surgeon, and a businesswoman. That said, in all cases, hints of traditionalism continued. For example, an article on Polish-immigrant-turned-business-mogul Helena Rubenstein presented her as the head of a global cosmetics empire tasked with a specific goal: to make women look and feel beautiful.[29] On four occasions, *Amerika* showcased female politicians or women associated with politics because of the men in their lives. September 1962's "The Lady Is a Senator" featured Gloria Schaffer, a state senator from Connecticut. The article referred to Schaffer, an accomplished woman in her own right, as both "Mrs. Eugene Schaffer" and a housewife, and stated that since her election she had learned to juggle a "daily schedule of domestic and legislative duties." September 1965's "Congresswoman from Hawaii" focused on Patsy Mink, June 1962's issue on First Lady Jacqueline Kennedy, and June 1965's issue on First Daughter Lucy Baines Johnson.[30] June 1964's "Mother Goes Back to School" reflected the new opportunities available to American women as it discussed a growing trend in the United States: the housewife's return to school. It depicted Mrs. Jane McKinlay of Minneapolis, one of six hundred housewives who were returning to school as part of the "University of Minnesota Plan" to draw women into post-secondary education. The article, however, made sure to note that these women returned to school only when their children reached school age.[31] The article that deviated most from *Amerika*'s conservative postwar stance was April 1961's "TV's Nancy Hanschman." The magazine noted that Hanschman, at age thirty-four, had a "dream of a career" as a political reporter and that her covering the 1960 presidential election reflected new opportunities for women in journalism. Unlike other articles, it did not discuss her feminine characteristics, domestic capabilities, or relationships, except to say that she was single.[32] Progress was made in reflecting real women's diverse lives and roles, but this progress was slow. October 1961's issue contained just its third article entirely on an African American female, when it profiled gospel singer Mahalia Jackson in "She Sings from the Heart."[33] It was not until July 1968 when it published its fourth, on fashion designer Ellen Stewart, in "One Intense Woman against the Tide."[34] There was not a single instance of the magazine featuring an ordinary African American woman.

However, this decade was a notable one for *Amerika* due to its increased concentration on African Americans as a whole, their status in society, continued racial discrimination, and the growing civil rights movement. These subjects had long been neglected in the magazine, but appeared more frequently in accordance with Kennedy's foreign policy objectives.[35] As Thomas Borstelmann notes, the African American and African freedom movements of the decade encouraged and reinforced each other. He argues that changes in Kennedy's approach towards the domestic civil rights movement were borne out of Cold War necessity, namely his desire to support decolonization in Africa in order to prevent the spread of communism on the continent. If racial inequality continued unabated, it could undermine US efforts to recruit Cold War allies and promote US models of democracy.[36] Indeed, during the decade, Kennedy was cautious in escalating his efforts to support the civil rights movement so as not to alienate southern segregationists; at the same time, he strengthened his relationships with Africa's nationalist leaders. Accordingly, *Amerika* began spotlighting African Americans more frequently, including well-known figures such as Rev. Dr. Martin Luther King Jr., actor Sidney Poitier, writer Ralph Ellison, jazz musician Louis Armstrong, and actress Diahann Carroll, who also appeared on May 1965's cover.[37] Other articles began to address the growing efforts of African Americans to end racial discrimination and violence. This editorial move may have appeared risky given the Soviet tendency to use US racial tensions to its advantage, but it was done carefully. Each of these articles addressed the issue, but consistently ended on a positive note in an effort to signal the progress the country was making. December 1961's issue provided its first direct acknowledgment of the US civil rights movement. "Civil Rights: The Strongest Revolt" noted that African Americans were waging a revolution without arms and barricades in the faith that the country would peacefully give them the full human rights to which the US "had always been committed."[38] In December 1962's "The American Negro and the Law," Arthur E. Sutherland, a constitutional law professor at Harvard, discussed civil rights and the legal methods which African Americans had used in their quest for equality.[39] February 1964's "Interview with a Civil Rights Leader, Roy Wilkins" was the first to depict a noted civil rights leader. This interview with Wilkins, the executive director of the National Association for the Advancement of Colored People (NAACP), pointed to the progress African Americans had made in the previous three decades. Wilkins appeared optimistic, noting that he hoped African Americans were on their way to achieving equal rights, and that recent demonstrations should be viewed not as the "result of desperation, but of rising expectations."[40] May 1964's "Ferment on the Campus: Civil Rights" acknowledged increased dissent on school campuses, noting that beginning with lunch counter sit-ins, students were increasingly devoting themselves to bringing down barriers to racial equality.[41] However, it was October 1964's issue that was most noteworthy. In honour of the June 1964 signing of the Civil Rights Act, *Amerika*'s first sustained attempt to address the civil rights movement was seen in a special thirty-five-page report called "Equal Rights for All," on the "effort to wipe out racial discrimination" in the United States.[42] The front cover showed a close-up of a female African American civil rights demonstrator surrounded by protest signs. However, the report's articles once again addressed racial discrimination in such a way that simultaneously emphasized US progress. Though "1954–1964: A Chronology" acknowledged the racial struggles of the past, it attempted to downplay the violence associated with the movement. It indicated that although these dramatic outbreaks were generating headlines, the less publicized "quiet constructive actions" were more common. "Civil Rights: The Continuing Struggle" reinforced this notion, as it depicted the "peaceful" struggle for civil rights, stating that US history had been characterized by a "series of peaceful revolutions," all of which ended by "incorporating another formerly underprivileged ethnic, racial or social group into the mainstream of national life." According to the article, the time had come for the African American to "join his predecessors."[43]

Later articles began focusing more heavily on the civil rights movement and racial discrimination, with its detrimental effects on society. July 1967's "Civil Rights 1967 – The Tough Phase Begins" was perhaps the most glaring admission on the part of the magazine that African Americans were frustrated, even angry, with the lack of progress. It noted that the quest for social, political, and economic equality had only just begun.[44] The issue also included "Other Voices, Other Views," which noted the different outlooks that civil rights organizations had embraced in recent months. It attributed this diversity of opinion to the goals and methods of the movement, and to its increasing strength and vitality.[45] June 1968's issue included "The Troubled Road to Equality," "The Nature of the Ghetto Crisis," "Cooling Down the Cities," and "Little Rock Revisited: Desegregated but Not Integrated." In light of Dr. King's recent assassination, these articles addressed his death, the complexity of the civil rights movement, and recent riots that had engulfed urban communities.[46] By August 1969, when "Black Power and White Liberals" appeared, the magazine had finally admitted to Russian readers that African American anger at the slow pace of change had forced many in the civil rights movement to become more radicalized. In the article, Congress of Racial Equality (CORE) founder and director James Farmer boldly wrote that in the face of a new separatist movement, white liberals would need to accept a more modest role in the civil rights movement than they had held in the past.[47]

Amerika became more progressive in its content during the 1960s, particularly in addressing racial inequality, but this did not extend to addressing gender inequality. While the status of women was largely ignored by *Amerika* throughout the decade, its counterpart, *USSR*, devoted its entire March 1962 issue to women.[48] This move was highly unusual, but timely, given the USIA's recent focus on conveying the "special status" of American women to their Russian counterparts, through its own magazine as well as the American National Exhibition. *USSR*'s initial issues focused on a multitude of topics related to what it referred to as "current events of major importance" in the country, as well as the lives of its people. News stories on the Communist Party Congresses, the reorganization of industrial management, virgin land cultivation, the seven-year plan for economic development, cuts in the armed forces, the new pension system, the abolition of income tax, cuts in the workday without pay reduction, and improvements in the education system were all covered. Other stories focused on specific factories, collective farms, cities, and republics, as well as the activities of young people, their schooling, and leisure time.[49] All of these articles related the lives of men and women to the broader Soviet system, only occasionally focusing solely on women. In contrast, March 1962's cover boldly included eleven colour images of Russian women, in distinctive dress, and seemingly of different backgrounds and occupations (figure 6.2).

Articles included "Our Women," "Three Questions for Soviet Women," "Beauty Salon," "Special for Women," and "Spring Fashions."[50] Other articles highlighted working women, including "Hamro Tairova," a feature on a typical woman of the Central Asian Republics, "Puppeteer," which showcased puppet designer Yekaterina Bekleshova, "Novelist," on Antonina Koptyayeva, and "Women in Sports," on female college-aged athletes.[51] "Our Women" was the issue's feature piece and its lengthiest at five pages. It began by offering American readers insight into the unique outlook the Soviet Union had towards women:

> It is simpler by far to offer a woman a seat in a bus than in a national legislature, to kiss a woman's hand than to give those hands work worthy

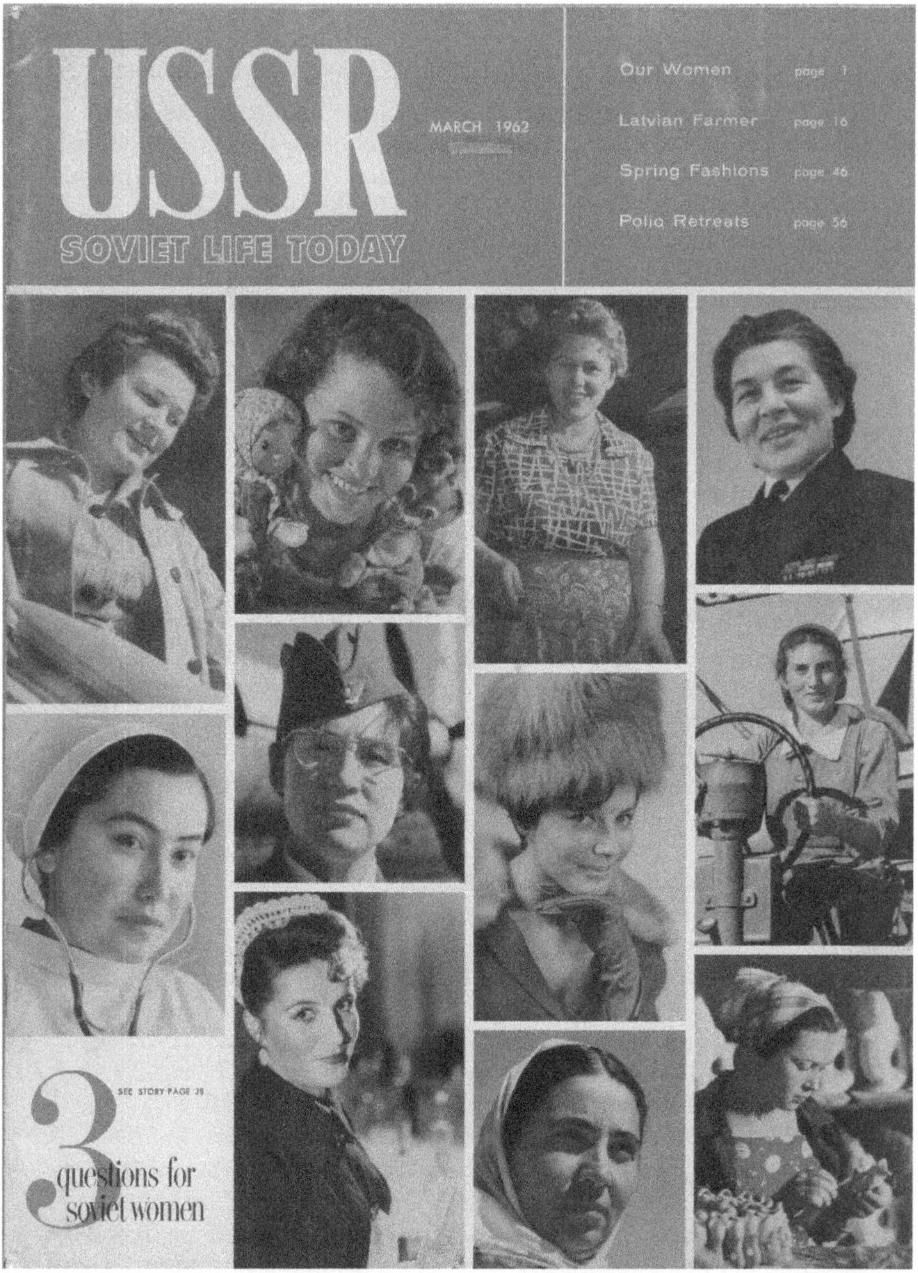

Figure 6.2. This *USSR* cover showcased the working women of the Soviet Union and included their diverse occupations that ranged from medicine to crane operating to modelling. *USSR*, March 1962.

of them – and pay for the labor at the same wage rate as a man gets. To do the first you merely have to be a well-bred person; to do the second, you must be a citizen of a civilized and genuinely democratic state. The "gallantry" of a society is measured not simply by its courtesies but by this essential criterion – whether the society gives its women equal rights with its men, gives them the material requisites, the respect, the motivation to develop their spiritual, vocational and civic capacities. Nor does the modern woman lose any of her feminine graces when she regards just and equal law as more important than serenades and madrigals.[52]

The message conveyed to the reader was clear: in spite of the Western Cold War language that suggested otherwise, the Soviet Union was more democratic than the United States because it provided its women with equal rights rather than the "special privileges" that emphasized their differences. According to *USSR*, Russian women were equal to men in all capacities: in employment, salaries, and education. They were given "equal opportunity in all economic, scientific, cultural and political spheres; and an equal right to elect and be elected to any public office." The article noted that Russian women held an honoured position in building and maintaining the socialist state. They fought alongside men in the revolution and against fascists during the war, and had rebuilt villages and cities after it. They made up 47 per cent of the workforce and worked in fields, automobile plants, universities, government, and the arts. They were everywhere and were the pride of the nation. According to *USSR*, these strides were possible due to the "socialist laws" that guaranteed women full equality, the opportunities presented to them, and their progressive social attitudes.[53] The article confirmed that many women were indeed happy with their "outside jobs" and believed that those jobs made a "larger social contribution than keeping house or raising children."[54] This, of course, contrasted with *Amerika*'s content, which frequently suggested that a woman's most important job was that of housewife and mother. According to *USSR*, women in the Soviet Union could no longer be called the "weaker sex."[55] It also countered US conceptions of Russian women by referring to them as both modern and feminine, and indicated that they now had more options as consumers.

In honour of their "hard work and loyalty," the article iterated that the Soviet government strove to give women a more prosperous and happy life, part of which lay in the production and availability of consumer goods. For example, in spite of Khrushchev's kitchen debate claims that convenient household items were unnecessary in the homes of working Russian women, and certain ones even made them lazier, the Soviet government was producing more appliances, including refrigerators, washing machines, and vacuum cleaners. Retail stores stocked more items that "appealed to women" and new women's shops and beauty salons opened frequently.[56] "Special for Women" and "Beauty Salon" highlighted these new consumer outlets and services available to Russian women in recent years. "Special for Women" depicted a new Moscow department store specifically for women that had opened in October 1961. It resembled urban American department stores seen in *Amerika*, such as Marshall Field's or J.L. Hudson's, albeit on a much smaller scale. The store contained several clothing departments, including "ready-made"; "semi-finished," which offered clothing in need of alterations; and "made to order." This last department is notable, given that Russian women had begun to replicate Western styles of dress. Russian women could bring to the "made-to-order" department images and patterns of the clothing and fashions seen in *Amerika* or Western fashion magazines. The article noted, however, that this department was often reserved for the "fussy." Resembling the ease and comfort of US retail outlets, the store employed helpful salesclerks and comfortable armchairs and fashion magazines for women who wanted to rest and read. According to the store's manager the store had become "very popular with the ladies." The article was accompanied by seven black-and-white images depicting the store's exterior, as well as women examining products such as clothing, hats, and jewellery, as well as women resting.[57] "Spring Fashions" was the only article in the issue to consist entirely of colour images. The article showcased six women in various styles of dress suitable for spring, a time when, as the article noted, a "multitude of colours come to life." It indicated that when creating women's clothing, designers at the All-Union House of Fashions kept both beauty and comfort in mind. Items were geared to the season, and as a result, unpredictable Soviet springs necessitated costumes for warm, cold, and rainy days. The fashions, however, while more modern than the clothing described by the American women who had visited and lived in the Soviet Union, failed to appear as colourful, diverse, or modern as US fashions. With the exception of a red raincoat, none reflected the bright colours of the season, and appeared in shades of black, beige, and green. All consisted of skirts or dresses to the knee, and none reflected recent trends in American women's attire, such as shorts or slacks.[58] In fact, *USSR* rarely, if ever, showed women in such untraditional clothing. Throughout this issue, the only time women appeared in pants was while engaged in factory work.

Western influence was also apparent in the new services offered to Russian women. "Beauty Salon" depicted a Moscow salon where women could receive a facial, hair treatment, manicure, or pedicure. The article noted that beauticians put in an extraordinary amount of effort to emphasize each women's facial features and make them look beautiful; customers left satisfied, walking out of the salon with their heads held high. The popularity of the beauty salon was clear, as the article indicated that long lines were the norm, and it was particularly busy at lunch and after work hours. Five black-and-white images of seemingly satisfied women getting their hair, makeup, and nails done were included.[59] Ironically, this issue, as the *Amerika* of the 1950s did, clearly attempted to strike a balance in its images of women. Russian women's equal status and work ethic were emphasized along with their desire to appear feminine and have access to more products and services. At the same time that *USSR* lauded the equal status of Russian women and showed pride in their work ethic, it attempted to show these women in a different light: they were now also living in a country that provided them with the modern luxuries they coveted (figure 6.3).

Perhaps *USSR*'s most telling article, however, was "Three Questions for Women." It asked sixteen women three questions including, "Do you believe the hearth should be a woman's main calling?" "How do you think children should be brought up?" and "What, in your opinion, is beauty in a woman?" The first question appeared to be the most revealing for the purposes of this study, particularly as it related to conceptions of the role of women in society, and how that role contrasted in the United States and the Soviet Union. Of the sixteen women surveyed, four – a biochemist, an actress, and two housewives – responded that the hearth was indeed a woman's main calling. Zinaida Kostina, a thirty-six-year-old housewife believed that every man and woman dreamt of a happy home and hearth. If that did not exist, it was a "woman's fault. She simply never bothered to learn her job as wife and mother." Lydia Serdyuk, a thirty-two-year-old housewife similarly responded that the family was a "woman's basic responsibility." Three women – a sea captain, a senior researcher, and a fashion model – adopted a mixed approach to this question, indicating while the woman was the central figure of the home, her life should also entail work. Two women – an airline hostess and a crane operator – noted that they could not answer properly, as they did not have proper homes; the former had grown up in a children's home and the latter currently lived in a rooming house. Perhaps the most emphatic stances, however, were given by the seven women who associated the home with boredom and monotony. Anastasia Goryushkina, a fifty-five-year-old pensioner, indicated that she had worked while raising her ten children because it was "dull to chain oneself to housework and lose contact with people."

194 Selling Women, Gender, and Consumer Culture

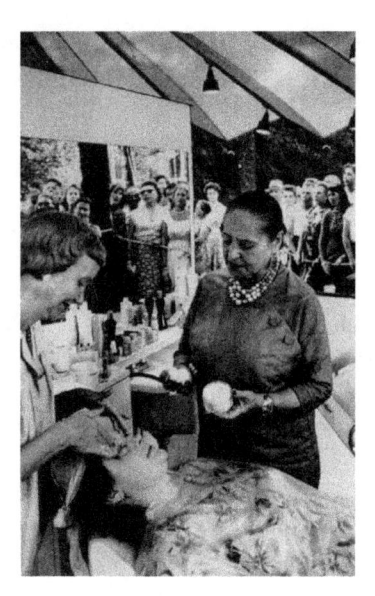

Figure 6.3. Images like this provided legitimacy to the idea that Russian women wanted to be beautiful as much as American women did. This photo shows Russian women waiting in long lines to receive free facial treatments at the Helena Rubenstein exhibit at the American National Exhibition, or looking on. *Life*, 10 August 1959.

Rasia Bobyleva, a thirty-three-year-old architect, noted that she would be unhappy if her life were "limited to the home." Nadezhda Ostrovskaya, a thirty-six-year-old surgeon, declared that she would "find it a bore to sit home and do nothing but keep house." Lydia Tuz, a twenty-three-year-old waitress, responded that to limit one's time and interests to a home and family was dull. It "makes life so monotonous, robs it of all its richness." Zoya Shevchenko, a twenty-five-year-old ceramics artist, indicated that she considered the home "a duty, rather than a calling." Perhaps most boldly, Nina Yevseyeva, a thirty-two-year-old dressmaker, argued for equitable relationships in the home for men and women, indicating that if there was such a "calling for women, it should be the same for men." Similarly, Jemma Khachatryan, a twenty-two-year-old architect, declared that a home and family was "just as much man's calling as woman's" and called for chores to be shared by all members of the family.[60] These responses made it clear that Russian women had diverse opinions and beliefs on the role of women in society. However, the dominant message was that women should develop their own interests and careers outside of their homes. *USSR* was attempting to show American readers that it was not that the home was unimportant, but rather a woman's life could be rich, meaningful, and happy with a home *and* a career, and that this was indeed possible within the Soviet Union.

Meanwhile, it was not until March of 1971 that *Amerika* finally made a bold move of its own, when it devoted thirty-four pages to "changes in the ideas, look and role of American women" (figure 6.4).

Prior to 1971, *Amerika* had devoted partial issues to special topics, including the seemingly non-controversial graphic arts, agriculture, architecture, and industrial design, as well as an entire issue on literature and publishing.[61] In the spirit of the turbulent 1960s, it acknowledged contentious movements on two occasions, in October 1964, with its special report titled "Equal Rights for All," and, in December 1967, with an entire issue devoted to "American youth."[62] However, during that time frame, *Amerika* only touched on the burgeoning women's movement once – in March 1967, when it included "For American Women: The Chance to Choose," written by Eli Ginzberg. A noted Columbia University economics professor and presidential adviser, Ginzberg was a firm believer that the United States lagged behind in its intellectual potential because more than half of the young population, including women, failed to complete college. In "awe" of the masses of Russian women who entered the paid workforce in the postwar period, he believed the United States needed to better utilize its womanpower, particularly in areas such as science and engineering. Coming from a desire to serve the national interest, rather than an acknowledgment of women's growing discontent, he wrote that while the social expectation for a young woman was still that she would marry and raise a family, this was no longer her only acceptable option.[63] Ginzberg's article aside, the decision by *Amerika* to blatantly avoid the discussion of women's rights prior to 1971 was likely intentional. In spite of Nixon's recent embrace of *détente*, a lessening of tensions between the United States and the Soviet Union, the Cold War still raged, and the magazine still acted as a tool of "polite propaganda" for the United States and its foreign policy goals. Devoting space to an article on the rampant gender inequality that existed in the United States could highlight the nation's weaknesses in the face of communist competition.[64] Just as it took the magazine some time to acknowledge the civil rights and youth movements, it was also slow in acknowledging that American women, who supposedly had "special privileges," were dissatisfied and had begun advocating for equal rights themselves.

Figure 6.4. This March 1971 issue of *Amerika*, which featured a special report on women, showed a lone woman standing before a seascape, appearing contemplative and looking ahead as the wind blew into her hair. *Amerika*, March 1971.

The timing of the March 1971 issue was key. In the past decade, civil rights–based movements had shaken the very foundation of the United States. The rise of second wave feminism, beginning with Betty Friedan's 1963 release of *The Feminine Mystique* and the 1966 creation of the National Organization for Women (NOW), had spurred American women to make tremendous political, economic, cultural, and social strides in a short time period.[65] Years after the second wave emerged, the magazine at long last addressed the issue of gender inequality, suggesting that the nation's leaders were rectifying past transgressions and moving forward. Previously, according to the magazine, American women had enjoyed special status, but now that they wanted and were advocating for equality, their government was responding positively to their aspirations. In fact, articles by noted experts in their fields, such as former editor Marion K. Sanders, anthropologist Margaret Mead, and psychologist Eleanor Macoby, implied that if women still experienced inequality, it may actually be *their* fault. In other words, the magazine, like the government that issued it, could feign ignorance to the discontent of Friedan's "happy housewife heroine," proclaim that it was addressing that discontent because women had finally voiced their concerns, and argue that any personal struggle for equality was now the responsibility of the individual. By 1971, it was appropriate, then, that *Amerika* decided to take the approach of devoting a special report to the newly emerging, but often controversial (at least in the United States), issue of women's equality. Failing to address a movement that affected over half of the US population simply would have been untenable. As Bonnie J. Dow has noted, by this point *McCall's*, the most popular women's magazine of the past decade, had a female editor at its helm and had begun to devote editorial content to the movement.[66] However, *Amerika* once again appeared to take its cues from the *Ladies' Home Journal*, which was considerably slower in addressing the movement. Its August 1970 issue contained an eight-page insert entitled "'Women's Liberation' and You: The Special Feminist Section Everyone's Been Talking About," which was only included after one hundred feminists took over its editorial offices on 18 March 1970 for eleven hours. They demanded that editor John Mack Carter be replaced by a woman and an all-female editorial and advertising staff be hired; they also called for an end to exploitative advertising and insisted that a free daycare centre be provided for employees' children.[67] Carter refused these demands, although he promised to consider the daycare centre and allowed the demonstrators to write an eight-page insert for the *Journal*'s August issue, for which he wrote the introduction and referred to the new women's liberation movement as both "daring and bizarre," and speculated that readers might find the section "enlightening, or baffling, or infuriating – or all three." According to him, the *Journal* had permitted these women to express how they felt, and while they did not "agree with many of the assumptions their arguments rested on," in 1970, "all peoples and both sexes are free to re-examine their roles."[68] The insert included six articles which discussed topics such as marriage, housekeeping, sex, work, and education.[69] Carter did not offer a ringing endorsement of the movement, but, as he acknowledged in 1971, "some of the complaints about our magazines made by the women's lib types were right. There has been a lot of silliness cranked out to sell products and lifestyles to women, but it will never happen in this magazine again." By 1972, both *McCall's* and the *Ladies' Home Journal* gave feminists regular columns.[70]

In March 1971, in their introduction to their own special report, *Amerika*'s own editors acknowledged the magnitude of the changes that were taking place:

> We live in a time of accelerating change, a period in which old values are being tested against the realities of the present. This search for "identity," for a meaningful lifestyle, is one in which everyone is involved. The quest is particularly noticeable in the cases of racial or ethnic groups or students, but there is another group which is equally engaged, equally determined to bring about a better way of life for itself. This group is American women. Comprising 51 per cent of the population, the women, like their sisters in many lands, are moving toward a new definition of just what being a woman should mean. And as they raise questions and begin to propound answers, tremors are felt through all of society – for there is no aspect of society that is not affected by what women do and think. In this issue, *America Illustrated* [sic] looks in on some of this ferment: changes in the ideas, look and role of American women.[71]

It should be noted that nowhere here or anywhere else in this issue did *Amerika*'s editors use the words women's movement, feminism, or anything resembling them. Recognizing their decision to address the women's movement directly was a bold one, the magazine apparently still approached the movement with trepidation. However, while *Amerika*'s editors never referred to the movement directly, its contributors did, most notably Sanders, Mead, and Macoby, albeit providing mixed messages about its members, goals, and outcomes. These articles were interwoven with the stories of ordinary women experiencing its effects on their daily lives.

There was nobody more fitting to write this issue's leading article than its first editor, Sanders. Sanders had done much since she left her position in 1952. In that year, she ran for Congress as a Democrat in Rockland County, New York, losing to the incumbent in a heavily Republican area; in 1956, she wrote *Women and the Vote*, a book on women in politics; and in 1958, she because a senior editor at *Harper's Magazine*. Rather ironically, in 1973 she went on to write *Dorothy Thompson: A Legend in Her Time*, the first biography on the legendary journalist and *Ladies' Home Journal* columnist who, in the magazine, had taken an aggressive stance against communism and the Soviet Union.[72] In "American Woman: Her Goals, Her Achievements, Doubts," Sanders attempted to gauge the state of mind of the American woman. She wrote that earlier feminists had "long since" battled many forms of discrimination, including in business, industry, government, and education, and, as a result, women like her combined career and family "without too much difficulty." Seemingly failing to recognize that obstacles to equality still existed, and that she, as a white, middle-class, heterosexual, educated woman had a privileged life, she wrote that the chief obstacle the American woman now faced was not an external barrier (a comment that conveniently appeared to absolve the US government of responsibility for women's unequal status) but rather "something going on in her own head." Women were asking themselves questions such as, "What is the American woman's self-image?" and "What does she want out of life?" She described the dilemma of the modern, middle-aged American woman: in spite of her labour-saving devices and helpful husband, and with the postwar cult of domesticity now receding, she found herself with the desire to re-enter the workforce, particularly as her children grew older, but struggled to find her place within it. Many found that college curriculums were suited to younger students, others opted to work only on a part-time basis, and others simply did not see themselves as "career women." Sanders discussed the ways in which this new movement of young, middle-class, college-educated women was changing American society. Expressing contempt for their mothers' lifestyles, they were waging war against the "remaining vestiges of 'male chauvinism.'" Sanders also discussed the revolutionary aspects of the birth control pill, arguing that it had caused significant changes in sexual attitudes, including a greater emphasis on sex as integral to a loving relationship and the gradual decline of the double standard. Young women, free of unwanted pregnancy, could experiment in their relationships and pursue careers.[73] While Sanders approved of these developments, she argued that this liberated period in a woman's life was limited; once a woman *did* have children, traditional gender norms and values would resurface. According to her, the majority of Americans still believed that a mother's love and care were essential to children, particularly at a young age, and that there was no adequate childcare substitute. As the success of postwar America's pronatalist ideology and coinciding baby boom indicated, and as Inkeles and Bauer's 1959 Harvard study on *The Soviet Citizen* pointed out, there were indeed women who expressed a desire to stay in the home and solely raise their children.[74] However, for the Russian mothers who read this special report and embraced the socialized daycare which allowed them to combine jobs and careers with motherhood, this mindset likely seemed outdated and hypocritical, coming from an author who had combined career and motherhood herself. Sanders also suspected it was unlikely for the marriage and family to go out of style altogether. She argued that while emancipated young women scorned beauty products that defined them as "sex objects," these items were still popular, as were items traditionally associated with the female's role in the home. Further, she posed a counterpoint to the new feminist, arguing that in the United States there was no lack of women who enjoyed their special feminine status in a patriarchal society. These women were content to let their husbands support the family while they cared for their children and tended to their domestic tasks. They also found ample outlets for their energy through their churches, clubs, and community organizations, which, according to Sanders, could not exist without the voluntary labour of "public-spirited housewives."[75] While *Amerika*'s issue on women seemed revolutionary, it walked a fine line as it perpetuated the traditional gender norms it had conveyed in the past. Sanders' article appeared to follow *Amerika*'s editorial line, concluding that American women had more options than ever. Yet she correctly believed they were divided as to their goals and ambitions. She blamed this division squarely on "some" – clearly the feminists she discussed throughout her article, who according to her were "creating a storm" as they struggled with their individual choices.

A second article in this special report was written by renowned anthropologist Margaret Mead. Known for her cross-cultural studies on human behaviour, Mead discussed the "new tide of feminism rising in the United States," and the societal changes its members were demanding. Like Sanders, Mead had successfully combined marriage, motherhood, and a career. And like Sanders, she took an ambiguous stance towards second wave feminism, critiquing its members and purpose but acknowledging its impact. She praised previous generations of feminists, but harshly called "new feminists" "stormy and obstreperous" women who were self-centred, hostile to men, and advocating for "women's rights for women's sake." Their views, perhaps, were a reflection of their similar ages and life circumstances. Mead was born in 1901 and Sanders in 1905, respectively, and they were both white, middle-class, heterosexual, educated women who came of age during and after the first wave, thus witnessing its promises, successes, and failures. According to Mead, this new movement did not have the potential for revolutionary change because women's roles had changed little over time. Societies had always reinforced the belief that women's tasks consisted of maintaining the home, childrearing, and caring for others. While many protested, the penalties given to "headstrong women who follow their own bent carried the message that those who follow the rules are better off." Ultimately, however, what prevented a different future for men and women was the fear of life without a family. She wrote that people look at "individuals without descendants and shudder," and a fear of loneliness was "potent in determining the individual's choice for marriage and a family." According to her, women's wishes for self-determination and personal fulfilment did "not outweigh their need for warmth and intimacy." Regardless of marital or employment status, women thought in terms of basic choices: "public role or private role – which is the more important? In an emergency which would you sacrifice?" "If your child was sick or unhappy, would you leave him in someone else's care?" If your husband's job took him to another country, would you give up a promising career to go with him? Would you go far away from friends and relatives for your career?" Mead determined that most women would put their families first (although she failed to suggest that men would do the same), regardless of career fulfilment. She did acknowledge, however, that some women preferred careers and the work-life balance they offered. Just as Sanders appeared to absolve the government of its long-entrenched role in perpetuating gender inequality, Mead did the same. According to her, for the movement to fulfil its goals, and for women to be treated as full human beings, they needed to look inwards. They needed to restructure how they saw each other and learn to trust and respect one another. This included developing a new regard for women's traditional occupations. She wrote that women were in peculiar positions, on the one hand denigrating the things "they knew best," namely housework, but on the other hand, unwilling to share these tasks with other women. She wrote that in postwar America, wives and mothers reigned over their private households and nuclear families, but in order for women to make careers a viable option, they needed to resign their homemaking roles to other women, particularly those who were professionally trained. They would have to dignify this work and recognize that it involved high-level skills. Only then could women's personal and professional lives grow. In contrast to Sanders,

Mead advocated for the professionalization of homemaking and, in an apparent acknowledgment of the postwar emphasis on masculine domesticity, she recognized that men may take on feminine caretaking roles in the future. She advocated for the nursery school as a modern and liberating system of childcare, for it could set the stage for future change. She described it as a setting which encouraged children to play together, forge new relationships, and take on different roles, regardless of their sex. She argued that the elimination of educational restrictions would ensure more diversified relationships between boys and girls, based on shared interests. These lessons could follow them into adulthood and lead to the lifestyle changes women's liberation groups were advocating.[76] Mead's arguments advocating for the professionalization of housework and use of nursery schools as a means to evoke future change were considered progressive at the time, and appeared to advocate for the socialist model of childcare seen in the Soviet Union.[77]

Eleanor Macoby's "Are Women That Different?" attempted to make further sense of this new movement and the societal debates it had invoked regarding a woman's place. A top child psychology professor at Stanford University and a self-proclaimed feminist, Macoby examined the views of feminists, who believed that biological differences between the sexes were not integral in shaping individual identities, and traditionalists, who argued that women's roles stemmed from their biological nature.[78] She addressed two questions. First, "What are the ways in which the sexes differ?" and second, "Is there any biological necessity behind their norms of behaviour?" Answering the first, she outlined three areas in which American girls and boys supposedly differed. She wrote that, intellectually, girls developed more quickly but, once out of school, their intellectual pursuits declined. Socially, boys were more aggressive and girls were more nurturing. In the area of self-esteem, boys had more confidence than girls did. Macoby noted that these differences could not result solely from a society's treatment of boys and girls, as many of the traits were found in diverse societies around the world. She cited studies done on sex differences in primates which showed that males were more aggressive while females were more nurturing. In one study, pregnant female monkeys received injections of a male hormone, resulting in female offspring that acted aggressively. According to Macoby, biochemical differences between the sexes *did* exist, and they could provide a foundation for temperamental differences, as well as shape individual personalities; there were, however, caveats. She acknowledged that it was possible for a society to create rigid masculine and female stereotypes that could actually produce the behaviour they portrayed. She also noted there were instances when males and females exhibited similar characteristics, encompassing both traditionally masculine and feminine behaviour. For example, popular boys *and* girls tended to be "animated, emotionally secure, busy, full of ideas, and good at doing things," without being pushy or easily angered. For girls, it appeared that competence was not incompatible with likeability; in fact, it was an asset. Into adulthood, there was evidence that active, energetic women with many interests had more affectionate and sexually satisfying relationships. An enduring relationship called for many of the same qualities in both sexes: consideration, warmth, humour, energy, and competence. In contrast to the beliefs of many of the traditionalists she discussed, Macoby wrote that a woman could be successful and independent, and still be feminine. In her concluding statements, Macoby took a more definitive stance on the woman's movement than both Sanders and Mead, acknowledging her own success in combining a career with being a wife and mother of five, and perhaps alluding to her own feminist beliefs. Optimistically, she wrote that modern women were fortunate in having more choices and opportunities than ever before. They could forgo marriage and children and have a career, or combine both. Macoby concluded that, if women did not allow themselves to be constrained by false conceptions of femininity, they could choose any path and be successful and in tune with themselves as women.[79]

Through "Facts Only," *Amerika*'s special report provided the Russian reader with concrete statistics, taken from the Women's Bureau of the US Department of Labor, on women's lives. It indicated that American women had made tremendous inroads since 1920, when only two out of every one hundred women aged twenty-one years old and older had graduated from university. Fifty years later, in 1970, that number was at nineteen. In 1920, the proportion of women in the labour force was 23 per cent, and in 1970 it had grown to 43 per cent. Fifty-nine per cent of women workers were married, 22 per cent were single, 19 per cent were widowed, divorced, or separated. The article noted that women were breaking out of traditional fields and taking up demanding positions in a variety of areas. One of these was the public service. There were thirteen women in the US Senate and Congress, twenty-three mayors in cities of 10,000 or more, and 306 in state legislatures. However, the majority of employed women aged sixteen and over were still in traditionally female occupations: 34.3 per cent were clerical workers and 21.6 per cent were service workers. In contrast, only 17.1 per cent were factory workers, 13.8 per cent were professional or technical workers, and 6.9 per cent were sales workers.[80]

To highlight women's progress, the issue featured biographies celebrating the accomplishments of extraordinary American women. It indicated that these women were "confident in their abilities, creative in their output, and serene in their femininity." Biographies included those of Jeannette Rankin, a Montana Republican who was the first woman to sit in Congress; Jacqueline Grennan Wexler, the president of New York City's Hunter College; Terry Hill, a graduate student at the University of California Berkeley and editor of its student newspaper, the *Daily Californian*; LaDonna Harris, the Native American wife of Senator Fred Harris (OH-D); Mary Ellen Mark, a photographer; Helen Frankenthaler, an abstract expressionist painter; Shirley Chisholm, a New York City Democrat and the first African American woman to sit in Congress; Helen Brooke Taussig, a pediatrician and professor at Johns Hopkins University and the first female president of the American Heart Association; Elinor Kaine, the only female member of the Professional Football Writers Association; and Dr. Mina Rees, a mathematics adviser in the US Navy.[81] All were professional women who had opinions on either the women's liberation movement or the place of women in society. The most notable was Rankin, who had been involved in the first wave feminist movement fifty years ago. She believed that women had advanced since that time, but regretfully admitted that women were still confronting many of the same issues they encountered back then. She lauded the movement, but claimed she "couldn't get excited about it because I got so excited so long ago." In spite of Rankin's reservations, *Amerika*'s biographies demonstrated that the women's movement was having an impact, particularly on young woman. For example, Hill's approach as editor of the *Daily Californian* reflected the organizational practices of women's liberation groups. These groups allowed her to realize that problems in her professional life, particularly the "invisibility syndrome" that resulted from women being ignored in the workplace, were cultural rather than personal. She stated that, as a newspaper editor, she had no desire to impose her will on others. Instead of competing with one another, her small team tried to make decisions collectively. According to her, the American cultural revolution needed new forms of organization, and it was women who could provide such inspiration. Further, Hill's personal life was also impacted by women's liberation. She indicated that it had forced women to value others for what they *did*, rather than how they looked. As a result, groups of women who had once been divided had now been brought closer together and sought validation from each other rather than through the men in their lives.[82]

Amerika's special report included pieces highlighting the experiences of women at various stages in their lives. One of these was "Motherhood," a first-hand account by Barbara Rosenfeld which recounted the joys, challenges, and doubts that accompanied childbirth, childrearing, and modern techniques in both countries.[83] In 1962, she had met her husband Stephen while she worked as a guide at the USIA's Medicine USA exhibition. For his part, Stephen had joined the *Washington Post* in 1952 as a foreign affairs columnist specializing in the Soviet Union. In 1964, he established the newspaper's Moscow bureau, but within one year it was shut down and he was expelled from the Soviet Union. In 1967, they published *Return from Red Square*, an account of their lives in Moscow.[84] It was clear that Rosenfeld's perceived negative experiences while living in the Soviet Union impacted her storytelling in this issue. Rosenfeld attempted to connect her role as a mother more broadly with Russian women, writing that the feelings of nervousness and excitement she experienced while awaiting the birth of her firstborn, David, in 1964, were the same feelings of "an expectant mother anywhere." However, she wrote that she was confident her skilled doctor would make the event easy and safe, thanks to modern medicine.[85] Rosenfeld relied, in particular, on the multitude of services and work-saving devices available in the United States to make motherhood "simple, even idyllic." They included prepared baby foods and formulas, diaper services, and washing machines and dryers. Upon returning home from the hospital, Rosenfeld had the (rare) assistance of a nurse who cared for her baby and household duties for ten days, so she could rest. Further, Rosenfeld relied on her pediatrician, friends, and Dr. Spock's *The Common Sense Book of Baby and Child Care* for up-to-date advice and techniques. Above all, she noted that her "greatest supporter, helper and inspiration" was her husband. According to Rosenfeld, he was "willing to share in the labor" to provide her with relief. She wrote that while some men viewed it as improper to help around the house, in her eyes, it never lessened a man's dignity or masculinity. They shared in the tasks of parenthood, as it was "their" son, and "their" job to raise him. Rosenfeld's language showed that, in spite of the seemingly enlightened views she and her husband shared, she still assumed childcare was *her* job as a mother. Her husband's "willingness" to "help" her, and to "share" in that labour did not appear to be a firm expectation, but rather something for which she was grateful. As a result, he was her "supporter" and her "inspiration." Rosenfeld's account of childbirth and motherhood differed from the one she provided to American readers in *Return from Red Square*. In this earlier telling, aptly titled "Birth, Soviet Style," she told of the uncomfortable and old-fashioned methods of Soviet medicine she experienced while giving birth to her second child, Rebecca. According to Rosenfeld, she debated leaving the country for her delivery, as many foreigners did, but believed that the birth of a baby in a Soviet hospital would introduce her to the "real Russia."[86] Indeed, she told of her difficulties in obtaining a bed at Moscow's Gynecological Institute, only receiving one with the assistance of US ambassador Foy D. Kohler. She told of the institute's subpar accommodations; among the privations were having to share a room with four other women, and one shower and toilet with ninety women, and a lack of Kleenex, toilet paper, and sanitary napkins.[87] She also told of the lack of modern medicine and techniques. For example, in spite of her pain, doctors refused to provide her with anaesthesia, which they believed to be unsafe; she was forced to breastfeed immediately as formula was not available; and her baby was swaddled, a traditional practice of wrapping a baby in tight blankets to ensure straight limbs.[88] Interestingly, these "old-fashioned" practices were ones that were reintroduced by the natural childbirth movement beginning in the 1960s and still remain popular, if somewhat controversial. Finally, Rosenfeld discussed the loneliness she felt at the hospital. In Washington, DC, she and her firstborn had stayed in the same room, and her husband visited. In Moscow, her baby stayed in a separate room, and her husband was prohibited from entering the hospital during her eight-day stay. Rosenfeld noted that although Rebecca's birth was a "good bargain" at seventy-eight dollars, that Soviet doctors were competent and efficient, and that post-childbirth she received kind and compassionate care, she "did not care to repeat her stay." It appeared, according to her account, that childbirth in the Soviet Union was not the joyful experience it was in the United States and was further exacerbated by the fact that mothers were expected to tolerate pain and loneliness.[89]

For her part, Rosenfeld wrote that in the United States she became skilled in infant care and began to consider herself a "model mother." She adopted a modern approach to mothering that included treating her children as people with unique characteristics, thoughts, and feelings. According to Rosenfeld's account in *Return from Red Square*, this laid-back approach differed from the rigid upbringing the Soviet government encouraged. In 1964, the Soviet Academy of Medical Sciences published *The Feeding of Children*. It suggested that a baby should be fed seven times a day for the first six months, five times a day until eighteen months, regardless of hunger. The baby should not be entertained at mealtime, allowed to speak, play with its food, or eat with its left hand. Further, Russian children were urged to walk and toilet train early. What made Rosenfeld's account unique was that, like many Russian women, she wanted and was able to maintain her professional interests after her children were born. She admitted the hours she worked outside the home were limited, but engaging in such work made her happier and gave her relief from the full-time job of childrearing which she found demanding, pressure-filled, and often frustrating. Her entire salary went to her babysitter, but she believed the personal rewards of paid employment made it worthwhile. For the Russian women who were used to working while leaving their children for long days at socialized daycare centres or elsewhere, Rosenfeld's account may have represented the perfect work-life balance. However, in a rare moment she also expressed criticism of the postwar mass exodus to the suburbs and its effect on women. She noted that, while families tended to move to the suburbs in search of affordability and space as well as amenities such as schools and shopping centres, mothers were "forced" to spend the most time there. She noted that the modern home had labour-saving devices, but much work still needed to be done. Further, she lamented the suburbs' lack of diversity and culture. Ultimately, according to Rosenfeld, the suburbs were pleasant but isolating. While Rosenfeld's piece focused predominantly on motherhood, her discussion of her professional interests and her concerns about suburban life were illuminating for the time. It reflected the growing dissatisfaction American women had experienced, and were finally beginning to express, as a result of the postwar emphasis on traditional gender roles. It also reflected the attempts of white, middle-class women to create a balance between their personal obligations and professional aspirations. Her account, which showed both gratitude and exasperation, demonstrated to the Russian reader that one could have it all under a capitalist system: a home, family, and satisfying career. Together, these admissions on the part of Rosenfeld also demonstrated *Amerika*'s divergence from the postwar gender norms it supported in its early years.[90]

Another article in March 1971's issue showed this divergence, and it was one that perhaps more directly resulted from the second wave feminist movement. The article tells the story of forty-year-old Paula, a woman who had embraced postwar gender norms for a time, but then decided they no longer suited her needs. "Divorce," by Elinor L. Horwitz, chronicled a hectic day in Paula's life as one of 2.5 million divorced American women. Raising her two children, seventeen-year-old Cissy and fifteen-year-old Steve, as well as working a full-time job, she experienced the feelings of many divorced women of her time, at times capable and optimistic, other times lonely and uncertain.[91] Horwitz noted that, while a divorced woman could expect court-protected legal and financial support, psychologically she needed to work out her own destiny. This was a feat which Paula had clearly managed to accomplish. While the article centred on a day in Paula's life, it also reflected on her decision to end her twelve-year marriage, starting over at the age of thirty-two, and embarking on a new life as a single mother. She discussed the difficult decisions a divorced woman faced, one involving her initial desire to keep their large home in the suburbs so her children could have the comfort of their same school and friends. Like Rosenfeld, she felt confined by the suburbs; one year later, she and her children moved into a semi-detached three-bedroom home in the city. One Sunday when her children were with their father, Paula repainted her bedroom a bright yellow, admired her work, and suddenly fell in love with her newfound freedom. She told herself that her children were healthy, intelligent, and loving; she was an excellent teacher, a job she had given up when her children were born; and that she was perfectly capable of paying her bills and maintaining her car. She no longer felt defeated, but instead felt capable and optimistic about her new life. Paula spoke of her children with pride. Cissy managed everything beautifully "but her waistline," and Steve was a good student, athletic and popular with his classmates. Both children earned their own spending money through respectable part-time jobs. Overall, she indicated to Horwitz that she no longer believed the problems associated with adjusting to divorced parents were as disturbing to children as she used to fear. In many ways, it made them stronger and more responsible. While divorce did have its economic pitfalls, these were problems she appeared to be overcoming. When the children were younger, she admittedly struggled, having to pay so much for household help and babysitting that she barely had any money left. She currently owned her home and car and managed to get by on her income and monthly alimony and child support payments. She recently took a two-month unpaid leave from work to complete her master's degree and was then promoted to a higher-paying position at the board of education, creating new school curriculums. She was even able to hire a cleaning lady for one day a week. When Paula met newly divorced women who asked her for advice, she told them that the most important thing was to find a job that was engrossing, stimulating, and satisfying. Of course, Paula's divorced life was not just filled with family and work. She discussed her robust social life, which included her wide circle of friends, as well as her dating life, in particular her weekly dates with a divorced lawyer and father of three. At the end of the article, Paula reflected on her day and stated that she felt lucky, particularly living in an urban environment where there was no stigma attached to divorce, women moved about freely, and were able to find rewarding jobs. In spite of this, however, she was aware that there was something about the divorced woman that made people uneasy, as if she were handicapped. While the article emphasized that a woman's single status could depend on any number of personal or practical reasons, it was clear that Paula embraced her choices. She pondered the future, as her two children would soon be away at school, and the prospect of remarriage. In a bold statement during a time when women still believed that a complete life included marriage, she concluded that she once prayed for a protective man who would save her from failure and loneliness, but right now, she simply enjoyed her freedom.[92] As a divorced woman, Paula appeared to be thriving and wholly satisfied with her life.

Amerika's special report included other short articles related to women. "Their Special Look" included eight images of women of various races and ethnicities, of all ages, and in all facets of life. All, it stated, had an "unmistakably American look and spirit."[93] "Farewell to Childhood" focused on twelve-year-old Michele DeLattre as she navigated adolescence, the period when she was no longer a child but not yet a woman. The article noted that when she was with her friends and brother she revelled in the "frolics, fantasy and fun of being a child," but while she was with her mother she talked of womanly things, like "clothes, shopping, family, boys," and the future.[94] "Where Is It Written" and "Married Is Better" contained poems on gender roles and married life, and a *New York Times* book review discussed Kate Millett's recent bestseller on women's liberation, *Sexual Politics*.[95] Overall, this special report on women was unique for a magazine that since its inception had promoted the idea of traditional gender roles and consumerism. Historically the magazine admitted that, at times, women engaged in paid labour, but the implication was that women's primary roles were those as wives, mothers, and consumers. If these were not their current roles, they were ones they aspired to. However, in March of 1971, *Amerika*, for the first time, acknowledged that a revolution of tremendous importance was taking place, and analysed its impact on women as well as its potential for society as a whole in the future. It cannot be ignored that, with the exception of LaDonna Harris and Shirley Chisholm, the women depicted were white and therefore did not represent diverse subsets of the nation's population.[96] And there were times that the issue's contents reflected an ambivalence towards second wave feminism. However, that *Amerika*'s editors chose to devote an entire issue to women was pivotal, particularly as the USIA rarely acknowledged its nation's faults. Further, the experiences of the seemingly ordinary women within its pages, of women such as Barbara or Paula, showed the ambiguity of these contentious times for women, the simultaneously happy, confusing, and frustrating moments of living during an era that continued to emphasize the postwar domestic ideology of the past, but was gradually attempting to rectify past injustices towards half of its population.

Russian women reading this issue had their own experiences navigating their ambiguous place in society. By taking on traditionally male roles during war, as well as after it, they had already showed they were capable of challenging stereotypes and taking on varied, challenging, and even physically demanding work. At the same time, American social scientists consistently reinforced the point that Russian women were burdened by a long workday, as well as housework, frequently without the "help" of the men in their lives, in spite of Soviet proclamations of gender equality.[97] As Lynne Attwood has noted, in spite of the Communist Party's "official" ideology proclaiming gender equality, an unofficial ideology awkwardly combined a "rational" and "romantic" approach towards women's status, one that simultaneously called for their involvement in the public sphere as well as their continued commitment to marriage and the family.[98] According to Mark G. Field, in addition to their full day at work and childrearing responsibilities, women spent as much as three hours a day shopping, preparing food, and cleaning.[99] A study of men's and women's time based on a sample of 1,477 families living in Moscow and Novosibirsk in 1959 found that women spent a total of five hours per day doing housework and self-care, with only one hour of free time, while men spent two hours on housework and self-care and had three hours of free time (table 6.1).

These figures, part of the 1959 Soviet census, indicate that in spite of official claims of gender equality, Russian women, just like their American counterparts, had ambiguous positions in society. While many worked full-time and often in arduous positions, they were expected to, and did, spend more time on childcare and housework than the men in their lives, in part because the latter were reluctant to take up these traditionally female tasks. Women's situations were exacerbated by Soviet proclamations of socialized daycare for all which did not, in reality, exist for all. Further, these women did not have the amenities available to the white, middle-class American women shown in *Amerika*, including single-family dwellings, modern technology and conveniences, an abundance of food, or even fashion choices. Inkeles and Bauer confirmed that women were the main consumers within the Soviet household, just as they were in the United States. They were the ones who did the shopping and waited in long lines for difficult-to-find products. Inkeles and Bauer affirmed the centrality of women and gender to US foreign policy objectives of inducing Russians to demand increased

Table 6.1. Time Budgets, Non-working Time, Men and Women.

	Men			Women		
	Hours	Minutes	% of Total	Hours	Minutes	% of Total
Free time	3	8	20.0	1	43	10.8
Housework and self-care	2	43	17.3	5	10	32.6
Time for sleep and meals	8	58	57.1	8	11	51.7
Expenditure of time connected with production work	0	53	5.6	0	47	4.9
Total non-working time	15	43	100.0	15	51	100.0

Note: Based on a sample of 1,477 families, Moscow and Novosibirsk, 1959
Source: "Questions Concerning the Calculation of Non-working Time in Budget Statistics, Statistical Handbook, No. 8, 1961," *Problems of Economics* 4, no. 12 (April 1962). Reprinted in Mark G. Field, "*Workers (and Mothers): Soviet Women Today*," in The *Role and Status of Women in the Soviet Union*, edited by Donald R. Brown (New York: Teachers College Press, 1968), 45.

consumer goods. If Soviet authorities improved the living standards of its people and provided them with more consumer goods, their negative view of capitalism would decrease.[100] Russian women got married, raised children, and worked at unprecedented rates, something which the white, middle-class elite in the United States had little conception of, rarely acknowledged, and never reflected on in the pages of *Amerika*, until that astounding issue of March 1971, which finally commented on and reflected the complex decisions, challenges, and lives that diverse groups of women faced on a daily basis.

Conclusion

Assessing *Amerika*'s Effectiveness: Soviet Promises for the Future and Its Failures

Throughout the 1950s, the US media depicted Russian women as being "graceless, shapeless, and sexless," often unable to properly fulfil their traditional roles as housewives and mothers, and lacking the consumer goods available in the West.[1] During a decade when US government contact with the Soviet Union was minimal, it was difficult for both the US media and USIA to ascertain *Amerika*'s reception among its female readers, as well as its overall effectiveness. Not only was the magazine's circulation limited due to the provisions of its reciprocal agreement, but circumstances made it impossible to interview Russian women and to conduct surveys on the magazine's impact. However, from its inception, US journalists and officials were convinced that *Amerika* appealed to ordinary Russian women and that it was an unqualified success in showing them how tantalizing traditional gender roles and consumer culture actually were, and how both could improve their lives. According to these officials, there was no reason to doubt the magazine's appeal to Russian readers.[2] Their sentiments were further corroborated by Khrushchev himself, who appeared to embrace consumerism by ushering in a new era characterized by a rise in living standards, particularly through the construction of *Khrushchevki*, as well as the increased availability of consumer goods for the Russian people.

In an October 1945 *New York Times* article, journalist Brooks Atkinson, stationed in Moscow, proclaimed that Russians were anxious to obtain copies of *Amerika*. He described a scene in which visitors lined the US embassy anxiously awaiting the release of the third issue.[3] Soyuzpechat, the Soviet agency responsible for distributing *Amerika*, regularly reported to the US embassy that all fifty thousand copies of each issue were sold out. Russians also found copies through US officials. In 1947, Ambassador Smith claimed that the magazine sold out regularly at Moscow newsstands and that the embassy received approximately twenty phone calls per day requesting subscriptions.[4] In 1950, M. Gordon Knox, first secretary of the US embassy, travelled by train from Moscow to Odessa to check the distribution and availability of *Amerika*. He brought copies of the magazine and claimed he encountered many individuals who were interested in viewing it. One woman who showed the "keenest interest" was the wife of a lieutenant colonel in the Soviet army. He wrote that the woman was from Leningrad, appeared cultured, and was well dressed by Soviet standards, wearing an expensive-looking blouse and skirt. Knox showed her a copy of *Amerika*, which she had never heard of, and according to him, examined it from cover to cover. In their subsequent conversation, she revealed that she most enjoyed the articles and images on women, particularly those related to fashion and those which showed women dancing and playing sports. She also enjoyed the articles on modern furnishings and new convertibles. According to Knox, she reluctantly handed back the issue of *Amerika*, but later returned to ask for additional copies, which her husband told her to return.[5] Knox's account supports the idea that women were most interested in the articles and images focused on women. Another group of young people, according to Knox, asked to view the magazine, noting that it was interesting, but "too good to be true." Ultimately, Knox declared that, based on his observations, *Amerika* was a "popular magazine."[6] Hans Tuch's responsibilities as press and cultural attaché at the US embassy in Moscow included monitoring the distribution of *Amerika* and counselling its editors in Washington about content. When the magazine was released every month, he checked Moscow's newsstands to see that copies were delivered and sold. He often saw long lines forming, but noted that the magazine was typically held underneath counters and sold to certain customers who had made prior arrangements to purchase it, usually for a higher price than five rubles.[7]

According to others, *Amerika*'s popularity was evidenced in the fact that Russian readers circulated copies of the magazine and discussed its contents among family and friends. Ambassador Harriman commented that in visiting Soviet homes throughout the years he saw worn copies of *Amerika* and was told by hosts that many read the magazine.[8] Two decades later, the Rosenfelds wrote that they saw long lines of people waiting to buy the magazine in advance.[9] Its popularity can be further evidenced in conversations during USIA exhibitions in the Soviet Union. In 1959, guides working at the American National Exhibition confirmed that many of the visitors they interacted with mentioned reading and enjoying *Amerika*.[10] In response both to magazine content and the exhibition, Soviet visitors frequently questioned guides about US consumer goods, including homes and appliances, if they owned such items, and their prices.[11] In the end, they appeared more concerned about "concrete living standards than about abstract ideologies."[12] Perhaps in response to such interest, the Soviet government banned *Amerika*'s distribution at US exhibitions throughout the 1960s.[13] Whether or not all Russian readers discussed *Amerika* in a positive or negative light is difficult to ascertain, but the point is that it was a topic of conversation, as were the high living standards and mass consumer goods highlighted throughout the magazine. Information about the United States, its way of life, and its people were circulated throughout Moscow, and to a lesser extent throughout the entire country, thus exerting US influence in the Soviet Union. By 1959 Moscow embassy diplomats reported that "with the exception of personal contacts, *Amerika* made the greatest contribution to the better understanding of America by the Russians and to the provision of accurate information about the US." Historians agree with these assessments. Laura Belmonte calls the magazine one of the US information program's earliest successes.[14] Walter Hixson writes that officials credited it with diminishing the effectiveness of Soviet internal propaganda.[15] Former diplomat turned historian Yale Richmond noted that readers were impressed with the standard of living portrayed in the magazine and, inevitably, compared it with their own. With an annual cost of just one million dollars, excluding staff salaries, *Amerika* was a "minor expense, but a major success, in the Cold War of ideas."[16]

These comments by journalists and officials were based on personal observations and informal discussions with Russian readers, which to them suggested that *Amerika* enjoyed wide popularity and was "accepted by readers as accurate, non-propagandistic information."[17] The magazine appeared to be so effective that they even sought to emulate its success in other Eastern European countries. In 1949 and 1951, when the magazine was run by the State Department, it began issuing similar magazines in Czechoslovakia and Yugoslavia, called *Amerika* and *Sad*, respectively. In 1959, the USIA began issuing a Polish version, called *Ameryka*.[18] The intention was to replicate *Amerika*, and gradually win over the hearts and minds of the women and men residing in those communist countries as well. With an abundance of resources, but limited access to the Russian people, *Amerika*'s reissuance in 1956 provided the newly minted USIA with the unique opportunity to create a magazine that finally reached Russian women and showed them the awe-inspiring benefits of a capitalist society that emphasized traditional gender norms. It was one that depicted American women in traditional roles as feminine wives, mothers, and consumers, and offered the possibility that one day the same could be possible for Russian women. Of course, the "special" role of full-time wife and mother was not one that all Russian women desired, but *Amerika* provided these hard-working women a brief glimpse of an easier way of life, made possible by a capitalist consumer culture.

By the end of the decade, US journalists and USIA officials began to take notice of changes in the attitudes of the Russian people as well as the interests of the Soviet government, particularly Khrushchev, in accommodating them. This included Russian women's desire for consumer goods, and to a lesser extent, their desire to adopt feminine roles akin to those seen within the United States. For the US media and government, the former was best evidenced in their interest in *Amerika* and the overwhelming response to 1959's American National Exhibition, which welcomed 2.7 million visitors. As the Rosenfelds acknowledged in their account, when these types of changes in Soviet society occurred, Westerners gloated as though an increased desire for higher living standards marked a "sellout of socialism and a vindication of capitalism."[19] Indeed, the press began to smugly suggest that a "new" Russian woman was emerging, one who more closely reflected her US counterpart. A December 1959 *New York Times* article entitled "New Soviet Plan – Feminine Females" argued that, regardless of political ideology, Russian women were still women at their core, and they had feminine aspirations. The article suggested that all women strived for a beautiful appearance and home. Their desire to purchase consumer goods, to be attractive and well dressed, was as "enduring as their natural desire to bear children."[20] According to the article, Russian women began imitating the styles worn by American women, particularly the fashion models and guides they saw at the American National Exhibition. They waited in long lines at Soviet beauty salons to dye their hair, replace their old-fashioned braids and buns with modern bobs, and have their nails done.[21] USIA officials noted that fashion models at GUM were wearing bright colours, shorter skirts, and Western-style shoes. Most importantly, they argued that Russian citizens and the Soviet press were emboldened in their critiques of Soviet consumer culture.[22] For the USIA, this was an astounding accomplishment, particularly since neither had ever been known to question, at least outwardly, governmental priorities. For example, during Khrushchev's 1959 Siberian tour Russians frequently asked him about the increased production of consumer goods and possibility of price reductions. USIA reports further noted that the Soviet newspaper *Iszestiya* had called for improvements in clothing, claiming that workmanship was poor, clothes did not fit properly, and styles were unimaginative and only consisted of dull, dark colours.[23] Both the US media and USIA officials noted that the Soviet government responded with planned increases in the volume and variety of goods available to Russian women, as well as a new emphasis on style and quality. The Soviet government also began importing Western-style items.[24]

By the 1960s, visitors to the Soviet Union wrote that the government had made noticeable improvements in women's fashion. Rosenfeld wrote that she saw more varied and brighter dresses, knitwear, plastic raingear, and stylish winter boots with heels and fur linings. She noted that fashion shows took place three times a day at the All-Union House of Fashion on Kuznetsky Most, Moscow's most fashionable street. They adopted an "international" style, similar to what was seen at the American National Exhibition, with young models and music playing in the background. However, she also noted that commentators suggested the age, size, and shape of a woman for whom a particular dress would be suitable. Although female audience members were delighted, they left disappointed as the House of Fashion sold only patterns, not clothing.[25] Doris Anderson, long-time editor of Canadian women's magazine *Chatelaine,* attended these fashion shows during her visit to Moscow in 1959 and wrote that audience members made note of the styles they liked and then bought the patterns to make them themselves, or took them to a dressmaker.[26] Even *USSR* appeared to jump on the fashion bandwagon. After its March 1962 issue on women, it began regularly including fashion articles in its last pages, under the category of "Miscellaneous." For example, July 1962's issue included an eleven-page spread on the latest "Summer Fashions." These fashions appeared modern and accentuated the shapes, including the waistlines, of the slim models who wore them. For a Soviet government that eschewed fashion for its frivolity this was a stunning inclusion within a state-sanctioned magazine. Further, given that these fashions were intended specifically for the summer, a limited time frame in a country known for its long and harsh winters, it appeared that the Soviet government had finally "given in" to Western standards, or at least to the demands of its women.[27] The irony of *USSR*'s inclusion of fashions was that by this time, *Amerika* had begun to slowly move away from its emphasis on fashionable females. Regardless, these state-sanctioned efforts on the part of the Soviet government were an important step towards a Western-style capitalist consumer culture. For readers, and citizens as a whole, they provided the hope that even if the Soviet government could not yet provide women with mass produced fashion, one day soon those items might appear in department stores. In the meantime, just as American women emulated fashions they saw in the

Ladies' Home Journal, Russian women could emulate those they saw, and in the process possibly influence the clothing choices of female family members, friends, colleagues, and even strangers on the streets of Moscow. For the USIA, it appeared that its efforts were slowly paying off. Rosenfeld wrote that with these developments, Khrushchev had officially sanctioned "choosiness."[28] In other words, the consumer "options" that Nixon had advocated for during the kitchen debates, and were advertised in *Amerika*, were finally making their way to the Soviet Union.

In addition to providing women with increased clothing options, Khrushchev made public pronouncements promising to provide them with more household appliances and food. An October 1959 decree raised production targets for all goods of "cultural household significance." It called for the production of twice as many refrigerators, vacuum cleaners, and television sets, and three times as many washing machines by 1961.[29] The USIA observed that the Soviet government was redesigning and modernizing refrigerators and washing machines to match the "best domestic and foreign models."[30] In January 1960, the Kremlin announced a 1.8-billion-ruble investment in machinery for the production of new food products, including canned, frozen, and dried foods, as well as distinctly US products, such as potato chips, corn flakes, and soft drinks.[31] According to Susan Reid, these improvements lent further credence to the idea that the American way was the "right way."[32]

US media and USIA accounts emphasized the Soviet government's efforts to raise the living standards of its citizens, particularly by providing them increased housing options. In September 1959, Harrison Salisbury, the *New York Times* reporter who won a Pulitzer Prize for his series on Russia and first documented the second kitchen debate, wrote an eight-part series called "Khrushchev's Russia."[33] Salisbury claimed that, although communists still aimed for "world rule," the country had changed considerably and that Russians lived in "better and freer" conditions than ever before.[34] While the shift towards addressing inadequate housing and creating higher living standards began before Stalin's death, this process was greatly accelerated by Khrushchev. Salisbury lauded the construction of *Khrushchevka*, private homes for the single, nuclear family.[35] He concluded that although it would be impossible for the Soviet government to duplicate US living standards, the lives of Russian citizens had improved.[36] It is unclear why Salisbury would characterize these developments as a sign that Russians were "freer," as political rights were still suppressed throughout the country, but it is clear that the government invested in attempting to better the housing conditions of its citizens. Western historians have estimated that during the 1956–60 Five-Year Plan over 145 million square metres of living space was built, more than during the entire period from 1918 to 1946. During the two Five-Year Plans that coincided with Khrushchev's leadership, from 1956 to 1965, over thirteen million apartments were built and approximately sixty-five million individuals experienced improvements in their housing conditions.[37]

With the introduction of the "feminine female" and higher living standards, the US media as well as USIA officials began applauding the Soviet government for its supposed recognition that women wanted to embrace their "special" status as housewives and mothers. US media reports claimed that the Soviet government began heralding women's "natural" roles as childbearers, informing them that motherhood was their "greatest contribution" to the communist cause.[38] Just as a pronatalist strategy subsumed postwar America, Soviet journalists wrote that the Soviet government had determined that population growth was "essential to national survival."[39] The truth was that the Soviet government had maintained this position for decades; in 1936, after sixteen years of legalized abortion, it issued a decree outlawing abortions because of concerns over a decrease in birthrates and the impact of repeat abortions on a woman's health and, therefore, her ability to effectively engage in paid labour.[40] As Wendy Goldman notes, this decree reflected a pronatalist strategy on the part of the Soviet government. It offered women incentives for childbearing by providing stipends for new mothers, bonuses for multiple children, longer maternity leaves, and an increase in the number of maternity clinics and daycare centres. Additionally, penalties were enacted for men who failed to pay alimony or child support, and divorces became more difficult to obtain.[41] This official position took on increased significance after the war, and the deaths of millions of able-bodied Russian men. However, by 1955, the Soviet government lifted this abortion ban during the first twelve weeks of pregnancy in a practical effort to combat the high post-abortion mortality rate among women who continued to seek illegal abortions.[42] While the Soviet government had never exalted traditional gender roles in the same way the US government had, the policy changes of these decades reflected its emphasis on a woman's ability to both reproduce and work for the sake of the nation.

The *New York Times* took this "new" Soviet mentality one step further, wondering whether, since former luxuries were becoming necessities, "family, food, fashions and furnishings" would distract Russian women from paid labour altogether.[43] As Reid confirms, under Khrushchev, Soviet culture became *"obsessed* with homemaking and domesticity," but this obsession did not necessarily lead to an embrace of American gender norms.[44] Rather it was the by-product of the construction of *Khrushchevki* and the promise of a higher standard of living. Historians have noted that *Khrushchevki* served as a catalyst for mass consumption. They led to an expectation, and frequently a desire, on the part of ordinary women to adequately furnish these new structures, particularly the kitchens that inevitably became their domain.[45] The house became a place of comfort for the nuclear family, a home. A sense of pride emerged that rarely existed in the communal apartments of Stalinist Moscow, and when the Soviet government failed to provide adequate furnishings to make them liveable, women were frequently left disappointed. However, *Khrushchevki* were never intended to imitate Western homes. Instead, they were intended to strike a balance between Western and Eastern notions of what was deemed adequate shelter. To the Soviet government, they signalled the fulfilment of the goals of the 1917 Russian Revolution and brought to fruition "a new everyday existence known as the 'communist way of life' (*kommunisticheskii byt*)."[46] They were to be comfortable, but functional, and include necessities rather than luxuries. While they contained private apartments similar to what you would find in the West, they also provided communal spaces, such as dining halls, childcare facilities, and courtyards, and organized group activities so residents could interact. Under Khrushchev, this new home was intended to bridge the gap between private and public, and demonstrate a communist, collectivist spirit.[47] For women, the building of the *Khrushchevka*, and the rise in living standards that accompanied them, was a double-edge sword. This newfound obsession with homemaking and domesticity fell on women, thus increasing their workload, just as the high expectations of postwar suburban living did for American women.[48] However, in spite of what appears to be an increased desire for consumer items, particularly for the household, there is no clear evidence that the majority of Russian women wished to adopt the role of full-time housewife. As Inkeles and Bauer pointed out, many women enjoyed their status within Soviet society, including their educational and employment opportunities. However, they also wanted the conveniences and products that came with a capitalist culture. This mentality was also iterated in *USSR*'s March 1962 special issue on women, which indicated that Russian women were not willing to give up their equal rights for the "special privileges" that American women supposedly possessed. Many women were happy with their "outside jobs," and believed they consisted of a "larger social contribution than keeping house or raising children."[49] The irony, of course, was that neither did Russian women enjoy full equality, nor did American women enjoy special privileges. Yet the US media heralded the effects of these US cultural activities as the beginning of a trend whereby Russian women caught a brief glimpse of what their lives could be like if they lived in a consumption-oriented society. This lifestyle meant not only increased access to goods and services but also the adoption of American gender norms. The USIA attributed these changes in attitudes to its information program.

These changes can also be attributed to Khrushchev himself, who became one of the most vigorous proponents of selected aspects of American consumer culture. Both the power of the USIA's efforts and his admiration for American consumption and high living standards became clear in September 1959, when he visited the United States. In the past, Khrushchev had sent Soviet delegations to the United States so they could learn more about its science, technology, and ways of life, but he had always expressed a desire to visit the country himself. When Eisenhower personally sent him an invitation to visit, he eagerly accepted, becoming the first Soviet head of state to visit the United States. In a well-publicized trip that lasted for two weeks, he brought a fifty-four-member delegation that included his wife, Nina Petrovna, and their children.[50] After being welcomed by Eisenhower in Washington, DC, on 15 September, Khrushchev travelled to New York, Los Angeles, San Francisco, Iowa, and Pittsburgh, before rejoining him at Camp David.[51] While he wanted to discuss a ban on nuclear weapons, the mutual reduction of armed forces, and the elimination of military bases and troops on foreign soil, he also admitted that he visited because he was just "curious to have a look at America."[52] Khrushchev's trip was filled with memorable moments, all well documented by the US media, and many showing his appreciation for US culture, or at the very least, its food.

The first occurred when Khrushchev toured International Business Machine's (IBM's) headquarters in San Jose, California. IBM's president, Thomas J. Watson Jr., wanted Khrushchev to see his RAMAC computer, which had been on display at the American National Exhibition; it stored countless facts on world history and "spoke" ten languages.[53] However, it was IBM's cafeteria, where Khrushchev had his first self-service dining experience, that became the most notable aspect of his plant tour. According to Khrushchev's son Sergei, his father enthusiastically picked up his tray, pushed it along the buffet line and piled it high with classic American food, including fried chicken, potatoes, apple pie, and iced tea. After lunch, Watson took him through his IBM plant, but his father left with a more favourable impression of the cafeteria than the computers.[54] In his speech that day, Khrushchev thanked Watson for the opportunity to visit his plant, and especially his self-service cafeteria.⁵⁵ In his memoirs, Khrushchev wrote of his admiration for the concept of the self-serve cafeteria, which allowed for fewer lines, a formal dining experience, more food options, and a "democratic structure" where everyone ate together.⁵⁶ Khrushchev wrote that upon his return home, he recommended to party leaders and trade-union organizations that they, too, adopt the American-style self-service cafeteria.⁵⁷ Other events strengthened Khrushchev's admiration of American culture. In Coon Rapids, Iowa, Khrushchev visited Roswell "Bob" Garst, a hybrid-corn grower who owned the town's largest farm, so he could view Garst's cattle, farming equipment, and growing techniques.⁵⁸ However, what once again stood out most for Khrushchev was the food, in particular the lunch that Garst's wife served. In his memoirs, he wrote, "Americans really know how to eat. They have delicious canned foods, not to mention all sorts of fresh dishes." According to him, the Garsts served turkey, which was "very much respected in the US, not just as a bird but as meat, too. The Americans ... even have a special 'turkey day' when every American absolutely has to eat roast turkey."⁵⁹ While in Iowa, Khrushchev also visited the Des Moines Packing Company, where he donned a butcher's gown and sampled his first hot dog, slathered in mustard. His approval was evident, as he proclaimed, "We have beaten you to the moon, but you have beaten us in sausage-making." In his memoirs, Khrushchev confirmed that the hot dogs were, in fact, delicious.⁶⁰ In one final notable incident, while in San Francisco, he spontaneously decided to tour Quality Foods, a recently opened supermarket. When word of Khrushchev's visit leaked, a crowd of two thousand quickly gathered to get a glimpse of him touring the quintessential symbol of postwar American consumer culture, the supermarket.⁶¹ Khrushchev calmly examined the displays and had discussions with shocked store clerks and housewives.⁶² Before he left, he shook hands with the store manager and told him, with approval, that he had a "fine organization – a good operation."⁶³

Khrushchev's escapades and comments proved amusing to the US media and public, but it was his wife, Nina Petrovna, that captured their hearts and minds. Little was known about Petrovna, but she prompted tremendous curiosity. She was often described as a short, plump, grey-haired woman who wore no makeup or jewellery and had little fashion sense. When she arrived in Washington, DC, the US media initially ridiculed her as a dowdy woman who exemplified the failures of the Soviet regime. However, her quiet demeanour, friendly smile, and photographs of her grandchildren endeared her to the US media and public. In spite of Khrushchev's kitchen debate declaration that the "capitalistic attitude" towards women did not exist in the Soviet Union,

Petrovna, in many ways, embodied America's traditional postwar gender norms. She had worked as a history teacher and then stayed home to raise their five children. Eric Johnston, president of the Motion Picture Association of America (MPAA), visited the Khrushchev's Georgian beach home in October 1958 and told the *New York Times* that she had a nicely furnished home, served a meal comparable to one found anywhere else, and ran a proper household.[64] The *New York Times*, writing of Khrushchev, suggested that anyone who had the good sense to "marry her, stay married to her, and bring her over here couldn't be all villain."[65] The article initially described her as a shy homemaker and mother who travelled to the US to support her husband, but as time progressed, she began to speak to the media in English, further endearing her to them. When asked what impressed her most about the United States, she responded that it was the people. They have "created beautiful things and they themselves are a noble, good-hearted people."[66] Petrovna, much like her husband, appeared lured by the many consumer items on display. While in San Francisco, she and her family members went to Sears and Macy's. A *New York Times* article, cheekily entitled "Mme. Khrushchev Breaks Away," reported that she "escaped" her official engagements and eluded the police and press to purchase items for her grandchildren.[67] Petrovna was so popular that by the end of the year she appeared to have single-handedly altered the US media portrayal of Russian women, extending it beyond the "graceless, shapeless, and sexless" stereotype of the past. Petrovna's visit, according to Robert L. Griswold, ushered in an alternative image of the Russian woman. She became known first and foremost as a "typical grandmother," a venerated title in the United States and one to which many women could relate.[68] Petrovna, in effect, put a human, female face on the leadership of a Soviet regime, one that was characterized by the rigid and repressive Stalin and then the erratic but humorous Khrushchev. Even if the US media did not fully embrace Khrushchev, they loved his wife. She reinforced and legitimized the wholesome and caring maternal figure that was epitomized in postwar America's pronatalist ideology, demonstrating that even across the world, Russian women embraced this role as well. By the end of 1959, Khrushchev was emboldened by recent Soviet technological achievements, his meetings with US leaders, and his visit to the United States. He was eager to see improvements in Soviet living standards, and confidently predicted that the Soviet Union would "pass the US" by the end of its next economic plan in 1965.[69] Of course, Khrushchev's attempts at economic reform largely failed, and he was ousted from power in 1964.[70] Nevertheless, his desire to improve Soviet living standards, and his efforts to do so, show that women, gender, and consumption were integral to international relations, particularly during the decade where he and President Eisenhower both held leadership positions.

USIA activities, particularly through *Amerika*, show that postwar representations of women and gender norms in the United States were heavily deployed in the federal government's overseas information program. The USIA utilized images of white, middle-class women as feminine housewives, mothers, and consumers to show Russian women the American way of life and the benefits that came with it. These tactics were extremely effective. By the end of the decade, it was evident that even if Russian women did not look approvingly at traditional gender roles, they certainly embraced a consumer-oriented lifestyle. Patrick Hyder Patterson correctly cautions scholars not to dismiss the impact of the consumer experience on the shaping of modern society. During a period when the American economy was the envy of the world, the lure and influence of its consumer culture cannot be underestimated, particularly for those who had experienced extreme hardship during World War II and in its immediate aftermath. In his case study on Yugoslavia, he underscores the importance of "Western exposure" and the desires and aspirations of individuals for a better life in the unravelling of a communist regime.[71] The Yugoslav government sought to achieve a "Good Life" for its citizens, but did so largely by obtaining credit from the West, in the process artificially boosting living standards and increasing consumer demand.[72] Consumerism became a stabilizing force in Yugoslav society, but by the 1980s, when that "Good Life" could no longer be sustained, it ultimately generated massive discontent in a people who had proudly believed their "Third Way," an alternative approach that bridged the gap between capitalism and communism, was the right way.[73] In other words, the Yugoslav people looked to their government to sanction, sustain, and prop up their way of life, much like the Russian people began to do by the end of the 1950s. Their newfound outlook was indeed reinforced by their nation's own leader and his wife during their whirlwind tour of the United States. Khrushchev began to recognize the demand for, and power of, consumer goods and made frequent declarations of his government's desire to increase their production and availability. Years later, when it had largely failed to do this, it bred widespread discontent on the part of the Russian people. Unlike military initiatives whose successes or failures can be gauged almost immediately, cultural diplomacy can take years, even decades, to reveal their effectiveness, and this certainly proved to be the case for the USIA's information program in the Soviet Union. *Amerika*'s second run did not end until 1994 (figure 7.1), outlasting the Cold War itself,

Figure 7.1. The cover of *Amerika*'s final issue, appearing in October 1994, featured an adult woman, presumably the grown image of the little girl that appeared on its first cover in October 1956 (figure 4.1). As in the first issue of its second run, she wore a red dress and gazed over the Pacific Ocean with her back turned to the reader.

and while upon first glance it can be difficult to gauge the success of such an initiative in a foreign country effectively blocked by the so-called Iron Curtain, its long-lasting impact cannot be underestimated. By the time *Amerika* folded, the Cold War was an event of the past, communism had collapsed in the Soviet Union, and the mission of the USIA, and *Amerika*, had been accomplished. In spite of this, there were many who still did not want to see the magazine end, with its glimpse into a way of life that the Russian people, and their government, had now embraced wholeheartedly. Thirty-four-year-old "housewife" Katya Chizhova noted that she had looked forward to reading the magazine each month. According to her, it was "interesting to read about scientific achievements and in general, about the American way of life."

She lamented that it would no longer be published: "I can tell you that for many, it meant a lot. People had very little information about life abroad, and their interest in America was great."[74]

This analysis of *Amerika* demonstrates the significance of women, gender, and consumption to international politics during the Cold War. Along with this and other attempts to connect domestic and foreign politics, there are still many enlightening avenues of potential research. While the history of consumption and gender has been studied, further research could discuss the US media's treatment of consumerism as a foreign policy asset. In the postwar era, the media consistently attempted to reconcile "classic" American values of hard work, industriousness, and thrift with the alluring and convenient, but often superficial, values of a modern consumer-oriented society. At times, this resulted in conflicting messages, particularly as they related to depictions of the women. Although America was portrayed as a land of opportunity for all, US womanhood was defined as white, middle-class, and heterosexual, and anyone considered "other" was consistently excluded from a postwar narrative that emphasized traditional gender norms and mass consumption. For the USIA, maintaining this narrative, however false, was especially important a during a time of increasingly violent racial tensions in the country. It was not only maintained at home through magazines such as the *Ladies' Home Journal*, but also abroad through *Amerika* and its equivalents in other nations. As for *Amerika*, it has been an integral, yet seriously understudied, component of the US overseas information program in the Soviet Union. The magazine should be analysed in its entirety to demonstrate how, as the years went on, it continued to reflect both the changing vision of each administration it fell under, as well as the broader foreign policy objectives of Cold War America. That it existed until 1994 shows its effectiveness, at least in the minds of USIA officials. The Czechoslovakian, Yugoslavian, and Polish versions of *Amerika* have not been studied; analysis of their contents would vastly contribute to a better understanding of the connections between the overseas information program, citizen demands for a consumer-oriented way of life, and the unrest that eventually occurred in each of these countries. This further analysis can only add to the immense contribution that cultural diplomacy had in the collapse of communism in both the Soviet Union and Eastern Europe. The Soviet Union was a vast entity that many people do not typically see as being easily "infiltrated" with Western propaganda, but propaganda, whether or not US officials liked to refer to it as such, was vital to their efforts in undermining the Soviet government. Historians have recently discussed the ways in which it sowed the seeds of unrest, and more work needs to be done in this area, especially as it relates to the print culture that was so much more accessible to ordinary Russians than the radio broadcasts that were frequently jammed, the cultural events (such as the opera, theatre, and musical concerts) that were inaccessible to most, or the foreign exhibitions that travelled across the country, often only for weeks or months at a time. All came together to contribute to the collapse of communism in the Soviet Union and its satellites. Similarly, it would be worthwhile to study the Soviet perspective to cultural diplomacy, particularly to compare US attempts to "infiltrate" the Soviet Union with Soviet attempts to do the same in the United States. Studies should include *Amerika*'s equivalent, *USSR*, later renamed *Soviet Life*, but also the Soviet National Exhibition that took place in New York's Coliseum in 1959, two other areas that have been largely neglected within existing scholarship. Studies of this nature can demonstrate that while the United States and the Soviet Union were vastly different in their political and economic systems, and in many cases their societies and cultures, they were in fact similar. During these early years of the Cold War, both nations attempted to reach the "other," to entice the people of each respective nation to understand the "other," to seek "friendships" as Khrushchev articulated in November 1960's issue of *USSR*, and ultimately to win over "hearts and minds."

According to the philosophy of the USIA, its cultural activities within the Soviet Union were integral to conveying information related to US gender norms and consumer culture for the purposes of winning over female hearts and minds. *Amerika* was unique through its ability to reach and show Russian women, for the first time, the gender-specific norms idealized in postwar American society, as well as the vast consumer goods available to women. These consumer goods would supposedly make women's roles as feminine housewives and mothers easier, and their lives, as a whole, happier. With them, they could receive the same "special privileges" that American women supposedly possessed. Much as the *Ladies' Home Journal* did for domestic readers, *Amerika* allowed the USIA to shape the messages and images Russian women received about the United States, at least those Russian women who had access to and read the magazine. By the time of the American National Exhibition in 1959, Russian women were finally able to see and interact with American women and observe and touch the consumer goods seen in the pages of *Amerika* first-hand. Further, they were also able to communicate with female guides and other employees in their native Russian. Moving into the next decade, just as US international political priorities moved from the Soviet Union and Eastern Europe to Latin America, Africa, and Asia, and as the second wave feminist movement altered the national discourse on a women's "proper place," the USIA changed *Amerika*'s approach. It largely ceased to promote postwar America's conservative gender ideology, and less frequently advertised its high standard of living and abundance of consumer goods. Instead, it began to more frequently include stories on America's political system, history, labour, farming, scientific and artistic achievements, sports, and religious life. During the 1950s, however, amid a hostile political climate, and a conservative domestic setting in which the United States adopted a pronatalist strategy that sought to maintain, and even advance, its civilization, *Amerika*'s approach was fitting. USIA officials firmly believed that the magazine whetted the appetites of Russian women. These factors, combined with a broader program of cultural diplomacy that sought to promote the American way of life and consumer culture within the Soviet Union, as well as Khrushchev's openness towards reform, contributed to the Soviet Union's efforts by the end of the decade to make consumer goods more available to its citizens and raise their living standards. In these ways, America's early Cold War cultural activities, part of what became known as a "golden age of diplomacy," may have accomplished more towards Soviet economic reform than political pressure or military force ever could. As the USIA boldly declared in reference to the Soviet Union in 1959, "It is not likely that this buying public will ever be the same again."[75]

Notes

Introduction: Why Women, Cold War Cultural Diplomacy, and *Amerika*?

1 "From the Editors," *Amerika* 1, October 1956, 2.
2 While this first issue referred to the magazine as *America Illustrated*, the majority of all other issues, articles and government documents referred to it as *Amerika*.
3 The Union of Soviet Socialist Republics, or the USSR, was composed of fifteen republics that consisted of modern-day Armenia, Azerbaijan, Belarus, Estonia, Georgia, Kazakhstan, Kyrgyzstan, Latvia, Lithuania, Moldova, Russia, Tajikistan, Turkmenistan, Ukraine, and Uzbekistan. Although all were controlled by a centralized government located in Moscow and most had once belonged to the former Russian Empire, they were diverse in their geographical landscapes, economies, populations, and the nature of their peoples and cultures. This study will focus on US activities targeting those citizens residing in the heart of the Soviet Union, the ones who felt the ramifications of the "Soviet Experiment" from its beginning: the Russian people. It will refer to them as Russians rather than Soviets, as the latter can apply to the citizens residing in any of the fourteen other republics. Exceptions have been made when historical documents, writers, or figures have referred to Soviet citizens as a whole. In these cases, the original language used has been retained. The Soviet government will still be referred to as such.
4 The articles under analysis in this study have been translated from the Russian language in one of three ways. Each issue of *Amerika* located at the National Archives at College Park (NACP) contains an English table of contents with brief descriptions of each published article. Articles under extensive analysis, particularly those discussed in chapters 3 and 4, were translated with the much-appreciated research assistance of Dima Sochnyev. The NACP holds full translations of the *Amerika* articles

discussed in chapter 6, ones which appear in the magazine during the 1960s and 1970s, including the March 1971 issue that contained a "special report" on women.
5. Michael L. Krenn, *The History of United States Cultural Diplomacy: 1770 to the Present Day* (New York: Bloomsbury Academic, 2017), 5.
6. David Riesman, "The Nylon War," *A Review of General Semantics* 8.3 (Spring 1951).
7. Emily Rosenberg, *Spreading the American Dream: Selling American Economic and Cultural Expansion, 1890–1945* (New York: Hill and Wang 1982), 7.
8. Lizabeth Cohen, *A Consumer's Republic: The Politics of Mass Consumption in Postwar America* (New York: Random House, 2003), 8.
9. Walter L. Hixson, *Parting the Curtain: Propaganda, Culture and the Cold War, 1945–1961* (New York: St. Martin's Press, 1998), 10.
10. Ibid.
11. Hans N. Tuch, *Communicating with the World: US Public Diplomacy Overseas* (New York: St. Martin's Press, 1990), 6.
12. International Educational Exchange Program, "The Citizens Role in Cultural Relations," September 1959; Box 2, p. 1; Organization, News Articles, 1955–1974 to Agency Mission, 1947–1969; Subject Files, 1953–2000; RG 306; NACP.
13. For more on the history of the USIA, see Nicholas J. Cull, *The Cold War and the United States Information Agency: American Propaganda and Public Diplomacy, 1945–1989* (New York: Cambridge University Press, 2008); Nicholas J. Cull, *The Decline and Fall of the United States Information Agency: American Public Diplomacy, 1989–2001* (New York: Palgrave Macmillan, 2012); Wilson P. Dizard Jr., *Strategy of Truth: The Story of the US Information Service* (Washington, DC: Public Affairs Press, 1961); Wilson P. Dizard Jr., *Inventing Public Diplomacy: The Story of the US Information Agency* (Boulder, CO: Lynne Rienner, 2004); Allen C. Hansen, *USIA: Public Diplomacy in the Computer Age*, 2nd ed. (New York: Praeger, 1989).
14. Theodore C. Streibert, New US Information Agency Program; Box 2, p. 2; Organization, News Articles, 1955–1974 to Agency Mission, 1947–1969; Subject Files, 1953–2000; RG 306; NACP.
15. Statement by President Dwight D. Eisenhower, 28 October 1953; Box 2; Organization, News Articles, 1955–1974 to Agency Mission, 1947–1969; Subject Files, 1953–2000; RG 306; NACP.
16. Theodore C. Streibert, The New US Information Agency Program; Box 2, p. 2; Organization, News Articles, 1955–1974 to Agency Mission, 1947–1969; Subject Files, 1953–2000; RG 306; NACP.
17. It should be noted that the Central Intelligence Agency (CIA) also ran Radio Free Europe/Radio Liberty (RFE/RL) as a method to communicate with citizens of the Soviet Union and its satellite states. RFE was created in 1949 to

broadcast to Soviet satellite states, and RL in 1951 to broadcast to the Soviet Union itself. They merged in 1976. Their most notable impact was likely in 1956, when RFE broadcasts encouraged Hungarian students to rebel, leading to a nationwide revolution in which Western countries ultimately provided little support, and which was eventually quashed by the Soviet Union. For more on RFE/RE, see A. Ross Johnson, *Radio Free Europe and Radio Liberty: The CIA Years and Beyond* (Washington, DC: Woodrow Wilson Press, 2010); Arch Puddington, *Broadcasting Freedom: The Cold War Triumph of Radio Free Europe and Radio Liberty* (Lexington: University of Kentucky Press, 2000); Gene Sosin, *Sparks of Liberty: An Insider's Memoir of Radio Liberty* (University Park: Penn State University Press, 1999).

18 The Voice of America (VOA) was created in 1942 to inform foreigners of US war aims. It began broadcasting to Russians in 1947 in order to discredit the Soviet government and counter Soviet propaganda. For more on the VOA during its early Cold War years, see David F. Krugler, *The Voice of America and the Domestic Propaganda Battles, 1945–1953* (Columbia: University of Missouri Press, 2000); and A. Ross Johnson and R. Eugene Parta, eds., *Cold War Broadcasting: Impact on the Soviet Union and Eastern Europe* (New York: Central European University Press, 2010).

19 Hixson, *Parting the Curtain*, xiv.

20 From 1959 to 1991, the USIA brought twenty-three exhibitions to nine cities in the Soviet Union. For more on these exhibitions, see Yale Richmond, *Cultural Exchange and the Cold War: Raising the Iron Curtain* (University Park: Penns State University Press, 2003); Jenny Thompson and Sherry Thompson, "Dueling Exhibitions," in *The Kremlinologist: Llewellyn E. Thompson, America's Man in Cold War Moscow* (Baltimore: Johns Hopkins University Press, 2018), 180–9; Tomas Tolvaisas, "Cold War 'Bridge-Building': Exchange Exhibits and Their Reception in the Soviet Union, 1959–1967," *Journal of Cold War Studies* 12.4; and Andrew James Wulf, *US International Exhibitions during the Cold War: Winning Hearts and Minds* (Lanham, MD: Rowman & Littlefield, 2015).

21 Kenneth A. Osgood, "Propaganda," in *Encyclopedia of American Foreign Policy*, ed. Alexander DeConde et al. (New York: Charles Scribner's Sons, 2001), 240.

22 Ibid.

23 Tuch, *Communicating with the World*, 9.

24 For more on Truman's psychological warfare strategy, see Sarah-Jane Corke, *US Covert Operations and Cold War Strategy: Truman, Secret Warfare and the CIA, 1945–1953* (New York: Routledge, 2008).

25 Paul M.A. Linebarger's definition appears in Martin J. Manning and Herbert Romerstein, *Historical Dictionary of American Propaganda* (Westport, CT: Greenwood Press, 2004), 229.

26 Kenneth A. Osgood, *Total Cold War: Eisenhower's Secret Propaganda Battle at Home and Abroad* (Lawrence: University Press of Kansas, 2006), 47.
27 Hixson, *Parting the Curtain*, 15.
28 Nicholas J. Cull, "Public Diplomacy: Lessons from the Past," in *CPD Perspectives on Public Diplomacy* (Los Angeles: Figueroa Press, 2009).
29 Tuch, *Communicating with the World*, 3.
30 Cull, "Public Diplomacy," 12.
31 Sarah Ellen Graham, *Culture and Propaganda: The Progressive Origins of American Public Diplomacy, 1936–1953* (Burlington, VT: Ashgate, 2015), 4.
32 This study will refer to the Soviet Union's own internal and external activities as propaganda.
33 Krenn provides a comprehensive study on the history of American cultural diplomacy from the eighteenth to the twenty-first century. See Krenn, *The History of United States Cultural Diplomacy*.
34 For more on America's wartime information program, see John D. Hench, *Books as Weapons: Propaganda, Publishing, and the Battle for Global Markets in the Era of World War II* (Ithaca, NY: Cornell University Press, 2010); Clayton R. Koppes and Gregory D. Black, *Hollywood Goes to War: How Politics, Profits and Propaganda Shaped World War II* (Berkeley: University of California Press, 1987); Darlene J. Sadler, *Americans All: Good Neighbor Cultural Diplomacy in World War II* (Austin: University of Texas Press, 2012); and Allan M. Winkler, *The Politics of Propaganda: The Office of War Information, 1942–1945* (New Haven, CT: Yale University Press, 1978).
35 For example, in 1956 Eisenhower established the "People-to-People" program to encourage Americans to develop friendships with foreigners for the purposes of encouraging mutual understanding between people and nations. For more information, see Osgood, *Total Cold War*; and Pam Perry, *Eisenhower: The Public Relations President* (Lanham, MD: Lexington Books, 2014).
36 Scott Lucas, *Freedom's War: The US Crusade Against the Soviet Union, 1945–1956* (New York: New York University Press, 1999).
37 Helen Laville. *Cold War Women: The International Activities of American Women's Organizations* (Manchester: University of Manchester Press, 2002).
38 During the interwar period, the newly created Soviet Union emerged as an area of interest to a segment of the American public, particularly African Americans, women, and intellectuals who were intrigued by the "Soviet Experiment" and its promise of equality. As a result, many of them voluntarily travelled to the Soviet Union, and wrote of their experiences in a positive light. As Stalin consolidated his power and his purges began, many began to question the inherent contradictions of the

socialist system. The onset of the Cold War and subsequent Red Scare only exacerbated this inner conflict among them. This topic is further explored in chapter 3.

39 See Michael David Fox, *Showcasing the Great Experiment: Cultural Diplomacy and Western Visitors to the Soviet Union, 1921–1941* (London: Oxford University Press, 2012); Nigel Gould-Davies, "The Logic of Soviet Cultural Diplomacy," *Diplomatic History* 27.2 (April 2003); Rosa Magnusdottir, "Mission Impossible? Selling Soviet Socialism to Americans, 1955–1958," in *Searching for a Cultural Diplomacy*, ed. Jessica C. E. Glenow-Hecht and Mark C. Donfried (New York: Berghahn Books, 2010).

40 See David Caute, *The Dancer Defects: The Struggle for Cultural Supremacy during the Cold War* (New York: Oxford University Press, 2005); Lisa E. Davenport, *Jazz Diplomacy: Promoting America in the Cold War Era* (Jackson: University Press of Mississippi, 2009); Michael L. Krenn, *Fall-Out Shelters for the Human Spirit: American Art and the Cold War* (Chapel Hill: University of North Carolina Press, 2005); Naima Prevots, *Dance for Export: Cultural Diplomacy and the Cold War* (Middletown, CT: Wesleyan University Press, 1999); and Damion Thomas, *Globetrotting: African American Athletes and Cold War Politics* (Champaign: University of Illinois Press, 2012).

41 Penny Von Eschen, *Satchmo Blows Up the World: Jazz Ambassadors Play the Cold War* (Cambridge, MA: Harvard University Press, 2006).

42 Mary L. Dudziak, *Cold War, Civil Rights: Race and the Image of American Democracy* (Princeton, NJ: Princeton University Press, 2000).

43 Elaine Tyler May, *Homeward Bound: American Families in the Cold War Era* (New York: Basic Books, 2008), 11.

44 Ibid., 30.

45 Ibid., 13.

46 Laura A. Belmonte, *Selling the American Way: US Propaganda and the Cold War* (Philadelphia: University of Pennsylvania Press, 2008), 5.

47 Robert Dean, *Imperial Brotherhood: Gender and the Making of Cold War Foreign Policy* (Amherst: University of Massachusetts Press, 2001), 13.

48 Stephanie Coontz, *The Way We Never Were: American Families and the Nostalgia Trap* (New York: Basic Books, 1992), 26. Coontz provides an excellent study on the persistence in the American psyche of the idealized white, middle-class, pro-family image of the postwar period, in spite of the fact that 25 per cent of Americans were poor.

49 Stuart Ewen, *All Consuming Images: The Politics of Style in Contemporary Culture* (New York: Basic Books, 1988), 60.

50 Emily S. Rosenberg, "Consuming Women: Images of Americanization in the 'American Century.'" *Diplomatic History* 23.3 (Summer 1999): 480.

51 Ewen, *All Consuming Images*, 46.

234   Notes to pages 11–13

52 Stuart Ewen, *Captains of Consciousness: Advertising and the Social Roots of the Consumer Culture* (New York: McGraw-Hill, 1976), 48.
53 Ewen, *All Consuming Images*, 49.
54 Dawn Spring, *Advertising in the Age of Persuasion: Building Brand America, 1941–1961* (New York: Palgrave Macmillan, 2011), 69. See also Daniel L. Lykins, *From Total War to Total Diplomacy: The Advertising Council and the Construction of the Cold War Consensus* (Westport, CT: Praeger, 2003).
55 Shawn J. Parry-Giles, "The Eisenhower Administration's Conceptualization of the USIA: The Development of Overt and Covert Propaganda Strategies," *Presidential Studies Quarterly* 24.2 (1994): 266.
56 See Cheyanne Cortez, "The American Girl: Ideas of Nationalism and Sexuality as Promoted in the Ladies' Home Journal during the Early Twentieth Century," in *Women in Magazines, Research, Representation, Production and Consumption*, ed. Rachel Ritchie et al. (New York: Routledge, 2016); Helen Damon Moore, *Magazines for the Millions: Gender and Commerce in the* Ladies' Home Journal *and* Saturday Evening Post, *1880–1919* (Albany: State University of New York Press, 1994); Jennifer Scanlon, *Inarticulate Longings: The* Ladies' Home Journal, *Gender and the Promises of Consumer Culture* (New York: Routledge, 1995); David Welky, "Defining Womanhood in the *Ladies' Home Journal*," in *Everything Was Better in America: Print Culture in the Great Depression* (Champaign: University of Illinois Press, 2008).
57 Scanlon, *Inarticulate Longings*, 1–2.
58 Kate A. Baldwin, *The Racial Imaginary of the Cold War Kitchen: From Sokol'niki Park to Chicago's South Side* (Lebanon, NH: University Press of New England, 2016), xvii. Baldwin discusses the place of race in Cold War domestic ideology, arguing that the use of the kitchen as a propaganda tool to symbolize US freedom and democracy ignored the historical experiences of racial minorities. As African American women were historically tied to the kitchen, their experiences with slavery, colonialism, and racial genocide were effectively erased to highlight the so-called benefits of a white, middle-class, consumer-oriented lifestyle.
59 Robert L. Griswold, "'Russian Blonde in Space': Russian Women in the American Imagination, 1950–1965," *Journal of Social History* 45.4 (2012): 882.
60 See Lydia Kirk, *Postmarked Moscow* (New York: Charles Scribner's Sons, 1952). Notable journalist Dorothy Thompson wrote a monthly column in the *Ladies' Home Journal* that regularly discussed the inadequacies of the Soviet regime.
61 For example, in 1989 future Russian president Boris Yeltsin visited a supermarket in Houston, Texas. He later noted in his autobiography that the experience was "shattering." The supermarket, with its long, food-filled aisles, made him sick with despair for the Russian people, whose

living standard had been lower than that of Americans for so many years. See Boris Yeltsin, *Against the Grain* (New York: Simon & Schuster, 1990).
62 See John Steinbeck and Robert Capa, "Women and Children in the USSR," *Ladies' Home Journal*, February 1948.
63 X, "The Sources of Soviet Conduct," *Foreign Affairs: An American Quarterly Review* (July 1947): 575.
64 Alan Nadel, *Containment Culture: American Narrative, Postmodernism and the Atomic Age* (Durham, NC: Duke University Press, 1995), 2–3.
65 May, *Homeward Bound*, 208.
66 Diana Cucuz, "Containment Culture: The Cold War in the *Ladies' Home Journal*, 1946–1959," in *Modern Print Activism in the United States*, ed. Rachel Schreiber (Burlington, VT: Ashgate, 2013), 146.
67 Laura McEnaney, *Civil Defense Begins at Home: Militarization Meets Everyday Life in the Fifties* (Princeton, NJ: Princeton University Press, 2000), 108–9.
68 May, *Homeward Bound*, 30.
69 Ewen, *Captains of Consciousness*, 213.
70 Betty Friedan, *The Feminine Mystique* (New York: W.W. Norton, 1963).
71 Nancy Walker, *Shaping Our Mothers' World: American Women's Magazines* (Jackson: University Press of Mississippi, 1995), viii.
72 Joanne Meyerowitz, "Beyond the Feminine Mystique: A Reassessment of Postwar Mass Culture, 1946–1958," *Journal of American History* 79.4 (March 1993): 1469.
73 See Valerie Korinek, *Roughing It in the Suburbs: Reading Chatelaine Magazine in the Fifties and Sixties* (Toronto: University of Toronto Press, 2000), 21.
74 Belmonte, *Selling the American Way*, 6.
75 There was a clear gender divide in the types of exhibition displays that men and women viewed as being favourable. While men tended to view science and technology displays approvingly, women tended to approve of those on home conveniences and consumer goods. In most cases, however, both sexes tended to believe that the Soviets surpassed the United States in science and technology.
76 USIA Research and Reference Service, "Visitor Reaction to the US versus Major Competing Exhibits at the 1958 Zagreb Trade Fair," December 1958; Box 25; History, 1938–1990 to Studies, 1942–1984; Subject Files, 1953–2000; RG 306; NACP.
77 Belmonte, *Selling the American Way*, 134–5.
78 Cohen, *A Consumer's Republic*, 119.
79 Ibid., 8.
80 Andrew L. Yarrow has written on changing messages in early Cold War print propaganda, but has focused broadly on *Amerika*'s first and second runs; *Free World*, a magazine distributed in East Asia; as well

as pamphlets, comic books, and other printed material. See Andrew L. Yarrow, "Selling a New Vision of America to the World: Changing Messages in Early Cold War Print Propaganda," *Journal of Cold War Studies* 11.4 (Fall 2009).

81 Thomas G. Paterson, "A Round Table: Explaining the History of American Foreign Relations," *Journal of American History* 77.1 (June 1990). This issue also included Akira Lriye, "Culture"; Michael H. Hunt, "Ideology"; Emily S. Rosenberg, "Gender"); Thomas J. McCormick, "World Systems"; Louis A. Perez Jr., "Dependency"; Melvyn P. Leffler, "National Security"; Michael J. Hogan, "Corporatism"; J. Garry Clifford, "Bureaucratic Politics"; Richard H. Immerman, "Psychology."
82 Leffler, "National Security."
83 Elaine Tyler May, "Commentary: Ideology and Foreign Policy: Culture and Gender in Diplomatic History," *Diplomatic History* 18.1 (January 1994); Emily S. Rosenberg, "'Foreign Affairs'" After World War II: Connecting Sexual and International Politics," *Diplomatic History* 18.1. This groundbreaking issue also included Laura McEnaney, "He-Men and Christian Mothers: The America First Movement and the Gendered Meanings of Patriotism and Isolationism," *Diplomatic History* 18.1; Geoffrey S. Smith, "Commentary: Security, Gender, and the Historical Process"; Susan Jeffords, "Commentary: Culture and National Identity in Foreign Policy"; Amy Kaplan, "Commentary: Domesticating Foreign Policy"; Anders Stephanson, "Commentary: Considerations on Culture and Theory"; Bruce Kuklick, "Commentary: Confessions of an Intransigent Revisionist."
84 Victoria De Grazia, *Irresistible Empire: America's Advance through Twentieth-Century Europe* (Cambridge: Harvard University Press, 2009), 5.
85 Reinhold Wagnleitner, *Coca-Colonization and the Cold War: The Cultural Mission of the United States in Austria after the Cold War* (Chapel Hill: University of North Carolina Press, 1994), xi.
86 Richard Pells, *Not Like Us: How Europeans Have Loved, Hated and Transformed American Culture since World War II* (New York: Basic Books, 1997), xv.
87 Roland Robertson, *Globalization: Social Theory and Global Culture* (Thousand Oaks, CA: Sage, 1992), 173–4.
88 Lynne Attwood, *Creating the New Soviet Woman: Women's Magazines as Engineers of Female Identity, 1922–1953* (New York: St. Martin's Press, 1999), 3. See also Lynne Attwood, "From the 'New Soviet Woman' to the 'New Soviet Housewife': Women in Post-War Russia," in *War-Torn Tales: Literature, Film and Gender in the Aftermath of World War II*, ed. D. Hipkins and G. Plain (Bern: Peter Lang, 2007).
89 Ibid., 134.
90 Natasha Kolchevska, "Angels in the Home and at Work: Russian Women in the Khrushchev Years," *Women's Studies Quarterly* 33.3/4 (Fall–Winter 2005): 132.

91 Attwood, *Creating the New Soviet Woman*, 12.
92 Melanie Ilic, "Women in the Khrushchev Era: An Overview," in *Women in the Khrushchev Era*, ed. Melanie Ilic, Susan E. Reid, and Lynne Attwood (New York: Palgrave Macmillan, 2004), 20.
93 Susan E. Reid, "Cold War in the Kitchen: Gender and the Destalinization of Consumer Taste in the Soviet Union under Khrushchev," *Slavic Review* 61.2 (Summer 2002): 246.
94 Ilic, "Women in the Khrushchev Era," 11.
95 For more on the double duty of Russian women, see Barbara Alpen Engel and Anastasia Posadskaya-Vanderbeck, eds., *A Revolution of Their Own: Voices of Women in Soviet History* (Boulder, CO: Westview Press, 1998); Wendy Z. Goldman, *Women at the Gates: Gender and Industry in Stalin's Russia* (New York: Cambridge University Press, 2002); Melanie Ilic, Susan E. Reid, and Lynne Attwood, eds., *Women in the Khrushchev Era* (New York: Palgrave Macmillan, 2004); and Melanie Ilic, "Equal Pay for Equal Work: Women's Wages in Soviet Russia," in *The Palgrave Handbook of Women and Gender in Twentieth-Century Russia and the Soviet Union*, ed. Melanie Ilic (London: Palgrave Macmillan, 2018).
96 Larisa Zakharova, "Soviet Fashion in the 1950s-1960s: Regimentation, Western Influences and Consumption Strategies," in *The Thaw: Soviet Society and Culture during the 1950s and 1960s*, ed. Denis Koslov and Eleonory Gilburd (Toronto: University of Toronto Press, 2013), 428.
97 Ibid., 403.
98 Djurdja Bartlett. *FashionEast: The Spectre That Haunted Socialism* (Cambridge, MA: MIT Press, 2010), 11–12.
99 Kristin Roth-Ey, *Moscow Prime-Time: How the Soviet Union Built the Media Empire That Lost the Cultural Cold War* (Ithaca, NY: Cornell University Press, 2012), 4.
100 Division of Research for Europe, Office of Intelligence Research, "Information Control and Propaganda in the USSR," 24 February 1948; Box 9, pp. 7–8; State Department Information Programs (1946–1948); Charles Hulten Papers; HST Library.
101 Riesman, "The Nylon War," 163.

1 The "Modern Woman": The "Special Privileges" of American Womanhood in the *Ladies' Home Journal*

1 Betty Friedan, "Have American Housewives Traded Brains for Brooms?" *Ladies' Home Journal*, January–February 1963, 24.
2 Phyllis McGinley, "10 Ways to Keep a Husband – Young," *Ladies' Home Journal*, January–February 1963, 87, 129, 132; Jean Freeman, "What Men Have Done for Love," *Ladies' Home Journal*, January–February 1963, 88–9, 93; Dorothy Cameron Disney, "Why Husbands Run Away," *Ladies' Home*

Journal, January–February 1963, 94; Betty Hannah, "Masculinity: What Is It? What Makes a Man Masculine?" *Ladies' Home Journal,* January–February 1963, 96, 98, 123–4.

3   It should be noted that Dr. Benjamin Spock was the most notable pediatrician of the postwar era, known for his "firm, but gentle" approach to parenting. In 1946, he released *The Common Sense Book of Baby and Child Care* (New York: Duell, Sloan and Pearce), which became an instant bestseller. To this day, it has gone through ten editions and been translated into thirty-nine languages. In this particular column, Dr. Spock focused on the question "Should Mothers Work?" ultimately concluding that a woman should discuss the issue with a professional counsellor before she made her decision. However, part-time work was a satisfactory compromise, as a child had a "vital need for a mother or for a loving, reliable substitute," especially at a young age. Dr. Benjamin Spock, "Doctor Spock Talks with Mothers: Should Mothers Work?" *Ladies' Home Journal,* January–February 1963, 21.
4   Friedan, "Have American Housewives Traded Brains for Brooms?" 26.
5   "Our Readers Write Us," *Ladies' Home Journal,* June 1963, 20.
6   The 1950 census indicated that of the 76,139,192 women living in the country, 89.1 per cent (67,894,638) identified as "white" and 10.8 per cent (8,244,554) identified as "nonwhite." Of these, 7,774,182 (10.2 per cent of the entire female population) identified as African American. The remainder consisted of Indians, Japanese, Chinese, Filipino, and what was referred to as "all other."
7   Scanlon, *Inarticulate Longings,* 7.
8   The term "American Dream" become popularized during the Great Depression, when author John Truslow Adams wrote his 1931 bestseller, *The Epic of America.* However, the concept of the American Dream has existed since the nation's founding as an ethos, a set of ideals for all citizens. They include religious liberty, equality, freedom, and independence from government tyranny, and the opportunity for upward mobility, both economically and socially. In the context of the postwar period that ethos extended to include a domestic life characterized by home ownership, particularly in the suburbs. However, the American Dream has largely been criticized for being unachievable for many, particularly an African American population that has experienced persistent racial discrimination throughout its history. Jim Cullen, *The American Dream: A Short History of an Idea That Shaped a Nation* (New York: Oxford University Press, 2004), 7–8.
9   As with the American Dream, the notion of "special privileges" has been highly contested given that working-class women, and women of colour, have not traditionally had the luxury of pursuing traditional gender roles, and always had to work to ensure the survival of their families.

The most notable advocate for women's "special privileges" was failed politician, attorney, and activist Phyllis Schlafly, who created STOP ERA (Stop Taking Our Privileges) in 1972 in order to combat the newly emerging second wave feminist movement in its effort to have the Equal Rights Amendment (ERA) passed. Schlafly, like other conservatives, believed that the ERA would destroy traditional gender roles. See Donald T. Critchlow, *Phyllis Schlafly and Grassroots Conservatism: A Woman's Crusade* (Princeton, NJ: Princeton University Press, 2005); David Farber, "Phyllis Schlafly: Domestic Conservatism and Social Order," in *The Rise and Fall of Modern American Conservatism: A Short History* (Princeton: NJ: Princeton University Press, 2012).

10 The *Ladies' Home Journal* rarely discussed the issue of homosexuality among girls and women. January 1941's "As the Twig Is Bent: XXI – Girlish Boys and Boyish Girls" was part of a twenty-four-part series by Dr. Leslie B. Hohman, a psychiatrist from Johns Hopkins Medical School, and was the first article that did so. However, while the title referenced girls, it focused on the case study of a boy who was "retrained" to avoid "homosexuality in adulthood" through military school. Similarly, subsequent articles addressed homosexuality only in relation to boys and men, frequently blaming children's upbringing, by mothers in particular, for these "tendencies," and positing that with early diagnosis and treatment they could be cured. See Leslie B. Hohman, "As the Twig Is Bent: XXI – Girlish Boys and Boyish Girls," *Ladies' Home Journal*, January 1941, 59–60; Amram Scheinfeld, "Are American Moms a Menace?" *Ladies' Home Journal*, November 1945, 36, 138, 140; Dorothy Thompson, "Some Observations on a Sensational Book," *Ladies' Home Journal*, May 1948, 11–12; Robert C. Taber, "Catch Them before They Kill! Spot and Stop Potentially Dangerous Criminals in Our Schools," *Ladies' Home Journal*, January 1954, 52, 60–2; Seward Hiltner, "Sex and Religion: Sex-Sins or Salvation," *Ladies' Home Journal*, February 1959, 41, 184–5; Frederic Wertham, "10 Ways a Child May Tell You He Is Headed for a Troubled Teen Age," *Ladies' Home Journal*, March 1959, 62–3, 194, 197, 199–200.

11 Friedan, *The Feminine Mystique*.
12 Walker, *Shaping Our Mothers' World*, viii.
13 Meyerowitz, "Beyond the Feminine Mystique," 1469.
14 Telegram from Senator Joseph McCarthy to President Harry S. Truman, 11 February 1950. https://www.archives.gov/files/education/lessons/mccarthy-telegram/images/telegram-page-1.gif.
15 For more on the second domestic Red Scare, particularly as it impacted white, middle-class, heteronormative values, see David K. Johnson, *The Lavender Scare: The Cold War Persecution of Gays and Lesbians in the Federal Government* (Chicago: University of Chicago Press, 2004); and Mary

Brennan, *Wives, Mothers, and the Red Menace: Conservative Women and the Crusade against Communism* (Boulder: University Press of Colorado, 2008).
16 Scanlon, *Inarticulate Longings*, 1–2.
17 Ibid.
18 John M. Lee, "Curtis Tries New Methods to Meet Challenge," *New York Times*, 26 March 1962.
19 John G. Morris, *Get the Picture: A Personal History of Photojournalism* (Chicago: University of Chicago Press, 2002), 101.
20 Welky, "Defining Womanhood in the *Ladies' Home Journal*," 125.
21 For more on the Goulds, see Bruce Gould and Beatrice Blackmar Gould, *American Story: Memories and Reflections of Bruce Gould and Beatrice Blackmar Gould* (New York: Harper & Row, 1968).
22 Meyerowitz, "Beyond the Feminine Mystique," 1469.
23 As beauty editor of the *Ladies' Home Journal*, Benjamin not only wrote on fashion and beauty, but also topics related to embracing one's femininity and attracting men. Appropriately, she was also the author of *Why Men Like Us: Your Passport to Charm* (New York: Stackpole Sons, 1937).
24 Louise Paine Benjamin, "Femininity Begins at Home," *Ladies' Home Journal*, January 1947, 136.
25 Ibid.
26 "Our Readers Write Us," *Ladies' Home Journal*, October 1952, 4.
27 Leo Guild, "The 'How to Get Married' Chart," *Ladies' Home Journal*, June 1952, 93.
28 Benjamin, "Femininity Begins at Home," 136.
29 During a time when Parisian fashion houses were suffering and many believed the country could lose its leading role in the fashion world, Dior's show debuted on 12 February 1947 to a select audience and much fanfare, revolutionizing postwar female fashions and inspiring countless designers. See Jeanne Perkins, "Dior," *Life*, 1 March 1948, 85–90.
30 Nora O'Leary, "Little Gem of a Wardrobe," *Ladies' Home Journal*, February 1953, 52.
31 "*Life* Presents a Review of Fall Fashions," *Life*, 22 September 1947, 115–25.
32 Dawn Crowell, "Welcome Change," *Ladies' Home Journal*, February 1948, 168.
33 Ruth Mary Packard, "Pretty Mother's Wardrobe ... $99.00," *Ladies' Home Journal*, March 1952, 172.
34 Ruth Packard, "Stay-in-Style Wardrobe ... $111.56," *Ladies' Home Journal*, April 1952, 190.
35 Dawn Crowell Norman, "Are You an Up-to-Date Beauty?" *Ladies' Home Journal*, April 1952, 187.
36 Paul Marcus, "They Learned to Love Again," *Ladies' Home Journal*, October 1952, 171–4, 184–6. This unusual "How America Lives" column

highlighting the Simons' marriage problems was used to launch a long-running column called "Can This Marriage Be Saved?" that began in January 1953.
37 Dawn Crowell Norman, "The Soft Touch," *Ladies' Home Journal*, October 1952, 177.
38 Nora O'Leary, "Year-Round Maternity Clothes," *Ladies' Home Journal*, May 1953.
39 The 1950 US census indicated that 37,695,757 of 57,289,039 women over the age of fourteen were married.
40 Betty Hannah Hoffman, "The Big Wedding," *Ladies' Home Journal*, May 1954, 194.
41 Joan Hafey, "The Best Things in Life Are Free," *Ladies' Home Journal*, September 1955, 183.
42 Ibid., 185.
43 Ibid.
44 Ibid., 174.
45 Ibid., 172.
46 Ibid., 185.
47 Laura McEnaney, *Civil Defense Beings at Home: Militarization Meets Everyday Life in the Fifties* (Princeton, NJ: Princeton University Press, 2000), 108–9.
48 Katherine Howard, "Civil Defense at Home and Abroad," speech presented to the Massachusetts Society of Colonial Dames of America, Boston, Massachusetts, 31 March 1955, KGH Papers, Box 5, DDEL. The Federal Civil Defense Administration was created in 1951 before it was consolidated in 1958 with the Office of Defence Mobilization, under the Office of Civil and Defense Mobilization.
49 Hildegarde Dolson, "The Scrambled Housewife," *Ladies' Home Journal*, August 1954, 120.
50 Ibid., 121.
51 Dorothy Canner, "Interesting and Inexpensive," *Ladies' Home Journal*, August 1954, 98.
52 Dolson, "The Scrambled Housewife," 120.
53 Ibid., 122.
54 Margaret Davidson, "How Not to Stay Broke," *Ladies' Home Journal*, August 1954, 100.
55 Canner, "Interesting and Inexpensive," 98.
56 Amram Scheinfeld, "Are American Moms a Menace?" *Ladies' Home Journal*, November 1945, 36.
57 The majority of these articles tended to deal with the impact of "bad motherhood" on boys, and only rarely addressed its impact on girls. For example, "Masculinity, What Is It?: What Makes a Man Masculine" was one of

the rare accounts in the *Ladies' Home Journal* that addressed homosexuality, albeit only lightly. It stated that some "minor homosexuality" during adolescence was common, attributed it to a child's relationship with his parents, and noted that much needed to be learned about the "causes and cures" of homosexuality. See Betty Hannah, "Masculinity, What Is It?: What Makes a Man Masculine, *Ladies' Home Journal*, June 1963, 96, 98, 123–4.

58 "Diary of Domesticity" ran from November 1937 to December 1957; "Ask Any Woman" ran from September 1941 to June 1963; and "There's a Man in the House" ran from June 1949 to June 1963.

59 Clifford R. Adams, "Making Marriage Work: Be Cautious about Marrying," *Ladies' Home Journal*, October 1947, 26.

60 Clifford R. Adams, "Marking Marriage Work: Are You Failing as a Wife?" *Ladies' Home Journal*, November 1947, 26.

61 Each of these columns appeared in the August 1948, January 1950, January 1951, and January 1955 *Ladies' Home Journal* issues, respectively.

62 Clifford R. Adams, "Making Marriage Work: Are You a Creative Wife?" *Ladies' Home Journal*, January 1955, 26.

63 Clifford R. Adams, "Making Marriage Work: Changes Husbands Would Make," *Ladies' Home Journal*, December 1948, 26.

64 Clifford R. Adams, "Making Marriage Work: What's Wrong with Husbands?" *Ladies' Home Journal*, March 1949.

65 While Dr. Popenoe's name was attached to the column, case studies were compiled by Dorothy Cameron Disney (Mrs. Milton MacKaye), a mystery-story writer, who also worked on the column "How America Lives." October 1978's column was the last one associated with Popenoe's name. After this point, case studies were taken from various counselling agencies across the country.

66 Betty Hannah Hoffman, "The Man Who Saves Marriages," *Ladies' Home Journal*, September 1960, 124.

67 Molly Ladd-Taylor, "Eugenics, Sterilisation and Modern Marriage in the USA: The Strange Career of Paul Popenoe," *Gender & History* 13.2 (August 2001): 300.

68 Ibid., 307–8.

69 Ladd-Taylor, "Eugenics, Sterilisation and Modern Marriage in the USA," 305, 321. As Ladd-Taylor notes, throughout his early career Popenoe opposed the birth control movement, denouncing it as a "quasi-religious cult." By the 1970s, he actively lobbied against both women's and gay liberation, arguing that the "survival of 'civilized' society depended on strengthening the heterosexual 'foundations of the home.'"

70 "Can This Marriage Be Saved?" *Ladies' Home Journal*, January 1953, 82.

71 October 1968's "Can This Marriage Be Saved? Alma Hid from the Truth" finally addressed the issue of homosexuality in the heterosexual

marriage, through the twenty-year partnership of Thad and Alma, a couple with two sons. Thad admitted to being "born a homosexual," but blamed his single, smothering mother for his "miserable sex urges." Indeed, Popenoe affirmed Thad had received a "bad start" in life, particularly because he lacked a father figure and because "Alma did not help him." In spite of his affairs, alcoholic tendencies, and absenteeism, any of which would have easily doomed any marriage, the article concluded that after months of counselling for both, and psychiatric and group therapy for Thad, the couple were "happier than ever." They also benefited as parents, as Thad was no longer an "absent father" and Alma no longer a "tyrannical mother." See "Can This Marriage Be Saved? Alma Hid from the Truth," *Ladies' Home Journal*, October 1968, 30, 35–6, 40.
72 "Our Readers Write Us," *Ladies' Home Journal*, March 1954, 4.
73 Mrs. D.L. Hubert, "Can This Marriage Be Spoiled?" *Ladies' Home Journal*, January 1955, 6.
74 See Paul Popenoe, *Modern Marriage: A Handbook for Men* (New York: Macmillan, 1925) and *Marriage: Before and After* (New York: Wilfred Funk, 1943).
75 Michael J. Kirkhorn, "Dorothy Thompson: Withstanding the Storm," *The Courier* 23.2 (1988): 7.
76 Dorothy Thompson, "Commercialism Takes – and Wears – a New Look," *Ladies' Home Journal*, June 1954, 11.
77 The Northland Center closed in 2015.
78 May, *Homeward Bound*, 208.
79 Dorothy Thompson, "A Primer on the Cold War," *Ladies' Home Journal*, August 1950, 11.
80 Ibid.
81 Dorothy Thompson, 'The Economical Man Is the Patriot," *Ladies' Home Journal*, April 1948, 11.
82 Ibid., 12.
83 Dorothy Thompson, "To Protect Civil Liberties," *Ladies' Home Journal*, February 1952, 12.
84 Dorothy Thompson, "What Price Liberty?" *Ladies' Home Journal*, May 1958, 11.
85 Ibid., 14.
86 Ibid.
87 Ibid.
88 Thompson, "The Economical Man Is the Patriot," 12.
89 Eleanor Roosevelt, "If You Ask Me," *Ladies' Home Journal*, April 1948, 77.
90 W.J. Fulbright, "How to Get Better Men Elected," *Ladies' Home Journal*, November 1951, 218.
91 Ibid., 52.

244 Notes to pages 45–50

92 Margaret Chase Smith, "No Place for a Woman?" *Ladies' Home Journal*, February 1952, 50.
93 Ibid.
94 "The Eyes of the World Are upon Us," *Ladies' Home Journal*, September 1952, 51.
95 Ibid.
96 Meyerowitz, "Beyond the Feminine Mystique," 1469.
97 Margaret Hickey, "14 Points for Beginners in Politics," *Ladies' Home Journal*, February 1952, 49.
98 Erwin D. Canham, "It's Time Women Took Direct Action," *Ladies' Home Journal*, January 1952, 18.
99 "You Can Ask Questions," *Ladies' Home Journal*, March 1952, 165.
100 Margaret Hickey, "What's the US to You?" *Ladies' Home Journal*, April 1950, 23.
101 Ibid.
102 William Benton, "Join a Party ... Either Party ... But Join," *Ladies' Home Journal*, May 1952, 55.
103 Harold W. Dodds, "Women's Place in Politics," *Ladies' Home Journal*, August 1952, 47.
104 Ibid.
105 "Who Cares?" *Ladies' Home Journal*, October 1951, 46–7.
106 Canham, "It's Time Women Took Direct Action," 18.
107 Rosemary Jones, "Kefauver's Secret Weapon," *Ladies' Home Journal*, November 1954, 208.
108 "Women Like You and Me in Politics," *Ladies' Home Journal*, February 1952, 48.
109 Ibid.
110 "They Say It with Action," *Ladies' Home Journal*, February 1953, 149.
111 Ibid., 150.
112 "The Eyes of the World Are Upon Us," 50–1.
113 "How America Lives" was a regular column that ran until November 1979.
114 "How America Lives," *Ladies' Home Journal*, February 1940, 47.
115 Ibid.
116 Roger Butterfield, "We're Polls Apart ... in Politics Only," *Ladies' Home Journal*, November 1952, 69.
117 Ibid., 70.
118 Ibid.
119 Ibid.
120 Ibid., 176.
121 In March 1962, the Goulds resigned from their positions as editors of the *Ladies' Home Journal* and Curtiss Anderson, managing editor, replaced them. He led the magazine through a "sweeping reorganization" after its

long-time rival, *McCall's*, had overtaken it in circulation. In April 1963, shortly after the Winter 1963 issue on men appeared, he was replaced by Hubbard H. Cobb (1963–4), editor of *American Home*, followed by Davis Thomas (1964–5), managing editor of the *Saturday Evening Post*, and John Mack Carter (1965–74), who had ironically formerly been the editor at *McCall's*. A *New York Times* article at the time alluded to differences of opinion over the "conduct of the magazine," with Anderson noting, "An editor has to run his own magazine." See "Goulds Quit the *Home Journal*, Curtiss Anderson, 34, is Editor," *New York Times*, 6 March 1962; and "Editor of *Ladies' Home Journal* Is Replaced by Curtis Publishing," *New York Times*, 23 April 1963.

122 "Decline of Key Magazines Rocked Curtis Empire," *New York Times*, 9 October 1964.
123 Jean E. Hunter, "A Daring New Concept: 'The *Ladies' Home Journal* and Modern Feminism,'" *NWSA Journal* 2.4 (Autumn 1990): 585.
124 See Mary P. Ryan, *Women in Public: Between Banners and Ballots, 1825–1880* (Baltimore: Johns Hopkins University Press, 1992).

2 The "Babushka": The "Special Hardships" of Russian Womanhood in the *Ladies' Home Journal*

1 For further information on these Cold War partnerships, see Nancy E. Bernhard, *US Television News and Cold War Propaganda, 1947–1960* (New York: Cambridge University Press, 1999); Lykins, *From Total War to Total Diplomacy*; and James Schwoch, *Global TV: New Media and the Cold War, 1946–69* (Champaign: University of Chicago Press, 2009).
2 Meyerowitz, "Beyond the Feminine Mystique," 1469.
3 Scholarship on the postwar era frequently focuses on "the other" as it relates to racialized minorities, and African Americans in particular. Racialized minorities rarely, if ever, appeared in mainstream postwar magazines, women's or otherwise, frequently for fear of showing an unpalatable America to readers at home and abroad. In contrast, for publishers, depictions of Russian women as "the other" could satisfy the curiosity of readers as well as juxtapose Soviet life with the supposedly good life which existed in America.
4 Studies on Stalinist era housing have been limited, as most historians tend to focus on the Khrushchev era and its attempts to alleviate the problems of urban housing. See Donald Filzer, *The Hazards of Urban Life in Late Stalinist Russia: Health, Hygiene and Living Standards, 1943–1953* (Cambridge: Cambridge University Press, 2010); and Mark B. Smith, *Property of Communists: The Urban Housing Program from Stalin to Khrushchev* (Dekalb: Northern Illinois University Press, 2010).

5 J.B. Phillips, "Typical Woman of Postwar Moscow," *Newsweek* 28, 4 November 1946, 52.
6 Griswold, "Russian Blonde in Space," 882.
7 Winter, an Australian-British journalist, was likely chosen to write this piece, the only one she ever wrote for the *Ladies' Home Journal*, because of her previous work on the Soviet Union during the interwar period. In her rather complimentary account, she praised the new regime for its progress in emancipating women in the workplace, the family, and in sexual relationships. See Ella Winter, *Red Virtue* (New York: Harcourt, Brace, 1933).
8 Ella Winter, "Our Allies, the Russians," *Ladies' Home Journal*, February 1943, 37, 152.
9 Phillips, "Typical Woman of Postwar Moscow," 52.
10 Americans got other glimpses of the Soviet Union during the war. In 1942, Artkino Pictures, the official distributor of Soviet documentaries, released *Moscow Strikes Back*, which focused on the Battle of Moscow. It was released to wide acclaim and won an Academy Award for Best Documentary Feature. More notably, the next year the Office of War Information (OWI) released *Why We Fight*, a seven-film series, directed by Frank Capra, which sought to persuade the American public of the necessity of the US war effort. It included a two-part film entitled "The Battle of Russia," directed by Capra and Russian-born Anatole Litvak, which focused on the Siege of Leningrad and the Battle of Stalingrad. Although it was controversial in its favourable depiction of the Soviet Union, it was nominated for an Academy Award for Best Documentary Feature that same year.
11 Peter Hopkinson, *Split Focus: An Involvement in Two Decades* (London: Rupert Hart-Davis, 1969), 81.
12 Ibid., 96.
13 Ibid., 90.
14 Ibid., 84–5.
15 Ibid., 86.
16 Ibid., 93.
17 Feiga Blekher, *The Soviet Woman in the Family and in Society (A Sociological Study)* (New York: John Wiley & Sons, 1979), 19.
18 Mark G. Field, "Workers (Mothers): Soviet Women Today," in Donald R. Brown, *The Role and Status of Women in the Soviet Union* (New York: Teachers College Press, 1968), 27.
19 Field, "Workers (Mothers): Soviet Women Today," 22.
20 In comparison, the 1960 US census indicated that the population of women (61.5 million) over the age of sixteen outnumbered that of men (55.6 million) by almost six million. In spite of this discrepancy, 83.3 per

cent of men over the age of sixteen were in the paid labour force, compared with only 37.7 per cent of women. See Mitra Toosi, "A Century of Change: the US Labor Force, 1950–2050," *Monthly Labor Review* (May 2002): 15–28, https://www.bls.gov/opub/mlr/2002/05/art2full.pdf.
21 Alex Inkeles and Raymond Bauer, *The Soviet Citizen: Daily Life in a Totalitarian Society* (Cambridge, MA: Harvard University Press, 1959), 3–4. Inkeles and Bauer launched the project during the summer of 1950, and ultimately conducted 764 interviews and disseminated questionnaires to almost 3,000 different respondents. As the authors noted, up to that point there had been many studies on the history of the Soviet Union, and the structure and functioning of its institutions, but little was known about the attitudes, values, and experiences of its citizens. The authors thus focused on evaluating certain aspects of Soviet citizens' daily lives; these include their occupation, education, and knowledge of current events and family life, as well as their relationship to the state, including support for and against it, and divisions as they related to social class, the Communist Party and secret police, and ethnicity. Inkeles and Bauer, *The Soviet Citizen*, 5.
22 Inkeles and Bauer, *The Soviet Citizen*, x.
23 Although this study refers to its subject matter as "Russian women," when discussing Inkeles and Bauer's study it will refer to them as "Soviet women," particularly since the refugees that were interviewed had migrated to the West from throughout the Soviet Union, not solely Russia.
24 Inkeles and Bauer, *The Soviet Citizen*, 208.
25 Ibid., 207.
26 Ibid., 204.
27 Ibid., 206.
28 Ibid., 207.
29 LaFell Dickinson, "Russian Women as I Saw Them," *Redbook*, February 1947, 54.
30 Bess Furman, "Women in Russia Said to Fear War," *New York Times*, 5 September 1946, 38.
31 Steinbeck's sympathetic accounts of Depression-era migrant workers through works such as *The Grapes of Wrath* and his critiques of modern-day capitalism earned him a devout following in the Soviet Union. Capa, a former *Life* photographer, had made a name for himself through his vivid images of the Spanish Civil War and the European front during World War II. He was also part of the prestigious group of photographers who founded Magnum Photos in 1947, a cooperative photography agency that provided pictures to international publications. The photographs included in "Women and Children in the USSR" were among its first works.

32 Steinbeck and Capa, "Women and Children in the USSR," 44.
33 See John Steinbeck, *A Russian Journal* (New York: Penguin Books, 1948).
34 This article demonstrates that children – invariably linked to the supposedly maternal female readers of the *Ladies' Home Journal* – were, like women, used as political tools during the Cold War. Children were used to evoke both outrage and sympathy from readers. For example, Steinbeck wrote of their wartime "patriotism," discussing their work as spies and runners, as well as on the farm, picking vegetables and tending to animals. These descriptions were ones which ran counter to the innocent images of America's wartime children. In contrast, he also discussed Russian children in relation to their school and leisure time activities, which included trips to museums, listening to concerts in the park, taking ballet and piano lessons, and playing chess. While these were not necessarily activities that American children would have engaged in, they demonstrated that Soviet children were relatable. Steinbeck wrote that just as in the United States, "the best of everything ... was reserved for the children." However, he noticed that children living in destroyed areas had eyes with a "haunted sadness" and smiles that came "reluctantly." He noted that "these children have lived a hundred years of tragedy when they should have been in grade school." Of Capa's images, seventeen focused on children; these included ones where they engaged in adultlike activities, such as marching alongside soldiers in Red Square, waiting in line to see Lenin's Tomb, and working in the fields. For more on the US and Soviet use of children as political tools to demonstrate the strength and future of their respective nations, as well as to highlight the "other," see Margaret Peacock, *Innocent Weapons: The Soviet and American Politics of Childhood in the Cold War* (Chapel Hill: University of North Carolina Press, 2014).
35 Steinbeck and Capa, "Women and Children in the USSR," 44.
36 Morris, *Get the Picture*, 114–19. Picture editor John G. Morris, a close friend of Capa's, notes in his autobiography that the Goulds were impressed with Capa's work for a twelve-part *Ladies' Home Journal* series on families around the world called "People Are People the World Over." The series was featured from April 1948 to March 1949 and included Capa's images of a typical American family in the Goulds' native Iowa. When Morris presented them with Capa's images of Russian women, they eagerly accepted the opportunity to seize this "exclusive" story from other major publications, including *Life*.
37 Morris, *Get the Picture*, 119.
38 Although Capa and Steinbeck travelled throughout parts of the Soviet Union – Russia, Georgia, and Ukraine in particular – they referred to the women they encountered as Russian, rather than Soviet.

39 Alex Kershaw, *Blood and Champagne: The Life and Times of Robert Capa* (New York: St. Martin's Press, 2003), 178.
40 Richard Wheelan, *Robert Capa: A Biography* (New York: Alfred A. Knopf, 1985), 150–1.
41 Kershaw, *Blood and Champagne*, 179.
42 Ibid., 187.
43 Ibid., 186.
44 Ibid., 191.
45 Steinbeck and Capa, "Women and Children in the USSR," 45.
46 Jay Parini, *John Steinbeck: A Biography* (New York: Henry Holt and Company, 1994), 311.
47 Steinbeck and Capa, "Women and Children in the USSR," 51.
48 Ibid., 52.
49 Ibid., 51.
50 During the postwar period, the *Ladies' Home Journal* was devoid of articles on female friendships. In fact, letters to the editor and articles suggested that a woman's best friend was her husband. For example, in 1951, Mrs. R.F. Buettner wrote into the magazine to tell readers that a second marriage could be "successful and beautiful." Indeed, it was her second husband, who had taken care of her after she suffered a mild stroke and had a bad fall, that was her "best friend." Mrs. R.F. Buettner, "A Husband Is a Girl's Best Friend," *Ladies' Home* Journal, June 1951, 5.
51 Steinbeck and Capa, "Women and Children in the USSR," 49.
52 Ibid., 45.
53 Ibid.
54 Ibid., 49.
55 Ibid., 59.
56 Wilbela Cushman, "Sun Fashion Here to Stay," *Ladies' Home Journal*, February 1948, 62–7.
57 Henrietta Murdock, "What Can Young Marrieds Afford?" *Ladies' Home Journal*, February 1948, 128, 214–15.
58 Ann Batchelder, "February Fare," *Ladies' Home Journal*, February 1948, 72–3, 202.
59 Historian Nancy A. Walker has analysed the "How America Lives" series, which first appeared in February 1940, demonstrating that its messages were fiercely nationalistic. Although featured families varied in their location and socio-economic status, the series only reflected the white, middle-class ideal that was predominant at mid-century. See Nancy A. Walker, "*The Ladies' Home Journal,* 'How America Lives' and the Limits of Cultural Diversity," *Media History* 6.2 (2000).
60 Lewis M. Dickson, "How America Lives: How We Save on $71 a Week," *Ladies' Home Journal*, February 1948, 160–1.

61 Ibid., 158–9.
62 Ibid., 170.
63 Filzer, *Hazards of Urban Life*, 32.
64 From 1947 to 1950, Stalin began construction of what became known as the "Seven Sisters" skyscrapers, all of which would tower over the city's skyline, and be built according to the elaborate principles of "Stalinist Architecture." After his death, an "eighth sister" was to have been built, but Khrushchev scrapped the plan. See Katherine Zubovich, *Moscow Monumental* (Princeton, NJ: Princeton University Press, 2020).
65 For more on the construction of, and everyday life within, *Khrushchevka*, see Steven E. Harris, *Communism on Tomorrow Street: Mass Housing and Everyday Life after Stalin* (Baltimore: Johns Hopkins University Press, 2013); Steven E. Harris, "Soviet Mass Housing and the Communist Way of Life," in *Everyday Life in Russia Past and Present*, ed. Choi Chatterjee et al. (Bloomington: Indiana University Press, 2015); Susan E. Reid, "Communist Comfort: Socialist Modernism and the Making of Cosy Homes in the Khrushchev Era," *Gender & History* 21.3 (November 2009); Christina Varga-Harris, "Moving towards Utopia: Soviet Housing in the Atomic Age," in *Divided Dreamworlds? The Cultural Cold War in East and West*, ed. Peter Romijn et al. (Amsterdam: Amsterdam University Press, 2012); Christine Varga-Harris, *Stories of House and Home: Soviet Apartment Life during the Khrushchev Years* (Ithaca, NY: Cornell University Press, 2015).
66 Dawn Crowell, "Welcome Change," *Ladies' Home Journal*, February 1948, 168.
67 Morris, *Get the Picture*, 119.
68 Lisa A. Kirschenbaum, "Constructing a Cold War Epic: Harrison Salisbury and the Siege of Leningrad," in *Americans Experience Russia: Encountering the Enigma, 1917 to the Present*, ed. Choi Chatterjee and Beth Holmgren (New York: Routledge, 2012), 73–4.
69 Harrison Salisbury, "Russia Re-Viewed: Life of a Soviet Common Man Is a Constant Struggle," *New York Times*, 24 September 1954.
70 Eleanor Roosevelt, "If You Ask Me," *Ladies' Home Journal*, August 1948, 44.
71 Steinbeck and Capa, "Women and Children in the USSR," 59.
72 Bruce and Beatrice Gould's article appeared as a transcribed interview, which outlined each question and reply.
73 "We Saw How Russians Live," *Ladies' Home Journal*, February 1957, 59.
74 Ibid., 60.
75 Robert Griscom, "Report on Russian Youth," *Ladies' Home Journal*, February 1957, 173.
76 Ibid., 170.
77 "We Saw How Russians Live," 176.
78 Ibid., 179.
79 Ibid.

Notes to pages 78–81   251

80 Molly Ladd-Taylor and Lauri Umansky, "Introduction" in *"Bad" Mothers: The Politics of Blame in Twentieth-Century America*, ed. Molly Ladd-Taylor and Lauri Umansky (New York: New York University Press, 1998), 13.
81 "They Let Us Talk to the Russians," *Ladies' Home Journal*, June 1955, 149.
82 "We Saw How Russians Live," 58.
83 Deborah A. Field, "Everyday Life and the Problem of Conceptualizing Public and Private during the Khrushchev Era," in Chatterjee et al., *Everyday Life in Russia*, 174–5.
84 Ibid., 176.
85 Griscom, "Report on Russian Youth," 170.
86 "We Saw How Russians Live," 176.
87 Ibid.
88 Lydia Kirk and Roger Kirk, *Distinguished Service: Lydia Chapin Kirk, Partner in Diplomacy, 1896–1985* (Syracuse, NY: Syracuse University Press, 2007), xiv.
89 Role of Psychological Strategy Board under 4/4/51 Presidential Directive, 28 September 1951; Box 13; 091.4 Southeast Asia File #2 to 091.411 Responsibilities and Precedents under NSC 10/5; Psychological Strategy Board Files; Harry S. Truman Papers, HST Library.
90 Kirk and Kirk, *Distinguished Service*, xiv.
91 Ibid., 251.
92 Lydia Kirk, "Letters from Moscow," *Ladies' Home Journal*, March 1952, 47.
93 Nona Bolakian, "Talk with Lydia Kirk," *New York Times*, 27 July 1952.
94 Kirk, "Letters from Moscow," March 1952, 198.
95 Ibid.
96 Ibid.
97 Ibid. Much had been said in the postwar media on the Soviet Union's repression of the Russian Orthodox Church and religion more broadly. However, by the post-Stalinist era, articles emerged that emphasized Khrushchev's increased acceptance of the place of religion in the lives of Russia's fifty million followers. Although Sunday schools and religious instruction for children were prohibited, women continued their religious traditions, including attending church and baptizing their children. See Charles C. Parlin, "Women versus the Kremlin," *Ladies' Home Journal*, October 1956, 46, 48, 50, 127.
98 Lydia Kirk, "Letters from Moscow," *Ladies' Home Journal*, April 1952, 132.
99 Kirk, "Letters from Moscow," March 1952, 201.
100 Lydia Kirk, *Postmarked Moscow* (New York: Charles Scribner's Sons, 1952), 189.
101 Alice Kessler-Harris, *In Pursuit of Equity: Women, Men and the Quest for Economic Citizenship in 20th-Century America* (New York: Oxford University Press, 2001), 205.

102 Alice Kessler-Harris, "Pink Collar Ghetto, Blue Collar Token," in *Sisterhood Is Powerful: The Women's Anthology for a New Millennium*, ed. Robin Morgan (New York: Washington Square Press, 2003), 360–1.
103 See Katarina Katz, *Gender, Work and Wages in the Soviet Union: A Legacy of Discrimination* (New York: Palgrave Macmillan, 2001).
104 Kirk, *Postmarked Moscow*, 109.
105 Ibid., 189.
106 Ibid., 47.
107 Ibid., 116.
108 Kirk, "Letters from Moscow," March 1952, 199.
109 Kirk, *Postmarked Moscow*, 210.
110 Ibid., 47–8.
111 Kirk, "Letters from Moscow," March 1952, 199.
112 Emily S. Rosenberg, "Another Mission to Moscow: Ida Rosenthal and Consumer Dreams," in Chatterjee and Holmgren, *Americans Experience Russia*, 131–2.
113 Ibid., 134.
114 Ibid., 132.
115 Ibid., 135.
116 Kirk, *Postmarked Moscow*, 138.
117 Kirk, "Letters from Moscow," March 1952, 193.
118 Kirk, *Postmarked Moscow*, 116.
119 Kirk, "Letters from Moscow," March 1952, 199.
120 Ibid., 217.
121 Kirk, *Postmarked Moscow*, 230.
122 Kirk, "Letters from Moscow," March 1952, 200.
123 Kirk, *Postmarked Moscow*, 212.
124 Ibid., 50–1.
125 In 1955, Levine's husband became the first US television correspondent to be accredited in the Soviet Union. He subsequently wrote three non-fiction books on the country. See Irving R. Levine, *Main Street USSR* (Garden City, NY: Doubleday, 1959); Irving R. Levine, *Travel Guide to Russia* (Garden City, NY: Doubleday, 1960); Irving R. Levine, *The New Worker in Soviet Russia* (New York: Macmillan, 1973).
126 Nancy Jones Levine, "American Bride in Moscow," *Ladies' Home Journal*, February 1958, 4.
127 Kirk, "Letters from Moscow," May 1952, 217–18.
128 Levine, "American Bride in Moscow," 4.
129 Gisela Kahn Gresser, "I Went to Moscow," *Ladies' Home Journal*, October 1950, 48–9, 142, 147, 144, 150. Gresser wrote that their five-star treatment included their stay at the Savoy, a luxury hotel in the heart of Moscow, transportation by limousine, and visits to the theatre and ballet. In 1956,

Notes to pages 86–91   253

Charles C. Parlin travelled to the Soviet Union as part of a delegation of nine American clergymen, invited by Alexei I, Patriarch of Moscow, to observe Russia's churches and meet with its religious leaders. Parlin noted the "lavish red-carpet welcomes" that awaited them throughout their ten-day stay and wrote that every meal was a "banquet in the grand style." See Parlin, "Women versus the Kremlin."
130 Ibid., 83.
131 "They Let Us Talk to the Russians," 152.
132 Dorothy Thompson, "America's Greatest Problem." *Ladies' Home Journal*, December 1946, 6.
133 Kirk, "Letters from Moscow," April 1952, 63.
134 Van Raalte advertisements, *Ladies' Home Journal*, March 1952, 202, 203.
135 Kirk, "Letters from Moscow," March 1952, 199.
136 Spring, *Advertising in the Age of Persuasion*, 47.
137 Brand Names Foundation, *Ladies' Home Journal*, March 1952, 198.
138 "They Let Us Talk to the Russians," 151.
139 Kirk, "Letters from Moscow," April 1952, 132.
140 Michael J. Kirkhorn, "Dorothy Thompson: Withstanding the Storm," *The Courier* 23.2 (1988): 7.
141 Dorothy Thompson, *The New Russia* (New York: Henry Holt, 1928), 15.
142 Thompson, *The New Russia*, 18.
143 Ibid., 270.
144 Ibid., 262.
145 Ibid., 264.
146 Other articles focused on English, French, and German women. See H.G. Wells, "The Woman and the War: What It Has Already Meant and What It Will Mean: A Remarkable Article," *Ladies' Home Journal*, June 1916, 10, 59–62; Sarah Bernhardt, "My France," *Ladies' Home Journal*, February 1917, 11–12; James W. Gerard, "What the German Women Have Done: What the American Women Can Now Do," *Ladies' Home Journal*, August 1917, 15.
147 Natalie De Bogary, "The Russian Woman That Is Coming," *Ladies' Home Journal*, March 1917, 16.
148 In the immediate postwar period, articles on Russia and its women were minimal, but those that appeared criticized the tyranny of the new Russian regime and the broken promises it had made to its women. See C. Berkeley Burnand, "How I Escaped through Russia: The Remarkable Experiences of a Young Bride with Her Baby," *Ladies' Home Journal*, September 1919, 25–6, 97–8, 100; and Maude Radford Warren, "Bolshevik Women," *Ladies' Home Journal*, December 1920, 16–17, 176.
149 Isaac Marcosson, "The After-the-War Woman: What Is She Going to Become, and Where, Too, Will Be Her Place?" *Ladies' Home Journal*, June 1918, 13, 90, 92.

150 Maurice Hindus, "What's What in Russia," *Ladies' Home Journal*, October 1931, 12–13, 178–9.
151 Eve Garette Grady, "The Twilight of Russian Family Gods," *Ladies' Home Journal*, November 1931, 12–13, 172–3, 175.
152 Anne O'Hare McCormick, "Russia Now Laughs," *Ladies' Home Journal*, April 1934, 8–9, 130–2, 135. McCormick was a *New York Times* columnist who wrote extensively on Europe during the interwar period and World War II.
153 Julia L. Mickenberg, *American Girls in Red Russia: Chasing the Soviet Dream* (Chicago: University of Chicago Press, 2017), 183, 31.
154 Ibid., 246. African American artists in particular were encouraged by the Soviet government to visit the country and were courted extensively for the purposes of drumming up pro-communist sentiment when they returned home to America. Many wrote of their positive experiences while there. For example, in 1995 writer Dorothy West wrote that 1932, the year she spent in Moscow, was perhaps the happiest one of her life. See Dorothy West, "An Adventure in Moscow," in *The Richer, the Poorer* (New York: Doubleday Anchor, 1995), 205.
155 Thompson wrote *I Saw Hitler* in 1932 after a 1931 interview with Hitler, in which she warned of his rise to power and its possible repercussions.
156 Kirkhorn, "Dorothy Thompson," 16.
157 Dorothy Thompson, "I Write of Russian Women," *Ladies' Home Journal*, March 1952, 11.
158 Ibid., 12.
159 Margaret Marsh, "Suburban Men and Masculine Domesticity, 1870–1915," *American Quarterly* 40.2 (June 1988): 166.
160 Dorothy Thompson, "What Is Wrong with American Woman?" *Ladies' Home Journal*, August 1953, 11.
161 Ibid.
162 Cucuz, "Containment Culture," 156.
163 Dorothy Cameron Disney, "Escape to Freedom," *Ladies' Home Journal*, April 1952, 181.
164 Ibid., 197.
165 Griswold, "Russian Blonde in Space," 882.
166 "We Saw How Russians Live," 187.
167 Historians of the Soviet Union have recently begun to study diary entries, released after the collapse of the USSR, to analyse "socialist subjectivity," but many of these studies have been undertaken in the context of the early Stalinist era. They show the complex inner struggles many went through to conform ideologically. More recently, Anatoly Pinsky has written on the Soviet writers and literary critics who wrote diary entries expressing hope of reforming socialism under Khrushchev. He argues that

with the recent study of Soviet diaries to gain insights into the past, historians should consider not just the content of diaries but also the purpose of their authors in writing them. See Jochen Hellbeck, *Revolution on My Mind: Writing a Diary under Stalin* (Cambridge, MA: Harvard University Press, 2006); and Anatoly Pinsky, "The Diaristic Form and Subjectivity under Khrushchev," *Slavic Review* 73.4 (Winter 2014): 805–27.

3 Selling the American Way Abroad: The Beginnings of Cold War Cultural Diplomacy in the Soviet Union

1. USIA, Basic Guidance and Policy Planning Paper No. 12, "Women's Activities (Part II)," 13 August 1959; Box 14; Correspondence, Cultural Exchange Program, 1972 to Interdepartmental Committee on Cooperation with American Republics, 1937–1938; Subject Files, 1953–2000; General Records of the US Information Agency, Record Group 306 (RG 306); NACP.
2. USIA, Basic Guidance and Policy Planning Paper No. 12, "Women's Activities (Part II)," 13 August 1959; Box 14; Correspondence, Cultural Exchange Program, 1972 to Interdepartmental Committee on Cooperation with American Republics, 1937–1938; Subject Files, 1953–2000; General Records of the US Information Agency, Record Group 306 (RG 306); NACP.
3. USIA, Basic Guidance and Policy Planning Paper No. 6, "Women's Activities," 31 March 1959; Box 14; Correspondence, Cultural Exchange Program, 1972 to Interdepartmental Committee on Cooperation with American Republics, 1937–1938; Subject Files, 1953–2000; RG 306; NACP.
4. Ibid.
5. Ibid.
6. Dean, *Imperial Brotherhood*, 13.
7. Executive Order 9182 of 13 June 1942, Establishing the Office of War Information. Gerhard Peters and John T. Woolley, *The American Presidency Project*, http://www.presidency.ucsb.edu/ws/?pid=16273.
8. For more on the creation of propaganda material to entice American women to support the war effort, see Tawnya J. Adkins Covert, *Manipulating Images: World War II Mobilization of Women through Magazine Advertising* (Lanham, MD: Lexington Books, 2011); Maureen Honey, *Creating Rosie the Riveter: Class, Gender and Propaganda during World War II* (Amherst: University of Massachusetts Press, 1984); and Leila J. Rupp, *Mobilizing Women for War: German and American Propaganda, 1939–1945* (Princeton, NJ: Princeton University Press, 1978).
9. For more on American women's wartime contributions, see Karen Anderson, *Wartime Women: Sex Roles, Family Relations and the Status of Women During World War II* (Westport, CT: Greenwood Press 1981); and

Susan M. Hartmann, *The Home Front and Beyond: American Women in the 1940s* (Boston: Twain Publishers, 1982).

10 Miller's poster, created for Westinghouse Electric Corporation, is the most commonly known image of Rosie the Riveter. However, in 1943, iconic American artist Normal Rockwell also created an image of Rosie which graced the 29 May 1943 issue of the *Saturday Evening Post*. In this slightly more masculinized version, she was seen wearing overalls, eating her lunch, and sitting in front of an American flag with a rivet gun in her lap and a copy of *Mein Kampf* under her feet.

11 Edward P. Lilly, The Development of American Psychological Operations, 1945–1951, 19 December 1951; Box 22, p. 23; Distribution of PSB Report to NSC to File #2 – Report by the PSB on the Status of the Psychological Program; Psychological Strategy Board Files, Harry S. Truman Library (HST Library).

12 Ibid., 24.

13 Ibid., 34.

14 Tuch, *Communicating with the World*, 6.

15 International Educational Exchange Program, "The Citizens Role in Cultural Relations," September 1959; Box 2, p. 1; Organization, News Articles, 1955–1974 to Agency Mission, 1947–1969; Subject Files, 1953–2000; RG 306; NACP.

16 United States Information and Educational Exchange Act of 1948, Public Law 402 (1948), http://www.state.gov/documents/organization/177574.pdf.

17 Ibid.

18 Hixson, *Parting the Curtain*, 11.

19 Division of Research for Europe, Office of Intelligence Research, "Information Control and Propaganda in the USSR," 24 February 1948; Box 9, p. 5; State Department Information Programs (1946–1948); Charles Hulten Papers; HST Library.

20 Ibid.

21 Hixson, *Parting the Curtain*, 10.

22 Division of Research for Europe, Office of Intelligence Research, "Information Control and Propaganda in the USSR," 24 February 1948; Box 9, p. 1; State Department Information Programs (1946–1948); Charles Hulten Papers; HST Library.

23 Central Intelligence Agency Report, "Soviet-Satellite Drive against Western Influence in Eastern Europe," 2 June 1950; ORE 17–50 Central Intelligence Reports; President's Secretary's Files: Intelligence File; HST Library.

24 Hixson, *Parting the Curtain*, 9.

25 Division of Research for Europe, Office of Intelligence Research, "Information Control and Propaganda in the USSR," 24 February 1948; Box 9, pp. 7–8; State Department Information Programs (1946–1948); Charles Hulten Papers; HST Library.

26 Ibid., 7.
27 Sanders had a long career as a journalist and speechwriter before coming to the Office of War Information and later *Amerika*. After leaving *Amerika*, in 1952, she unsuccessfully ran for Congress in New York's 28th District; in 1958, she became a senior editor at *Harper's Magazine*, and, in 1973, she wrote the first biography on Dorothy Thompson.
28 Telegram from James E. Webb to American Embassy, 18 May 1950; Box 2430; From 511.61/1–551 to 511.61/12–3154; Decimal File; Department of State, Record Group 59 (RG 59); NACP.
29 Edward D. Kuekes, "Better Than Bombs," *Cleveland Plain Dealer*, 25 January 1951.
30 Marion K. Sanders, "*Amerika* Magazine: An Affirmative Tool of the US Overseas Information Program," *The American Foreign Service Journal*, June 1949; Box 2453; Decimal File 1950–1954; RG 59; NACP.
31 Ibid.
32 These issues included 13 (August 1946); 14 (September 1946); 16 (November 1946); 17 (December 1946); 18 (January 1947); 20 (March 1947); 22 (May 1947); 26 (September 1947); and 31 (February 1941).
33 This article explicitly stated that it intended to refute Soviet propaganda on American race relations and discussed the "impressive strides" African Americans had made since the turn of the century. It was the only instance in which *Amerika* addressed African American life during the magazine's first run and one of the magazine's rare attempts to acknowledge the issue of race and race relations under Truman. "The Negro in American Life," *Amerika* 50, 2–15.
34 Sanders, "*Amerika* Magazine."
35 Creighton Peet, "Russian '*Amerika*,' a Magazine about US for Soviet Citizens," *College Art Journal* 11.1 (Autumn 1951): 20.
36 Ralph S. Collins, USIE Report for the Months April, May, and June 1950, Report 3, 14 August 1950; Box 2425; Department of State Central Decimal File 1950–1954, Records of the State Department, RG 59; NACP.
37 Foreign Service Despatch, Communication for Soviet Distributor of Magazine *Amerika*, 7 September 1951; Box 28; *Amerika Illustrated*, 1950–1956 to National Security Directive 51, 17 October 1990; Records Relating to Select USIA Programs, 1953–1999; RG 306; NACP.
38 Robert I. Owen to State Department, 7 December 1951, Box 28; *Amerika Illustrated*, 1950–1956 to National Security Directive 51, 17 October 1990; Records Relating to Select USIA Programs, 1953–1999; RG 306; NACP.
39 Ibid.
40 Telegram from Dean Acheson to US Embassy in Moscow, 20 July 1950; Box 2430; From 511.61/1–551 to 511.61/12–3154; Decimal File; RG 59; NACP.
41 Peet, "Russian '*Amerika*,'" 9.

42 Ibid., 11.
43 Telegram from Alan G. Kirk to Dean Acheson; 23 June 1950; Box 2430; From 511.61/1–551 to 511.61/12–3154; Decimal File; RG 59; NACP.
44 Telegram from Dean Acheson to US Embassy in Moscow; 5 September 1950; Box 2430; From 511.61/1-551 to 511.61/12-3154; Decimal File; RG 59; NACP.
45 Memorandum from Marion K. Sanders to Jack McDermott, 27 February 1950; Box 28; *Amerika Illustrated*, 1950–1956 to National Security Directive 51, 17 October 1990; Records Relating to Select USIA Programs, 1953–1999; RG 306; NACP.
46 "Propaganda Steps by US Criticized," *New York Times*, 1 June 1952.
47 Role of Psychological Strategy Board under 4/4/51 Presidential Directive, 28 September 1951, Section 1 "Torrential" File #1, Psychological Strategy Board, box 13, Truman Library, 4969.
48 Manning and Romerstein, *Historical Dictionary of American Propaganda*, 229.
49 Presidential Directive, 4 April 1951, Section 1 "Torrential" File #1, PSB, Box 13, Truman Library.
50 Former secretary of the US Army Gordon Gray became the PSB's first director. In interviews, he indicated that the PSB was inhibited by the State Department belief that the PSB was merely an extension of its own foreign policy objectives, and not an autonomous agency tasked with creating a national plan for the Cold War. Further, he notes that the PSB lacked support and advocacy from key officials. According to Gray, on the occasions he spoke with the president regarding the PSB, Truman's feedback consisted simply of "do the best you can." Richard D. McKinzie, Oral History Interview with Gordon Gray, Washington, DC, 18 June 1973, http://www.trumanlibrary.org/oralhist/gray.htm.
51 Ed Edwin Interview with Mr. and Mrs. Abbott Washburn, 20 April 1967 and 5 January 1968; Files of Special Assistant to the Office of Coordinator of Government Public Service Advertising (James M. Lambie, Jr.) Red Cross – 1957; Staff Files; DDE Library.
52 Dwight D. Eisenhower, State of the Union Address, 2 February 1953, DDE Library, https://www.eisenhower.archives.gov/all_about_ike/speeches/1953_state_of_the_union.pdf. http://www.eisenhower.archives.gov/all_about_ike/speeches/1953_state_of_the_union.pdf.
53 Kenneth A. Osgood, "Total Cold War: US Propaganda in the 'Free World,' 1953–1960" (PhD diss., University of California, Santa Barbara, 2001), 23.
54 Dwight D. Eisenhower, "The Chance for Peace Speech," 16 April 1953, DDE Library, http://www.eisenhower.archives.gov/all_about_ike/speeches/chance_for_peace.pdf.
55 Osgood, "Total Cold War," 41.

56 For more on C.D. Jackson, see John Allen Stern, *C.D. Jackson: Cold War Propagandist for Democracy and Globalism* (Lanham, MD: University Press of America, 2012).
57 Hixson, *Parting the Iron Curtain*, 22.
58 Ibid., 20.
59 US Information Agency First Report to Congress, August–December 1953; Box 39, ii; Posts Publications, 1953–1999; RG 306; NACP.
60 Don North, Oral History Interview with Theodore Streibert, 10 December 1970; DDE Library.
61 Ibid.
62 US Information Agency First Report to Congress, August–December 1953; Box 39, ii; Posts Publications, 1953–1999; RG 306; NACP.
63 The President's Committee on International Information Activities Report to the President, 30 June 1953; Box 14; US President's Committee International Information Activities (Jackson Committee) Records, 1950–1953; DDE Library.
64 A Report to the National Security Council – NSC-68, 12 April 1950; President's Secretary's Files; HST Library.
65 X, "The Sources of Soviet Conduct," 575.
66 Elizabeth Edwards Spalding, *The First Cold Warrior: Harry Truman, Containment and the Remaking of Liberal Internationalism* (Lexington: University of Kentucky Press, 2006), 186.
67 The President's Committee on International Information Activities Report to the President, 30 June 1953; Box 14; US President's Committee International Information Activities (Jackson Committee) Records, 1950–1953; DDE Library.
68 James C. Hagerty, Press Release, The White House, 8 July 1953; Box 63, p. 3; C.D. Jackson Papers, 1931–67; DDE Library.
69 Executive Order 10483 Establishing the Operations Coordinating Board, 2 September 1953; Box 22; White House Office: Office of the Staff Secretary, 1952–61; Eisenhower Library.
70 Executive Order 10483 Establishing the Operations Coordinating Board, 2 September 1953, Box 17, Eisenhower Library.
71 Executive Order No. 10598, Amending Executive Order No. 10483, Establishing the Operations Coordinating Board, 28 February 1955, Box 17, Eisenhower Library.
72 Operations Coordinating Board Handbook, September 1955; Box 22; White House Office: Office of the Staff Secretary, 1952–61; Eisenhower Library.
73 Executive Order No. 10598 Amending Executive Order No. 10483 Establishing the Operations Coordinating Board, 28 February 1955; Box 22; White House Office: Office of the Staff Secretary, 1952–61; DDE Library.

260 Notes to pages 113–15

74 Truman created the Psychological Strategy Board in 1951, but it was plagued with problems, which included a lack of funding and office space as well as high turnover rates. It folded in 1953, when Eisenhower became president.
75 It should be noted that the USIA's existence, funding, and efficacy varied under each Cold War administration. Throughout the 1950s and 1960s the USIA was well funded and had expanded, particularly as Kennedy sought to rebuild America's international image in Latin America and Africa, and Johnson sought to continue that trend during a tumultuous decade. During the 1970s, the agency's work was undermined by Nixon and National Security Advisor and Secretary of State Kissinger, and as a result, it declined in influence. Under Carter, the agency went through a major reorganization, and in 1977 its functions, along with those of the State Department's Bureau of Cultural and Educational Affairs (CU) were subsumed by the newly created United States International Communication Agency (ICA). It also faced the foreign policy challenges of the Carter years. In 1982, Reagan changed the agency's name back to the USIA; its foreign policy influence was restored, its budget expanded, and it played a vital role in restoring the US image abroad, particularly after the "malaise and self-doubt" of the 1970s. Cull, *The Cold War and the United States Information Agency*, 189, 294, 361, 404–6, 442.
76 James C. Hagerty, Press Release, The White House, 8 July 1953; Box 63, p. 3; C.D. Jackson Papers, 1931–67; DDE Library.
77 The President's Committee on International Information Activities Report to the President, 30 June 1953; Box 14; US President's Committee International Information Activities (Jackson Committee) Records, 1950–1953; DDE Library.
78 Ibid.
79 Ibid.
80 Ibid.
81 Ibid.
82 James C. Hagerty, Press Release, The White House, 8 July 1953; Box 63, p. 4; C.D. Jackson Papers, 1931–67; DDE Library.
83 USIA, Basic Guidance and Planning Paper No. 2, The Cultural Program of USIA – A Basic Paper, 17 September 1958; Box 14, p. 1; Correspondence, Cultural Exchange Program, 1972 to Interdepartmental Committee on Cooperation with American Republics, 1937–1938; Subject Files, 1953–2000; RG 306; NACP.
84 USIA, Basic Guidance and Planning Paper No. 12, Women's Activities (Part II), 13 August 1959; Box 14, pp. 4–5; Correspondence, Cultural Exchange Program, 1972 to Interdepartmental Committee on Cooperation with American Republics, 1937–1938; Subject Files, 1953–2000; RG 306; NACP.
85 Ibid., 6.

86 Ibid.
87 USIA, Press Release No. 113, 26 July 1956; Box 28; *Amerika Illustrated*, 1950–1956 to National Security Directive 51, 17 October 1990; Records Relating to Select USIA Programs, 1953–1999; General Records of the US Information Agency, Record Group 306 (RG 306); NACP.
88 Fyodor Konstantinov to the Central Committee of the Communist Parties of the Union Republics, Oblast and Territorial Committees of the CPSU, "Letter to Party Organizations Concerning the Dissemination of the Magazine *America* in the USSR, Secretariat of Central Committee, 30 July 1956, CT 19/2, translated by Marta D. Olynyk, http://bukovsky-archives.net/pdfs/usa/1200_us56-6-Eng-Olynyk.pdf.
89 Magnusdottir, "Mission Impossible?" 52–3.
90 Konstantinov, "Letter to Party Organizations."
91 Ibid.
92 *Soviet Life* also ran throughout the duration of the Cold War. Its final issue appeared in December 1991 and coincided with the collapse of the Soviet Union. A lack of government funding forced the publication to fold. However, just one year later, it re-emerged as *Russian Life*. Funded by Russian Information Services, a privately owned Vermont company, it is published on a bimonthly schedule.

4 Modelling the American Dream: Fashion and Femininity in *Amerika*

1 USIA, Press Release No. 113, 26 July 1956; Box 28; *Amerika Illustrated*, 1950–1956 to National Security Directive 51, 17 October 1990; Records Relating to Select USIA Programs, 1953–1999; General Records of the US Information Agency, Record Group 306 (RG 306); NACP.
2 Scanlon, *Inarticulate Longings*, 7.
3 "Brief Survey of American Magazines," *Amerika* 49, October 1960, 18–19. Of the eight magazines depicted in this article, the *Ladies' Home Journal* was the only one that was specifically geared towards women and was billed first. The others were *The Atlantic, Foreign Affairs, Holiday, Life, Newsweek, Partisan Review,* and *Scientific American*.
4 USIA, Basic Guidance and Policy Planning Paper No. 12, "Women's Activities (Part II)," 13 August 1959; Box 14; Correspondence, Cultural Exchange Program, 1972 to Interdepartmental Committee on Cooperation with American Republics, 1937–1938; Subject Files, 1953–2000; General Records of the US Information Agency, Record Group 306 (RG 306); NACP.
5 USIA, Basic Guidance and Policy Planning Paper No. 6, "Women's Activities," 31 March 1959; Box 14; Correspondence, Cultural Exchange Program, 1972 to Interdepartmental Committee on Cooperation with American Republics, 1937–1938; Subject Files, 1953–2000; RG 306; NACP.

6 USIA, Basic Guidance and Planning Paper No. 12, Women's Activities (Part II), 13 August 1959; Box 14, pp. 4–5; Correspondence, Cultural Exchange Program, 1972 to Interdepartmental Committee on Cooperation with American Republics, 1937–1938; Subject Files, 1953–2000; RG 306; NACP.
7 Griswold, "Russian Blonde in Space," 882.
8 Loudon Wainwright, *The Great American Magazine: An Inside History of Life* (New York: Alfred A. Knopf, 1986), 179.
9 Ibid., 81.
10 Henry Luce, "The American Century," *Life*, 17 February 1941.
11 Wainwright, *The Great American Magazine*, 180. Throughout the 1950s *Life*, just like *Amerika*, rarely dealt with the complex issues of race, class, or gender. For example, it only included African Americans on its cover twice: Jackie Robinson on 8 May 1950 and Willie Mays on 28 April 1958. The Robinson issue discussed racial integration in Major League Baseball only minimally, noting that in Robinson's first year with the Brooklyn Dodgers fans taunted him and that he tried to keep out of quarrels with umpires to avoid interracial friction. The article painted his experience in a mostly positive light, portraying him as a national hero who was popular with fans and was starring in a film based on his life. Coverage on Willie Mays focused on the celebrations surrounding the New York Giants 1958 move to San Francisco, neglecting to mention race altogether.
12 Erika Doss, *Looking at Life Magazine* (Washington, DC: Smithsonian Press, 2001), 11.
13 Ibid.
14 Kershaw, *Blood and Champagne*, 179.
15 Alan Brinkley, *The Publisher: Henry Luce and His American Century* (New York: Alfred A. Knopf, 2010), 391–2.
16 *Amerika*'s first issue of its second run contained sixty-four pages, as did *USSR*'s. Gradually, the length of each magazine expanded to approximately eighty pages.
17 Hixson, *Parting the Curtain*, 118.
18 See Olga Moore, "The Fourth of July," *Amerika* 22, July 1958, 30–8; Virginia Evans, "Thanksgiving: A Nostalgic Holiday," *Amerika* 26, November 1958, 4–8; Henry F. Pringle and Katherine Pringle, "Mr. President," *Amerika* 24, September 1958, 8–11.
19 Clinton Rossiter, "The Role of the President," *Amerika* 6, March 1957, 13–18, "The Congress of the United States," *Amerika* 16, January 1958, 34, Clinton Rossiter, "The Supreme Court of the United States," *Amerika* 17, February 1958, 14–17.
20 *Amerika* 1, October 1956, 1.

21 For example, "Revolution in the Kitchen" appeared in the 15 February 1957 issue of *US News and World Report* and contained eleven pages and three black-and-white images of a grocery store. A condensed version of the article appeared in *Amerika*'s February 1958 issue and consisted of five pages and only one image of convenience foods, which never appeared in the original publication. *Amerika*'s March 1958 issue contained the remainder of the article, renamed "Kitchen Appliances: Today and Tomorrow." It consisted of five pages and eleven images of various kitchens and appliances, none of which appeared in the original publication.
22 While each issue's table of contents reveals, if applicable, each article's original source of publication, it gives no other information such as original author, title, and date, making it difficult to assess the extent to which articles were altered, as "Revolution in the Kitchen" was.
23 Tuch, *Communicating with the World*, 136.
24 Ibid., 136.
25 First Secretary of Embassy M. Gordon Knox to Ambassador Alan Kirk, Embassy's Despatch 6 Observations Concerning VOA and Magazine, *Amerika*, During 10 Day Trip from Moscow to Odessa via Kharkov and Return, May 1950, 25 July 1950; Box 2453; Decimal File 1950–1954; RG 59; NACP.
26 M. Gordon Knox, "USIE Report for the Months October, November and December 1949," 17 January 1950; Box 2425, p. 12; Department of State Central Decimal File 1950–1954, Records of the State Department, RG 59; NACP.
27 Bureau of Social Science Research, Yugoslavian Reactions to *SAD*, a New USIS Magazine; Box 10; USSR Yugoslavia General; Office of Research and Evaluation International Survey Research Reports, 1950–1964; RG 306; NACP.
28 Ibid.
29 Department of State Instruction, John Foster Dulles to American Embassies in Warsaw and Prague, 20 April 1956; Box 2170; 1955–1959 Central Decimal File; From 511.593/1-457 to 511.602/12-1257; RG 59; NACP.
30 Office of Research and Analysis, "What Works and What Does Not Work in Communicating with the Soviet People," 1 April 1960; Box 1, p. 6; "R" Reports, 1960–1963; Office of Research; RG 306; NACP.
31 Yarrow, "Selling a New Vision of America to the World," 35.
32 Telegram from US Embassy in Moscow to John Foster Dulles, 27 July 1956; Box 28; *Amerika Illustrated*, 1950–1956 to National Security Directive 51, 17 October 1990; Records Relating to Select USIA Programs, 1953–1999; General Records of the US Information Agency Bureau of Programs; NACP.
33 "From the Editors," 2.

34 "America Today," *Amerika* 1, October 1956, 3–7.
35 Ibid.
36 For further analysis of these messages, see Meyerowitz, "Beyond the Feminine Mystique," and Walker, *Shaping Our Mothers' World*.
37 Walter Hixson does not explicitly state main themes in *Amerika*, but notes that its editors likely realized that articles on fashion and technology would be more appealing to Russian readers. See Hixson, *Parting the Curtain*, 118.
38 "Summer Fashions," *Amerika* 1, October 1956, 36. Originally published in *Mademoiselle*,
39 "New Member of the Family," *Amerika* 1, October 1956, 2–7. Originally published in *McCall's*.
40 "America's 1956 Model Automobiles," *Amerika* 1, October 1956, 40–4.
41 "Ten Young Women of Distinction," *Amerika* 1, October 1956. Originally published in *Mademoiselle*.
42 "*USSR* Magazine Is Five Years Old," *USSR* 61, October 1961, 37–40.
43 Nikita Khrushchev, "Khrushchev's Letter to Our American Readers," *Amerika* 62, November 1960.
44 Nikita Sergeyvich Khrushchev, *Khrushchev Remembers* (New York: Little Brown, 1970), 365.
45 Visitor comment books allow us to gauge Soviet reactions to the exhibition. While comments are wide-ranging, there are comments written by women which indicate they enjoyed viewing household appliances and the Miracle Kitchen. For example, one female visitor wrote that these items were "impressive" and expressed the sentiment that "our housewives had the chance to own such things." Visitors Comments on ANE in Moscow 25 July–5 September 1959; Box 11, p. 11; Comment Books and Lists of Visitors Related to US Exhibits in the USSR, Rumania and Bulgaria; Office of Exhibits; RG 306; NACP.
46 Yekaterina Sheveleva, "The Standard of Living and the Standard of Happiness," *USSR*, March 1962, 36–7.
47 Hellbeck, *Revolution on My Mind*, 13.
48 "*USSR* Magazine Is Five Years Old," 40.
49 Polina Korobova, "Woman's Place in Soviet Life," *Amerika* 3, December 1956, 18–23.
50 Alexis Peri, "New Soviet Woman: The Post-World War II Feminine Ideal at Home and Abroad," *Russian Review* 77 (October 2018): 23.
51 Dudziak, *Cold War, Civil Rights*, 38.
52 Keith Gilyard, *Louise Thompson Patterson: A Life of Struggle for Justice* (Durham, NC: Duke University Press, 2017), 77–9.
53 Ibid., 83, 89. The film was eventually cancelled when the Soviet government decided to forgo its strategy of embarrassing the US government in

favour of prioritizing its diplomatic relationship with the country. This strategy changed by the beginning of the Cold War.
54 Ibid., 94.
55 Kate A. Baldwin, *Beyond the Color Line and the Iron Curtain: Reading Encounters between Black and Red, 1922–1963* (Durham, NC: Duke University Press, 2002), 1–2.
56 *Amerika 9*, June 1957; and *Amerika 17*, February 1958.
57 "Ten Young Women of Distinction," *Amerika* 1, October 1956; originally published in *Mademoiselle*. "First Ball," *Amerika* 6, March 1957, 48–50; originally published in *Picture Post*.
58 Anderson's April 1939 concert in front of the Lincoln Memorial was surrounded by controversy. She had been asked by Howard University to perform as part of its annual concert series, but given Anderson's popularity, a suitable venue could not be found. The use of Constitution Hall, the largest venue in the city at 4,000 seats, was denied by its owners, the Daughters of the American Revolution (DAR), because they only permitted white performers. In protest, First Lady Eleanor Roosevelt resigned from the organization and arranged for Anderson to sing outdoors in front of the Lincoln Memorial. The controversy surrounding the performance, as well as Roosevelt's resignation, attracted national attention and an audience of 75,000 on Easter weekend. See Allan Keiler, *Marion Anderson: A Singer's Journey* (Champaign: University of Illinois Press, 2000).
59 Von Eschen, *Satchmo Blows Up the World*, 7.
60 Marian Anderson, "My Lord, What a Morning," *Amerika* 27, December 1958, 28–33.
61 "Facts about the US: The Negro Today," *Amerika* 29, February 1959, 26–7.
62 "Facts about the US: Organized Labor," *Amerika* 32, May 1959, 45.
63 Dudziak, *Cold War, Civil Rights*, 118.
64 In certain instances, articles featuring children or items related to them are included in these categories. For example, if children's fashions were shown in the magazine they are included in the totals, as women were the main consumers of the household, and such fashions were in reality designed to appeal to them as readers and consumers. Articles on children in relation to the family, rather than in school or camp, for example, are included under "Marriage and Family."
65 It should be noted that, in similar fashion, *USSR* also rarely showed women in pants or shorts, both in photographs of its women and in its fashion pages.
66 "Practical Fashions," *Amerika* 2, November 1956, 52. Originally published in *Mademoiselle*.
67 "Fashions," *Amerika* 6, March 1957, 10–12. Originally published in *Vogue*.

68 "Fashions under Twenty Dollars," *Amerika* 11, August 1957, 25–7. Originally published in *Glamour*.
69 "Holiday Fashions," *Amerika* 12, September 1957, 10–11. Originally published in *Charm*.
70 According to the US census, these exact figures consisted of 18.389 million working women in 1950, and 23.240 million in 1960. See Mitra Toosi, "A Century of Change: The US Labor Force, 1950–2050," *Monthly Labor Review* (May 2002): 15–28, https://www.bls.gov/opub/mlr/2002/05/art2full.pdf. This number had increased significantly from 1940, when 13.015 million women worked, or 25.7 per cent of the labour force. See Census, 1940: "Estimates of Labor Force, Employment, and Unemployment in the United States, 1940 and 1930," by Dr. Leon E. Truesdell (Washington, DC: Government Printing Office, 1944), https://www2.census.gov/library/publications/decennial/1940/population-labor-force/population-labor-force.pdf.
71 "Tailored for the City," *Amerika* 8, May 1957, 45–7. Photographs from *Charm*.
72 "Wear Them to Work," *Amerika* 18, March 1958, 11. Photographs from *Mademoiselle* and *Glamour*.
73 "Office Dresses," *Amerika* 20, May 1958, 27. Photographs from *Charm*.
74 "College Girls Dressed Up," *Amerika*, 17, February 1958, 29–33. Originally published in *Life*.
75 It should be noted that these statistics do not indicate whether or not these women completed college during those four years. See US Census Bureau, No. 1426. Educational Attainment, by Sex: 1919 to 1998," in *Statistical Abstract of the United States: 1999*.
76 The All-Union Census Bureau's 1959 census was the first in twenty years. Like the US census, it indicated there was a slight gap between female and male students, where 21 per cent of men completed college, slightly above female rates of completion. *Itogi vsesoiuznoi perepisi naseleniia 1959 goda* (Results of the All-Union Census of 1959) (Moscow: Gosstatizdat, 1962), 81. Reprinted in Field, "Workers (Mothers)," 40.
77 "College Girls Like These Shirts," *Amerika* 21, June 1958, 51. Originally published in *Mademoiselle*.
78 "Best Dressed College Girls," *Amerika* 30, March 1959, 50. Originally published in *Glamour*.
79 "College Girls Dressed Up," *Amerika*, 17, February 1958, 29–33. Originally published in *Life*.
80 Zakharova, "Soviet Fashion in the 1950s–1960s," 403; Peet, "Russian '*Amerika*.'"
81 "Soviet Students Visit Washington D.C.," *Amerika* 30, March 1959, 48.
82 Zakharova, "Soviet Fashion in the 1950s–1960s," 403.

83 "Wardrobe for Mother-to-Be," *Amerika* 28, January 1959, 40. Originally published in *Glamour*.
84 *Soviet Woman* also regularly contained sewing patterns.
85 Mabel Hill Souvaine, "A Smart Coat You Can Make Yourself," *Amerika* 39, December 1959, 39.
86 The institution of 4-H clubs dates back to 1902. During a time when agricultural methods were being modernized, members were called on to devote their heads to clearer thinking, hearts to greater loyalty, hands to larger service, and health to better living, in service of their clubs, communities, country, and the world. For more on the history of 4-H and its place in American culture, see Gabriel N. Rosenberg, *The 4-H Harvest: Sexuality and the State in Rural America* (Philadelphia: University of Pennsylvania Press, 2016).
87 "4-H Girls' Fashions," *Amerika* 10, July 1957, 52–3.
88 "Patch Fashions," *Amerika* 4, January 1957, 52–3. Originally published in *McCall's*.
89 Zakharova, "Soviet Fashion in the 1950s–1960s," 429.
90 Ibid.

5 Living the American Dream: The Happy Homemaker in *Amerika*

1 USIA, Basic Guidance and Planning Paper No. 12, Women's Activities (Part II), 13 August 1959; Box 14, pp. 4–5; Correspondence, Cultural Exchange Program, 1972 to Interdepartmental Committee on Cooperation with American Republics, 1937–1938; Subject Files, 1953–2000; RG 306; NACP.
2 There is a rich literature on the history of postwar American motherhood. See Rima Dobrev Apple, *Perfect Motherhood: Science and Childrearing in America* (New Brunswick, NJ: Rutgers University Press, 2006); Mary Frances Berry, *The Politics of Parenthood: Child Care, Women's Rights, and the Myth of the Good Mother* (New York: Viking, 1993); Ladd-Taylor and Umansky, *"Bad" Mothers*; Rebecca Jo Plant, *Mom: The Transformation of Motherhood in Modern America* (Chicago: University of Chicago Press, 2010); Jodi Vandenberg-Daves, *Modern Motherhood: An American History* (New Brunswick, NJ: Rutgers University Press, 2014).
3 Interestingly, March 1962's issue of *USSR*, a special issue on women, contained "The Male in the Apron." The article was unique in that it included cartoons of a dishevelled-looking Russian husband, father, and scientist caring for his baby as his wife was writing a paper on volcanoes, which according to the article, was "a man's job." The male author provided mixed messages, writing, "That's one of the things our sex has got

to get used to. When the wife's busy, it's up to us to do the housekeeping and baby-sitting." The author commended the supposed "rationality" that men had brought into housekeeping with their revolts against the dictates of daily cleaning, an argument which could also be attributed to laziness. However, he concluded, "as one man to another, personally I'd feel happier with a woman in the house." See Yuriev, "The Male in the Apron," 60–1.

4 Debutante balls had their roots in sixteenth-century England when aristocratic families began formally presenting their daughters before vetted audiences to ensure they married into suitable families. During the eighteenth century, when families newly established in America were looking to differentiate between the social classes, they adopted the practice themselves. See Karal Ann Marling, *Debutante: Rites and Regalia of American Debdom* (Lawrence: University of Kansas Press, 2004); and Kristen Richardson, *The Season: A Social History of the Debutante* (New York: W.W. Norton, 2019).

5 While October 1956's "Ten Young Women of Distinction" included twelve-year-old spelling whiz Gloria Lockerman and singer Leontyne Price, they were not the main focus of the article.

6 These images would have been in direct contradiction to those of Russian girls, who in official pictures were frequently depicted in school or engaged in state-sanctioned cultural or leisure time activities, and were certainly never shown engaging in religious activities or in the presence of religious figures.

7 "First Ball," *Amerika* 6, March 1957, 48–50. Originally published in *Picture Post*.

8 Jo Campbell, "A Young Couple Gets Married," *Amerika* 21, June 1958, 14–18.

9 "Golden Wedding Anniversary," *Amerika*, May 1957, 2–5.

10 "New Member of the Family," *Amerika* 1, October 1956, 2–7. Originally published in *McCall's*.

11 Unlike postwar women's magazines, which occasionally alluded to the supposed dangers of homosexuality when warning of the consequences of "bad mothering" and its ramifications for US society and culture, *Amerika* neither discussed nor even alluded to homosexuality. This is likely because it had the potential of framing American mothers, and broader American society, in a negative light.

12 "Sister from the Far East," *Amerika* 50, November 1960, 35–7.

13 "Adopting a Five-Year-Old," *Amerika*, March 1957. Originally published in *Look*.

14 Kenneth Jackson, *Crabgrass Frontier: The Suburbanization of the United States* (New York: Oxford University Press, 1984), 244.

15 Robert Phillips, "Housing Ideas on Display," *Amerika*, 25, October 1958, 12.
16 This issue's (*Amerika* 47, August 1960) ten housing-related articles comprised "The Human Frontier: Shelter," 21; Charles E. Silberman, "Housing in America," 22–5; Robert W. Carrick, "Tomorrow's Building Materials," 26; "Second Homes for Family Vacations," 27–31 (originally published in *Life*); "Builders Cut Costs," 32–5 (originally published in *Living for Young Homemakers*); Gardner Soule, "A Family Buys a House"; Albert Roland, "Home Improvement Is Big Business"; Leon Wellstone, "A Man of Sweeping Vision," 42–4; Richard E. Saunders, "A Key to Home Ownership," 45; and Marjorie Parsons and Anthony G. Bowman, "A Day in an Apartment House."
17 Silberman, "Housing in America."
18 Parsons and Bowman, "A Day in an Apartment House."
19 "Second Homes for Family Vacations."
20 Stephen Lovell, *Summerfolk: A History of the Dacha, 1710–2000* (Ithaca, NY: Cornell University Press, 2016), 1.
21 Christine Frederick, *Selling Mrs. Consumer* (New York, Business Bourse, 1929), 169. For more on Frederick and the emergence of the field of home economics, see Janice Williams Rutherford, *Selling Mrs. Consumer: Christine Frederick and the Rise of Household Efficiency* (Athens: University of Georgia Press, 2003); Barbara Ehrenreich and Deirdre English, *For Her Own Good: Two Centuries of the Experts' Advice to Women* (New York: Anchor Books, 2005); and Carolyn M. Goldstein, *Creating Consumers: Home Economics in Twentieth-Century America* (Chapel Hill: University of North Carolina Press, 2012).
22 See Ruth Schwartz Cowan, *More Work for Mother: The Ironies of Household Technology from the Open Hearth to the Microwave* (New York: Basic Books, 1983); and Jessamyn Neuhaus, *Housework and Housewives in American Advertising: Married to the Mop* (New York: Palgrave MacMillan, 2011).
23 Neuhaus, *Housework and Housewives in American Advertising*, 5.
24 Gail Warshofsky Lapidus, *Women in Soviet Society: Equality, Development and Social Change* (Berkeley: University of California Press, 1978), 5–6.
25 "Farm Wife," *Amerika* 9, June 1957, 48–51. Originally published in *Harvester World*.
26 Ibid.
27 May 1959's issue of *Amerika* depicted men partaking in an unusual task: cooking. The short one-page article "Teaching Men Their Place in the Kitchen" featured the two hundred students enrolled at the Culinary Institute of America in New Haven, Connecticut, called the American equivalent of Paris's Cordon Bleu. In contrast to the housewives and mothers seen in the pages of the magazine cooking in their home kitchens, the article noted that these men were not "cooks"; rather their

two years of study would prepare them to become skilled chefs, presumably with the intention of owning their own restaurants. See "Teaching Men Their Place in the Kitchen," *Amerika* 32, May 1959, 21.
28 "Kitchen Appliances: Today and Tomorrow," *Amerika* 18, March 1958, 34–8. Originally published in *US News and World Report*.
29 William Howland, "Kitchen Workroom," *Amerika* 46, July 1960, 20–2. Originally published in *House Beautiful*.
30 Harrison E. Salisbury, "Nixon and Khrushchev Argue in Public as US Exhibit Opens: Accuse Each Other of Threats," *New York Times*, 25 July 1959.
31 For more on the political usefulness of the kitchen, see Cristina Carbone, "Staging the Kitchen Debate: How Splitnik Got Normalized in the United States," in *Cold War Kitchen: Americanization, Technology and European Users*, ed. Ruth Oldenziel and Karin Zachmann (Cambridge, Massachusetts: Massachusetts Institute of Technology, 2009); Greg Castillo, *Cold War on the Home Front: The Soft Power of Midcentury Design* (Minneapolis: University of Minnesota Press, 2010); Sarah T. Phillips and Shane Hamilton, *The Kitchen Debate and Cold War Consumer Politics: A Brief History with Documents* (New York: Bedford/St. Martin's Press, 2014); and Susan E. Reid, "'Our Kitchen Is Just as Good': Soviet Responses to the American Kitchen," in Oldenziel and Zachmann, *Cold War Kitchen*.
32 Kirk, *Postmarked Moscow*, 83.
33 "We Saw How Russians Live," 59.
34 Laura Shapiro, *Something from the Oven: Reinventing Dinner in 1950s America* (New York: Penguin, 2004), 8.
35 "Revolution in the Kitchen," *Amerika* 17, February 1958, 34–7. Originally published in *US News and World Report*.
36 Shapiro, *Something from the Oven*, 44–5.
37 Anna Zeide, *Canned: The Rise and Fall of Consumer Confidence in the American Food Industry* (Berkeley: University of California Press, 2018), 2.
38 Olga Arnold, "From Pelmeni to Sukiyaki," *Amerika* 20, May 1958, 15–17.
39 Laura Winslow, "The Fair in Moscow," *Amerika* 41, February 1960, 2–9.
40 This issue's (*Amerika* 41, February 1960) ten food-related articles comprised "The Human Frontier: Nutrition," 17; Timothy D. McEnroe, "The Supermarket in an Age of Distribution," 18–24; Richard Montague, "Farming the Water," 25; Donald W. Lief, "We Are What We Eat," 26–7; "Easy Cooking in Today's Kitchen," 28–31; Olga Arnold, "Food Invades the Arts," 32–4; Marjorie Parsons, "It's Lunch Time," 35–7; Anthony G. Bowman, "Protecting the Consumer," 38; "Notes about Nutrition," 39; "The Pushbutton Cornucopia" 40–3 (originally published in *Time*).
41 Andrew F. Smith, *Eating History: 30 Turning Points in the Making of American Cuisine* (New York: Columbia University Press, 2009), 178. The concept of the supermarket, which offered prices lower than those of

independent grocers and other chains, grew in popularity during the Great Depression. That popularity only accelerated after World War II.

42 Soviet leaders have a long history of touring supermarkets during their visits to the United States. In January 1959, Soviet deputy minister Anastas Mikoyan had also visited a supermarket in White Oak, Maryland. Years later, in 1989, future Russian President Boris Yeltsin visited one in Houston, Texas.

43 Timothy D. McEnroe, "The Supermarket in an Age of Distribution," *Amerika* 41, February 1960, 18–24.

44 For example, *Life* magazine contained detailed accounts of these exhibitions and included images of visitors viewing the American supermarkets on display.

45 Seymour Freidin, "The Wonderful Supermarket," *New York Post*, 27 September 1957.

46 Shane Hamilton. "Supermarket USA Confronts State Socialism," in Oldenziel and Zachmann, *Cold War Kitchen*, 152.

47 Patrick Hyder Patterson, *Bought & Sold: Living and Losing the Good Life in Socialist Yugoslavia* (Ithaca, NY: Cornell University Press, 2011), xvi.

48 Patterson writes that by the 1960s Yugoslavs were permitted to travel throughout most European nations without a visa. As a result, they freely and frequently crossed directly into nations such as Italy and Austria to obtain household items and groceries that were unavailable or more expensive in Yugoslavia, further exposing them to Western consumer culture. Moreover, this ease of travel also allowed for workers, typically young men, to travel across borders, earn money, and return home with a disposable income and new ideas regarding consumption and capitalism. Ibid., 4–6, 318.

49 Ibid., 128.

50 For more on the place of supermarkets in Cold War propaganda efforts, see Tracey Deutsch, *Building a Housewife's Paradise: Gender, Politics and American Grocery* (Chapel Hill: University of North Carolina Press, 2010).

51 Emily Coleman, "Ballerina – and Actress, Too," *Amerika* 4, January 1957, 32–3(originally published in *The New York Times Magazine*); "Nurse Harding," *Amerika* 9, June 1957, 29–32 (originally published in *Cosmopolitan*); Phil Cameron, "Writers of the American South," *Amerika* 10, July 1957, 18–20; Agnes DeMille, "Rhythm in My Blood," *Amerika* 10, July 1957, 42–5 (originally published in *Atlantic Monthly*); Samuel Grafton, "Two Girls and the Poets," *Amerika* 13, October 1957, 21–3 (originally published in *Good Housekeeping*); Roland Gelatt, "Wanda Landowska, *Amerika* 17, February 1958, 26–8; Maria Tallchief, "Prima Ballerina," *Amerika* 18, March 1958, 47–9; "Miss Wilson, I Know! I Know," *Amerika* 18, March 1958, 39–42 (originally published in *Look*); "Two Outstanding Teachers,"

Amerika 19, April 1958, 52–3 (originally published in *McCall's*); Donald W. Lief, "New Faces in Women's Tennis," *Amerika*, 21, June 1958, 52–4; Rochelle Girson, "Gentle Classicist in a Modern Age," *Amerika*, 25, October 1958, 42–5; Marion Anderson, "My Lord, What a Morning," *Amerika*, 27, December 1958, 26–7; Mabel Hill Souvaine, "Lady with a Loom," *Amerika* 31, April 1959, 14–17; "Three Famed Actresses on Broadway," *Amerika* 33, June 1959, 24–5; Mabel Hill Souvaine, "Claire McCardell," *Amerika* 33, June 1959, 44–8; John Christopher, "Roberta Peters – A Success Story," *Amerika* 34, July 1959, 50–1; "Actress Audrey Hepburn," *Amerika* 35, August 1959, 9; "Alicia Alonso: Ballerina Tourist," *Amerika* 37, October 1959, 8–11; Carol Heiss, "Ballerina of the Ice," *Amerika* 37, October 1959, 18–19 (originally published in *Look*); Mabel Hill Souvaine, "An Interview with Sally Victor," *Amerika* 37, October 1959, 40–3; "Pets Assist Nurses," *Amerika* 38, November 1959, 24–5; Olga Moore "Mattiwilda Dobbs," *Amerika* 38, November 1959, 55; "Man and Wife Teams," *Amerika*, 42, March 1960, 49; Mabel Hill Souvaine, "Artist of the Textile Mill," *Amerika* 48, September 1960, 36–8; and "Young Record Breaker," *Amerika* 48, September 1960, 54 (originally published in *Sports Illustrated*).
52 "New Teacher," *Amerika*, 24, September 1958, 39–41.
53 "2,700 Lives of an Office Building," *Amerika* 18, March 1958, 55; originally published in *Life*.
54 "Two New Doctor's in Town," *Amerika* 14, 52–5; and "Judge Ann Mikoll," *Amerika* 50, 24–6; originally published in *Redbook*.
55 "Busy Mother," *Amerika* 40, January 1960, 11–13; originally published in *McCall's*.
56 Steinbeck and Capa, "Women and Children in the USSR," 49.
57 Patrick Hyder Patterson, "Risky Business: What Was Really Being Sold in the Department Stores of Socialist Eastern Europe?" in *Communism Unwrapped: Consumption in Cold War Eastern Europe*, ed. Paulina Bren and Mary Neuburger (New York: Oxford University Press, 2012), 117.
58 Violet Wood, "Give the Lady What She Wants," *Amerika* 45, June 1960, 14–19.
59 J.L. Hudson's was also the subject of Dorothy Thompson's "Commercialism Takes – and Wears – a New Look," *Ladies' Home Journal*, June 1954, discussed in chapter 1.
60 Richard Montague, "Shopper's Paradise," *Amerika* 36, September 1959, 20–2.
61 Tom Mahoney, "Sears, Roebuck and Company," *Amerika* 33, June 1959, 56–61.
62 Violet Wood, "Woolworth's House of Pennies," *Amerika* 48, September 1960, 16–20.

63 Thompson, "Commercialism Takes – and Wears – a New Look," 11.
64 Cohen, *A Consumer's Republic*, 278–9.
65 Jan Whitaker, *Service and Style: How the American Department Store Fashions the Middle Class* (New York: St. Martin's Press, 2006), 28.
66 For more on the history of US department stores, see Susan Porter Benson, *Counter Cultures: Saleswomen, Managers and Customers in American Department Stores 1890–1940* (Champaign: University of Illinois Press, 1998); Christopher Faircloth, *Images of America: Cleveland's Department Stores* (Charleston, SC: Arcadia Publishing, 2009); William Lancaster, *The Department Store: A Social History* (Leicester: Leicester University Press, 1995); and Michael J. Lisicky, *Baltimore's Bygone Department Stores: Many Happy Returns* (Charleston, SC: History Press, 2012).
67 Rollie McKenna and Mary Cook, "City of Stores for the Suburbs," *Amerika* 19, April 1958, 2–10.
68 "Four Family Budgets," *Amerika* 29, February 1959, 12–17; originally published in *Pageant*.
69 Carl Rieser, "Great Shopping Game," *Amerika* 32, May 1959, 28–33.
70 USIA, Basic Guidance and Policy Planning Paper No. 12, "Women's Activities (Part II)," 13 August 1959; Box 14; Correspondence, Cultural Exchange Program, 1972 to Interdepartmental Committee on Cooperation with American Republics, 1937–1938; Subject Files, 1953–2000; General Records of the US Information Agency, Record Group 306 (RG 306); NACP.
71 USIA, Basic Guidance and Policy Planning Paper No. 12, "Women's Activities (Part II)," 13 August 1959; Box 14; Correspondence, Cultural Exchange Program, 1972 to Interdepartmental Committee on Cooperation with American Republics, 1937–1938; Subject Files, 1953–2000; General Records of the US Information Agency, Record Group 306 (RG 306); NACP.
72 See Zinovi Yuriev, "The Male in the Apron," 60–1.

6 *Amerika*, *USSR*, and a Woman's Proper Place in the 1960s

1 Betty Friedan, "Woman: The Fourth Dimension," *Ladies' Home Journal*, June 1964, 48–55.
2 Hunter, "A Daring New Concept," 586–9.
3 "They Met in Moscow," *Amerika* 58, July 1961, 8–9.
4 "Wedding Bells of America," *Amerika* 136, January 1968, 51.
5 "Housewife on the Go," *Amerika* 138, March 1968, 14–16; other articles on motherhood in the 1960s included "Mother and Child: A Vast New

Study," *Amerika* 73, October 1962, 29–31; and Joyce Lubold, "Why Mothers Don't Get Sick," *Amerika* 146, November 1968, 45.
6 "Farm Women's Festival," *Amerika* 58, July 1961, 6–7.
7 "Women of the American Farm," *Amerika* 70, July 1962, 56–60.
8 "Facts about the US: The American Home," *Amerika* 59, August 1961, 8.
9 "Shopping for a New House," *Amerika* 74, November 1962, 56–61; originally published in *Life*.
10 "Homes Full of Light and Easy Living," *Amerika* 89, February 1964, 32–5; "Facts about the US; A Nation of Homeowners," *Amerika* 89, February 1964, 40–1. This issue contained a "special survey" on architecture and also included Wolf Von Eckardt, "American Architecture in Transition," *Amerika* 89, February 1964, 16–31; and Mary Sayre Haverstock, "A Young Architect Speaks Out," *Amerika* 89, February 1964, 36–9.
11 "A Place of Our Own," *Amerika* 102, March 1965, 2–5.
12 "Ready-made Pastries with Homemade Taste," *Amerika* 121, October 1966, 18–21.
13 "There's a Factory in the Kitchen," *Amerika* 144, 42–3.
14 "Technology Tackles the Package," *Amerika* 125, February 1967, 10–15; originally published in *Fortune*.
15 Richard Montague, "Grocery Chain Brings Food to Market, *Amerika* 88, January 1964, 42–5; "Mrs. Dixon Buys Her Groceries," *Amerika* 88, January 1964, 48–51.
16 Lynn Marett, "What Do Americans Eat?" *Amerika* 126, March 1967, 53–8.
17 The following articles in *Amerika* were devoted to fashion: "Warm, Comfortable, Smart," 52, January 1961, 40–1; "The Furry Look," 53, February 1961, 27; "For That Happy Day," 57, June 1961, 28–9; Laura Thurston, "Bright as the Sunfish," 59, August 1961, 14–15; "The Bride's Gown," 61, October 1961, 42; "Fashions for Living," 66, March 1962, 42–4 (originally published in *Life*); "For a Rainy Day," 68, May 1962, 26 (originally published in *Mademoiselle*); "It Tops Them All," 71, August 1962, 52–3; "A Warm Welcome for Winter," 73, October 1963, 9–11 (originally published in *McCall's*); "Hairstyles: Long and Lovely," 79, April 1963, 46–7; "Fashions in the Sun," 81, June 1963, 56–7 (originally published in *McCall's*); Madelyn Hunter, "Lovely to Look at," 86, November 1963, 20–1; "For Well-Travelled Feet," 90, March 1964, 52–3 (originally published in *Look*); "From the Coed's Closet," 92, May 1964, 48–9; "Winter Glamour, 98, November 1964, 29–32 (originally published in *McCall's*); "Fashion on the Slopes," 99, December 1964, 38–9 (originally published in *Vogue*); "The Long Look of Autumn," 100, January 1965, 36–7; "Four Seasons for Teenage Fashions," 108, September 1965, 42–5; "She Flipped Her

Wig," 109, October 1965, 53; "Two Sweaters for One," 110, November 1965, 50; "Young and Fancy," 114, March 1966, 30–2 (originally published in *Seventeen*); "Fashions in 'Op'" 115, April 1966, 10–12; Phyllis Levin, "The Instant Dress: All-American Fashion," 131, August 1967, 42–4; "Topped with Elegance," 134, November 1967, 58. As in the past, the majority of these articles focused on women's fashions, the exception being the following, which focused on men's fashions: "Cold Weather Wear," 54, March 1961, 48–9 (originally published in *Men's Wear Magazine*); "Progress Report: Men's Fashions," 55, April 1961, 52–3; "Fancy Footwork," 58, July 1961, 51; "Walking on Air," 69, June 1962, 22 (originally published in *New York Times Magazine*); "Fashion Report: Men's Wear," 89, February 1964, 48–9; "To Suit the Occasion," 112, January 1966, 41–4; and "Functional Fashions for the Future," 159, December 1969, 54–5.

18 Clarence Newman, "No Blues for Jeans," *Amerika* 116, May 1966, 47; originally published in the *Wall Street Journal*.
19 Much has been written on the rise in popularity of blue jeans not just in Russia, but throughout the Soviet Union and Eastern Europe during the decade and up to the fall of communism. Youth embraced this article of clothing as a symbol of a carefree Western lifestyle and abundant consumer culture that appeared less rigid than their own. See Robert Hornsby, *Protest, Reform and Repression in Khrushchev's Soviet Union* (Cambridge: Cambridge University Press, 2013); Uta G. Poiger, *Jazz, Rock, and Rebels: Cold War Politics and American Culture in a Divided Germany* (Berkeley: University of California Press, 2000); Gregor Tomc, "A Tale of Two Subcultures: A Comparative Analysis of Hippie and Punk Subcultures in Slovenia," in *Remembering Utopia: The Culture of Everyday Life in Socialist Yugoslavia*, ed. Breda Luthar and Maruša Pušnik (Washington DC: New Academic Publishing, 2010); and Radina Vučetić, "Džuboks (Jukebox): The First Rock'n'roll Magazine in Socialist Yugoslavia," in Luthar and Pušnik, *Remembering Utopia*.
20 Newman, "No Blues for Jeans," 47.
21 "Short and Snappy," *Amerika* 122, November 1966, 50–1; originally published in *Vogue*. "High Style – Then and Now," *Amerika* 131, August 1967, 45–8; originally published in *Harper's Bazaar*.
22 "Behind the Scenes of Fashion," *Amerika* 98, December 1964, 56–61.
23 Robert S. Becksmith, "Shoppers' Mecca," *Amerika* 63, December 1961, 50–5.
24 "How the World's Number One Retailer Got to the Top," *Amerika* 149, February 1969, 36–41; originally published in *Business Week*.

25 Daniel Yankelovich, "Finding Out What the Consumer Really Wants, *Amerika* 125, February 1967, 7–9.
26 Malcolm Henry, "The Lure and Fascination of Seven Fabulous Stores," *Amerika* 125, February 1967, 20–3.
27 Jeff Stansbusy, "Tyson's Corner: Everything and Anything in One Package, *Amerika* 125, February 1967, 24–9.
28 For articles in *Amerika* on American working women see the following: Jean Simmons, "Where Girls Get Wings," 53, February 1961, 15–17; Suzanne Bailey, "Sister Mary Corita," 54, March 1961, 29–32; "Marjorie Parsons, "Doris Day: For Millions She Is the Girl Next Door," 56, May 1961, 35–7; Olga Arnold, "Miracles and Miracle Workers, 57, June 1961, 38–41; Richard Montague, "A Dancer, a Legend, 64, January 1962, 57; Marcy Learns She's a Winner," 66, March 1962, 21–3; "Richard Montague, "Garment Worker," 65, February 1962, 54–9; Madelyn Hunter, "Three Models, Then and Now, *Amerika* 76, 1963, 55; John Haskins, "Soprano with Glamour and Talent," 78, March 1963, 54–5; "Teacher of the Year," 82, July 1963, 14–16 (originally published in *Look*); "Designed to Dazzle," 84, September 1963, 15–17; "Registered Nurse," 84, September 1963, 23–6; "TV's Bouncing Belles, 86, November 1963, 46–7 (originally published in *Saturday Evening Post*); "Teacher of the Year," 98, November 1964, 51–3; Anthony G. Bowman, "Little Lady of Song," 102, March 1965, 24; Richard Meryman, "The Rewards of a Fine Teacher," 103, April 1965, 14–19; "Mother's in the Opera, 104, May 1965, 26–7; Walter Terry, "What Makes a Ballerina Great," 108, September 1965, 57; Irving Penn, "Prima Donna," 111, December 1965, 11; "Actress on the Move," 113, February 1966, 28–9; Richard Lemon, "Anne Bancroft: 'Hey, Ma, I Can Do That,'" 118, July 1966, 10–12; Mary Wingaire, "I've Got My Own Song," 123, December 1966, 8–10; "This Nurse Doesn't Wear White," 152, May 1969, 48–51; and "TV Glamour Girl," 156, September 1969, 46–7.
29 See "Girl Scientist," *Amerika* 52, January 1961, 17–20 (originally published in *Life*); "They Know Where They're Going," *Amerika* 89, February 1964, 34–5; "The Lady Is a Logger," *Amerika* 114, March 1966, 6–9; and Virginia Olsen, "Helena Rubenstein: Ageless Little Monarch from Krakow," *Amerika* 97, October 1964, 48–53.
30 See Jacqueline Kennedy," *Amerika* 69, June 1962, 2–4; "The Lady Is a Senator," *Amerika* 72, September 1962, 2–12; Jane Ries, "Teenager in the White House," *Amerika* 107, August 1965, 2–6; and "Congresswoman from Hawaii," *Amerika* 108, September 1965, 49–51.
31 "Mother Goes Back to School," *Amerika* 93, 46–7; originally published in *Look*.

32 "TV's Nancy Hanschman," *Amerika* 55, April 1961, 25. Nancy Hanschman went on to become Nancy Dickerson, a pioneer in the field of television journalism, who reported first for CBS and then NBC News, before becoming an independent producer.

33 Olga Arnold, "She Sings from the Heart," *Amerika* 62, November 1961, 49–51. October 1956's "Ten Young Women of Distinction" briefly included twelve-year-old spelling whiz Gloria Lockerman and singer Leontyne Price, but it was not until March 1957's "First Ball" that an African American female was the main focus of an article, when eighteen-year-old Jean Walburg was prominently featured. The December 1958 issue featured an excerpt from opera singer Marion Anderson's autobiography, "My Lord, What a Morning," as well as a picture of her on the cover.

34 Josh Greenfield, "One Intense Woman against the Tide," *Amerika* 142, July 1968, 2–6; originally published in the *New York Times Magazine*.

35 Unlike his predecessors, Kennedy focused much of his foreign policy attention on Africa. He believed that the recent wave of independence movements overtaking the continent turned it into an important Cold War battleground, and he consequently sought to court nationalist leaders. See Richard D. Mahoney, *JFK: Ordeal in Africa* (London: Oxford University Press, 1983); Philip E. Muehlenbeck, *Betting on the Africans: John F. Kennedy's Courting of African Nationalist Leaders* (New York: Oxford University Press, 2012); and Thomas J. Noer, "New Frontiers and Old Priorities in Africa," in *Kennedy's Quest for Victory: American Foreign Policy, 1961–1963*, ed. Thomas G. Paterson (New York: Oxford University Press, 1989).

36 Thomas Borstelmann, *The Cold War and the Color Line: American Race Relations in the Global Arena* (Cambridge, MA: Harvard University Press, 2001), 2, 268.

37 "Martin Luther King Wins Nobel Peace Prize," *Amerika* 102, March 1965, 17; Hollis Alpert, "Sidney Poitier: Wanted Actor," *Amerika* 103, April 1965, 52–5; "On Becoming a Writer," *Amerika* 112, December 1966, 20–1 (originally published in *Commentary*); Robert Penn, "Who Speaks for the Negro?" *Amerika* 127, April 1967, 59–64; and Richard Meryman, "Half a Century of Satchmo," *Amerika* 128, May 1967, 30–5.

38 Wallace Westleigh, Jr., "Civil Rights: The Strongest Revolt," *Amerika* 63, December 1961, 28–31.

39 Arthur E. Sutherland, "The American Negro and the Law," *Amerika* 75, December 1962, 33–7.

40 Nathan Glick, "Interview with a Civil Rights Leader, Roy Wilkins," *Amerika* 89, February 1964, 2–6.

41 August Meier, "Ferment on the Campus: Civil Rights," *Amerika* 92, May 1964, 44–7.

42 This special report in *Amerika* included "The Resolute Years," 97, October 1964, 14–19; John P. Roche, "Civil Rights: The Continuing Struggle," 97, October 1964, 20–5; "1954–1964: A Chronology," 97, October 1964, 26–8; "A Giant Step Forward," 97, October 1964, 29; Matt Herron, "Interracial Youth Group in Birmingham," 97, October 1964, 30–1; A.P. Richmond, "City in Transition," 97, October 1964, 32–6; "The Big Five," 97, October 1964, 40–2; "We Shall Not Be Moved," 97, October 1964, 43; "Problems, North and South," 97, October 1964, 44–5; and "Many Voices ... Speak Out on the Morals and Mores of Segregation," 97, October 1964, 46–7.

43 John P. Roche, "Civil Rights: The Continuing Struggle," *Amerika* 97, October 1964, 20–5.

44 Leo Janos, "Civil Rights 1967 – The Tough Phase Begins," *Amerika* 130, July 1967, 19–20.

45 Malissa Radfield, "Other Voices, Other Views," *Amerika* 130, July 1967, 21–5.

46 John Jacobs, "The Troubled Road to Equality," *Amerika* 141, June 1968, 1–2; "Nathan Glazer, "The Nature of the Ghetto Crisis," *Amerika* 141, June 1968, 3–5; "Cooling Down the Cities," *Amerika* 141, June 1968, 6–7; and "Little Rock Revisited: Desegregated but Not Integrated," *Amerika* 141, June 1968, 8–13.

47 James Farmer, "Black Power and White Liberals," *Amerika* 155, August 1969, 30–1. For the most part, during the decade articles in *Amerika* depicted interracial cooperation. They included Neal Gregory, "Memphis Is My Home," 86, November 1963, 2–6; Chester Morrison, "Integration in a Southern City," 93, June 1964, 51–3 (originally published in *Look*); "The Johnsons' Busy Life," 105, June 1965, 52–3; David R. Jones, "Detroit: How a Big City Eases Racial Tension," 114, March 1966, 10–13; Georgia B. Leonard, "A Final Interview with Lillian Smith," 128, May 1967, 20–1; and Robert Canzoneri, "Charles Evers: Mississippi's Black Catalyst," 152, May 1969, 32–5.

48 Cover, *USSR*, March 1962.

49 "*USSR* Magazine Is Five Years Old," 37–40.

50 See "Our Women," *USSR* 66, March 1962, 1–6; "Three Questions for Women," *USSR* 66, March 1962, 38–41; Galina Vasilyeva, "Beauty Salon," *USSR* 66, March 1962, 42–3; Valentina Beletskaya, "Special for Women," *USSR* 66, March 1962, 44–5; and Yelena Raizman, "Spring Fashions," *USSR* 66, March 1962, 46–7.

51 See Arnold Odintsov, "Hamro Tairova," *USSR* 66, March 1962, 6–9; Olga Ignatovich, "Puppeteer," *USSR* 66, March 1962, 51; Bertha Brainina, "Novelist Antonina Koptyayeva," *USSR* 66, March 1962, 52; and Victor Kuprianov, "Women in Sports," *USSR* 66, March 1962, 62–5.

52 "Our Women," 2.

53 Ibid., 2–4.
54 Ibid., 4.
55 Ibid., 4.
56 Ibid., 3.
57 Valentina Beletskaya, "Special for Women," *USSR* 66, March 1962, 44–5.
58 Yelena Raizman, "Spring Fashions," *USSR* 66, March 1962, 46–7.
59 Galina Vasilyeva, "Beauty Salon," *USSR* 66, March 1962, 42–3.
60 "Three Questions for Women," *USSR* 66, March 1962, 38–41.
61 On several occasions prior to 1971 *Amerika* delved into special topics at length; issue 90 (March 1964) contained a special report on architecture; issue 125 (February 1967), on industrial design, was timed to coincide with the Industrial Design USA exhibit touring the Soviet Union; similarly issue 83 (August 1963) was devoted entirely to the graphic arts, and was timed to coincide with the Graphic Arts USA exhibition in the Soviet Union; issue 88 (January 1964) was entirely on agriculture; and issue 127 (April 1967) was entirely on literature and publishing.
62 Issue 97 (October 1964) included a special thirty-five-page report entitled "Equal Rights for All"; issue 135 (December 1967) was devoted entirely to youth.
63 Eli Ginzberg, "For American Women: The Chance to Choose," *Amerika* 125, February 1967, 13–15. For more on Ginzberg's views on the topic, see Eli Ginzberg et al., "Human Resources and National Security," *Scientific Monthly* 82.3 (March 1956): 121–35.
64 Prior to 1971, there were articles in *Amerika* that reflected the discontent and discord of the previous decade. Most notably these were devoted to civil rights and the youth movement, and to a lesser extent, the farm workers and consumer movements. In addition to the "special" reports and issues indicated above, these articles included Clifford Laird, "A New University President Addresses Restless Students," 112, January 1966, 2–4; "Protest and Progress," 112, January 1966, 5–9; Virginia Olsen, "Voices of the Students," 121, October 1966, 50–1; "Strike!" 131, August 1967, 2–5; Patrick Anderson, "Ralph Nader, Public Defender No. 1" 145, October 1968, 39–41; Joel R. Kramer, "What Lies Behind Student Rebellion," 146, November 1968, 36–7; and Kenneth Kenniston, "What the Students Want and Why," 159, December 1969, 14–16.
65 For more on the emergence and impact of the second wave feminist movement, see Alice Echols, *Daring to Be Bad: Radical Feminism in America, 1967–1975* (Minneapolis: University of Minnesota Press, 1989); Sara M. Evans, *Personal Politics: The Roots of Women's Liberation in the Civil Rights Movement and the New Left* (New York: Alfred A. Knopf, 1979); Sara M. Evans, *Born for Liberty: A History of Women in America* (New York: Simon & Schuster, 1989); Sara M. Evans, *Tidal Wave: How Women*

Changed America at Century's End (New York: Simon & Schuster, 2003); Estelle B. Freedman, *No Turning Back: The History of Feminism and the Future of Women* (New York: Ballantine Books, 2002); Stephanie Gilmore, ed., *Feminist Coalitions: Historical Perspectives on Second-Wave Feminism in the United States* (Champaign, 2008); Cynthia Harrison, *On Account of Sex: The Politics of Women's Issues, 1945–1968* (Berkeley: University of California Press, 1988); Nancy A. Hewitt, *No Permanent Waves: Recasting Histories of US Feminism* (New Brunswick, NJ: Rutgers University Press, 2010); and Ruth Rosen, *The World Split Open: How the Modern Women's Movement Changed America* (New York: Penguin Books, 2000).

66 Bonnie J. Dow, *Watching Women's Liberation, 1970: Feminism's Pivotal Year on the Network News* (Champaign: University of Illinois Press, 2014), 13.

67 Grace Lichtenstein, "Feminists Demand 'Liberation' In *Ladies' Home Journal* Sit-In," *New York Times*, 19 March 1970.

68 John Mack Carter, "Why You Find the Next Eight Pages in the *Ladies' Home Journal*," *Ladies' Home Journal*, August 1970, 63.

69 The August 1970 *Ladies' Home Journal* insert included "Hello to Our Sisters," 64; "Women and Work," 64–5; E.M. "This Woman Is Anti-Semantic," 65; "Your Daughter's Education," 65–6; "Babies Are Born, Not Delivered," 66–7; and "Help Wanted: Female," 67–8.

70 Dow, *Watching Women's Liberation, 1970*, 117.

71 "Introduction to Women's Packet," *Amerika* 173, March 1971.

72 See Marion K. Sanders, *Dorothy Thompson: A Legend in Her Time* (Boston: Houghton Mifflin Company, 1973).

73 This was a questionable statement on the part of Sanders, as *Eisenstadt v. Baird*, the Supreme Court case that established the right of unmarried women to obtain contraceptives for the purpose of preventing pregnancy on the same basis as married ones, was not passed until March of 1972. Married women could easily obtain contraceptives from June 1965 onwards as a result of *Griswold v. Connecticut*.

74 Inkeles and Bauer, *The Soviet Citizen*, 206.

75 Marion K. Sanders, "American Woman: Her Goals, Achievements, Doubts," *Amerika* 173, March 1971.

76 Margaret Mead, "An Anthropologist's View," *Amerika* 173, March 1971, 12–13.

77 In fall 1971, Congress passed the Comprehensive Child Development Act, co-sponsored by Minnesota senator Walter Mondale and Indiana representative John Brademas, with strong bipartisan support. It would create a comprehensive network of nationally funded, locally administered childcare centres that would provide education, meals, and medical treatment to all children, regardless of socio-economic status and family background This bill addressed recent feminist demands and the needs

of working mothers and their children. However, President Richard Nixon vetoed it, arguing that it would implement a "communal approach to child rearing over against the family-centered approach" thus weakening the family unit and the mother-child bond, both of which were frequently cited by US government officials eager to distance themselves from anything that may have been interpreted as resembling socialism. See Andrew Karch, "A Watershed Episode: The Comprehensive Child Development Act," in *Early Start: Preschool Politics in the United States* (Ann Arbor: University of Michigan Press, 2013).

78 For more on Macoby's views on this subject, see Eleanor E. Macoby and Roy G. D'Andrade, *The Development of Sex Differences* (Stanford, CA: Stanford University Press, 1966); and Eleanor E. Macoby and Carol N. Jacklin, *The Psychology of Sex Differences* (Stanford, CA: Stanford University Press, 1974).
79 Eleanor Macoby, "Are Women That Different?" *Amerika* 173, March 1971, 20–1.
80 "Facts Only," *Amerika* 173, March 1971, 10–11.
81 "Current Biographies," *Amerika* 173, March 1971, 14–18.
82 Ibid.
83 Barbara Rosenfeld, "Motherhood," *Amerika* 173, March 1971, 29–33.
84 Emma Brown, "Post Editor, Columnist Opened Newspaper's First Moscow Bureau," *Washington Post*, 3 May 2010. Rosenfeld was expelled in retaliation for the *Washington Post*'s serialization of *The Penkovsky Papers* (Doubleday, 1965), which purported to be the memoirs of Oleg V. Penkovsky, a Russian colonel who was executed in 1963 for spying for Britain and the United States. The papers were later shown to have been compiled, unbeknownst to the *Washington Post*, by the Central Intelligence Agency.
85 Barbara Rosenfeld, "Motherhood," *Amerika* 173, March 1971, 29–33.
86 Stephen and Barbara Rosenfeld, *Return from Red Square*, 53–4.
87 Ibid., 58–61.
88 Ibid., 60.
89 Ibid., 60–3.
90 Ibid.
91 Elinor L. Horwitz, "Divorce," *Amerika* 173, March 1971, 26–8.
92 Ibid.
93 "Their Special Look," *Amerika* 173, March 1971, 4–9.
94 "Farewell to Childhood," *Amerika* 173, March 1971, 22–5.
95 Julia Viorst, "Where Is It Written" and "Married Is Better," *Amerika* 173, March 1971, 19; and "Reviews: Books-Films-Theater-Music," *Amerika* 173, March 1971, 55.
96 As the predominately white, middle-class, second wave feminist movement emerged, American African women struggled to find their place

282 Notes to pages 209–13

within both the civil rights and feminist movements. Much has been written about their marginalized place within both, as well as the creation of their own separate movement. See Winifred Breines, *The Trouble between Us: An Uneasy History of White and Black Women in the Feminist Movement* (New York: Oxford University Press, 2006); Benita Roth, *Separate Roads to Feminism: Black, Chicana, and White Feminist Movements in America's Second Wave* (New York: Cambridge University Press, 2004); Kimberly Springer, *Living for the Revolution: Black Feminist Organizations, 1968–1980* (Durham, NC: Duke University Press, 2005); and Anne M. Valk, *Radical Sisters: Second-Wave Feminism and Black Liberation in Washington D.C.* (Champaign: University of Illinois Press, 2008).
97 See Brown, *The Role and Status of Women in the Soviet Union*; Carola Hansen and Karin Liden, *Moscow Women: Thirteen Interviews* (New York: Pantheon Books, 1983); and I.A. Kurganoff, *Women in the USSR* (London, ON: SBONR Publishing House, 1971).
98 Attwood, *Creating the New Soviet Woman*, 3.
99 Questions Concerning the Calculation of Non-working Time in Budget Statistics, Statistical Handbook No. 8, 1961, in *Problems of Economics*, IV (April 1962), in Field, "Workers (Mothers): Soviet Women Today," 22.
100 Inkeles and Bauer, *The Soviet Citizen*, x.

Conclusion: Assessing *Amerika*'s Effectiveness: Soviet Promises for the Future and Its Failures

1 Griswold, "Russian Blonde in Space," 882.
2 Hugh S. Cumming, Jr., "Continuation of Magazine '*Amerika*,'" Foreign Service Despatch, 13 November 1951, Box 2431, RG 59. NACP.
3 Office of Public Affairs Department of State. "Foreign Affairs: Background Summary: America – A Full and Fair Picture," January 1947; Box 2, p. 46; Organization, News Articles, 1955–1974 to Agency Mission, 1947–1969; Subject Files, 1953–2000; RG 306; NACP.
4 Telegram from Ambassador William Bedell Smith to John Foster Dulles, 4 March 1947; Box 28; *Amerika Illustrated*, 1950–1956 to National Security Directive 51, 17 October 1990; Records Relating to Select USIA Programs, 1953–1999; RG 306; NACP.
5 M. Gordon Knox, "Conversations Concerning VOA and Magazine, *Amerika*, during 10 Day Trip from Moscow to Odessa via Kharkov and Return, May 1950," Foreign Service of the United States, 25 July 1950, Box 2432; Decimal File 1950–1954; RG 59; NACP.
6 First Secretary of Embassy M. Gordon Knox to Ambassador Alan Kirk, Embassy's Despatch 6 Observations Concerning VOA and Magazine, *Amerika*, During 10 Day Trip from Moscow to Odessa via Kharkov and

Return, May, 1950, 25 July 1950; Box 2453; Decimal File 1950–1954; RG 59; NACP.
7 Tuch, *Communicating with the World*, 52.
8 Richmond, *Cultural Exchange and the Cold War*, 151.
9 Stephen and Barbara Rosenfeld, *Return from Red Square*, 194.
10 Summary of the Impression of Guides at the American National Exhibition Concerning attitudes of Visitors Toward the US; Box 11; Comment Books and Lists of Visitors Related to US Exhibits in the USSR, Rumania and Bulgaria; Office of Exhibits; RG 306; NACP.
11 Ibid., 25.
12 Ibid., 30.
13 Tolvaisas, "Cold War 'Bridge-Building,'" 18. Other magazines, including *Vogue* and the *Sears Roebuck* catalogue, were also banned from distribution, reinforcing the belief that magazines showing America's high standard of living threatened the status quo.
14 Belmonte, *Selling the American Way*, 11.
15 Hixson, *Parting the Curtain*, 32.
16 Richmond, *Cultural Exchange and the Cold War*, 151.
17 Hixson, *Parting the Curtain*, 119.
18 *America Illustrated* (Polish), January 1959; *America Illustrated* (Polish) (English Translations of Articles) Volume 1 (1959 Numbers 1–5); Publications About the United States, 1953–1999; RG 306; NACP.
19 Stephen and Barbara Rosenfeld, *Return from Red Square*, 34–6.
20 Max and Tobia Frankel, "New Soviet Plan – Feminine Females," *New York Times*, 6 December 1959.
21 Ibid.
22 James J. Halsema to Mr. Albert P. Toner, "Item for Staff Report for the President: No. 353 Soviet Consumer Gains," February 1960; Box 21; White House Staff Research Group (Albert P. Toner and Christopher H. Russell) Records, 1956–61; DDE Library.
23 "Some Developments Affecting the Soviet Countries since Summer 1959, 11 February 1960"; Container 3; Research Notes, 1958–1962; Office of Research and Analysis; RG 306; NACP.
24 Max and Tobia Frankel, "New Soviet Plan – Feminine Females."
25 Stephen and Barbara Rosenfeld, *Return from Red Square*, 34–6.
26 Doris Anderson, "The Russian Housewife: She Never Had It So Good," *Chatelaine*, February 1960.
27 "Summer Fashions," *USSR* 70, July 1962, 45–55.
28 Ibid.
29 "Some Developments Affecting the Soviet Countries since Summer 1959, 11 February 1960"; Container 3; Research Notes, 1958–1962; Office of Research and Analysis; RG 306; NACP.

30 Ibid.
31 Ibid.
32 Reid, "Communist Comfort," 469.
33 Salisbury had spent significant time in the Soviet Union during and after Stalin's regime, including four months travelling the country during the American National Exhibition.
34 Harrison E. Salisbury, "Khrushchev's Russia – 1," *New York Times*, 8 September 1959.
35 Harrison E. Salisbury, "Khrushchev's Russia – 6," *New York Times*, 13 September 1959.
36 Martin McCauley, *Khrushchev and Khrushchevism* (London: Macmillian, 1987), 68.
37 Varga-Harris, *Stories of House and Home*, 2.
38 Max and Tobia Frankel, "New Soviet Plan – Feminine Females."
39 Ibid.
40 Wendy Z. Goldman, *Women, the State and Revolution: Soviet Family Policy and Social Life, 1917–1936* (Cambridge, Cambridge University Press, 1993), 289.
41 Ibid., 291–3. Goldman notes that the government position on abortion was misguided. Although official rhetoric dictated that women sought abortions because they were unmarried, unemployed, or impoverished, the majority were actually married and wanted to limit the size of their families. In spite of the ban, women continued to seek the procedure illegally, resulting in increased complications, higher death rates, and a failure on the part of the state to raise its birthrate substantially.
42 Liubov Denisova, *Rural Women in the Soviet Union and Post-Soviet Russia* (New York: Routledge, 2010), 78.
43 Frankel, "New Soviet Plan – Feminine Females."
44 Reid, "Communist Comfort," 469.
45 Harris, *Communism on Tomorrow Street*; Reid, "Communist Comfort"; and Varga-Harris, *Stories of House and Home*.
46 Harris, "Soviet Mass Housing and the Communist Way of Life," 181.
47 Ibid., 186.
48 Reid, "Communist Comfort," 477.
49 Inkeles and Bauer, *The Soviet Citizen*, 4.
50 Elizabeth Ford, "Out of the Shadows: US Visits Lift Soviet Curtain on K.'s Family," *New York Times*, 1 September 1959.
51 Ibid., 375.
52 Ibid., 369.
53 "Goodman to Jazz Up US Showing at Fair," *Sunday News*, 16 February 1958.
54 Peter Carlson, *K Blows His Top: A Cold War Comic Interlude, Starring Nikita Khrushchev, America's Most Unlikely Tourist* (New York: Public Affairs, 2009), 195.

Notes to pages 221–3 285

55 Khrushchev in America, "Full Texts of the Speeches Made by N.S. Khrushchev on His Tour of the US, 15–27 September 1959," State Department, https://archive.org/stream/khrushchevinamer006997mbp/khrushchevinamer006997mbp_djvu.txt.
56 Khrushchev, *Khrushchev Remembers*, 127.
57 Ibid. August 1961's *USSR* included "Home Service Kitchen," an article depicting a service counter which carried a large selection of ready-made food. The article indicated that sixty such counters had opened in Moscow in the past year, and they were popular with Soviet housewives, who used them to have dinner on the table within minutes.
58 Ibid., 396.
59 Ibid., 400.
60 Ibid., 403.
61 "Khrushchev Takes Over, Now Running Show," *Toronto Daily Star*, 22 September 1959.
62 Carlson, *K Blows His Top*, 199.
63 "Howya Doin'? Is Query: Supermarket Bedlam as Khrushchev Visits," *Globe and Mail*, 22 September 1959.
64 "Wife of Premier History Teacher," *New York Times*, 15 September 1959.
65 "A Motherly Visitor," *New York Times*, 28 September 1959.
66 Ibid.
67 Edith Evans Asbury, "Mme. Khrushchev Breaks Away," *New York Times*, 22 September 1959.
68 Griswold, "Russian Blonde in Space," 882. Griswold argues that, by 1963, a third image emerged of the Russian woman as the "professional"; this coincided with twenty-six-year-old cosmonaut Valentina Tereshkova's solo space flight in June of that year, as well as the Kennedy administration's efforts to better utilize American women in the workforce. The US media began to assure women that, like Tereshkova, they could work and be feminine. In its September 1963 issue, the *Ladies' Home Journal* interviewed Tereshkova, discussing her career, but still highlighting her femininity. The article noted her single status and questioned her marriage prospects, concluding that she would probably make a "competent housewife" due to her ability to clean, mend, do laundry, and cook. See Edmund Stevens, "Comely Cosmonaut," *Ladies' Home Journal*, September 1963, 60–1.
69 Vice President Richard Nixon and Premier Nikita Khrushchev, The Kitchen Debate – transcript, 24 July 1959, https://www.cia.gov/library/readingroom/docs/1959–07–24.pdf.
70 See Jeremy Smith and Melanie Ilic, *Khrushchev in the Kremlin: Policy and Government in the Soviet Union, 1953–64* (New York: Routledge, 2011).
71 Patterson, *Bought & Sold*, 15.

72 Ibid., 42.
73 Ibid., 318.
74 Jennifer Griffin, "Cold War Thaw Closes '*Amerika*' Magazine," *Austin American Statesman*, 20 August 1994.
75 "Some Developments Affecting the Soviet Countries since Summer 1959, 11 February 1960"; Container 3; Research Notes, 1958–1962; Office of Research and Analysis; RG 306; NACP.

Bibliography

Primary Sources

Dwight D. Eisenhower Presidential Library (DDE Library)

Abbott Washburn Papers
C.D. Jackson Papers
Clarence Francis Papers
James M. Lambie Jr. Papers
Library Staff Files
National Security Council Staff Papers
Office of the Staff Secretary Records
Operations Coordinating Board Central File Series
Psychological Strategy Board Files
US President's Committee on Information Activities Abroad (Sprague Committee)
US President's Committee International Information Activities (Jackson Committee) Records
White House Central Files, General File
White House Staff Files
White House Staff Research Board Records

Harry S. Truman Presidential Library (HST Library)

Charles S. Hulten Papers
President's Secretary's Files

National Archives at College Park (NACP)

State Department Records
United States Information Agency Records

Magazines and Periodicals

The American Foreign Service Journal
Amerika
Cleveland Plain Dealer
Globe and Mail
House Beautiful
Ladies' Home Journal
Life
Newsweek
Saturday Evening Post
Time
Toronto Daily Star
US News and World Report
USSR
The Washington Post

Secondary Sources

Adams, James Truslow. *The Epic of America*. Boston: Little Brown and Co., 1931.
Anderson, Barbara A. "The Life Course of Soviet Women Born 1905–1960." In *Politics, Work and Daily Life in the USSR: A Survey of Former Soviet Citizens*, edited by James R. Millar, 203–40. Cambridge: Cambridge University Press, 1985.
Anderson, Karen. *Wartime Women: Sex Roles, Family Relations and the Status of Women During World War II*. Westport, CT: Greenwood Press 1981.
Apple, Rima Dobrev. *Perfect Motherhood: Science and Childrearing*. New Brunswick, NJ: Rutgers University Press, 2006.
Atkinson, Dorothy, Alexander Dallin, and Gail Warshofsky Lapidus, eds. *Women in Russia*. Stanford, CA: Stanford University Press, 1977.
Attwood, Lynne. *Creating the New Soviet Woman: Women's Magazines as Engineers of Female Identity, 1922–1953*. New York: St. Martin's Press, 1999.
Attwood, Lynne. "From the 'New Soviet Woman' to the 'New Soviet Housewife': Women in Post-War Russia." In *War-Torn Tales: Literature, Film and Gender in the Aftermath of World War II*, edited by D. Hipkins and G. Plain, 143–62. Bern: Peter Lang, 2007.
Baldwin, Kate A. *Beyond the Color Line and the Iron Curtain: Reading Encounters between Black and Red, 1922–1963*. Durham, NC: Duke University Press, 2002.
Baldwin, Kate A. *The Racial Imaginary of the Cold War Kitchen: From Sokol'niki Park to Chicago's South Side*. Lebanon, NH: University Press of New England, 2016.
Bartlett, Djurdja. *FashionEast: The Spectre That Haunted Socialism*. Cambridge, MA: MIT Press, 2010.

Belmonte, Laura A. *Selling the American Way: US Propaganda and the Cold War*. Philadelphia: University of Pennsylvania Press, 2008.
Benson, Susan Porter. *Counter Cultures: Saleswomen, Managers and Customers in American Department Stores, 1890–1940*. Champaign: University of Illinois Press, 1998.
Bernhard, Nancy E. *US Television News and Cold War Propaganda, 1947–1960*. New York: Cambridge University Press, 1999.
Berry, Mary Frances. *The Politics of Parenthood: Child Care, Women's Rights, and the Myth of the Good Mother*. New York: Viking, 1993.
Blekher, Feiga. *The Soviet Woman in the Family and in Society*. New York: Wiley Press, 1979.
Borstelmann, Thomas. *The Cold War and the Color Line: American Race Relations in the Global Arena*. Cambridge, MA: Harvard University Press, 2001.
Breines, Winifred. *The Trouble between Us: An Uneasy History of White and Black Women in the Feminist Movement*. New York: Oxford University Press, 2006.
Brennan, Mary. *Wives, Mothers, and the Red Menace: Conservative Women and the Crusade against Communism*. Boulder: University Press of Colorado, 2008.
Brinkley, Alan. *The Publisher: Henry Luce and His American Century*. New York: Alfred A. Knopf, 2010.
Brown, Donald R., ed. *The Role and Status of Women in the Soviet Union*. New York: Teachers College Press, 1968.
Carbone, Cristina. "Staging the Kitchen Debate: How Splitnik Got Normalized in the United States." In *Cold War Kitchen: Americanization, Technology and European Users*, edited by Ruth Oldenziel and Karin Zachmann, 59–81. Cambridge, MA: Massachusetts Institute of Technology, 2009.
Carlson, Peter. *K Blows His Top: A Cold War Comic Interlude, Starring Nikita Khrushchev, America's Most Unlikely Tourist*. New York: Public Affairs, 2009.
Castillo, Greg. *Cold War on the Home Front: The Soft Power of Midcentury Design*. Minneapolis: University of Minnesota Press, 2010.
Caute, David. *The Dancer Defects: The Struggle for Cultural Supremacy during the Cold War*. New York: Oxford University Press, 2005.
Chessel, Marie-Emmanuelle. "From America to Europe: Educating Consumers." *Contemporary European History* 11.1 (February 2002): 165–75.
Clifford, J. Garry. "Bureaucratic Politics." *Journal of American History* 77.1 (June 1990): 161–8.
Cohen, Lizabeth. *A Consumer's Republic: The Politics of Mass Consumption in Postwar America*. New York: Random House, 2003.
Coontz, Stephanie. *The Way We Never Were: American Families and the Nostalgia Trap*. New York: Basic Books, 2016.
Corke, Sarah-Jane. *US Covert Operations and Cold War Strategy: Truman, Secret Warfare and the CIA, 1945–1953*. New York: Routledge, 2008.

Cortez, Cheyanne. "The American Girl: Ideas of Nationalism and Sexuality as Promoted in the Ladies' Home Journal during the Early Twentieth Century." In *Women in Magazines, Research, Representation, Production and Consumption*, ed. Rachel Ritchie et al. New York: Routledge, 2016.

Covert, Tawnya J. Adkins. *Manipulating Images: World War II Mobilization of Women through Magazine Advertising*. Lanham, MD: Lexington Books, 2011.

Cowan, Ruth Schwartz. *More Work for Mother: The Ironies of Household Technology from the Open Hearth to the Microwave*. New York: Basic Books, 1983.

Critchlow, Donald T. *Phyllis Schlafly and Grassroots Conservatism: A Woman's Crusade*. Princeton, NJ: Princeton University Press, 2005.

Cucuz, Diana. "Containment Culture: The Cold War in the *Ladies' Home Journal*, 1946–1959." In *Modern Print Activism in the United States*, edited by Rachel Schreiber, 145–60. Burlington, VT: Ashgate, 2013.

Cull, Nicholas J. *The Cold War and the United States Information Agency: American Propaganda and Public Diplomacy, 1945–1989*. New York: Cambridge University Press, 2008.

Cull, Nicholas J. *The Decline and Fall of the United States Information Agency: American Public Diplomacy, 1989–2001*. New York: Palgrave Macmillan, 2012.

Cull, Nicholas J. "Public Diplomacy: Lessons from the Past." In *CPD Perspectives on Public Diplomacy*. Los Angeles: Figueroa Press, 2009. http://uscpublicdiplomacy.org/sites/uscpublicdiplomacy.org/files/legacy/publications/perspectives/CPDPerspectivesLessons.pdf.

Cullen, Jim. *The American Dream: A Short History of an Idea That Shaped a Nation*. New York: Oxford University Press, 2004.

Curtis, Glenn E., and Marian Leighton. "The Society and Its Environment." In *Russia: A Country Study*, edited by Glenn E. Curtis, 237–94. Washington, DC: Federal Research Division, Library of Congress, 1998.

Davenport, Lisa E. *Jazz Diplomacy: Promoting America in the Cold War Era*. Jackson: University Press of Mississippi, 2009.

Dean, Robert. *Imperial Brotherhood Gender and the Making of Cold War Foreign Policy*. Amherst: University of Massachusetts Press, 2001.

De Grazia, Victoria. *Irresistible Empire: America's Advance through Twentieth-Century Europe*. Cambridge: Harvard University Press, 2009.

Denisova, Liubov. *Rural Women in the Soviet Union and Post-Soviet Russia*. New York: Routledge, 2010.

Deutsch, Tracey. *Building a Housewife's Paradise: Gender, Politics and American Grocery*. Chapel Hill: University of North Carolina Press, 2010.

Dizard, Wilson, Jr. *Inventing Public Diplomacy: The Story of the US Information Agency*. Boulder: Colorado: Lynne Rienner, 2004.

Dizard, Wilson, Jr. *Strategy of Truth: The Story of the US Information Service*. Washington, DC: Public Affairs Press, 1961.

Doss, Erika. *Looking at Life Magazine*. Washington, DC: Smithsonian Press, 2001.
Dow, Bonnie J. *Watching Women's Liberation, 1970: Feminism's Pivotal Year on the Network News*. Champaign: University of Illinois Press, 2014.
Dudziak, Mary L. *Cold War, Civil Rights: Race and the Image of American Democracy*. Princeton, NJ: Princeton University Press, 2000.
Echols, Alice. *Daring to Be Bad: Radical Feminism in America, 1967–1975*. Minneapolis: University of Minnesota Press, 1989.
Ehrenreich, Barbara, and Deirdre English. *For Her Own Good: Two Centuries of the Experts' Advice to Women*. New York: Anchor Books, 2005.
Eichengreen, Barry. *Europe's Postwar Recovery*. New York: Cambridge University Press, 1995.
Eisenhower, Dwight D. *White House Years: Waging Peace, 1956–1961*. Garden City: Double Day, 1963.
Engel, Barbara Alpen, and Anastasia Posadskaya-Vanderbeck, eds. *A Revolution of Their Own: Voices of Women in Soviet History*. Boulder, CO: Westview Press, 1998.
Engerman, David C. *Know Your Enemy: The Rise and Fall of America's Soviet Experts*. New York: Oxford University Press, 2009.
Eschen, Penny Von. *Satchmo Blows Up the World: Jazz Ambassadors Play the Cold War*. Cambridge, MA: Harvard University Press, 2006.
Evans, Sara M. *Born for Liberty: A History of Women in America*. New York: Simon & Schuster, 1989.
Evans, Sara M. *Personal Politics: The Roots of Women's Liberation in the Civil Rights Movement and the New Left*. New York: Alfred A. Knopf, 1979.
Evans, Sara M. *Tidal Wave: How Women Changed America at Century's End*. New York: Simon & Schuster, 2003.
Ewen, Stuart. *All Consuming Images: The Politics of Style in Contemporary Culture*. New York: Basic Books, 1988.
Ewen, Stuart. *Captains of Consciousness: Advertising and the Social Roots of the Consumer Culture*. New York: McGraw-Hill, 1976.
Faircloth, Christopher. *Images of America: Cleveland's Department Stores*. Charleston, SC: Arcadia Publishing, 2009.
Farber, David. "Phyllis Schlafly: Domestic Conservatism and Social Order." In *The Rise and Fall of Modern American Conservatism: A Short History*, 119–58. Princeton: NJ: Princeton University Press, 2012.
Farnsworth, Beatrice, and Lynne Viola, eds. *Russian Peasant Women*. New York: Oxford University Press, 1992.
Field, Deborah A. "Everyday Life and the Problem of Conceptualizing Public and Private during the Khrushchev Era." In *Everyday Life in Russia Past and Present*, edited by Choi Chatterjee et al., 163–80. Bloomington: Indiana University Press, 2015.

Field, Mark G. "Workers (Mothers): Soviet Women Today." In *The Role and Status of Women in the Soviet Union*, edited by Donald R. Brown, 7–56. New York: Teachers College Press, 1968.

Filzer, Donald. *The Hazards of Urban Life in Late Stalinist Russia: Healthy, Hygiene and Living Standards, 1943–1953*. Cambridge: Cambridge University Press, 2010.

Fox, Michael David. *Showcasing the Great Experiment: Cultural Diplomacy and Western Visitors to the Soviet Union, 1921–1941*. London: Oxford University Press, 2012.

Freedman, Estelle B. *No Turning Back: The History of Feminism and the Future of Women*. New York: Ballantine Books, 2002.

Friedan, Betty. *The Feminine Mystique*. New York: W.W. Norton, 1963.

George, George St. *Our Soviet Sister*. Washington, DC: Robert B. Luce, Inc., 1973.

Gilmore, Stephanie, ed. *Feminist Coalitions: Historical Perspectives on Second-Wave Feminism in the United States*. Champaign: University of Illinois Press, 2008.

Gilyard, Keith. *Louise Thompson Patterson: A Life of Struggle for Justice*. Durham, NC: Duke University Press, 2017.

Goldman, Wendy Z. *Women at the Gates: Gender and Industry in Stalin's Russia*. New York: Cambridge University Press, 2002.

Goldman, Wendy Z. *Women, the State and Revolution: Soviet Family Policy and Social Life, 1917–1936*. Cambridge: Cambridge University Press, 1993.

Goldstein, Carolyn M. *Creating Consumers: Home Economics in Twentieth-Century America*. Chapel Hill: University of North Carolina Press, 2012.

Gould, Bruce, and Beatrice Blackmar Gould. *American Story: Memories and Reflections of Bruce Gould and Beatrice Blackmar Gould*. New York: Harper & Row, 1968.

Gould-Davies, Nigel. "The Logic of Soviet Cultural Diplomacy." *Diplomatic History* 27.2 (April 2003): 193–214.

Graham, Sarah Ellen. *Culture and Propaganda: The Progressive Origins of American Public Diplomacy, 1936–1953*. Burlington, VT: Ashgate, 2015.

Griswold, Robert L. "Russian Blonde in Space": Russian Women in the American Imagination, 1950–1965. *Journal of Social History* 45.4 (2012): 881–907.

Haddow, Robert. *Pavilions of Plenty: Exhibiting American Culture Abroad in the 1950s*. Washington, DC: Smithsonian Institution Press, 1997.

Hamilton, Shane. "Supermarket USA Confronts State Socialism." In *Cold War Kitchen: Americanization, Technology and European Users*, edited by Ruth Oldenziel and Karin Zachmann, 137–59. Cambridge, MA: MIT Press, 2009.

Hansen, Allen C. *USIA: Public Diplomacy in the Computer Age*, 2nd ed. New York: Praeger, 1989.

Hansen, Carola, and Karin Liden. *Moscow Women: Thirteen Interviews*. New York: Pantheon Books, 1983.

Harris, Steven E. *Communism on Tomorrow Street: Mass Housing and Everyday Life after Stalin*. Baltimore: Johns Hopkins University Press, 2013.

Harris, Steven E. "Soviet Mass Housing and the Communist Way of Life." In *Everyday Life in Russia Past and Present*, edited by Choi Chatterjee et al., 181–202. Bloomington: Indiana University Press, 2015.

Harrison, Cynthia. *On Account of Sex: The Politics of Women's Issues, 1945–1968*. Berkeley: University of California Press, 1988.

Hartmann, Susan M. *The Home Front and Beyond: American Women in the 1940s*. Boston: Twain Publishers, 1982.

Hellbeck, Jochen. *Revolution on My Mind: Writing a Diary Under Stalin*. Cambridge, MA: Harvard University Press, 2006.

Hench, John D. *Books as Weapons: Propaganda, Publishing, and the Battle for Global Markets in the Era of World War II*. Ithaca, NY: Cornell University Press, 2010.

Hewitt, Nancy A. *No Permanent Waves: Recasting Histories of US Feminism*. New Brunswick, NJ: Rutgers University Press, 2010.

Hixson, Walter L. *Parting the Curtain: Propaganda, Culture and the Cold War, 1945–1961*. New York: St. Martin's Press, 1998.

Hogan, Michael J. "Corporatism." *Journal of American History* 77.1 (June 1990): 153–60.

Honey, Maureen. *Creating Rosie the Riveter: Class, Gender and Propaganda during World War II*. Amherst: University of Massachusetts Press, 1984.

Hopkinson, Peter. *Split Focus: An Involvement in Two Decades*. London: Rupert Hart-Davis, 1969.

Hornsby, Robert. *Protest, Reform and Repression in Khrushchev's Soviet Union*. Cambridge: Cambridge University Press, 2013.

Hunt, Michael H. "Ideology." *Journal of American History* 77.1 (June 1990): 108–15.

Hunter, Jean E. "A Daring New Concept: 'The *Ladies' Home Journal* and Modern Feminism." *NWSA Journal* 2.4 (Autumn 1990): 583–602.

Ilic, Melanie. *The Palgrave Handbook of Women and Gender in Twentieth-Century Russia and the Soviet Union*. London: Palgrave Macmillan, 2018.

Ilic, Melanie, Susan E. Reid, and Lynne Attwood, eds. *Women in the Khrushchev Era*. New York: Palgrave Macmillan, 2004.

Immerman, Richard H. "Psychology." *Journal of American History* 77.1 (June 1990): 169–80.

Inkeles, Alex, and Raymond Bauer. *The Soviet Citizen: Daily Life in a Totalitarian Society*. Cambridge, MA: Harvard University Press, 1959.

Jackson, Kenneth. *Crabgrass Frontier: The Suburbanization of the United States*. New York: Oxford University Press, 1984.

Jeffords, Susan. "Commentary: Culture and National Identity in Foreign Policy." *Diplomatic History* 18.1 (January 1994): 91–6.

Johnson, A. Ross, and R. Eugene Parta, eds. *Cold War Broadcasting: Impact on the Soviet Union and Eastern Europe*. New York: Central European University Press, 2010.

Johnson, A. Ross. *Radio Free Europe and Radio Liberty: The CIA Years and Beyond*. Washington, DC: Woodrow Wilson Press, 2010.

Johnson, David K. *The Lavender Scare: The Cold War Persecution of Gays and Lesbians in the Federal Government*. Chicago: University of Chicago Press, 2004.

Kaplan, Amy. "Commentary: Domesticating Foreign Policy." *Diplomatic History* 18.1 (January 1994): 97–105.

Karch, Andrew. "A Watershed Episode: The Comprehensive Child Development Act." In *Early Start: Preschool Politics in the United States*, 59–85. Ann Arbor: University of Michigan Press, 2013.

Katz, Katarina. *Gender, Work and Wages in the Soviet Union: A Legacy of Discrimination*. New York: Palgrave Macmillan, 2001.

Keiler, Allan. *Marion Anderson: A Singer's Journey*. Champaign: University of Illinois Press, 2000.

Kershaw, Alex. *Blood and Champagne: The Life and Times of Robert Capa*. New York: St. Martin's Press, 2003.

Kessler-Harris, Alice. *In Pursuit of Equity: Women, Men and the Quest for Economic Citizenship in 20th-Century America*. New York: Oxford University Press, 2001.

Kessler-Harris, Alice. "Pink Collar Ghetto, Blue Collar Token." In *Sisterhood Is Powerful: The Women's Anthology for a New Millennium*, edited by Robin Morgan, 358–67. New York: Washington Square Press, 2003.

Khrushchev, Nikita Sergeyevich. *Khrushchev Remembers*. New York: Little Brown, 1970.

Kirk, Lydia. *Postmarked Moscow*. New York: Charles Scribner's Sons, 1952.

Kirk, Lydia, and Roger Kirk. *Distinguished Service: Lydia Chapin Kirk, Partner in Diplomacy, 1896–1985*. Syracuse, NY: Syracuse University Press, 2007.

Kirkhorn, Michael J. "Dorothy Thompson: Withstanding the Storm." *The Courier* 23.2 (1988): 3–21.

Kirschenbaum, Lisa A. "Constructing a Cold War Epic: Harrison Salisbury and the Siege of Leningrad." In *Americans Experience Russia: Encountering the Enigma, 1917 to the Present*, edited by Choi Chatterjee and Beth Holmgren, 67–86. New York: Routledge, 2012.

Kolchevska, Natasha. "Angels in the Home and at Work: Russian Women in the Khrushchev Years." *Women's Studies Quarterly* 33.3/4 (Fall–Winter 2005): 114–37.

Koppes, Clayton R., and Gregory D. Black. *Hollywood Goes to War: How Politics, Profits and Propaganda Shaped World War II*. Berkeley: University of California Press, 1987.

Korinek, Valerie. *Roughing It in the Suburbs: Reading Chatelaine Magazine in the Fifties and Sixties*. Toronto: University of Toronto Press, 2000.

Kravets, Olga, and Ozlem Sandikci. "Marketing for Socialism: Soviet Cosmetics in the 1930s." *Business History* 87 (Autumn 2013): 591–612.

Krenn, Michael L. *Fall-Out Shelters for the Human Spirit: American Art and the Cold War.* Chapel Hill: University of North Carolina Press, 2005.

Krenn, Michael L. *The History of United States Cultural Diplomacy: 1770 to the Present Day.* New York: Bloomsbury Academic, 2017.

Krugler, David F. *The Voice of America and the Domestic Propaganda Battles, 1945–1953.* Columbia: University of Missouri Press, 2000.

Kuklick, Bruce. "Commentary: Confessions of an Intransigent Revisionist." *Diplomatic History* 18.1 (January 1994): 121–4.

Kurganoff, I.A. *Women in the USSR.* London, ON: SBONR Publishing House, 1971.

Ladd-Taylor, Molly. "Eugenics, Sterilisation and Modern Marriage in the USA: The Strange Career of Paul Popenoe." *Gender & History* 13.2 (August 2001): 298–327.

Ladd-Taylor, Molly, and Lauri Umansky. *"Bad" Mothers: The Politics of Blame in Twentieth-Century America.* New York: New York University Press, 1998.

Lancaster, William. *The Department Store: A Social History.* Leicester: Leicester University Press, 1995.

Lapidus, Gail Warshofsky. *Women in Soviet Society: Equality, Development and Social Change.* Berkeley: University of California Press, 1978.

Laville. Helen. *Cold War Women: The International Activities of American Women's Organizations.* Manchester: University of Manchester Press, 2002.

Leffler, Melvyn P. "National Security." *Journal of American History* 77.1 (June 1990): 143–52.

Levine, Irving R. *Main Street USSR.* Garden City, NY: Doubleday, 1959.

Levine, Irving R. *The New Worker in Soviet Russia.* New York: Macmillan, 1973.

Levine, Irvine R. *Travel Guide to Russia.* Garden City, NY: Doubleday, 1960.

Lisicky, Michael J. *Baltimore's Bygone Department Stores: Many Happy Returns.* Charleston, SC: History Press, 2012.

Lovell, Stephen. *Summerfolk: A History of the Dacha, 1710–2000.* Ithaca, NY: Cornell University Press, 2016.

Lriye, Akira. "Culture." *Journal of American History* 77.1 (June 1990): 99–107.

Lucas, Scott. *Freedom's War: The US Crusade against the Soviet Union, 1945–1956.* New York: New York University Press, 1999.

Lykins, Daniel L. *From Total War to Total Diplomacy: The Advertising Council and the Construction of the Cold War Consensus.* Westport, CT: Praeger, 2003.

Macoby, Eleanor E., and Roy G. D' Andrade. *The Development of Sex Differences.* Stanford, CA: Stanford University Press, 1966.

Macoby, Eleanor E., and Carol N. Jacklin. *The Psychology of Sex Differences.* Stanford, CA: Stanford University Press, 1974.

Magnusdottir, Rosa. "Mission Impossible? Selling Soviet Socialism to Americans, 1955–1958." In *Searching for a Cultural Diplomacy*, edited by

Jessica C.E. Glenow-Hecht and Mark C. Donfried, 50–72. New York: Berghahn Books, 2010.

Mahoney, Richard D. *JFK: Ordeal in Africa*. London: Oxford University Press, 1983.

Manning, Martin J., and Herbert Romerstein. *Historical Dictionary of American Propaganda*. Westport, CT: Greenwood Press, 2004.

Marling, Karal Ann. *As Seen on TV: The Visual Culture of Everyday Life in the 1950s*. Cambridge: Harvard University Press, 1994.

Marling, Karal Ann. *Debutante: Rites and Regalia of American Debdom*. Lawrence: University of Kansas Press, 2004.

Marsh, Margaret. "Suburban Men and Masculine Domesticity, 1870–1915." *American Quarterly* 40.2 (June 1988): 165–86.

Masey, Jack, and Conway Lloyd Morgan. *Cold War Confrontations: US Exhibitions and Their Role in the Cultural Cold War*. Zurich: Lars Muller Publishers, 2008.

May, Elaine Tyler. "Commentary: Ideology and Foreign Policy: Culture and Gender in Diplomatic History." *Diplomatic History* 18.1 (January 1994): 71–8.

May, Elaine Tyler. *Homeward Bound: American Families in the Cold War Era*. New York: Basic Books, 2008.

McCauley, Martin. *Khrushchev and Khrushchevism*. London: Macmillan, 1987.

McCormick, Thomas J. "World Systems." *Journal of American History* 77.1 (June 1990): 125–32.

McEnaney, Laura. *Civil Defense Beings at Home: Militarization Meets Everyday Life in the Fifties*. Princeton, NJ: Princeton University Press, 2000.

McEnaney, Laura. "He-Men and Christian Mothers: The America First Movement and the Gendered Meanings of Patriotism and Isolationism." *Diplomatic History* 18.1 (January 1994): 47–57.

McGaffey, Christina Frederick. *Selling Mrs. Consumer*. New York: Business Bourse, 1929.

Meyerowitz, Joanne. "Beyond the Feminine Mystique: A Reassessment of Postwar Mass Culture, 1946–1958." *Journal of American History* 79.4 (March 1993): 1455–82.

Mickenberg, Julia L. *American Girls in Red Russia: Chasing the Soviet Dream*. Chicago: University of Chicago Press, 2017.

Moore, Helen Damon. *Magazines for the Millions: Gender and Commerce in the Ladies' Home Journal and Saturday Evening Post, 1880–1919*. Albany: State University of New York Press, 1994.

Morris, John G. *Get the Picture: A Personal History of Photojournalism*. Chicago: University of Chicago Press, 2002.

Muehlenbeck, Philip E. *Betting on the Africans: John F. Kennedy's Courting of African Nationalist Leaders*. New York: Oxford University Press, 2012.

Nadel, Alan. *Containment Culture: American Narrative, Postmodernism and the Atomic Age*. Durham, NC: Duke University Press, 1995.

Neuhaus, Jessamyn. *Housework and Housewives in American Advertising: Married to the Mop*. New York: Palgrave MacMillan, 2011.

Noer, Thomas J. "New Frontiers and Old Priorities in Africa." In *Kennedy's Quest for Victory: American Foreign Policy, 1961–1963*, edited by Thomas G. Paterson, 253–83. New York: Oxford University Press, 1989.

Olson, Laura J., and Svetlana Adonyeva. *The Worlds of Russian Village Women: Tradition, Transgression, Compromise*. Madison: University of Wisconsin Press, 2012.

Osgood, Kenneth A. "Propaganda." In *Encyclopedia of American Foreign Policy*, ed. Alexander DeConde et al., 239–54. New York: Charles Scribner's Sons, 2001.

Osgood, Kenneth A. "Total Cold War: US Propaganda in the 'Free World,' 1953–1960." PhD diss., University of California, Santa Barbara, 2001.

Osgood, Kenneth A. *Total Cold War: Eisenhower's Secret Propaganda Battle at Home and Abroad*. Lawrence: University Press of Kansas, 2006.

Parini, Jay. *John Steinbeck: A Biography*. New York: Henry Hold, 1994.

Parry-Giles, Shawn J. "The Eisenhower Administration's Conceptualization of the USIA: The Development of Overt and Covert Propaganda Strategies," *Presidential Studies Quarterly* 24.2 (1994): 263–76.

Paterson, Thomas G. "A Round Table: Explaining the History of American Foreign Relations." *Journal of American History* 77.1 (June 1990): 93–8.

Patterson, Patrick Hyder. *Bought & Sold: Living and Losing the Good Life in Socialist Yugoslavia*. Ithaca, NY: Cornell University Press, 2011.

Patterson, Patrick Hyder. "Risky Business: What Was Really Being Sold in the Department Stores of Socialist Eastern Europe?" In *Communism Unwrapped: Consumption in Cold War Eastern Europe*, edited by Paulina Bren and Mary Neuburger, 116–39. New York: Oxford University Press, 2012.

Peacock, Margaret. *Innocent Weapons: The Soviet and American Politics of Childhood in the Cold War*. Chapel Hill: University of North Carolina Press, 2014.

Peet, Creighton. "Russian '*Amerika*,' a Magazine about US for Soviet Citizens." *College Art Journal* 11.1 (Autumn 1951): 17–20.

Pells, Richard. *Not Like Us: How Americans Have Loved, Hated and Transformed American Culture since World War II*. New York: Basic Books, 1997.

Pepchinski, Mary. "Women's Buildings at European and American World's Fairs, 1893–1939." In *Gendering the Fair: Histories of Women and Gender at World's Fairs*, edited by T.J. Boisseau and Abigail M. Markwyn, 187–207. Chicago: University of Chicago Press, 2010.

Perez, Louis A., Jr. "Dependency." *Journal of American History* 77.1 (June 1990): 133–42.

Peri, Alexis. "New Soviet Woman: The Post-World War II Feminine Ideal at Home and Abroad." *Russian Review* 77 (October 2018): 2–25.

Perry, Pam. *Eisenhower: The Public Relations President*. Lanham, MD: Lexington Books, 2014.

Phillips, Sarah, and Shane Hamilton. *The Kitchen Debate and Cold War Consumer Politics: A Brief History with Documents*. New York: Bedford/ St. Martin's Press, 2014.

Pinsky, Anatoly. "The Diaristic Form and Subjectivity under Khrushchev." *Slavic Review* 73.4 (Winter 2014): 805–27

Plant, Rebecca Jo. *Mom: The Transformation of Motherhood in Modern America*. Chicago: University of Chicago Press, 2010.

Poiger, Uta G. *Jazz, Rock, and Rebels: Cold War Politics and American Culture in a Divided Germany*. Berkeley: University of California Press, 2000.

Popenoe, Paul. *Marriage: Before and After*. New York: Wilfred Funk., 1943.

Popenoe, Paul. *Modern Marriage: A Handbook for Men*. New York: Macmillan, 1925.

Prevots, Naima. *Dance for Export: Cultural Diplomacy and the Cold War*. Middletown, CT: Wesleyan University Press, 1999.

Puddington, Arch. *Broadcasting Freedom: The Cold War Triumph of Radio Free Europe and Radio Liberty*. Lexington: University Press of Kentucky, 2000.

Reid, Susan E. "Cold War in the Kitchen: Gender and the De-Stalinization of Consumer Taste in the Soviet Union under Khrushchev." *Slavic Review* 61.2 (Summer 2002): 211–52.

Reid, Susan E. "Communist Comfort: Socialist Modernism and the Making of Cosy Homes in the Khrushchev Era." *Gender & History* 21.3 (November 2009): 465–98.

Reid, Susan E. "Everyday Aesthetics in the Khrushchev-Era Standard Apartment." In *Everyday Life in Russia Past and Present*, edited by Choi Chatterjee et al., 203–33. Bloomington: Indiana University Press, 2015.

Reid, Susan E. "'Our Kitchen Is Just as Good': Soviet Responses to the American Kitchen." In *Cold War Kitchen: Americanization, Technology and European Users*, edited by Ruth Oldenziel and Karin Zachmann, 83–112. Cambridge: MA: MIT Press, 2009.

Richardson, Kristen. *The Season: A Social History of the Debutante*. New York: W.W. Norton, 2019.

Richmond, Yale. *Cultural Exchange and the Cold War: Raising the Iron Curtain*. University Park: Penn State University Press, 2003.

Riesman, David. "The Nylon War." *A Review of General Semantics* 8.3 (Spring 1951): 163–70.

Robertson, Roland. *Globalization: Social Theory and Global Culture*. Thousand Oaks, CA: Sage, 1992.

Rosen, Ruth. *The World Split Open: How the Modern Women's Movement Changed America*. New York: Penguin Books, 2000.

Rosenberg, Emily S. "Another Mission to Moscow: Ida Rosenthal and Consumer Dreams." In *Americans Experience Russia: Encountering the Enigma, 1917 to the Present*, edited by Choi Chatterjee and Beth Holmgren, 127–38. New York: Routledge, 2012.

Rosenberg, Emily S. "Consuming Women: Images of Americanization in the 'American Century.'" *Diplomatic History* 23.3 (Summer 1999): 479–97.

Rosenberg, Emily S. "'Foreign Affairs'" After World War II: Connecting Sexual and International Politics." *Diplomatic History* 18.1 (January 1994): 59–70.

Rosenberg, Emily S. "Gender." *Journal of American History* 77.1 (June 1990): 116–24.

Rosenberg, Emily S. *Spreading the American Dream: Selling American Economic and Cultural Expansion, 1890–1945*. New York: Hill and Wang, 1982.

Rosenberg, Gabriel N. *The 4-H Harvest: Sexuality and the State in Rural America*. Philadelphia: University of Pennsylvania Press, 2016.

Rosenfeld, Stephen, and Barbara Rosenfeld. *Return from Red Square*. Washington, DC: Robert B. Luce, 1967.

Roth, Benita. *Separate Roads to Feminism: Black, Chicana, and White Feminist Movements in America's Second Wave*. New York: Cambridge University Press, 2004.

Roth-Ey, Kristin. *Moscow Prime-Time: How the Soviet Union Built the Media Empire That Lost the Cultural Cold War*. Ithaca, NY: Cornell University Press, 2012.

Rupp, Leila J. *Mobilizing Women for War: German and American Propaganda, 1939–1945*. Princeton, NJ: Princeton University Press, 1978.

Rupp, Leila J., and Verta Taylor. *Survival in the Doldrums: The American Women's Rights Movement, 1945 to the 1960s*. Columbus: Ohio State University Press, 1987.

Rutherford, Janice Williams. *Selling Mrs. Consumer: Christine Frederick and the Rise of Household Efficiency*. Athens: University of Georgia Press, 2003.

Ryan, Mary P. *Women in Public: Between Banners and Ballots, 1825–1880*. Baltimore: Johns Hopkins University Press, 1992.

Sadler, Darlene J. *Americans All: Good Neighbour Cultural Diplomacy in World War II*. Austin: University of Texas Press, 2012.

Salisbury, Harrison E. *The Soviet Union: Fifty Years*. New York: Harcourt, Brace and World, 1967.

Sanders, Marion K. *Dorothy Thompson: A Legend in Her Time*. Boston: Houghton Mifflin, 1973.

Scanlon, Jennifer. *Inarticulate Longings: The* Ladies' Home Journal, *Gender and the Promises of Consumer Culture*. New York: Routledge, 1995.

Schwoch, James. *Global TV: New Media and the Cold War, 1946–69*. Champaign: University of Illinois Press, 2009.

Scrivano, Paolo. "Signs of Americanization in Italian Domestic Life: Italy's Postwar Conversion to Consumerism." *Journal of Contemporary History* 40.2 (April 2005): 317–40.

Shapiro, Laura. *Something from the Oven: Reinventing Dinner in 1950s America*. New York: Penguin, 2004.

Smith, Andrew F. *Eating History: 30 Turning Points in the Making of American Cuisine*. New York: Columbia University Press, 2009.

Smith, Geoffrey S. "Commentary: Security, Gender, and the Historical Process." *Diplomatic History* 18.1 (January 1994): 79–90.

Smith, Jeremy, and Melanie Ilic. *Khrushchev in the Kremlin: Policy and Government in the Soviet Union, 1953–64*. New York: Routledge, 2011.

Smith, Mark B. *Property of Communists: The Urban Housing Program from Stalin to Khrushchev*. Dekalb: Northern Illinois University Press, 2010.

Sosin, Gene. *Sparks of Liberty: An Insider's Memoir of Radio Liberty*. University Park: Penn State University Press, 1999.

Spalding, Elizabeth Edwards. *The First Cold Warrior: Harry Truman, Containment and the Remaking of Liberal Internationalism*. Lexington: University of Kentucky Press, 2006.

Spock, Benjamin. *The Common Sense Book of Baby and Child Care*. New York: Duell, Sloan and Pearce, 1946.

Spring, Dawn. *Advertising in the Age of Persuasion: Building Brand America, 1941–1961*. New York: Palgrave Macmillan, 2011.

Springer, Kimberly. *Living for the Revolution: Black Feminist Organizations, 1968–1980*. Durham, NC: Duke University Press, 2005.

Steinbeck, John. *A Russian Journal*. New York: Penguin Books, 1948.

Stephanson, Anders. "Commentary: Considerations on Culture and Theory." *Diplomatic History* 18.1 (January 1994): 107–19.

Stern, John Allen. *C.D. Jackson: Cold War Propagandist for Democracy and Globalism*. Lanham, MD: University Press of America, 2012.

Thomas, Damion. *Globetrotting: African American Athletes and Cold War Politics*. Champaign: University of Illinois Press, 2012.

Thompson, Dorothy. *I Saw Hitler!* New York: Farrar and Rinehart, 1932.

Thompson, Dorothy. *The New Russia*. New York: Henry Holt, 1928.

Thompson, Jenny, and Sherry Thompson. *The Kremlinologist: Llewellyn E. Thompson, America's Man in Cold War Moscow*. Baltimore: Johns Hopkins University Press, 2018.

Tolvaisas, Tomas. "Cold War 'Bridge-Building': Exchange Exhibits and Their Reception in the Soviet Union, 1959–1967." *Journal of Cold War Studies* (12.4): 3–31.

Tomc, Gregor. "A Tale of Two Subcultures: A Comparative Analysis of Hippie and Punk Subcultures in Slovenia." In *Remembering Utopia: The Culture of Everyday Life in Socialist Yugoslavia*, edited by Breda Luthar and Maruša Pušnik, 165–98. Washington, DC: New Academic Publishing, 2010.

Toosi, Mitra. "A Century of Change: The US Labor Force, 1950–2050." *Monthly Labor Review* (May 2002): 15–28. https://www.bls.gov/opub/mlr/2002/05/art2full.pdf.

Tuch, Hans N. *Communicating with the World: US Public Diplomacy Overseas.* New York: St. Martin's Press, 1990.
Valk, Anne M. *Radical Sisters: Second-Wave Feminism and Black Liberation in Washington D.C.* Champaign: University of Illinois Press, 2008.
Vandenberg-Daves, Jodi. *Modern Motherhood: An American History.* New Brunswick, NJ: Rutgers University Press, 2014.
Varga-Harris, Christina. "Moving towards Utopia: Soviet Housing in the Atomic Age." In *Divided Dreamworlds? The Cultural Cold War in East and West*, edited by Peter Romijn et al., 133–54. Amsterdam: Amsterdam University Press, 2012.
Varga-Harris, Christine. *Stories of House and Home: Soviet Apartment Life during the Khrushchev Years.* Ithaca, NY: Cornell University Press, 2015.
Vučetić, Radina. "Džuboks (Jukebox): The First Rock 'n' Roll Magazine in Socialist Yugoslavia." In *Remembering Utopia: The Culture of Everyday Life in Socialist Yugoslavia*, edited by Breda Luthar and Maruša Pušnik, 145–64. Washington, DC: New Academic Publishing, 2010.
Wagnleitner, Reinhold. *Coca-Colonization and the Cold War: The Cultural Mission of the United States in Austria after the Cold War.* Chapel Hill: University of North Carolina Press, 1994.
Wainwright, Loudon. *The Great American Magazine: An Inside History of Life.* New York: Alfred A. Knopf, 1986.
Walker, Nancy A. "*The* Ladies' Home Journal, 'How America Lives' and the Limits of Cultural Diversity." *Media History* 6.2 (2000): 129–38.
Walker, Nancy A. *Shaping Our Mothers' World: American Women's Magazines.* Jackson: University Press of Mississippi, 1995.
Welky, David. *Everything Was Better in America: Print Culture in the Great Depression.* Champaign: University of Illinois Press, 2008.
West, Dorothy. "An Adventure in Moscow." In *The Richer, the Poorer.* New York: Doubleday Anchor, 1995.
Wheelan, Richard. *Robert Capa: A Biography.* New York: Alfred A. Knopf, 1985.
Whitaker, Jan. *Service and Style: How the American Department Store Fashions the Middle Class.* New York: St. Martin's Press, 2006.
Williams, William Appleman. *The Tragedy of American Diplomacy.* New York: W.W. Norton, 1959.
Winkler, Allan M. *The Politics of Propaganda: The Office of War Information, 1942–1945.* New Haven, CT: Yale University Press, 1978.
Winter, Ella. *Red Virtue.* New York: Harcourt, Brace, 1933.
Wulf, Andrew James. *US International Exhibitions during the Cold War: Winning Hearts and Minds.* Lanham, MD: Rowman & Littlefield, 2015.
X. "The Sources of Soviet Conduct." *Foreign Affairs: An American Quarterly Review* (July 1947): 566–82.

Yarrow, Andrew L. "Selling a New Vision of America to the World: Changing Messages in Early US Cold War Print Propaganda." *Journal of Cold War Studies* 11.4 (Fall 2009): 3–45.

Yeltsin, Boris. *Against the Grain*. New York: Simon & Schuster, 1990.

Zakharova, Larisa. "Soviet Fashion in the 1950s–1960s: Regimentation, Western Influences and Consumption Strategies." In *The Thaw: Soviet Society and Culture during the 1950s and 1960s*, edited by Denis Koslov and Eleonory Gilburd, 402–35. Toronto: University of Toronto Press, 2013.

Zeide, Anna. *Canned: The Rise and Fall of Consumer Confidence in the American Food Industry*. Berkeley: University of California Press, 2018.

Zubovich, Katherine. *Moscow Monumental*. Princeton, NJ: Princeton University Press, 2020.

Index

Adams, Clifford R., 37–9
advertising, 114, 171, 185, 197; in *Amerika*, 15–16, 118, 122, 129, 217; gender norms and, 15–16, 50–1, 167; in *Ladies' Home Journal*, 50, 87–9; in *Life* magazine, 121; shifts in image use, 11, 121, 181; targeting women, 11, 15, 87, 89, 118, 155
African Americans: artists, 128, 132–4, 186; civil rights struggles and (*see* civil rights movement); drawn to Soviet Union, 93, 132, 232n38, 254n154; lack of media representation, 12, 106, 181, 186–7, 245n3; women, 12, 93, 106, 128, 204, 238n6; workers, 132, 147, 234n58
African nations, 44–5, 226
Alhoff, Mary Jo, 33–4, 147–8
American Dream, 175; conceptualizations of, 26, 152, 154, 172, 238n8; pursuing the, 71, 95, 127, 149–53; Yugoslav Dream versus, 166
American Institute of Family Relations (AIFR), 39–41
American National Exhibition, 129, 153, 161–2; *Amerika* and, 6, 161, 213, 215, 226; kitchen debate, 6, 163; Russian attendance, 6, 169, 181, 194, 215; shopping and, 166, 169, 215; USIA at, 166, 189
Amerika, 53, 166; African American representation in, 131–4, 181, 187–9; article topics, 106, 132–6, 138–42, 146–7, 180–3; consumerism, coverage of, 120–3, 168–77, 183–5, 210, 214–17; content of, 4, 121–5, 148, 155, 180, 224–7; discontinuation of, 6, 108–9, 117; distribution of, 3, 6, 104, 106, 108, 118, 212–13; family and children, focus on, 127–8, 135, 151–2, 157–8, 177, 191; fashion showcased in, 119–21, 127, 135–45, 177, 183; food, coverage of, 146, 157, 162–6, 182–3, 210; gender equality, discussion of, 189, 195, 197–204, 207; gender norms, reinforcement of, 10, 129–32, 147, 151, 158, 186, 223–5; goals of, 3–4, 21, 107, 122, 146–7, 214, 224; homemaking, representation of, 135, 146–7, 154–61, 180, 191–2; housing, discussion of, 152–4, 159–60; launch and first run of, 96, 104, 106, 126; marriage, representation of, 127, 135, 146, 149–50, 167, 181; middle-class focus of, 127–8, 132, 134, 139–40, 152,

210; postwar women's magazines versus, 4, 154–5, 214, 216; reception among Russian women, 134, 136–7, 145–7, 207, 212–14; representations of women in, 16, 50–1, 127–35, 138–40, 180, 196, 223; revitalization of, 112, 116–19, 223–4; Russian women, appeals to, 6, 123–7, 138–45, 192, 210–12, 226–7; shopping malls and department stores in, 128, 168–77, 183, 185, 207; shifts in 1960s, 180–6, 193, 207, 226–7; Soviet regime versus, 117–18, 122–4, 129, 161, 214; special report of, 180, 195, 197–205, 209; USIA use of, 15–16, 21, 116–24, 146–7, 161–2, 223–6; *USSR* versus, 128–32, 135, 178, 189–93, 216, 226; women's employment, discussion of, 120, 135, 138, 166–7, 177, 185–6. *See also* Sanders, Marion K.

anti-Americanism: claims of, 27, 45; Soviet, 5–6, 132

anti-communism, 13, 43–4, 50, 112; *Amerika* on, 75–6, 161, 166, 214; campaigns (*see* anti-communism campaigns); "good housekeeping" and, 14, 35; *Ladies' Home Journal* on, 53–4, 61, 75–6, 90–3, 199

anti-communism campaigns, 4–5, 121, 143, 187; domestic politics and, 14, 27, 35, 50; women's involvement in, 8, 10, 14–15, 26–7, 90

Armstrong, Louis, 9

Asian nations: Soviet Union and, 44, 189; United States and, 45, 226

attitudes: "capitalistic," 73, 99, 161, 215, 221; femininity and, 28–30; on propaganda, 7, 99, 102; Russian, 81, 103, 129, 215, 247n21; sexual, 199; shifts in, 102, 199; on women's roles, 17, 99, 177, 191

Attwood, Lynne, 17, 131, 210

Bauer, Raymond, 56–8, 200, 210, 219, 247nn21, 23
Belmonte, Laura, 10, 15, 214
Benjamin, Louise Payne, 28–30, 240n23
Better Homes and Gardens, 27, 124
Bolshevism, 17, 91. *See also* Revolution, Russian
budgeting, 211; advice on, 36–8, 161, 174; lack of, 36, 164; *Ladies' Home Journal* on, 31–3, 36, 71–2

Canner, Dorothy and Bill, 36–7
"Can This Marriage Be Saved?," *Ladies' Home Journal*, 39–40
Capa, Robert, 77, 79, 85, 121, 168, 248nn34, 36; photography of Russian women and children, 59–70, 74–5, 82, 173, 247n31; Russian authorities versus, 60, 62

capitalism, 142, 221, 223; allegiance to, 16, 44, 94, 207; *Amerika*, portrayal of, 4, 51, 114–15, 120, 147–9, 214–15; corporate promotion of, 169–72; criticism of, 41–2, 92, 129, 161, 172, 247n31; democracy and, 41, 51–2, 87, 96; exposure to, 95, 172, 207, 211, 271n48; happiness and, 3–4, 10–12, 87, 128–29, 214–15, 219; *Ladies' Home Journal*, portrayal of, 41–3, 73, 86–7, 94–6; media portrayals of, 10–12, 86–7; US government selling of, 4, 10, 20, 52, 100, 210–11; women's promotion of, 10, 16, 94

careers, women's: combining mothering with, 49, 166–8, 177, 195, 199–204, 207; homemaking versus, 35, 38, 41, 167, 203; lack of, 25–6, 120; men's opinions on, 33–4; pursuit of, 58, 100, 128, 180, 186, 192–5

Carter, John Mack, 197–8
Central Intelligence Agency (CIA), 103, 109, 111
childcare, 36, 155; Russian women and, 78, 82, 90–2, 129–31, 197, 218–19; women's time devoted to, 18, 156, 173, 199–200, 208–11
childrearing, 94, 167; community involvement and, 46, 100, 200, 207; feminist movement and, 201–3; patriotism and, 10, 35, 40; Russian women and, 12, 54, 59, 75, 142, 178, 193; women's careers and, 48–9, 78, 115, 120, 166–8, 186, 191
children: advice on, 36–7, 120, 128, 151–3, 205–6, 238n3; expected commitment to, 17, 31–5, 40–1, 63, 146–53, 215; lack of desire for, 38, 58; maladjusted, 36–8; women's homemaking and, 26, 37, 115, 120, 135, 177, 222
chores, household, 25, 131, 155–6; family sharing of, 36, 194
churches: attendance at, 29, 35, 55, 149–50; communism versus, 43, 81, 115, 136–7, 251n97; women's roles in, 47, 49, 63, 200
citizens, 223; childrearing and, 10, 35, 78, 200; creating anti-communist, 43, 101, 103; housewives as, 43, 47, 49; interacting with Russian, 6–9, 56–7, 76, 104; notions of good, 10, 15–17, 46–7, 78, 191; patriotism and, 10, 35, 46, 101; as purchasers, 15–16, 225–7; Russian provision for, 56, 76, 105, 129, 217–18; US influence of Russian, 5, 101, 105, 110, 166, 215–16; women's imperatives as, 48–9, 101, 130
civic politics, 41–2, 172; women's involvement in, 14, 44–9, 115, 191

civilization, 43, 191, 227; "proper" childrearing and, 11, 35, 40, 242n69
civil rights movement: *Amerika* coverage and, 132, 134, 187–9, 195, 279n64; international advocacy, 9, 132; legislation, passage of, 9, 187; public struggles, 187–9, 197, 238n8, 257n33; women in, 180, 188, 281n96
class, 40, 100, 262n11; capitalism and, 42, 58; divisions between Russian women, 76, 84–5, 91, 247n21; middle (*see* middle-class women); working (*see* working-class women)
clothing: affordable, 65, 136, 138–9; class divisions in, 84–5; handmade, 30, 34, 73, 143; purchasing new, 30, 32, 36, 125; worn-out, 56, 215. *See also* fashion
Cohen, Lizabeth, 15–16, 172
Cold War: *Amerika* (see *Amerika*); definition of, 43; as ideological battle, 5, 8, 43, 214; journalism during, 52, 54, 74–6, 91, 214; *Ladies' Home Journal* on (see *Ladies' Home Journal*); propaganda (*see* propaganda); state-private network during, 8, 112
communism: accusations of, 27; *Amerika* on, 75–6, 161, 166, 214; anti- (*see* anti-communism); attempts to destabilize, 4–5, 15, 90, 121, 143, 187; capitalism versus, 12, 52, 93–6, 129, 161, 195; civil liberties versus, 43–4, 52; collapse of, 21, 224–7; containment policy toward, 13–14, 35, 43–4, 50, 112; curiosity about, 54, 58, 67, 111, 221, 245n3; *Ladies' Home Journal* on, 54, 61, 75–6, 90–3, 199; life under, 62, 75–6, 78–9, 217, 219; propaganda

explicitly against, 8, 13, 27, 53, 121, 143, 166; Russian women in, 12, 19, 55, 78, 89, 92–3, 218; safety from, 10, 26, 43, 45, 94–5; support for, 56, 76, 105, 129–31, 217–19, 254n154; threat of (*see* communist threat); women's role against, 10, 26–7, 43, 223

Communist Party (CP), Soviet Union, 5, 82, 116–17, 189, 210, 247n21

communist threat, 43–4, 112; housewives countering, 26–8, 45–6; *Ladies' Home Journal* on, 43, 52, 94–5

Congress, United States, 109, 122, 142, 280n77; funding for programs, 5, 7, 44, 102–3, 119; women in, 48, 186, 199, 203–4, 257n27

consumer culture, American: gender and, 9–10, 15–16, 74, 83, 212; government policy and, 5–6, 16, 216–22, 225; images of women, 4, 9–12, 74; Russian women and, 18, 81, 93, 127, 146–7, 191–2; shifting media coverage of, 180, 182–3; US government promotion of, 100, 116, 163–4, 178–9, 223

consumer goods, 177; availability of, 84–6, 128–9, 212–14, 226–7; benefits of, 19, 90, 96, 118, 122, 155, 182; new markets for, 138, 169–70, 210; Russian deprivation of, 13, 53–4, 91, 105, 168; Russian eagerness for, 9, 67, 77, 86, 131, 210–11

consumerism, 123, 209, 216; mass, 4, 9–11, 26, 52, 177–8, 214; US government selling of, 17–18, 52, 80, 120, 134, 215

consumer's republic, notion of, 15–16

consumption, American, 135, 155; gender and, 8, 26, 51, 125, 143, 209, 225; happiness and, 11–16, 28, 87, 169, 185; images of, 4, 10–12, 172–5; promotion of, 3–4, 10, 41–2, 185; women in narratives of, 10, 28–9, 89, 115, 135, 161

containment: domestic, 14, 27, 35, 50; policy of, 13–14, 112

cultural diplomacy: history of, 8–10, 18, 225; notions of, 7–8, 161, 223; programs for, 8–9, 223; Soviet, 8–9, 117, 161, 226; US government use of, 8, 110, 227; women and, 9–10. *See also* diplomacy

Czechoslovakia: communist, 32, 94–6; USIA publication for, 214, 225

democracy, 91, 103, 221; anti-communism and, 44, 50, 94–5; capitalist consumption and, 11, 41–2, 87, 115, 120, 172; racism and, 134, 187, 191; US government selling of, 6, 45, 52, 96, 100, 127, 166; women's civic involvement and, 44–7, 49–50

Democratic Party, 180; women's support for, 45, 49, 80, 199, 204

department stores, Russian, 192, 216; American versus, 168–73, 175, 185; GUM, 67, 86, 215; lack of availability of items, 65, 82, 86

Diana and Guy, 40–1

Dickinson, LaFell, 55, 58–9

Dickson, Mary and Lewis, 31–2, 70–4

Dior, Christian, 30–1, 240n29

diplomacy, 16, 214; cultural (*see* cultural diplomacy); definitions of, 5, 7–8, 102; golden age of, 3–4; public, 7–8, 102; traditional, 5, 102; Western, 79, 84, 89, 103–4, 109, 116–17

discourse on women, postwar, 10, 16; of domesticity, 25–6, 43, 49–50,

227; magazines and, 26, 49–50, 53; Russian, 17–18, 80–1
divorce: in Soviet Union, 54, 90, 92, 218; as undesirable, 39–40; for women, 203, 207–9
domesticity, 199; anti-communism and, 9, 43, 50; discourse of (*see* discourse); emphasis on women's, 35, 155, 218–19; *Ladies' Home Journal* on, 29, 37, 43–5, 50, 68, 100; masculine, 94, 202; US norms of, 9, 27, 49–50, 227; wartime promotion of, 10, 46
Dudziak, Mary, 9

Eastern Europe, 225; American focus on, 214, 226; Russian influence in, 102–4
education, 33, 134; American women's advocacy for, 46–7, 93, 208; feminist movement and, 186, 191, 198–9; free Russian, 13, 19, 54, 75, 129–30, 189; magazine messaging on, 13, 26, 29, 43, 53, 186; Russian women's, 18, 58, 77, 81, 191, 219; US government propaganda and, 7, 102, 115, 118
Eisenhower, Dwight D.: "Chance for Peace" speech, 110–11; cultural diplomacy and (*see* cultural diplomacy); electoral politics and, 45, 48–9; foreign policy approaches, 4–6, 8, 56, 113–14, 116, 220, 223; overseas information program, 4–8, 106, 110–15, 121–2. *See also* United States Information Agency (USIA)
electoral politics, 122; *Amerika* and, 134, 180; women's involvement in, 44–9, 186, 191
emancipation, women's: American, 197–202, 204, 209, 242n69; Russian Revolution and, 91–3, 132, 246n7

embassy, US: officials, 7, 80, 85; shipments of *Amerika*, 108, 116, 123, 212–14
employment, women's, 10, 76–7, 207; absence of, 26, 52, 117, 123; American, 28, 136, 166–7, 197, 201–3; Russian, 18–19, 54, 56–8, 67, 91, 191–5, 219. *See also* careers, women's
equality, 161, 195; gender (*see* gender inequality); racial (*see* racial inequality); Russian policy of, 4, 17–18, 58–9, 191–3, 210, 219
eugenics, 40
Europe, 90; Eastern (*see* Eastern Europe); US consumer culture in, 17, 48, 116; views of United States, 17, 73, 94; wartime, 48, 55, 101, 110; Western (*see* Western Europe)

families, 79–80, 146; in *Amerika*, 127–30, 135, 151–2, 168–78, 181–2; balancing careers and, 49, 166–8, 177, 195, 199–203, 207; capitalist consumption and, 10, 15–16, 128, 170–6; conservative idealization of, 6, 34, 40, 147; happiness and, 25–6, 35, 96, 120, 156; housing for, 21, 52–3, 92–3, 153, 192, 217–19; *Ladies' Home Journal* focus on, 34–7, 40–1, 45–6, 72–3; norms, reinforcement of, 9–10, 31–2, 94, 115, 120; Russian, 56, 58–9, 89–90, 146, 193; societal emphasis on, 25–6, 63, 99–100, 162, 210; US campaigns based on, 6, 10, 14, 127; in *USSR*, 193–4; women's imperatives with, 15–17, 26, 36–8, 155, 166–7
fashion: advertising imagery and, 11, 95, 138, 171; *Amerika* on, 106, 120–1, 135, 177, 183–4; focus on, 30, 33,

106, 213, 215; *Ladies' Home Journal* on, 28, 30–3, 68–9; maternity, 33, 143–4; practicality and, 30, 84, 135–40, 210; Russian approach to, 18, 82–3, 127, 142–5, 189, 216–17; Western influence in, 18, 84, 124, 141, 192. *See also* clothing

female friendship, 208; American downplaying of, 53, 63, 139, 249n50; Russian, 63, 65, 213

Feminine Mystique (Friedan), 14, 180, 197; criticism of, 25–6

femininity, 99; activism and, 46, 50, 68; *Amerika*, messaging on, 15–16, 50, 120, 127–9, 214–15; capitalist consumption and, 12, 16, 41–2, 52, 134, 215, 226; definitions of, 28–9; etiquette and, 29; fashion and, 30–3, 68–9, 135–6, 177; global desire for, 52, 65–7, 96, 193, 215; housewives and, 4, 26, 29–32, 50, 74, 100, 134, 214–15; ideal notion of, 120, 131, 200; images of fulfilment and, 25–6, 29, 61, 223; lack of, 12, 77, 82–4, 92, 96, 115, 146; *Ladies' Home Journal* on, 25–33, 61, 68, 74, 87; makeovers (*see* makeovers, women's); men's roles and, 202–3; "new," 25, 30–2; Russian women and, 53, 61, 67–8, 89, 191, 218; working women and, 185–6, 203–4

feminism: *Amerika* and, 102, 207, 226–7; *Ladies' Home Journal* and, 15, 28, 50, 181, 197–9; subversive form of, 14–15, 238n9; views of second wave, 26, 197, 200, 203–4, 209

films, 18, 132; government production of, 101, 103, 112, 246n10; magazine coverage of, 121, 128, 262n11; newsreels on Russian life and, 55; as propaganda, 7, 27, 55

food, 35, 263n21; *Amerika* articles on, 16, 162–6, 182; availability of, 67, 71, 85, 205, 217–18; class distinctions, 86, 132; convenience, 26, 37, 146, 162–3, 182, 205; Khrushchev and, 217–18, 220–1; *Ladies' Home Journal* on, 28, 71–3, 162; media portrayals of Russian, 67, 85–6, 164–6, 210; shortages, 13, 53–6, 91, 102. *See also* supermarkets

foreign policy, US. *See* policymaking, US

freedom, notions of, 92, 125, 187, 238n8; for American women, 19, 99–100, 107, 208, 234n58; *Amerika* portrayals of, 114, 121, 124, 208–9; consumerism and, 17, 89, 96; Soviet Union versus, 44, 52, 54, 58, 94–6, 100; USIA activities and, 6, 95–6, 100, 114, 124

Friedan, Betty (*Feminine Mystique*), 14, 25, 180; on happy housewife heroines, 19, 26–7, 50, 197

Fulbright, William J., 44–5

Garst, Roswell "Bob," 221
gender inequality, 17–18, 81, 92–4, 195–201
gender norms, 12; conservative, 3–6, 15–16, 26–7, 214–20, 227; consumer culture and, 8–10, 51, 74, 83, 118, 212, 223–7; on family life, 33–4, 78, 147, 151, 209; in postwar magazines, 14, 26–7, 51–2, 77–8, 199, 212
gender roles, traditional, 207; advertising messaging and, 11; *Amerika* and, 4, 16, 100, 118, 147, 212, 223; divergence from, 37, 100, 207; *Ladies' Home Journal* and, 13, 26–8, 37, 52, 74, 199; Russian

versus American, 3–6, 52–3, 58, 77, 147, 214–20; "special privileges" and (*see* "special privileges," American womanhood)
General Federation of Women's Clubs, 55, 58–9
glocalization, 17–18
Gorrie, Pat and Eddie, 34–6
Gould, Bruce and Beatrice: editorship of, 28–9, 37, 41, 244n121; portrayals of Russian life, 59–60, 75–80, 161; travel to Russia, 75–6. See also *Ladies' Home Journal*
Great Depression, 26, 60, 238n8, 270n41
"Great Shopping Game," 175–6
Gresser, Gisela Kahn, 86, 252n129
Griscom, Robert, 76, 79
Griswold, Robert L., 13, 222, 285n68

happiness, notions of, 28, 185; *Amerika* on, 15, 118, 131, 135–6, 146, 152–3; capitalist consumption and, 3–4, 10–16, 87, 169, 214–15, 219; family life and, 25–7, 35, 96, 120, 146, 152–6; feminine gender norms and, 34–8, 58–61, 84, 96; housewives and, 35–7, 50, 73, 147, 177, 197; *Ladies' Home Journal* on, 29–31, 34–41; overseas information program and, 12, 15; Russian women's lives, 12, 53–61, 64, 84, 94, 128–9; *USSR* on, 129–30, 178, 195; women's careers and, 166–8, 177, 199–203, 207, 219
Harlem Renaissance, 93, 132
Harriman, Averill, 104, 213
health, 56; American women's advocacy for, 46, 81, 208; Russian women's, 81, 218; women's role in familial, 37–8, 155, 162–3

healthcare, 67; universal, 13, 54, 129; women's magazines on, 26, 128
Hellbeck, Jochen, 95, 130
heterosexuality, 40; consumption, 8, 52, 225; cultural messaging of, 11–12, 40, 152, 201; norm of, 17, 19, 26–8, 151, 199, 242n71; women's compulsory, 15, 28, 52, 120, 242n69
Hitler, Adolf, 40, 45, 93
Hixson, Walter, 5, 103, 122, 214
homemaking: advice on, 36–7, 73, 162, 201–2; *Amerika*, promotion of, 120, 127, 131, 135, 146; class divisions and 58, 152–4; emphasis on women's, 15, 18, 36–7, 115, 156; happiness and, 146, 161; *Ladies' Home Journal* on, 28, 34–7, 41; Russian culture and, 161, 218–19, 222
Hopkinson, Peter (*The Russians Nobody Knows*), 55–6
household labour, 82, 131; labour-saving devices, 4, 115, 122, 129, 155–2, 217–19; media portrayals of, 25–7, 32, 53, 74, 172–5; men helping with, 34, 40, 93–4, 167–8, 177, 183, 205; women's, 18, 25, 53, 58, 93, 146, 201–5
housekeeping: anti-communism and, 14, 27, 35, 50; civic involvement, 46–50, 183, 191, 200; notions of good, 35–8, 40, 160–2, 219
housewives: complicating narratives of, 32, 48–50, 164, 180–1; femininity and, 4, 15–16, 28, 74, 100, 134, 223–6; as frivolous, 36–7, 41; gender norms and, 14–15, 35, 219, 226; glorification of, 25, 31, 43, 52, 193; as happy heroines, 19, 26–7, 31, 50, 73, 147, 177, 197; portrayals of, 29, 32, 35–7, 147–51, 172; Russian, 53, 62–8, 83, 146,

166, 178, 210–12; US government imagery, 4, 15, 120, 218–19, 223–6
housing, 181; American, 31–4, 48, 70–2, 94, 127, 153–5; media portrayals of, 70–3, 78–9; Russian, 68, 73, 78–9
"How America Lives," *Ladies' Home Journal*, 31–2, 48, 70, 72, 94–5
Hudson's, J.L., 169–70, 192
husbands, 200; addressing problems with, 36–9, 41; assumed desire for, 25, 35, 140; attracting, 25, 29, 40, 120; household help from, 93–4, 155, 167–8, 177, 183, 205; independence from, 33–4, 38–9, 48–9, 199; magazine articles on, 25, 29, 41, 63, 92; women's responsibility for, 12, 17, 32, 39, 41

ideals, 52; advancing American, 4, 7, 50, 119–23, 127, 131, 180; consumer culture, 4, 118, 121; domestic, 26, 33, 37–8, 100, 154, 182; of femininity, 30, 134; Russian, 130–1; suburban, 68, 100; women's roles and, 30, 50, 100, 119, 226; white, middle-class heterosexual, 15, 40, 94–5, 119–20, 127
ideological battles, 43; Cold War, 5, 8–10, 109, 145; postwar US, 5, 102; women in, 10, 45, 199
imagery, 74, 148, 226; of American women, 9–12, 17–18, 29, 99–101, 140, 176; in *Amerika*, 15–16, 51, 96, 119–29, 174, 209, 223; consumer culture and, 4, 9–12, 32, 87, 147, 165–6; domesticity and, 96, 99, 146–7, 153–6, 162, 177; fashion, 11, 95, 135–40, 142–3, 171; gender norms and, 15, 32, 74, 140, 145, 151, 167; in *Ladies' Home Journal*, 15, 28–9, 50–2, 68–9, 100; power of, 59–61, 63–5, 92, 134, 147; of Russian women, 13, 17, 53–68, 82, 95, 178, 189, 194; shifts in, 11, 121, 181–4
independence, women's, 203; abandonment of, 26; discouragement of, 38–9; Russian, 58, 90
information activities, 16; use of term, 7; US wartime administration, 6, 110–14
Inkeles, Alex, 56–8, 200, 210, 219, 247nn21, 23
institutions, 10; *Amerika*'s coverage of, 106, 108, 122, 125; communist versus democratic, 43–5, 57, 94, 247n21; cultural, 7, 37, 43
international relations, 79; culture, importance in, 9, 16, 117; gender analysis of, 10, 26, 101, 222–3; magazine coverage of, 4, 44, 225–7; postwar shifts in, 5–7, 102, 110, 116–18
Iron Curtain: American attempts to influence, 8, 104, 224; life behind, 6–7, 57, 124; magazine coverage on, 13, 53, 76, 80, 101

Jackson, Charles Douglas (C.D.), 111, 122
Jackson Committee Report, 112–14
Jackson, William, 111
Jamison, Edna, 47
jazz music, 9, 77, 187
journalism, 50, 199; Cold War, 52, 103, 106, 212–14, 218; women in, 26, 41, 92–3, 104, 129–30, 186

Kennan, George F., 13–14, 112
Kennedy, John F., 180, 186–7, 260n76
Kershaw, Alex, 60, 122
Khrushchev, Nikita: kitchen debate, 6, 129–30, 161, 163, 191; policies of, 5,

21, 73, 116, 129, 226–7; rise to power, 5, 21, 116; Russian life under, 53, 79, 164, 212, 215–23; Stalin versus, 5, 73, 79, 116, 156; women's equality, discourse on, 17–18, 156, 191–2
Khrushchevki, construction of, 21, 73, 152–3, 212, 219
Kiev, living conditions in, 55, 63, 66
Kirk, Alan G., 79–80
Kirk, Lydia, 79–87, 89, 108, 161; on Russian women, 79–82
kitchens, 95, 166; appliances for, 16, 156, 159–62, 177, 185; easing women's labour in, 34, 48, 161–3, 182, 219; shared Russian, 73, 79, 162; women's dislike of being stuck in, 36, 58, 92, 164
Knox, M. Gordon, 213
Konstantinov, Fyodor, 116–17
Kremlin, the, 80, 86, 112, 217; Western officials versus, 13–14, 76
Kutvirt, Duda and Oktar, 32, 94–6

Ladies' Home Journal: advice columns 30–3, 36–41, 71–2; anti-communism in, 52–4, 61, 75–6, 90–3, 199; on domesticity, 29, 37, 43–5, 50, 68, 100; families, focus on, 34–7, 40–1, 45–6, 72–3; on fashion, 28, 30–3, 68–9; femininity, notions of, 25–33, 61, 68, 74, 87–9; on food, 28, 71–3, 162; on gender roles, 13, 26–8, 37, 52, 74, 199; on happiness, 29–31, 34–41; on homemaking, 28, 34–7, 41; makeovers (*see* makeovers, women's); mixed messaging of, 48–50; readership, 12, 27–8, 50; representations of American women, 12–14, 27–8, 69–70; representations of Russian women, 54, 59–68, 79–89, 92; special issue on men, 25–6

La Falce, Alfonso and Rosaria, 149
League of Women Voters, 46–7, 49
leisure activities, women's, 3, 46, 125; Russian versus American, 62–3, 82, 155, 248n34
Leningrad, 109, 213, 246n10; journalist visits to, 58, 78
Levine, Nancy Jones and Irving R., 85–6, 252n125
liberal developmentalism, 4
Life magazine, 28, 77, 111, 121–3, 140, 194
"Little Gem of a Wardrobe," *Ladies' Home Journal*, 30–2, 136
Lockerman, Gloria, 128, 132, 268n5, 277n33
Luce, Henry Robinson, 111, 121–2

Macoby, Eleanor, 197–8, 202–3
Mademoiselle, 27, 123
makeovers, women's, 31–2, 73–4
Malenkov, Georgi, 110–11
marriage: advice, 32–3, 37–41, 68, 208–9; *Amerika* on, 106, 120, 127, 135, 167, 181, 208–9; careers and, 48, 58, 100, 200, 203; counselling, 39–40, 201; focus on, 26, 29, 39–40, 52, 68, 146–9; homemaking and, 35–7, 50, 140; *Ladies' Home Journal* on, 29–30, 32–8, 49, 120, 198; Russian, 54, 210–11, 222; unhappy, 37, 41, 208; USIA representations of, 18–19, 115. *See also* weddings
Marshall Field's, 169–70, 192
masculinity, 10, 25; household tasks and, 37, 94, 202–3, 205
mass production, 71, 177; consumer goods, 11, 128, 163, 216; of Russian housing, 21, 73, 152, 218–19
May, Elaine Tyler (*Homeward Bound*), 10, 14, 16
McCall's, 27, 50, 123, 197–8, 244n121

McCarthy, Joseph, 27
McEnaney, Laura, 14, 35
Mead, Margaret, 197–8, 200–3
media, 27, 134; American consumer culture in, 4, 15, 87, 155, 225; critiques of Russian system, 12–13, 101, 104–5, 178; portrayal of Russian living, 60–70, 72–6, 94–5, 212; shifting views on Soviet Union, 54–5, 146, 215–22; USIA partnership with, 52–3, 100–1, 103–4, 111, 122. See also *Amerika*; *Ladies' Home Journal*
men: articles on, 25, 37, 178; electoral politics, 10–12, 44–6; equality with, 59, 135, 178, 191, 194; household work, 18, 82, 166, 178, 201–2, 205; portrayals of Russian versus American, 44–6, 56, 62–5, 93–4, 210–11; supporting women in politics, 46–8, 186; women's femininity and, 17, 28–30, 33, 86, 89; women's independence from, 58, 92, 200, 218; work roles, 30, 153, 155, 167
middle-class women, 40, 172, 201, 207; lack of Russian, 76, 210–11
media idealization of American, 8–12, 26–8, 120, 127, 134–6, 223–5
messaging for, 14–15, 50, 91, 140, 155, 199
Millett, Kate (*Sexual Politics*), 209
Minsk, living conditions in, 55–6
modernity, 217, 267n86; Russian women's lack of, 13; US association with, 4, 11, 17; women and, 11, 32
morality: communist threat to, 14, 43–6, 77, 110; women and, 45–6, 81, 102
Morris, John G., 28, 59, 74–5, 248n36
Moscow, 73, 162, 173, 181, 192; *Amerika* distribution in, 106, 108, 123–4, 145, 212–17; diplomatic events in, 6, 58, 83–6, 129, 163, 166; living conditions in, 60–5, 78–81, 88–90, 192, 210; travel to, 58, 60, 75–6, 86–7, 216
motherhood, 17, 30; careers and, 49, 166–8, 177, 195, 199–203, 207; happiness and, 25–7, 35, 96, 120, 146, 152–6; importance of, 25–6, 31–5, 40–1, 63, 146–53, 215
mothers, 4, 177; *Amerika*, depictions in, 13–15, 127–8, 135, 151–2, 157–8, 191; menace of overbearing, 36–7
motion pictures. *See* films

nationalism, 43, 187; women's role in, 15–17, 249n59
National Security Council (NSC), 109, 112
national security issues, 9, 14; policymaking and, 16, 109, 113
New York Times, 209, 217, 254n152
portrayals of Russian life, 75, 77, 80, 212, 222
Russian women in, 59, 215, 218
Nixon, Richard, 195, 260n76; Khrushchev, debate with, 6, 129, 161, 163, 217
norms, 15–16, 50–1, 167; in *Amerika*, 10, 129–32, 147, 151, 158, 186, 223–5; of domesticity, 9, 27, 30, 49–50, 227; of heterosexuality, 17, 19, 26–8, 151, 199, 242n7; in *Ladies' Home Journal*, 3, 26–8, 37, 52, 74, 199
Northland Center, 42, 243n77
nuclear attack, threat of, 14, 44, 220
nuclear families, 73, 182, 201, 217, 219

Office of War Information (OWI), 101–2, 104, 246n10
Operations Coordinating Board (OCB), 113–14, 122

Osgood, Kenneth A., 8, 110–11
"other" the, 225; racialized women as, 12, 245n3; Russian women as, 12, 52–3, 245n3
overseas information program: development of, 3–4, 10–12, 101–3, 109–13, 119; imagery of domesticity in, 53, 58, 99–100, 178, 225; principles of, 114, 122, 223. See also *Amerika*; United States Information Agency (USIA)

patriotism: appeals to readers', 43–4, 87–9, 102; depictions of, 48–9, 80, 248n34; domestic containment and, 14, 35, 44–5
Patterson, Patrick Hyder, 166, 223
Petrovna, Nina, 220–2
Poland, 93, 186; food from, 163; USIA involvement in, 15, 164, 214, 225
policymaking, Russian, 5, 9, 56–7, 218; shifts in, 115–16, 161
policymaking, US, 102, 112, 122; Cold War information programs, 5, 8–9, 13, 96, 101, 113–15, 225; gender and, 16, 44, 181, 210–11; women's magazines on, 44, 101, 187, 195
political involvement, women's: anti-communist, 8, 14–15, 26–7, 45, 90; community-based, 14, 28, 44–9, 115, 191; magazines on, 44–9, 186, 191; men's support for, 46–8, 186; nationalism and, 26
Popenoe, Paul, 39–41, 242nn65, 71
Price, Leontyne, 128, 132, 268n5, 277n33
private enterprise, 54, 56; cooperative planning versus, 42; support for, 4, 42

private sphere. *See* public versus private spheres
propaganda: *Amerika* as polite, 122, 195; constructions of Russian, 5–6, 96, 214; cultural infiltration and, 5, 8, 80, 178–9, 225–6; funding for, 101, 109, 111–13; notion of, 7; Soviet Department of (*see* Soviet Union); US versus Russian, 53–4, 116–18, 132
psychological operations: government policies and, 79–80, 109; use of term, 6–7
Psychological Strategy Board (PSB), 79–80, 109, 113, 258n50
public opinion, 124; attempts to shape, 7, 103, 121; gauging, 188, 193–5; recognizing power of, 5, 7, 103, 110; on women's roles, 193–5, 204
public versus private spheres: communist, 17, 78–9, 191, 210; domesticity and, 10, 16, 63; women's political involvement in, 14, 43, 50
purchaser as citizen. *See* citizens

racial discrimination: inequality and, 9, 132, 187–9, 232n38; lack of coverage of, 117, 153, 234n58, 245n3. *See also* racism
racism: as national security issue, 9, 134, 225; Russian critiques of US, 9, 123, 132, 134; Russian outlawing of, 93, 134
radio programming: access to Russian audiences, 6–7, 104, 124, 226; American, 27, 54, 101, 104, 111; Russian censorship of, 76, 81, 104, 109; Russian propaganda on, 113
Redbook, 27, 55, 58
refugees, Russian, 56–7, 247n23

Republican Party, 122, 199; women's support for, 27, 49, 204
Revolution, Russian, 132, 219; American media critiques of, 90–2; women after the, 17, 57–8, 92–3, 130. *See also* Bolshevism
Riesman, David ("The Nylon War"), 4, 21
Roosevelt, Eleanor, 44, 75, 93, 265n58
Roosevelt, Franklin, 101–2
Rosenberg, Emily, 4, 11, 16, 83
Rosenberg, Julian and Ethel, 27
Rosenfeld, Barbara, 205–8, 213–17
Rosenthal, Ida (Maidenform founder), 83–4
Rosie the Riveter (J. Howard Miller), 102, 256n10
rural communities: American, 48, 100, 143, 155–6, 169–73; Russian, 53, 57, 59, 65
Russia, 59; American accounts of, 75, 80–1, 89–90, 206, 217; magazine critiques of, 90–2, 95, 156. *See also* Soviet Union
Russians, 104, 163, 226; American media portrayals of, 60–70, 72–81, 94–5, 117, 212; American critiques of, 52, 59, 80–1, 103; on life under communism, 44, 95–6, 124, 129–30; embracing American culture, 9, 18, 67, 77, 86, 105, 123, 210–15; standard of living, 53, 78–80, 86–7, 153, 217; US consumer targeting of, 3–4, 8, 120–3, 168–77, 183–5, 214–17; USIA activities for, 5–6, 8, 21, 55, 109, 114–15, 178–9
Russians Nobody Knows (Time Inc.), 55–6

Sad magazine, 124, 214
Salisbury, Harrison, 75, 217, 284n33
Samuelson, Dick and Polly, 152

Sanders, Marion K.: editorship of *Amerika*, 104, 106; resignation of, 108–9, 257n27; women's movement and, 197–201, 203, 280n73
Schmidt, Don, 33–4, 147–8
Scoville, Peg, 155–8
Sears, Roebuck and Company, 170–1, 222; catalogue, 80, 106, 124
Seven Corners Shopping Center, 173–4
sex, 79; men's desire for, 39, 41; Russian women's lack of, 13, 41, 53, 95, 120, 145, 212; women's relationships with, 92–3, 199, 203, 222
Sheveleva, Yekaterina, 129–30
shoes, 56, 215; availability of, 84–5, 170–3; fashionable, 106, 135, 139; quality of, 31, 85
shopping: in American centres, 41–2, 128, 168–76, 185, 207; portrayals of American, 36, 136, 138, 157, 166, 207; in Russian department stores, 65–7, 85–6; Russian women's, 85, 87–9, 210; women's supposed desire for, 25, 65–7, 86, 163–6, 209
Silberman, Charles E., 152–3
Simons, Eugenia, 32, 241n36
Smith-Mundt Act, 102–3
socialism, 54, 75, 142, 145; criticisms of capitalism, 41–2, 93, 95–6, 130, 202; Russian attempts to sell, 9, 18, 73, 131, 142, 191
socialist subjectivity, 95–6
Soviet Citizen: Daily Life in a Totalitarian Society (Inkeles and Bauer), 56–7, 200, 247n21
Soviet Experiment, 93, 132, 229n3, 232n38
Soviet regime, 4, 222; American policies toward, 5, 8–9, 13–14, 96, 101, 113–15, 225; censorship

under, 6, 17, 76–7, 81, 103–4, 109; discourse of, 17–18, 80–1; gender equality under, 4, 17–18, 81, 89; hardship under, 59–70, 74–5, 80–2, 173, 223; limiting American influence, 5, 103, 117; US delegitimization of, 4–7, 10, 62, 74–7, 105, 109; women, messaging about, 4, 12–13, 17–18, 221

Soviet Union, 44; American dissatisfaction in, 62, 79–87, 89–94, 234n60; *Amerika* in, 3, 6, 104, 106, 108, 116–18, 212–13; consumer culture in, 17, 67, 86, 143, 168, 192, 215–16; curiosity about American life, 67, 77, 124, 220; defensiveness of, 116–17; Department of Propaganda and Agitation, 116–17; food shortages, 53–4, 56, 89; intentions of global dominance, 44, 117; standard of living in, 13, 53–7, 78–80, 86–7, 153, 217; women's roles in, 13–18, 58, 78–82, 89, 95–6

Soviet Woman, 131

Soyuzpechat, 104, 106–8, 212

"special hardships," Russian womanhood, 12, 53–5

"special privileges," American womanhood, 4, 12, 195, 238n9; Soviet system versus, 52–3, 90, 191, 219–20, 226; traditional gender roles and, 26, 71, 254n9

Spock, Benjamin, 205, 238n3

Stalingrad, 58, 65, 68, 246n10

Stalinism, 85, 95, 232n38; life under, 17, 53, 62, 73–5, 79, 222; post-, 9, 43, 77, 110–11, 115–17, 178; women under, 17, 156, 217, 219

Stalin, Josef, 45, 54; death of, 5, 43, 73, 110, 217; Truman versus, 101

State Department, US, 27, 57, 123; *Amerika* distribution and, 6, 104, 108–9; guidance from, 13, 57, 102–4, 111–12; *Sad* distribution, 124, 214

Steinbeck, John, 59–60, 62–3, 65–70, 74–5, 79; *A Russian Journal*, 59–60; *Ladies' Home Journal* article, 59

Streibert, Theodore, 6, 112

suburban life, 184–5; accounts of, 36, 94, 152–5, 177, 182, 207–8; norms of, 9, 52, 100, 127–8; shopping in, 42, 128, 138, 164, 172–3, 176; Soviet system versus, 13, 68, 161, 219

supermarkets, 156, 164–6, 173, 183, 221, 234n61

"They Let Us Talk to the Russians" (Humphrey and Curran), 78, 86, 89

Thompson, Dorothy, 94, 199; anti-communist articles, 43, 90, 93, 234n60; on shopping centres, 41–2, 172

Time Inc., 55, 111, 121

Truman, Harry, 101; administration of, 7–10, 79, 102–3, 118; overseas information program, 109–14

Tuch, Hans, 7, 123, 213

Ukraine, 66, 229n3, 248n38; hardships in, 59–60

undergarments, women's, 82, 87; critiques of Russian, 83–4

United Nations Relief and Rehabilitation Agency (UNRRA), 55–6

United States, 53, 96, 122, 214–15; government of (*see* United States government); way of life, selling, 3–12, 48, 68–71, 115–18, 132, 146–7; women in (*see* women, American)

United States government: access to Russian people, 3, 5–7, 104,

124, 226; cultural diplomacy (*see* cultural diplomacy); democracy, selling of (*see* democracy); media outlet partnerships, 52–3, 100–1, 103–4, 111, 122; promotion of consumer culture, 100, 116, 163–4, 178–9, 223

United States Information Agency (USIA): *Amerika*, use of (*see Amerika*); channels and strategies of, 6, 15–16, 99–102, 114–15; claims of legitimacy, 5–7, 95–6, 100, 114, 124; creation and purpose of, 5–6, 11, 15–16, 110–15, 121–2; cultural program of, 53, 96, 99–102, 119, 178–9; Russian propaganda versus, 5–6, 8, 21, 55, 109, 114–15, 179; Voice of America (*see* Voice of America [VOA]); "Women's Activities" policy paper, 99–101, 114–15

Upshaw, Catherine and Banks, 48–9

urban living, 57, 82, 208; American, 48–9, 100, 138, 169–73, 192; Russian, 21, 53, 59, 73, 79, 153, 156

USSR, 178; *Amerika* versus, 128–31, 135, 189, 216, 226; special issue on women, 189–93, 219; US distribution of, 6, 116–18

veterans, 10, 70

Vogue, 27, 123–4

Voice of America (VOA), 6, 103, 109, 112, 231n18

volunteerism, female, 29, 47, 91, 172; American homemaking and, 19, 63, 100, 115, 156; government calls for, 14, 45, 102

Von Eschen, Penny, 9

voting, women's involvement in, 45–7, 199

Vyborg, 83

Walburg, Jean, 132, 147, 277n33

warfare: psychological, 7, 109, 111, 114; training for, 35; use of term, 6–7

weddings, 70, 181; idealized process for, 33, 147–50; *Ladies' Home Journal* articles on, 33–4

Weir, Arvella, 31–2

Western culture: appeal to Russians, 9, 11, 130, 183, 192; fashion, 18, 84, 124, 141–4, 192, 215–16; global influence of, 43–4, 103, 166, 223–5

Western Europe, 17, 56

white-collar workers, Russian women as, 57–8

white, middle-class women, 15, 127, 223–5; idealized representations of, 8–12, 40, 94–5, 119–20, 134–6

Wilkins, Roy, 187–8

Wilson, Woodrow, 101

Winter, Ella, 54, 246n7

wives. *See* housewives

womanhood, notions of, 26; relationships with men, 28–9; twentieth-century, 12, 119–20; US versus Russian, 89–90, 225

women: American (*see* women, American); bonds between Russian and American, 95–6, 115; of colour, 15, 128, 238n9 (*see also* African Americans); freedom to choose and, 19, 99–100, 107, 208, 234n58; idealized objectives of, 30, 50, 100, 119, 226; Russian (*see* women, Russian)

women, American, 93, 176, 180; idealized images about, 3–4, 9–12, 17–18, 29, 99–101, 140, 223; removal from workforce, 10, 35, 38, 41, 167, 203; Russian versus, 18, 62–70, 72–4, 81, 127, 146–7, 191–2; "special privileges" of (*see*

"special privileges," American womanhood); use against communism, 8, 10, 14–15, 26–7, 90; USIA portrayals of, 16, 50–1, 127–35, 138–40, 196
"Women and Children in the USSR" (Steinbeck and Capa), 59–70, 73–5, 82, 173, 247n31
women, Russian, 93, 192; American depictions of, 11, 13, 52–6, 60–70, 72–5; *Amerika*, appeals to, 6, 123–7, 138–45, 210–12, 226–7; childcare (*see* childcare; childrearing); class divisions between, 76, 84–5, 91, 247n21; consumerist targeting of, 4, 6, 10, 18, 81, 127, 146–7, 191–2; labour of, 18–19, 54–9, 79–82, 92–4, 191, 219; older generations of, 57–8; outnumbering men, 56–7, 62, 65; postwar living conditions, 53, 62–3, 74–5, 164, 212, 215–23; Russian Revolution, roles in, 17, 57–8, 90–3, 130; "special hardships" (*see* "special hardships," Russian womanhood); as unfeminine, 12, 17, 53, 77, 84, 89–90, 191, 218; USIA portrayals of, 13, 53–68, 82, 95, 100, 178, 189, 194; workforce participation, postwar, 55–7, 62–4
Woolworth's, 171–2
working-class women, 15, 17, 58, 238n9
World War I, 11; propaganda use during, 7–8, 101
World War II, 14; cultural diplomacy in, 8, 79, 101, 110; impact on Soviets, 55–7, 75, 130–1, 223; US media representation during, 52–4, 115, 247n31

Yugoslavia, 15, 124, 164–6, 214, 223; *Sad* magazine (see *Sad* magazine)
youth, 124; propaganda for, 113, 195; Russian versus American, 76–7, 183

Zakharova, Larisa, 18, 142, 145

Lightning Source UK Ltd.
Milton Keynes UK
UKHW041441201222
414218UK00015B/168/J